The Collected Works of Joh

John Dewey

The Later Works, 1925–1953

Volume 8: 1933

EDITED BY JO ANN BOYDSTON

TEXTUAL EDITOR, BRIDGET A. WALSH

ASSOCIATE TEXTUAL EDITOR,

HARRIET FURST SIMON

With an Introduction by Richard Rorty

Southern Illinois University Press

Carbondale

The Collected Works of John Dewey

COMMITTEE ON
SCHOLARLY EDITIONS

AN APPROVED EDITION

MODERN LANGUAGE
ASSOCIATION OF AMERICA

Editorial expenses for this edition have been met in part by grants
from the Editions Program of the National Endowment for the
Humanities, an independent Federal agency, and from the John
Dewey Foundation. Publishing expenses have been met in part by
a grant from the John Dewey Foundation.

ISBN-10: 0-8093-1246-8 (cloth: alk. paper)
ISBN-13: 978-0-8093-1246-7 (cloth: alk. paper)
ISBN-10: 0-8093-2818-6 (pbk.: alk. paper)
ISBN-13: 978-0-8093-2818-5 (pbk.: alk. paper)

The Library of Congress has cataloged the original issue of this book
as follows:
Dewey, John, 1859–1952.
The later works, 1925–1953.
Vol. 8 has introd. by Richard Rorty.
Continues The middle works, 1899–1924.
Includes bibliographies and indexes.
CONTENTS: v. 1. 1925—v. 2. 1925–1927—[etc.]—v. 8. 1933.
1. Philosophy—Collected works. I. Boydston, Jo Ann, 1924–. II. Title.
B945.D41 1981   191   80-27285
ISBN 0-8093-1246-8 (v. 8)

Contents

Introduction
By Richard Rorty

The material collected in this volume does not show Dewey working out new lines of thought, changing his mind, or exploring new areas. It is tempting to describe the volume as consisting of more or less popular expositions of views which he had previously developed. The articles on "Logic" and "Philosophy" for the *Encyclopaedia of the Social Sciences* are condensed versions of stories previously told in such books as *Reconstruction in Philosophy* and *The Quest for Certainty*.[1] The coauthored contributions to *The Educational Frontier* do not break fresh ground in the philosophy of education. Revision and enlargement of *How We Think*,[2] a book whose first edition had become the bible of those who came to be called "progressive" educators, gave Dewey an occasion to clear up some misunderstandings, as well as the chance to make the book even more readable. So we might describe Dewey, in these writings, as repackaging his thought in the interest of greater accessibility.

But the notion of "popular exposition" is misleading and rather un-Deweyan, as is that of "repackaging." Dewey was not inclined to distinguish between serious, "professional," work and "popularization." For him, to write up old ideas for a new audience was to produce new ideas, new instruments for advancing the projects he was promoting. He thought of himself as reshaping

1. *Reconstruction in Philosophy* (New York: Henry Holt and Co., 1920) [*The Middle Works of John Dewey, 1899–1924*, ed. Jo Ann Boydston (Carbondale and Edwardsville: Southern Illinois University Press, 1982), 12:77–201]; *The Quest for Certainty* (New York: Minton, Balch and Co., 1929) [*The Later Works of John Dewey, 1925–1953*, ed. Jo Ann Boydston, vol. 4 (Carbondale and Edwardsville: Southern Illinois University Press, 1984)].
2. *How We Think* (Boston: D. C. Heath and Co., 1910) [*Middle Works* 6:177–356]; *How We Think: A Restatement of the Relation of Reflective Thinking to the Educative Process* (Boston: D. C. Heath and Co., 1933) [*Later Works* 8:105–352].

tools for use on new materials rather than as providing "applied" versions of a previously "pure" body of knowledge. He did not think of his fellow philosophy professors as his "real" audience, nor of elementary school teachers, or readers of the *New Republic*, as supplementary constituencies to be supplied with a "popular," less demanding, version of the same material. Rather, he thought that philosophy professors had their special problems, teachers theirs, and politically conscious citizens theirs, and that there were no relations of precedence among these sets of problems.

Nevertheless, there is a certain inevitable tension which runs through Dewey's relation to his various audiences, and also through his own presentation of his work: the tension between the image of the philosopher as social activist, concerned to keep the spirit of reform alive by constant criticism of the adequacy of current practises and institutions, and the philosopher as politically neutral theoretician—a specialist in, and authority upon, such peculiarly philosophical topics as the rules of logic, the nature of science, or the nature of thought.

From a theoretical angle, this tension can be viewed as a special case of the tension between pragmatism's conception of inquiry (in any sphere, not just in philosophy) as a response to particular historical circumstances, and the traditional conception of inquiry as the discovery of eternal "objective" truths. This theoretical tension is one which Dewey discussed often—usually under the rubric of the "pragmatist theory of truth." Much of his work among his fellow philosophy professors was devoted to reconciling the purported "intuition" that truth is a timeless property of beliefs with the pragmatist claim that beliefs are rules for action, to be judged in terms of their effectiveness in resolving problems.[3]

But a theoretical resolution of a theoretical tension cannot, by itself, resolve the tension between two public images. The tension between the image of the philosopher as activist and as sage is between rhetorical tropes rather than between contradictory doctrines. It was one which Dewey never entirely resolved. Sometimes he presents himself as saying "Here are philosophical

---

3. See, for example, "A Short Catechism concerning Truth," in his *The Influence of Darwin on Philosophy and Other Essays in Contemporary Thought* (New York: Henry Holt and Co., 1910), pp. 154–68 [*Middle Works* 6:3–11].

views adhesion to which by the public would advance my socio-political projects; the point of formulating and propagating such views is to break up the crust of convention which impedes social reform." But sometimes he seems to be saying "You should share my desire for social reform, for it is grounded upon my philosophical research, certified by that 'scientific method' which I have identified as the best way of thinking." The former style gave occasion for attacks from Dewey's enemies—those who considered him a dangerous radical. The latter style comforted his radical friends, who liked to think that their socio-political outlook was more "reflective" or "intelligent" or "scientific" than that of their conservative opponents.

Dewey was quite happy with both images, and moved insouciantly back and forth between them. He saw no need to choose between these two self-conceptions, no need to find a natural order of precedence between, for example, his view about the current socio-economic order and his view of the nature of logic. It was one of his chief tenets that there is no natural order of priority and posteriority among subject-matters of inquiry or among disciplines. But since this view was not widely shared, since his various audiences were inclined to take for granted, for example, the political and moral neutrality of such subject-matters as "logic" and "psychology," Dewey was, in some measure, forced to acquiesce in the role of neutral specialist. He had to accept, and make use of, his role as sage, even while insisting that the image of the sage was a relic of undesirable and obsolete ways of thinking.[4]

Dewey sometimes did not bother with the pretense of neutrality. For example, the chapters of *The Educational Frontier* which Dewey coauthored with John L. Childs are remarkably frank in commending the philosophy of education embodied in *How We Think* as one calculated to change the character of American institutions—to move society to the political left by

4. Dewey was, of course, neither the first nor the last philosopher to be caught in this position. Any thinker who is historicist enough to question the traditional conception of truth as a relation between the human mind and an unchanging reality is going to be challenged by the same dilemma: is your historicism ahistorically true, or are you saying merely that historicism is an appropriate attitude in our present historical circumstances? The challenge is as appropriate a response to Protagoras, Hegel, Heidegger, or Nelson Goodman as to Dewey.

moving successive generations of students to the left of their parents. Dewey and Childs write that the philosophies of education which they oppose buttress "legal and economic institutions which encourage an exaggerated and one-sided development of egoistic individuality in a privileged few, while militating against a full and fair opportunity for a normal individuality in the many" (this volume, p. 81). Such a passage leaves Dewey wide open to the charge, often made by his enemies, that he is making socialist propaganda and disguising it as a "philosophical," and thus presumably neutral, discussion of the nature of thought.

At other times, however, Dewey writes as if there were some neutral, more or less professional, ground which he occupies in his capacity as philosopher or psychologist, rather than as social critic. From this high ground, he suggests, we can survey ways of thinking and discriminate the better from the worse. This was his typical stance when commending the virtues of what he sometimes called "scientific method" and sometimes, as in *How We Think*, "reflective thinking." But his description of this method is marked by an ambiguity—the same ambiguity between the descriptive and the normative which plagues his metaphilosophical account of his own activity.

Sometimes it seems as if Dewey is telling us that the seventeenth century discovered not only the true layout of the solar system and the laws of motion but a new method of inquiry, one with spectacular advantages over previous methods. Dewey recommends that we try this method out in areas where it has not been previously applied—that we "generalize the experimental side of natural science into a logical method which is applicable to the interpretation and treatment of social phenomena."[5] When Dewey writes in this vein, it sounds as if he were saying "All of us, no matter whether we would prefer a more religious or a more secular culture, or whether we are politically radical or politically conservative, naturally want to use the best possible tools in our work. The method discovered in the seventeenth century is a better, unfortunately neglected, tool. A study of the nature of thought, of how we think, will make the virtues of this tool clear to us."

Yet at other times it seems obvious that this tool is much more

5. "Logic," *Encyclopaedia of the Social Sciences*, this volume, p. 11.

suited to the projects of the secularizing and left-leaning intellectual than to those of his conservative, religious, counterpart, and
that this is precisely why Dewey is commending it. For in these
passages it sounds as if there is little more to this "method" than
an innovative and experimental attitude, a willingness to re-
describe things in a new vocabulary and see what happens. What
Dewey describes as "reflective thinking" sometimes sounds like
something everybody does quite naturally, something which is
the common property of the ancients and the moderns, and of
any reasonably literate and articulate person, no matter what
his or her persuasion. But sometimes, particularly when Dewey
is comparing this sort of thinking invidiously with "intellec-
tualism" and "rationalism," reflective thinking sounds like something quite particular, something which the moderns do more of
than the ancients did, something more commonly found among
laboratory scientists than among medieval schoolmen, and more
prevalent among liberals than among conservatives.

This ambiguity is not a surface phenomenon. It presents Dewey
with a real problem. To resolve it Dewey would have to find some
sort of middle ground between a well-defined procedure—a
method in the sense of a set of directions for what to do next,
something like a recipe—and a mere recommendation to be
open-minded, undogmatic, critical, and experimental. This is
what he tries to do in *How We Think*, as in the earlier *Essays in
Experimental Logic* and the later *Logic: The Theory of Inquiry.*[6]
In all these books, he wants to broaden the idea of "logic" so as
to make it more than a collection of rules for judging the validity
of inferences, yet not to broaden it so far that it becomes just a
set of platitudinous maxims, encouraging one to think hard,
gather lots of data, try out different theories, etc. He wants, on
the one hand, to claim that most attempts to specify a "method
for correct thinking" have merely hypostatized the vocabulary
and practises of a certain period or of a certain preferred area of
culture.[7] But, on the other hand, he does not wish to conclude (as
such recent writers as Paul Feyerabend have concluded) that the

6. *Essays in Experimental Logic* (Chicago: University of Chicago Press, 1916);
   Logic: The Theory of Inquiry (New York: Henry Holt and Co., 1938).
7. See, for example, his polemic against the idea that we can lay down a pre-
   formed grid upon a subject-matter in order to divide it up into its "elements":
   chapter 5 of *How We Think*, this volume, pp. 177ff.

way to encourage experimental thinking is to give up the very idea of "method" as an outdated shibboleth.[8] He is torn between the temptation to say that the only rule of logic we require is Peirce's "Do not block the road of inquiry!" and the need to lay out some procedures which, if adopted, will improve people's thinking.

To put the problem slightly differently: Dewey wants to praise certain ways of thinking which he thinks have become more common since the seventeenth century, but he cannot specify these ways too narrowly, for fear of erecting an abstract formalism as constrictive as any of those erected by his more "rationalistic" predecessors.[9] He thinks that any specific patterns of analysis— any *recipes* for how to think—will inevitably be parochial and thus potentially restrictive, likely to discourage inventive problem-solving. But he nevertheless writes *How We Think* in the conviction that teachers can train students to think better: "The better way of thinking that is to be considered in this book is called reflective thinking: the kind of thinking that consists in turning a subject over in the mind and giving it serious and consecutive consideration" (p. 113).

The trouble with this characterization of "reflective thinking" is that the only people who do *not* practise it are those whom we think of as either mentally deficient or morally flawed. Putting aside the former—those who, because of physiological incapacity, cannot focus on a topic long enough to perform con-

8. See Paul Feyerabend, *Against Method* (London: New Left Books, 1975). There are many "against method" passages in *How We Think*, as, for example, the critique of "overconscious formulation of methods of procedure" at p. 217 and the emphasis on the importance of inarticulatable skill at pp. 213–14. But there are also many pro-method passages, as at p. 249. One difficulty in interpreting Dewey in this area is his tendency to use "method" synonymously with "procedure," with "style," and with "philosophy"—to describe stages in the development of children, of individual disciplines, and of Western intellectual history in terms of the use of different "methods." See, for example, his use of "method" interchangeably with "logical theory" and with "climate of philosophical opinion" in his article on "Logic," pp. 3–12.

9. Thus in this second edition of *How We Think*, we find him cautioning those who took the famous description of "the five phases of reflection" too seriously. He is clearly worried that over-enthusiastic readers of the first edition have begun to treat his divisions of the process of thought with the same reverence that over-enthusiastic readers of the *Prior Analytics* brought to Aristotle's syllogistic. "There is nothing especially sacred," he says, "about the number five" (p. 207).

secutive inferences—as ineducable, the target of instruction and reform must be those who are dogmatic, opinionated, unwilling to listen, difficult to converse with. Yet it is inappropriate to say to such people "Come, I shall teach you something to your advantage: a new method." For such an invitation would appeal only if the method commended were a method for doing something which those addressed already want to do. Yet people of this kind do not want to be critical and experimental. They cherish their certainties; the last thing they want is to change the vocabularies in which they are habituated to describing things. Such people may conceivably be converted by an exhibition of the concrete advantages of particular changes in particular vocabularies, but it is hard to see how they could be converted by a general *methodological* exhortation.

It is easy to dislike this character type, and to view it as morally flawed—as exemplifying what it was once fashionable to call "an authoritarian personality." It is natural to hope that our children will not have such personalities, and to try to raise them so that they do not. *How We Think* was written precisely in order to encourage teachers to encourage children not to have such a personality, but instead to be critical and experimental in their reception of traditional practises and institutions. But it is not evident that there is a subject called "psychology," or one called "logic"—a discipline charged with studying "the nature of thought"—which can be called upon to underwrite such an attempt. It is not clear that we can ground a judgment about the ends of education—about the character-types we wish the schools to develop—upon an inquiry into the nature of thought.

The attempt to do so runs into the difficulty sketched above: the problem of whether one is trying to describe or reform, whether one is doing "science" or "politics." More specifically, it runs into the problem of whether one can find some way of describing the difference between, e.g., the laboratory scientist and the medieval schoolman (one of Dewey's favorite contrasts) which makes the difference sound like one of "logic" or "method." It is hard to find in *How We Think* a description of "reflective thinking" which could not be used to describe the activity of, say, Duns Scotus. Scotus and Charles Darwin certainly differed in their self-characterization—in the terms they used to describe the nature and purpose of their intellectual labors. They also differed in what they thought relevant—what sorts of evidence and objection they were prepared to take seriously. But it is not clear that, apart from having different goals and therefore different criteria of relevance, they *thought* differently—that we can find an interesting contrast between their intellectual activities at a level of description which might plausibly be called "psychological" or "logical."

Dewey defines "reflective thought"—the better way of thinking he wishes to recommend—as *"Active, persistent, and careful consideration of any belief or supposed form of knowledge in the light of the grounds that support it and the further conclusions to which it tends"* (p. 118). He contrasts this sort of thinking with reliance on "tradition, instruction, imitation"—with "prejudices; that is, prejudgments, not conclusions reached as the result of personal mental activity, such as observing, collecting, and examining evidence" (p. 116). Can one accuse Scotus of the latter sort of thinking? Not if one looks at his activity in his own specialty: his handling of certain philosophical and theological questions is as reflective (in Dewey's sense) as anyone's thought has ever been. One can, of course, point out that he did not question a lot of beliefs which he would have done well to question— e.g., those which the Enlightenment was later to question. But it would not make sense to suggest that Scotus (or anyone else) question *all* beliefs. Nor would Dewey, who shared Peirce's conviction that "Cartesian doubt" was a pointless exercise, make such a suggestion. Yet is there any "method" by which Scotus could have known *which* beliefs he should have questioned?

Dewey does not offer one, and it seems evident that there can be no general procedure for deciding which of the beliefs one has picked up from "tradition, instruction, and imitation" to treat skeptically and which to leave alone. So, for example, Dewey's praise of Columbus for being skeptical about the flatness of the earth seems unfair to Columbus's contemporaries. Dewey says that these contemporaries held a belief which "rested on laziness, inertia, custom, absence of courage and energy in investigation" (p. 117). Granted that it was fortunate that somebody should eventually have become skeptical about the shape of the earth, should we really say that those who were not skeptical were unreflective, lazy, or cowardly? Was it lazy for physicists prior to Einstein not to question Newtonian absolute time? Unreflective for muralists prior to Giotto not to envisage the greater realism which he was to achieve? Cowardly for medieval theologians not to envisage the possibility of a secular and democratic polity? Is it unreflective of us contemporary secularists, brought up on Dewey, not to ponder the evidences of the Christian religion?

Dewey would, if challenged, probably have agreed that we cannot formulate a strategy which will help one be skeptical about all and only the right things—one which will encourage a Columbus or a Darwin while simultaneously discouraging (for example) childish resistance to harmless conventions, scatter-brainedness, Pyrrhonism, paranoia, and Cartesian doubt. He was aware that no study of how we think can produce any formula, or set of formulae, which would serve as such a panacea. But in *How We Think* and elsewhere he constantly talks as if he were offering us such a strategy. He verges on the "intellectualist" assumption (one he elsewhere combats vigorously) that all the intellectual options—all possible hypotheses, all possible ideas—are out there, waiting for skeptical and experimental minds to come upon them. He speaks as if a correct account of the nature of thought would make possible the sort of improvement in thinking which had been promised in the past by others who explicitly held that assumption (e.g., Ramus and Descartes).

To make this criticism of *How We Think* is not to cast doubt on Dewey's goals, nor on his claim that something new and important came into the world with Bacon and the New Science. It is only to cast doubt upon his attempt to identify this new thing with a "way of thinking" (as opposed to some concrete suggestions about new hypotheses to try out) and upon his attempt to promote the goals he cherished by an appeal to a putatively descriptive, ideologically neutral, discipline called "psychology" or "logic." That attempt should be viewed as an unfortunate aftereffect of the nineteenth-century philosophical vocabularies on which Dewey was raised, vocabularies which suggested that "the nature of judgment" or "of reasoning" or "of thought" or "of science" were suitable topics for "philosophical research."

Dewey did a great deal to break up these vocabularies, and thus to make obsolete the idea of a discrete, permanent, range of problems which formed the distinctive subject-matter of a discipline called "philosophy" (or, for that matter, of one called "psychology"). But, like all of us, he could not question all his beliefs at once. So, part of the time, he worked with a set of distinctions, and a rhetoric, which was ill suited to his own purposes. This rhetoric led him to blinker his own sense of the relativity of thought to particular concrete problems and historical situations, in order to offer something like a general, abstract, characterization of a "better way of thinking."

Insofar as philosophy has "advanced" since Dewey, the advance may consist in the realization that, like the logical empiricists, Dewey overdid the attempt to make the natural scientist a model for the rest of culture. Both were too concerned to isolate a "method of experimental action called natural science" (p. 68). Both overestimated the differences between science, art, and politics. Recent philosophy of science (e.g., the work of Kuhn and Hesse) has been concerned to emphasize the similarities between these areas. Such emphasis has, however, helped increase our appreciation of Dewey's attack on the subject-object model of knowledge and on the cluster of Platonic and Cartesian ideas which buttress this model. It has also given us new intellectual tools to use in promoting the socio-political goals which Dewey cherished, and which provided the impetus (and, despite his occasional pretense of neutrality, the best justification) for his philosophical doctrines.

Contributions to
Encyclopaedia of the Social Sciences

Logic

The conditions under which logical theory originated are indicated by the two words still generally used to designate its subject matter—logic and dialectic. Both of these words have to do with speech, not of course with speech in the form of mere words but with language as the storehouse of the ideas and beliefs which form the culture of a people. Greek life was peculiarly characterized by the importance attached to discussion. Debate and discussion were marked by freedom from restrictions imposed by priestly power and were emphasized with the growth of democratic political institutions. In the Homeric poems the man skilled in words which were fit for counsel stands side by side with the man skilled in martial deeds. In Athens not merely political but legal issues were settled in the public forum. Political advancement and civic honor depended more upon the power of persuasion than upon military achievement. As general intellectual curiosity developed among the learned men, power to interpret and explain was connected with the ability to set forth a consecutive story. To give an account of something, a logos, was also to account for it. The logos, the ordered account, was the reason and the measure of the things set forth. Here was the background out of which developed a formulated theory of logic as the structure of knowledge and truth.

Of itself, however, it was only a background. Definite formulation of theory was the product of fermentation introduced by the philosophers. In the sixth and fifth centuries B.C. the Greek world of the Mediterranean basin was the scene of travel, commerce and social intercourse. The result was the development among the intellectual class of a kind of cosmopolitanism. Scholars, called wise men (sophists), subjected the various arts—

[First published in *Encyclopaedia of the Social Sciences*, ed. Edwin R. A. Seligman and Alvin Johnson (New York: Macmillan Co., 1933), 9:598–603.]

military, civic and industrial—to analysis and report. In consequence these arts, which formerly had a local meaning and scope, resting upon the tradition and customs of a particular community, were given a theoretical treatment. They were lifted out of their special environments and subjected to rationalization. The period was characterized by the preparation of an enormous number of dissertations covering all the arts. Traveling scholars as they went about offered to teach the arts by methods which rendered slow practical apprenticeship unnecessary. Finally, some of the more ambitious of these men offered their services to the young men of Athens, claiming that they could teach the "virtues"—an English word which gives only an awkward rendering of the Greek term, since the latter denotes skilled excellence in the arts, especially the political arts, combined with that power to command the attention of others which would assure civic preeminence. For those going into political life this promise involved training in ability to speak in private groups and in the public forum and formed the beginnings of a kind of practical logic.

Under the merciless attacks of Plato the name sophist took on an invidious meaning. He claimed that the method of the sophists was one of sham; that it was the art of appearing wise, not of being so. It aimed not at truth but at persuasion by whatever specious arguments would silence an opponent. Plato insisted therefore that the method of the sophists was one of contention, aiming at victory over others and hence assuming ultimate division in the structure of the mind. A true method, on the other hand, is a cooperative search, assuming an objective unity beneath all divisions of opinion and belief and terminating in the production of a common understanding sustained by grasp of the one relevant objective truth. Hence Plato called his method dialectic, a term obviously derived from the dialogue of those engaged in the exchange of ideas.

Part of the logical work of Plato consisted in pointing out some of the tricks by which the sophists made "the worse appear the better reason." This material was formulated by his successor Aristotle and remains today in logical treatises under the caption of fallacies. His positive contribution was his theory of the universal, the principle underlying the differences of different instances. Aristotle thus gives the Platonic Socrates credit for the discovery of induction and definition. Induction (better termed eduction) was the process by which the universal was extracted from a number of varying cases, definition the process by which this principle was fixed for use in all subsequent thinking. In Plato's system this universal constituted the "essence" or true and ultimate reality of the things in question. Aristotle criticized the resulting isolation of the universal from particular things. This isolation agreed both with Plato's mathematical interests and with his desire to obtain a method for social reform, since the separate universal provided an ideal reality which could be placed in contrast with existing things.

Aristotle was above all a naturalist. He asserted that the universal is united with particular existences, binding them together into a permanent whole (the species) and keeping within definite and fixed limits the changes which occur in each particular existence. The species is the true whole of which the particular individuals are the parts, and the essence is the characteristic form. Species fall within a graded order of genera as particular individuals fall within the species. Thinking is the correlate of these relations in nature. It unites and differentiates in judgment as species are united and separated in reality. Valid knowledge or demonstration necessarily takes the form of the syllogism because the syllogism merely expresses the system in which, by means of an intervening essence, individuals are included in species. Definition is the grasp of the essence which marks one species off from another. Classification and division are counterparts of the intrinsic order of nature.

Thus the logical theory which furnished the intellectual method of Europe for almost two thousand years was formulated when the appliances of observation and experimentation upon which modern scientific inquiry and testing depend were lacking. Moreover the only mathematics available was geometry, upon the model of which Alexandrian scientists constructed the astronomical frame. The traditional logic was a logic for clarifying and organizing that which was already known or that which was supposed to be known and hence currently believed. For putting this material in rational form, placing upon it the stamp of rational authenticity, logic was an unrivaled instrument. But it could not furnish means for breaking through the limits of the intellectual content of current culture so as to make discoveries

in new fields. The ultimate premises, or validating principles (beginnings), of all knowledge were assumed to be already in the
possession of the mind. Sense perception supplied the demonstrative material on the side of the particulars, and rational perception of self-evident truths, or axioms, performed the same
office on the side of universals. Human learning, or discovery,
was limited to putting these two given things together.

In its own intention the Aristotelian logic was a logic of truth.
It set forth the structure of valid knowledge, which corresponded
in turn to the systematic structure of reality. But when after the
decline of interest in nature ancient culture became introspective
and retrospective, logic declined more and more to a mere formal instrumentality of exposition and communication. The ethical schools, skeptic, Epicurean and stoic, either deprecated the
study of logic as of no importance (or even harmful in distracting
attention from the supreme business of the conduct of life) or else
reduced it to a mere device for avoiding error in moral judgments. Higher learning, as in the universities of Athens and Alexandria, devoted itself to organizing and interpreting the litera-
tures of the classic past and put logic on a level with rhetoric as a
formal aid in this task.

The administrative genius of Rome had little use for inquiry
and reflection for their own sakes. It was interested in the method
of thought as far as it could be used as a tool of political life. At
first this was in form largely subordinate to rhetoric in the guidance of oratory when, as in the time of Cicero, oratory played
a crucial part in civic rivalries. During the empire logic was the
instrument for organizing the complex legal body of rules and
decisions under fixed general principles, derived if possible from
the "law of nature." Logic thus became definitely a formal discipline useful in arranging material for purposes of argument, exposition and instruction.

The Christian church took over this conception of logic and
employed it as an agency for similar purposes of attack and defense, especially the defense of doctrine against pagan without
and heretic within. During the great scholastic period of the
twelfth and thirteenth centuries there was, however, a striking
revival in the scope and vitality of formal logic. The writings of
Aristotle came to Christendom through the Arabs. Intellectual
activity was stimulated to undertake a comprehensive organic

survey and formulation of Christian doctrine, with a view to showing its intrinsic harmony with reason even when the material of revelation was above reason. The relatively scanty axioms and first principles of Aristotle were expanded to include the authoritative truths of the Scriptures, fathers, church councils and popes. An extraordinarily stringent method of demonstrative exposition was built up in which all possible objections were considered and refuted in syllogistic fashion until the authorized body of doctrine was intellectually organized into a system. The universities, which were the centres of intellectual life, played their part. Great teachers met all comers in intellectual tournaments. Teaching was influenced by the method of doctrinal discussion while it also contributed to the perfecting of the latter method. The constructive intellectual movement which gave meaning and point to the development of formal logic degenerated after the work of unifying Christian dogma and rationalizing its structure had effected its purpose. There followed that period of hair splitting and refining which tended for a long time to throw the term scholastic into disrepute. What was even more important, the centre of intellectual gravity was shifting. Secular and humane interests were taking the place of ecclesiastical and theological concerns. Satisfaction of the new interests directed man toward nature and new intellectual methods were demanded. The cry went up that the old logic was one of words only and that what was required was a logic which would enable men to cope with things. New physical instruments and materials were invented or were introduced from the Orient. Travel and exploration extended the scope of intellectual data. The demand arose for a logic of discovery and new inquiry. Literary persons joined with reformers of society and of science in ridiculing the pretensions of syllogistic logic. Mathematical concepts, in conjunction with the apparatus of the newly developing technology, replaced the ideas of essences, genera and species as central in the constitution of nature.

The full history of the revolt and of the many more or less inchoate and antagonistic attempts to formulate a new logic is practically identical with the intellectual history of the period from the seventeenth century to the present. There soon appeared a division which, while technical in outer appearance, may be said to have had an almost tragic effect upon the intellect of the western world. This was the split between those who appealed exclusively to experience in the form of sense peception as the source of valid beliefs and those who appealed to reason in the form of mathematical concepts as the ultimate authority. Ignoring refinements one may regard Francis Bacon and Descartes as the representatives of the two movements. On the whole, with some notable excursions from each side into the territory of the other, Great Britain adhered to the empirical school and the continent to the rationalistic.

The tendency of the latter school was to engage in conceptual constructions and dialectic manipulations. Aside from mathematics and the subordination of physical phenomena to mathematical formulae (a field in which it won some notable triumphs) the rationalistic school took almost complete possession of the fields of morals, jurisprudence, political theory and rational theology, theology supposedly emancipated from supernatural bonds. It was thus supreme in the entire realm of what would now be termed the social sciences. The devastating wars of the seventeenth century, civil and religious, fostered a demand for a rational and moral standard as an authority above and untouched by shifting temporal struggles. Norms were demanded which could be applied securely to empirical social and political phenomena. To this end they must proceed from the source of reason which was superior to mundane and human vicissitudes. Grotius, for example, revamped the law of nature of the mediaeval period to help rationalize international relations, and his successors in various fields of jurisprudence and morals made his method of appeal more and more stringently logical.

The tendency of the rationalistic method was optimistic and justificatory or apologetic. The underlying assumption was that empirical social phenomena, however much they might fall short of rational norms, were yet subject to their authority. Actual institutions might be criticized in their detail as coming short of the law of reason, but their essential nature was justified as a manifestation of universal rationality. Thus Spinoza, who was anything but a political conservative in his ultimate ideal, held that the function of the state as a representative of law and therefore of reason and universality is so intimate and necessary that no conceivable abuse of authority justifies rebellion.

The religious civil wars of the seventeenth century had an opposite effect in Great Britain. They strengthened the empirical school because they created an atmosphere of moderation and compromise. The necessity for toleration was so evident that desire to carry through any comprehensive set of beliefs to its logical end was effectively dulled. The Revolution of 1688 not only established John Locke as the official intellectual apologist of popular rights (including the right and duty of rebellion) but made the empirical method developed by Locke in his *Essay concerning Human Understanding* supreme in the fields of morals, politics and natural theology until the early part of the nineteenth century.

David Hume detected what was logically the weak point in Locke's empiricism by showing that it left no place for intrinsic relations and thus resulted in an intellectual atomism whose only justifiable philosophic conclusion is complete skepticism. Nevertheless, Hume appealed to habit and custom as practical if irrational unifying and relating forces. Thus he really succeeded in strengthening rather than upsetting the empirical spirit in British thought. At most he gave it a conservative turn by insisting that habit is the sole ultimate principle of unity and coherence and so prevented the critical liberalism of the school of Locke from taking a radical turn. Hume's work bore its distinctly philosophic fruit in Germany. It destroyed rationalistic complacency in the mind of Kant and started him on the way to producing a philosophy which would give sense experience the function of supplying the matter of all justifiable beliefs and practical acts, while reason would furnish its rational forms, its justifying norms and inescapable imperatives. Kant's successors in Germany all felt that Kant's reconciliation of sense and reason in logical method as well as in the practical and moral applications of the new logic was mechanical, leaving the two factors in unstable equilibrium. The movement toward their organic union culminated in what may not unfairly be called the institutional idealism of Hegel.

The technical transformations wrought by Hegel in logical theory, with his dialectic movement of thesis, antithesis and synthesis, lie beyond the scope of this article. In substance it may be said, however, that Hegel sought a logic which would avoid the abstract, non-historical character of the earlier semimathematical rationalism. He wished in effect to make the movement of history the supreme rational manifestation. If philosophical and terminological technicalities are ignored, his work may be characterized as an attempt at a logical apotheosis of the historical method; indeed it was largely through his influence that the historical method was in the first half of the nineteenth century brought to consciousness in the fields of law, politics, morals, language, religion and political economy. Hegel piously retained the rationalistic idea of the supremacy of reason and absolute mind in history.

As far as fundamental logic was concerned, however, there was no great upset when Marx "stood Hegel on his head," as he said, and treated the ultimate logic and dialectic of history as essentially economic in character. The growing importance of evolution in biological science, with its stress on biological realism or biological materialism, was largely responsible for this rise of economic realism or materialism as an interpretation of human history. With Marx' official successors the materialistic dialectic of history was developed in an absolutistic spirit which made the complete downfall of bourgeois and capitalistic society inevitable, leading so necessarily to the social synthesis of communism as seemingly to free human action and planning from any responsibility in producing social change. The net tendency of the logic of historicism in its identification with evolutionism was to elevate an automatic movement of history to the position of supreme arbiter.

In Great Britain during the nineteenth century there was a rehabilitation of empirical method. It is noteworthy that Mill's logic was originated by his desire to introduce scientific method into social and moral subjects. He was offended by the adherence to dogmatic authoritarian methods in this field as well as by the position, typified by Macaulay, that in morals and politics we must depend only upon precedent and individual insight, political phenomena as such being outside the scope of scientific method. According to Mill, we can rise from observations to hypotheses, develop these hypotheses deductively and then apply them to social as well as to physical material. Mill's particularistic assumptions led him, however, into an extreme individualism which prevented realization of his scientific aim. On the other hand, the increasingly dispersive and disintegrative tendencies of social life led a group of English thinkers to rely upon the "organic" logic of the German idealistic school as the best means

of combating atomistic individualism. For a generation in the latter part of the nineteenth and the early part of the twentieth century this philosophy and logic were almost dominant in English
thought. Their influence coincided with the ebbing of the liberalism of the type of Locke and Mill and the growing desire for
state regulation of private enterprise. Whether Hegel so intended
or not, there is no doubt that the premises of his logical method
are conducive to collectivistic policies in social matters.

The split in schools of method earlier referred to as characteristic of modern life continues into the present. On the whole at
the present time the conceptualistic methods of the rationalist
school find little favor in the social sciences. The latter are devoted largely to empirical fact finding and to the attempt to arrive at social laws "inductively." Abstinence from general ideas is
accompanied, however, by remoteness of social method from
guidance of social, legal and economic phenomena. The split is
called tragic because it is the sign of failure to find a generally
accepted method which will do in control of social forces what
scientific method has accomplished in control of physical energies. We now oscillate between a normative and rationalistic logic
in morals and an empirical, purely descriptive method in concrete matters of fact. Hence our supposed ultimate ideals and
aims have no intrinsic connection with the factual means by
which they must be realized, while factual data are piled up with
no definitely recognized sense of their bearing on the formation
of social policy and the direction of social conduct.

Consciousness of this situation has been a main factor in a
new attempt to generalize the experimental side of natural science into a logical method which is applicable to the interpretation and treatment of social phenomena. So far this recent movement remains almost entirely American in character. It was
initiated by Charles S. Peirce and carried out especially in morals
and religion, under the name of pragmatism, by William James. It
is characteristic of this logical school to insist upon the necessity
of conceptions which go beyond the scope of past experience for
guidance of observation and experiment, while it also insists that
ideas are only tentative or working hypotheses until they are
modified, rejected or confirmed by the consequences produced
by acting on them. Emphasis upon experiment differentiates this
method from historic empiricism as well as from present fact

finding methods. The latter treat social inquiry as wholly outside the facts investigated and merely survey and record data in a certain field. The *novum organum* called for by the experimental logic insists that no such separation is possible in social matters, and that ideas and principles must be employed to deal overtly and actively with "facts" if, on one side, the facts are to be significant and if, on the other, ideas and theories are to receive test and verification. Experimental logic would resolve the controversies, now four centuries old, between reason and sense experience by making both concepts and facts elements in and instruments of intelligently controlled action.

See: METHOD, SCIENTIFIC; SCIENCE; PHILOSOPHY; SOPHISTS; SCHOLASTICISM; PRAGMATISM; MATERIALISM; POSITIVISM.

Consult: Prantl, Carl von, *Geschichte der Logik im Abendlande*, 4 vols. (Leipsic 1855–70; reprinted 1927); Harms, Friedrich, *Geschichte der Logik*, ed. by Adolf Lasson in Harms' *Die Philosophie in ihrer Geschichte*, 2 vols. (Berlin 1879–81) vol. ii; Adamson, Robert, *A Short History of Logic*, ed. by W. R. Sorley (Edinburgh 1911); Enriques, Federigo, *Per la storia della logica* (Bologna 1922), tr. by Jerome Rosenthal as *The Historic Development of Logic* (New York 1929); Dewey, John, *Essays in Experimental Logic* (Chicago 1916), and *Philosophy and Civilization* (New York 1931); Schiller, F. C. S., *Logic for Use* (London 1929); Peirce, C. S., *Collected Papers*, ed. by Charles Hartshorne and Paul Weiss, vols. i–ii (Cambridge, Mass. 1931–32) vol. ii; Cohen, M. R., *Reason and Nature* (New York 1931); Marck, Siegfried, *Die Dialektik in der Philosophie der Gegenwart*, 2 vols. (Tübingen 1929–31); Engels, Friedrich, "Dialektik und Natur," ed. by D. Rjazanov in *Marx-Engels Archiv*, vol. ii (1927) 117–395; Bradley, F. H., *The Principles of Logic*, 2 vols. (2nd ed. London 1922); Social Science Research Council, Committee on Scientific Method in the Social Sciences, *Methods in Social Science*, ed. by Stuart A. Rice (Chicago 1931).

Outlawry of War

On April 6, 1927, Foreign Minister Briand of France, in
a message to the American people on the occasion of the tenth
anniversary of American entrance into the World War, said that
"France would be willing to subscribe publicly with the United
States to any mutual engagement tending 'to outlaw war,' to use
an American expression, as between these two countries." Not
officially noticed at the time by the State Department of the
United States, this statement later became a subject of diplomatic
exchange of notes; and Briand formally submitted to the United
States government a proposal that the two governments "condemn recourse to war and renounce it respectively as an instrument of their national policy towards each other." On December
28, 1927, Secretary of State Kellogg suggested in reply that the
treaty be multilateral and an effort be made to secure "the adherence of all of the principal powers of the world to a declara-
tion renouncing war as an instrument of national policy." Mean-
while Senator Borah in a speech in Cleveland on May 10, 1927,
had urged this idea as a precondition of the adherence of the
United States. The French government demurred at first, urging
that while there was no obstacle to such a treaty between France
and the United States, the treaties by which other nations had
bound themselves under the Covenant of the League and the Lo-
carno agreements of October, 1925, stood in the way of a multi-
partite treaty; it desired also to limit the proposal to "outlawry
of aggressive wars," so-called. Further negotiations adjusted the
points of difference, however, and on August 27, 1928, the Paris
Pact was signed; there were fifteen original signatories including
France, the United States, Great Britain, Germany, Japan and a

[First published in *Encyclopaedia of the Social Sciences*, ed. Edwin R. A. Seligman and Alvin Johnson (New York: Macmillan Co., 1933), 11:508–10.]

number of secondary powers. War as a means of solving international controversies was condemned; it was renounced as an instrument of national policy, and the contracting parties agreed "that the settlement or solution of all disputes or conflicts of whatever nature or of whatever origin they may be, which may arise among them, shall never be sought except by pacific means." The United States Senate ratified the treaty on January 15, 1929, with but one dissenting vote. By the summer of that year practically every nation had declared its adherence, and President Hoover set July 24 as the date of its formal proclamation.

The history behind this action, which reversed the entire previous course of thought regarding the legitimacy of the institution of war, included ten years of agitation and discussion carried on by the American Committee for the Outlawry of War. The "American expression," as Briand justly called it, was first used by the founder and chairman of this committee, S. O. Levinson, a Chicago lawyer, in an article published in the *New Republic*, March 9, 1918. The article pointed out that while most people took it for granted that war was resorted to illegally or criminally, actually under existing international law it was recognized as the final method for settling disputes between nations; that international law provided rules "of" war but no rule "against" war; and that since social development had been marked by the continued extension of juridical methods for settling disputes and since now only international disputes remained outside the juridical sphere and hence were lawfully settled by force, the next step was to outlaw the institution of war.

The complete project of outlawry developed by Levinson and the Committee for Outlawry included four main points: first, modification of international law to take war out of the category of legitimate means of solving disputes, this change to be effected or attended by national plebiscites to insure the education and registration of public opinion; second, revision and codification of international law to insure harmony of all its parts with the new action; third, the formation of an international court of justice which should have affirmative jurisdiction with respect to disputes likely to lead to war; fourth, provision that, in accord with the tenor of article 1, section 8, of the Constitution of the United States, each nation should make offenses against the law of nations crimes under domestic law, so that war breeders would be tried and punished in their own country. All through the period of discussion and agitation the advocates of the outlawry principle insisted that its adoption be secured by mutual adhesion to a treaty. The whole course of the discussion shows that the original outlawry movement directly instigated the Paris Pact, which is historically inconceivable without it.

In his first article, written while the war was still being waged, Levinson advocated that the organized force of the world be used against a nation which violated the new provision of international law. But from 1921 he and the Committee for Outlawry took the position that the sole reliance was the organized moral sentiment of the world and that even if nations should agree to use force against a recalcitrant nation, there would be no assurance save good faith that that compact in turn would be kept. They held that there was a fallacy in the analogy between the use of force against a domestic offender and against a nation, since the latter signified the use of military force on a large scale and constituted war. Since that time, the supporters of the outlawry movement have always opposed any appeal to "sanctions."

Largely influenced by Levinson, Senator Knox, a former secretary of state, became a convert to the idea of outlawry, took part in formulating the four points already mentioned and in addresses in the Senate in 1919 and 1920 proposed and endorsed the outlawry principle. On February 14, 1923, Senator Borah, likewise a supporter of outlawry, introduced in the Senate a resolution which declared that "it is the view of the Senate . . . that war between nations should be outlawed as an institution or means for the settlement of international controversies by making it a public crime under the law of nations." It called for the preparation of a code of international law of peace based upon equality and justice; and it proposed that a judicial substitute for war be created in the form of an international court modeled on the United States Supreme Court and having affirmative jurisdiction to decide all purely international controversies, "the enforcement of its decrees" being the same as with the Supreme Court, "namely, the respect of all enlightened nations for judgments resting upon open and fair investigations and impartial decisions and the compelling power of enlightened public opinion." This document, which Senator Borah reintroduced in December, 1927, became the Magna Carta of the outlawry movement and was directly and indirectly the prototype of the action concluded in Paris in 1928. From 1923 an active popular educational campaign for outlawry was carried on in the United States, some of its chief supporters in addition to Senator Borah being Raymond Robins, Judge Florence Allen, John Haynes Holmes, C. C. Morrison and John Dewey. Senator Walsh of Montana was a strong defender of the idea in the Senate.

The movement throughout the earlier period met opposition and ridicule as well as indifference. To some extent the former were based upon misunderstanding between the critics and the adherents of the movement. The critics represented outlawry as merely a legalistic device constructed on the theory that wars could be banished by the passing of a statute. Adherents of the movement answered that they had never claimed that outlawry could prevent by legal fiat the occurrence of wars. They argued that, as had happened in the case of private combat, it represented the substitution of law for force as the authorized method of settling disputes and that it would deprive war of its authorized social status and consolidate public opinion against it. It was argued that the moral sentiment of the world was increasingly opposed to war but was now helpless, juridically speaking, law and morals being opposed to each other, while outlawry would bring the moral and the legal into harmony with each other; and that since formulation in law has always been a great educational agency, this change would serve to crystallize the popular sentiment for peace and test its genuineness. To the criticism therefore that the legal change would not touch the causes of war, which at present are almost always economic in nature, it was replied that while law and courts have never attempted to remove the causes of disputes, outlawry would provide the conditions for a much freer and more energetic educational campaign against economic injustice than now exists; it was urged that directly, because of its economic effects, and indirectly, because of the temper of mind it breeds, the war system is the greatest foe of economic reform, that it is a cause as well as an effect of economic injustice and that to wait for the abolition of war until economic wrongs are remedied might mean to wait until civilization is destroyed. Finally, to the objection that outlawry contemplated a legal method in substitution for all political methods of settling disputes, such as negotiation, conference, arbitration and conciliation, the defenders of outlawry replied that the abolition of the legal status of war would on the contrary give a direct stimulus to the use of these political methods and that it would make them franker and more effective by doing away with the threat of war, in the shadow of which they had always operated.

The immediate moral effect of the Paris Pact and its potential diplomatic effect were somewhat weakened by comments made by a few nations in exchange of notes, reserving certain territorial areas in the case of Great Britain and of the United States, and the "neutrality treaties" in the case of some continental nations, particularly France. There was also some ambiguity attending the notion of self-defense by a nation. The Committee for the Outlawry of War had strenuously opposed making a distinction between aggressive and defensive wars, pointing out that all nations claimed that their own wars were defensive and holding to the idea that it was the institution of war and not particular wars which were to be outlawed. As a concession to nationalist and militarist elements in various nations it was admitted in the course of the negotiations that each nation is its own judge as to whether a war in self-defense is necessary; the idea does not, however, appear in the pact itself and its legal status is doubtful in comparison with the sweeping agreement to resort to pacific means of settlement of all international disputes. In the original outlawry plan it was pointed out that the right of self-defense is extralegal and cannot therefore be touched by any law. But it was held that the actual facts of a case rather than a mere assertion of action in self-defense should be presented to the International Court for a decision as to whether a plea of self-defense was justified. This move has still to be made. In spite of these limitations, as compared with the broader scope of the original outlawry plan, the pact has been a fruitful source of international cooperation. It provides a common ground upon which nations may draw more closely together in coordination of efforts for peace. The doctrine of international non-recognition of territorial and other gains made in violation of the pact, already virtually endorsed by the League of Nations and a corollary of the pact itself, serves as an illustration of this achievement. If it is considered that for many centuries war has been the recognized means of settling disputes between nations, that it is one of the oldest of all historic institutions and that the minds of statesmen and diplomats as well as of the military have become adjusted to war as the ultimate juridical method of settlement, the change that has been effected in the legal status of war in a short period of ten years is striking.

See: War; Aggression, International; Pacifism; Peace Movements; International Law; International Organization; League of Nations; Arbitration, International; Permanent Court of International Justice; Permanent Court of Arbitration; Sanction, International; Disarmament; Militarism; National Defense.

Consult: Levinson, S. O., "The Legal Status of War" in *New Republic*, vol. xiv (1918) 171–73, "Can Peace Be 'Enforced'?" and "The Sanctions of Peace" in *Christian Century*, vol. xlii (1925) 46–47, and vol. xlvi (1929) 1603–06; Hard, William, "The Nonstop Peace Advocate" in *World's Work*, vol. lviii (1929) no. 3, 76–83; Dewey, John, "Political Combination or Legal Cooperation," "If War Were Outlawed," "What Outlawry of War Is Not," "War and a Code of Law," and "'As an Example to Other Nations'" in *New Republic*, vol. xxxiv (1923) 89–91, 234–35, vol. xxxvi (1923) 149–52, 224–26, vol. liv (1928) 88–89, and letters headed "Divergent Paths to Peace" by J. T. Shotwell and John Dewey, p. 194–96; Morrison, C. C., *The Outlawry of War* (Chicago 1927); Shotwell, J. T., *War as an Instrument of National Policy and Its Renunciation in the Pact of Paris* (New York 1929), especially ch. x; Madariaga, S. de, *Disarmament* (New York 1929) pt. i, ch. iii, pt. ii, ch. xv and pt. iii, ch. iii; Lippmann, Walter, "'The Outlawry of War'" in *Atlantic Monthly*, vol. cxxxii (1923) 245–53; Kellor, F., and Hatvany, A., *Security against War*, 2 vols. (New York 1924) vol. ii, ch. xxxix; Wright, Q., "The Outlawry of War" in *American Journal of International Law*, vol. xix (1925) 76–103; Fenwick, C. G., "War as an Instrument of National Policy" in *American Journal of International Law*, vol. xxii (1928) 826–29; Page, Kirby, *The Renunciation of War*, Christianity and World Problems, no. 16 (New York 1928); "The Preservation of Peace" ed. by Parker T. Moon in Academy of Political Science, *Proceedings*, vol. xiii (1929) no. 2; Miller, D. H., *The Peace Pact of Paris* (New York 1928); Myers, D. P., *Origin and Conclusion of the Paris Pact*, World Peace Foundation Pamphlets, vol. xii, no. 2 (Boston 1929); Council on Foreign Relations, *Survey of American Foreign Relations* (New Haven 1929) sect. ii; Wheeler-Bennett, J. W., *The Renunciation of War*, Information Service on International Affairs, Information Series, no. 4 (London 1928); Wehberg, Hans, *Die Aechtung des Krieges* (Berlin 1930); Schücking, Walther, *Die Revision der Völkerbundssatzung im Hinblick auf den Kelloggpakt*, Wissenschaftliche Beiträge zu aktuellen Fragen, no. 1 (Berlin 1931).

Philosophy

Definitions of philosophy are usually made from the standpoint of some system of philosophy and reflect its special point of view. For the purposes of this account the difficulty may be avoided by defining philosophy from the point of view of its historical role within human culture. Since the survey is confined to western civilization, the origin of European philosophy in Greece supplies the natural beginning. For not only does the name "philosophy" come from Greek thought, but also the explicit consciousness of what is denoted by the term. Greek thinkers moreover distinguished the branches into which philosophy is still conventionally divided; they laid the foundations of logic, cosmology, metaphysics, ethical and political philosophy, and to a lesser degree, aesthetic theory. Even if these foundations are not always built upon, it is impossible to understand departures and innovations apart from some reference to Greek thought. In Greek philosophy the problems of western philosophy are either formulated or adumbrated.

The reason for the primacy of Greek thought is not accidental, nor is it for the most part a mere matter of chronological priority. On the contrary, the reason for it is an essential part of a definition of philosophy from the cultural point of view. For Greece was a ground for exhibiting and proving most of the difficulties and predicaments that arise in the collective relation of man to nature and fellow man. This condition would not of itself have generated philosophy without the extraordinary capacity of the Greek mind for observation and statement. An explanation of this fact would here be irrelevant and perhaps impossible. Such is not the case, however, with respect to the traits of Greek culture that called forth the reflections that initiated western philosophy: these exhibit in striking fashion the typical conflicts of col-

[First published in *Encyclopaedia of the Social Sciences*, ed. Edwin R. A. Seligman and Alvin Johnson (New York: Macmillan Co., 1934), 12:118–29.]

lective human experience. Consequently, in spite of the limitations of the Greek world in space and time, Greek traits form the very stuff out of which philosophy is made. Greece, and especially Athens, was an intellectual looking glass in which the western world became conscious of its essential problems. The Greek origins of the European philosophical tradition dispose completely of the notion that philosophical problems evolve in the consciousness of lonely though brilliant thinkers. These origins prove that such problems are formulations of complications existing in the material of collective experience, provided that experience is sufficiently free, exposed to change and subjected to attempts at deliberate control to present in typical form the basic difficulties with which human thought has to reckon.

Greece was distinguished from other ancient civilizations in that priests lacked political authority, having indeed become subordinate civic officers. Equally important was the fact that religious beliefs were early set forth in literature of great artistic merit, never in the form of dogmas. The resulting intellectual freedom furnished the primary condition for the production of philosophy. The cosmogonies that characterized Greek mythology in common with all other religions were emancipated with comparative ease from a predominant religious setting and were transformed into reasoned attempts at a rational account of the origin and constitution of the known world. The early thinkers in the Grecian colonies in Asia Minor and Italy and its islands were geographers, astronomers, geologists, meteorologists, founders of the natural sciences quite as much as they were philosophers. Their generalized and comprehensive stories of the cosmos and its origin created an idea of completeness and breadth of view that remained as part of philosophy after the sciences had become specialized. The physical interest of these early thinkers persists today in that branch of philosophy called cosmology.

It was probably natural that interest in physical nature should have predominated in the adventurous, seafaring, trading Greek colonists, especially as their political life was borrowed. In Athens, however, cosmology was definitely subordinated to moral and political interests. Throughout Greece generally, with the exception of Sparta, civic matters were adjusted through the medium of discussion. Athens was moreover a pure democracy in that all citizens rather than a delegated body took part in public affairs.

Party conflict was rife and changes in type of government were frequent. The situation was expressed, on the intellectual side, in consciousness of a number of problems defined in terms of antitheses. There were, for example, the problems of stability versus change, of harmony and order versus conflict, of reason (represented by discussion and consultation with a view to persuasion) versus force. Intermingled with these were other questions brought to the fore by the traveling scholars called sophists. Although, chiefly owing to the attacks made upon them by Plato, the term sophist has now a distinctly derogatory significance, the sophists were only the learned men of the day who traveled about offering their intellectual wares for sale—and with the Greeks all important education was adult education. Disputes regarding the role assumed by these men evoked such further antitheses as tradition versus innovation, the relations between custom and conscious thought, between nature and culture, between nature and art—since the sophists professed to teach all of the arts that were in good repute; that is, those above the level of the manual craftsman, such as the military art and the art of managing the household and the city-state.

Socrates, the initiator of Athenian philosophic reflection, deliberately strove to limit theoretical discussion to moral and political subjects. Apparently the direct stimulus to his conversations on these topics came from the sophists. His primary question was whether the various forms of social excellence, the "virtues," which command recognition by others, can be taught and if so how. Consideration of this theme led him to consideration of the relation of the various virtues to one another and to their unity in understanding, or rational insight. Since rational insight was found by him to be practically non-existent among politicians, among the poets, who were the acknowledged moral teachers of the community, as well as among the sophists, his teaching came to its climax in a demand for the pursuit of understanding or wisdom.

The philosophical tradition of the western world did not originate because of a mere taste for abstract speculation or yet because of pure interest in knowledge divorced from application to conduct. On the contrary, wisdom, in its material and goal, was something more than science even though it was not possible without science. It was science enlisted in the service of conduct, first communal, or civic, and then personal. Most of the distinctive traits of philosophy through the ages are intimately connected with this fact. The connection is not external or due to the accident of its origin in Greece, but is intrinsic. The Greeks brought to consciousness three problems that are bound to emerge whenever civilization becomes reflectively turned back upon itself: What are the place and role of knowledge and reason in the conduct of life? What are the constitution and structure of knowledge and reason by virtue of which they can perform the assigned function? And, growing out of this question, what is the constitution of nature, of the universe, which renders possible and guarantees the conceptions of knowledge and of good that are reached? Upon the whole, in course of time, philosophy began with the last question, and this fact often disguises the initial problem as to the guidance of life and conduct. But the tie that unites the seemingly most remote speculations with this issue has never been completely cut.

The problem of the organization and direction of personal and community conduct was still uppermost with Plato, although he took steps which led to an apparent relegation of that issue to a secondary position, a fact that has frequently caused his modern interpreters to place him in a perspective foreign to his own intent. Instead of excluding or neglecting speculations about the constitution of nature in formulating the end of the organized state and individual, he asserted that the problem of the end and of good can be solved only when the inquiry is extended to include the totality of things and when the final conclusion is reached by understanding the constitution of nature. This latter problem moreover can be solved only as the problem of the structure and method of knowledge is solved. Thus the ethico-political problem was widened to include cosmology and logic. Dialectic became central, not merely auxiliary, in the philosophic scheme, for it was the means by which insight into the good was to be attained. By reason of the place of the good in the structure of the universe this fact instituted a necessary connection between logic and metaphysics.

Because of the inherent relation set up by Plato between cosmology, science (especially mathematics), logic and political ethics, his fundamental distinctions, such as those between being and becoming, reality and appearance, form and matter, whole and part or universal and particular, were not presented by him as detached intellectual distinctions. While he defines philosophy as desiderated science of the whole, he defines it also as the legislative science, or science of the state, since social organization is the form in which man is most directly concerned with the whole.

The distinction of reality and appearance has an ethical import as well as one running through knowledge—where it appears in connection with the distinction between science and mere opinion—and through metaphysics. Morally it involves the question of the individual in his relations to others, since evil never offers itself as such but disguises itself as a good: the bad man strives to *seem* good in order to obtain recognition, while the truly good man is content to *be*, without regard to appearance, that is, the impression made on others. Starting from this ethical distinction, Plato was able to follow the difference and relation of the two throughout a series of logical and cosmological terms, such as one and many, permanent and changing and so on. Being with Plato always has the connotation of the stable, the dependable, while change imports instability and variation— departure from a standard which is fixed. In a similar way his distinction of universal and particular is not merely logical or merely metaphysical, but is concerned with the relation of law— which is legislative and normative—to application to the individual in judicial decision and administration. Such points are arbitrarily selected examples of the interpenetration of the politico-moral with the logical and metaphysical, which is evidenced on a larger scale in his most systematic work, the *Republic*, since this is at once a treatise on metaphysics, theory of knowledge, politics and education.

It is evident that the interpenetration which, in the case of Plato, gave meaning to philosophy as the search for wisdom could not long be maintained in the form in which he set it forth. Philosophy was in a condition of unstable equilibrium with respect to the various factors contained in it. To Plato it seemed still possible, at least as an intellectual and moral aspiration, to reform and preserve the city-state. The fact that Aristotle was a tutor of Alexander the Great indicates that the failure of this dream was imminent and consequently a redistribution of the constituents of the whole inevitable. The direction it took, especially in the subordination of morals and politics to metaphysics and science and of practise in general to theory defined as contemplative cognitive possession and enjoyment of being, was connected with Aristotle's own naturalistic interests. It thus happened that while he could retain and utilize most of the leading distinctions of Plato, he gave philosophy as a whole a radically different turn and form. While to Plato the apprehension of real being was not complete until the insight was reembodied in control of phenomena through the appropriate organization of the latter, to Aristotle science was its own end, and everything in the sphere of action dealing with persons and things was relegated to an inferior order of probability and opinion. The separation thus effected by Aristotle enabled him to distinguish, define, and classify in a way not open to Plato, since the latter's problem was to institute actual connection between matters assigned by Aristotle to different classes or realms. The outcome was a marvel of systematization, which much later, at the height of scholasticism, became the model for the summing up and organization of knowledge from the standpoint of the prevailing theologies, Jewish and Christian.

Subsequent to the dissolution of Greece, during the time of the supremacy of Rome in politics, of Alexandria and oriental beliefs in religion, the values assigned by Aristotle became as unreal to his successors as the Platonic social aspirations had been to Aristotle. During the period which Gilbert Murray describes as "failure of nerve," the chief interest of thinkers was in the supernatural. There ensued of necessity a period of acute metaphysical speculation with all phenomena arranged and interpreted in hierarchical descent from supreme being, a reality unattainable by way of scientific thought but capable of being at least occasionally grasped in mystic intuition. Thus neo-Platonism effected a further distinctive redistribution of the constituents of philosophic reflection, because of a new centre of dominant value. Thinkers in Rome, more removed from oriental influence, translated philosophy into a practical direction of conduct, a tendency common to stoic, Epicurean and skeptic schools. The domination of western European life by the Roman church introduced another factor, and from the time of St. Augustine through the twelfth century there was a systematic distribution of metaphysical, logical, cosmological and ethical factors worked out on the basis of the supremacy of the values characteristic of religious faith.

The purpose of the foregoing is not to sketch, even in outline, the history of philosophic thought, but to suggest the features that have always been characteristic of philosophy, and to indicate that cultural causes have produced the main changes in the direction and content of philosophic systems. If the movement of modern philosophy were followed, its tendencies would be seen to be connected with the new values that emerged with the revival of scholarship in the Renaissance, and especially with the growth of the natural sciences and the secularization of interest that mark recent centuries. Such a historical survey shows the necessity of defining philosophy from the standpoint of value, since the changes of philosophy are all inherently bound up with problems that arise when new emphases and new redistributions in the significance of values take place. For example, it is as certain as anything can be that if science, at present a dominant interest, were to become subordinated to some value that may emerge in the future, there will be produced a new set of problems and hence of philosophies.

The connection of philosophies and of change in the aim and method of philosophizing with changes in culture and social organization, which bring about redistributions of collective valuations and prestige, makes it possible to explain the fact that each system has a definition of philosophy couched in its own terms. For each philosophy is in effect, if not in avowed intent, an interpretation of man and nature on the basis of some program of comprehensive aims and policies. The generality and comprehensiveness claimed for philosophy have their origin in this fact. Each system has of necessity an exclusive aspect, often expressing itself in a controversial way, because it is, implicitly, a recommendation of certain types of value as normative in the direction of human conduct.

This intimate connection of philosophy with the values that interpret existence and direct conduct explains certain matters related to it. Philosophy has always, for example, been associated with religion either by way of derivation and justification or by way of criticism, and religious beliefs evidently claim to be concerned with ultimate values while religious attitudes claim to be supreme in conduct. But since philosophy must formulate its conceptions and interpretations in rational form, each philosophy depends necessarily upon the intellectual currents and the best authenticated knowledge of its time—in other words, upon science. As a consequence of its relation to religion and morals on one side and to science on the other, philosophy occupies a peculiar position with respect to literature. While philosophies have not as a rule been presented in an especially satisfactory form, they have aimed at appeal and persuasion more general and more moving than those of the specialized sciences. They have striven to bring about adoption of certain basic attitudes, not merely to convey information.

Finally, philosophy has a close connection, in some cases direct and in others indirect, with matters of conduct. The connection is direct when those studying or accepting a given philosophy are thereby committed to a certain way of life, including personal discipline. This was the case, for example, with the Pythagoreans, cynics and stoics, and Epicureans. A trace of the idea remains in the popular notion (derived from stoicism) that a philosopher should be able to endure pain and the vicissitudes of life better than others. The indirect connection is illustrated in what has been said about the socio-ethical setting of philosophy in the case of Socrates and Plato. It is exemplified also with the scholastics, with Spinoza and John Locke, with the materialistically inclined *philosophes* of the eighteenth century, with Rousseau, Karl Marx, John Stuart Mill, Herbert Spencer and most great names in the history of thought. In spite of Aristotle's deviation from Plato, concern with the good, with value, is characteristic of the Stagirite thinker as well. For he asserts that the life of *theoria* is higher than that of *praxis*, so much higher that it defines the being and activity of God. Distinctions of higher and lower are found indeed throughout all his professedly purely cognitive distinctions and classifications. The philosophies that most emphasize scientific form and content also set forth a conception of the value of science.

It is a generic definition of philosophy to say that it is concerned with problems of being and occurrence from the standpoint of value, rather than from that of mere existence. There are of course various and varying types of philosophy that claim to connect philosophy directly and exclusively with science. Some of them regard philosophy as the ultimate science, holding that it deals with reality as a totality or as perfect being, in contrast with the special sciences, which deal with it piecemeal or with mere phenomena. Others hold that it is concerned with effecting a comprehensive synthesis of the results of the special sciences. Still others assert that it is concerned with analysis of the unexamined concepts and postulates that lie at the base of the special sciences. It would not be just to say that the conflict of these views with one another throws out of court any view that connects philosophy exclusively with science. But upon examination it will be found that the cause of the divergence of views resides in some difference of valuation or else that the theory of science is itself enclosed in a tacit context of valuation.

The connection of philosophy with conflicts of ends and values serves to explain two criticisms frequently brought against the enterprise of philosophy. One of them points to the diverging and controversial character of philosophy in contrast with the definite trend toward unity in the sciences. If, however, valuation enters into philosophy, divergence is inevitable. It could not be eliminated except by attainment of a complete consensus as to universal ends and methods. If those who hold up different values as the directive aims of life were to agree with one another in their interpretations of existence, it would be a sure sign of insincerity. Relativists and absolutists, radicals and conservatives, spiritualists and materialists, differ primarily in their systems of value, and their strictly intellectual differences follow logically. How can those who believe in the necessity of a transcendent source of authority agree with those who believe that the seat of authority is and should be in the processes and operations of actual experience? In spite of conflicts philosophy serves the purpose of clarifying the source of opposition and the problems attendant upon it; while with respect to some problems articulation and clarification are more significant than formal solution.

The other indictment of philosophy, that it mills around among the same problems without settling any of them, may be met, on the basis of the relation of philosophy to value, by pointing out that no phase of culture can settle the problems that arise in and for another phase of culture. General problems regarding aims and the means appropriate to their realization arise in every type of social life. They have formal features in common, and these are stated in philosophical generalizations. But in actual content they differ, and hence they have to be dealt with in the terms both of the science and of the dominant practical tendencies of each period. Only if social institutions and the culture attending them were wholly static would it be possible to carry over completely the solutions or even the methods of one epoch into the conditions of another.

A striking illustration of the formal constancy of certain problems along with tremendous change in content is found in the question of the relation between the individual and the universal. Conflicts between the individual and the total order of which he is a part are bound to arise in every complex and changing culture. Wherever reflection is free and energetic, these conflicts will be generalized and will take conceptual form as the problem of the relation of universal and particular. In this conceptual form they will have a certain independent dialectical career of their own. But the state of knowledge and the state of institutions are the variables of the formal relationship, and they will inevitably color the meaning of the problem. One has only, for example, to contrast Greek, mediaeval and contemporary culture with respect to the knowledge of nature bearing upon this problem and with respect to the political and economic conditions that determine the actual status of individuals, to see how constancy of the problem in formal terms is compatible with great variability in content, so that the issue must be approached from a new point of view, never repeated in subsequent history.

The same considerations explain the diversity of solutions propounded. For difference of valuation signifies difference of interest, of emphasis and hence of weight and perspective. For example, one who at the present time gives primary weight to the findings of the physical sciences will still have at least two opposite courses open to him. From one point of view he will see how careless nature is of the conservation and development of complex highly organized individuals, and will rate low the place of individuality in the scheme of things. On the other hand, he may be impressed by the breakdown of the Newtonian philosophy of ultimate atoms, inherently all alike and differing from one another only in external matters, such as spatial position and rate of motion, and by the tendency to regard all laws as statistical norms not exactly applicable to any individual particle, and hence will infer that unique individuality is rooted in the very nature of things. And one who approaches the problem from the side of material organized biologically and socially has open to him also a choice in valuations. He may esteem development as higher than order and identify individuality with the principle of progress. Or he may be troubled by disorder and disturbance and thus be led to subordination of individuality to the whole on the ground that individuality by itself leads to anarchy and chaos. There will be other times in which a fair equilibrium of the two principles will obtain and this particular problem will temporarily sink into the background, some other widely felt predicament directing attention and interest to the need of conceptual formalization of another conflict.

The conception of philosophy that results from the account just presented is in fundamental contrast to that view of philosophy which regards it as an ultimate science disclosing the intrinsic nature of reality as distinguished from the special sciences, physical and social, which reveal only phenomenal manifestations. Even, however, if the latter view is held, it must be admitted that it can apply literally only to some one of the diverse systems characterizing the history of thought, and that other systems have to be accounted for, if at all, in cultural terms. Presumably also one may find in the contemporary state of culture at least the causes for the emergence of the particular view of reality assumed to be correct.

In other words, whatever else philosophies are or are not, they are at least significant cultural phenomena and demand treatment from that point of view. When philosophy is so approached, a highly important role must be given to any intellectual effort which seizes upon the characteristic disturbances and needs manifested in a particular culture (including of course its scientific resources as well as its institutions) and which formulates them in the most generalized terms the epoch has at its command. The conception of philosophy reached from a cultural point of view may be summed up by a definition of philosophy as a critique of basic and widely shared beliefs. For belief, as distinct from special scientific knowledge, always involves valuation, preferential attachment to special types of objects and courses of action. Beliefs moreover are intimately attached to customs and institutions, partly as effects, partly as causes, so that forces which impinge upon institutions and tend to unsettle them have a disturbing impact upon beliefs, and vice versa. Thus philosophies are generated and are particularly active in periods of marked social change, provided of course that the people undergoing change have sufficient powers of reflection to undertake the task of abstraction and generalization.

This last statement obviously applies to the origin and development of philosophy in Greece; to the twelfth century, when Christian doctrine received comprehensive formulation; to the Renaissance; to the seventeenth century, when the scientific revolution occurred; to the eighteenth, when there dawned a conception of the applicability of science to a progressive determination of social life. When once the principles underlying beliefs and valuations have received formal statement, the resulting concepts obtain a certain independent intellectual existence of their own and are capable of having their own career without reference to the cultural conditions of their origin. This secondary and derived existence is accentuated when, as so often happens, professional teachers are the chief guardians and representatives of philosophy.

From one point of view, then, the chief role of philosophy is to bring to consciousness, in an intellectualized form, or in the form of problems, the most important shocks and inherent troubles of complex and changing societies since these have to do with conflicts of value. Viewed with reference to this highly general function, historic systems tend to divide into the conserving and the revolutionary. The tendency of some is to preserve the values that are already embodied in the traditional, relatively established order. They accomplish this task by giving these values a reasoned statement and by setting forth their rational justification. Other thinkers, sometimes the most important of an entire generation, are acutely conscious of the deficiencies and corruptions of the existent order. They shape their logical methods, their interpretations of knowledge and even their interpretations of the cosmic order, with a view to showing the necessity of radical changes and to pointing out the character of needed reforms.

In this general sense the philosophy of Plato is "revolutionary," that of Aristotle is "conserving." The so-called transcendentalism of Plato, his insistence upon pure forms apart from concrete incarnation as standards of existence, is directly associated with his desire for thoroughgoing reform. To change the actual he required leverage outside of the actually existent, an independent realm of possibilities higher in value and potency than anything found in existence. Aristotle's insistence that forms have no existence apart from their actual embodiment corresponds, on the other hand, with his general tendency to rationalize the existent world by exhibiting it as containing upon the whole (special aberrations excepted) all the meaning and value that the nature of the case permits. His oft cited justification of slavery, for example, does not indicate a private harsh preference on his part, but an attempt to find a rational meaning in a universally established institution. The formulations of scholasticism are of the same rationalizing import, finding an underlying meaning to justify the beliefs and practises sanctioned by the church. The general tendency of eighteenth century thought, on the contrary, was determined by Locke and also, as regards the *encyclopédistes* and Condorcet, by Bacon; it was critical of if not actually hostile to existing institutions, and it used the new sciences of nature to project ideals of a new and better future. In contrast, the philosophy of Germany in the first half of the nineteenth century, culminating in Hegel, was distinctively justificatory of the main types of existence, exhibiting them as necessary stages in the self-manifestation of absolute mind and treating the French Revolution as proof of the bankruptcy of the opposite empirical philosophy.

The opposition is never as polar in fact as are the tendencies in the abstract. There is always a certain amount of adverse criticism and of implicit condemnation in the philosophies whose main purport it is to exhibit the meaning implicit in the existent forms of nature and culture. For in justifying the logical content of their philosophies, thinkers are usually compelled to indicate the transitory and relatively unimportant character of some of the particular forms in which they are embodied, regarding them as husks in comparison with the inner kernel. Thus Hegel, for example, treated the doctrines and institutions of Christianity; their rational meaning was sound, but their garb was that of the pictorial imagination. Since his interpretation excluded acceptance of the supernatural in its received sense, the effect was "revolutionary" as far as popular belief was concerned. On the other hand, thinkers who are most critical of the status quo are compelled, in order to get a foothold for intentional change, to accept and justify some features of the existing order, although their usual method is to resort to an idealized view of the ideas of an earlier epoch. Thus historic philosophies constitute a spectrum rather than cluster about opposite poles.

Irrespective of the tendency of a reforming philosophy to resort to a prior culture in which it is assumed that its own doctrines and ideals were embodied in a "pure" form, the generalized character of a philosophic statement renders it peculiarly available for formal transfer from one cultural situation to another. The actual state of the world and of science in the mediaeval period, when Christian doctrine was formulated in a metaphysical theology that also embraced the entire universe of extant knowledge, had little similarity to the culture of the time in which Aristotle wrote. Nevertheless, the abstract generality of the latter made it possible for the scholastics to use Aristotelian doctrines as the intellectual framework of their system. The administrative genius of Rome was alien to free speculation, but it fell back upon Greek philosophers to achieve a formulation which would be sufficiently comprehensive to meet the complex needs of the empire. The dawning science of the Renaissance reverted to Platonic and pre-Socratic thought in order to achieve emancipation from fossilized Aristotelianism. In spite of the distance that separated the territorial national state of the nineteenth century from the small city-state of antiquity, Hegel and his followers employed the political philosophy of Plato and Aristotle to interpret and justify the structure and procedures of the European states of their day. The thought of Spinoza, contemned in his own time, came to life in the non-mathematical organic vitalism of Herder and Goethe. In general it may be said that the philosophies that seem to their immediate contemporaries to be wilful novelties (because they depart from doctrines that have become conventionally current) are more often in line with some great traditional current than are the intellectual fashions that cry out against them. For the former go back and lay hold upon some leading generalization that has become obscured.

The specific cultural contributions of philosophy have been in natural science and the social disciplines, the latter including education. Philosophy has been the matrix within which the conceptions that have given new direction in both the physical and the human fields were conceived and nourished. It has served this purpose in two ways, the first of which is comparatively accidental and external, although one that has at times been practically helpful to the progress of scientific inquiry. For example, there can be little doubt that the acceptance of mathematical mechanics for interpreting physical phenomena was facilitated (in its struggle with the qualitative teleological science inherited from Aristotle) by Descartes' dualistic separation of the material world from mind and by the use that he made of a thoroughly spiritualistic rationalism and theism to explain the nature and justify the role of mathematical conceptions.

The really important role of philosophy in science, however, is intrinsic. The notion that science proceeds merely by the accumulation of observations unregulated by theory has no support from the history of scientific inquiry. There is a basic reason for this. Fruitful observations cannot be made nor can their results be arranged and coordinated without the use of hypotheses, of ideas that go beyond the existing state of knowledge. The origin of modern science is to be understood as much by the substitution of new comprehensive guiding ideas for those which had previously obtained as by improvement of the means and appliances of observation. By the necessity of the case, comprehensive directive hypotheses belong in their original formulation to philosophy rather than to science. For they outrun past knowledge and even the possibility of adequate test by contemporary means to such an extent that they are speculative in nature. Only later do they become an accepted part of that body of beliefs that is termed science.

Cases in point are the mathematico-mechanical conceptions that played such a part from the time of Descartes and Newton; the idea of evolution that was developed speculatively and applied to human history long before it could be used to direct specific inquiries in geology and biology; the doctrines of the conservation of matter and energy and so on. Indeed conceptions that are now the commonplace foundations of science and that seem to be self-evident in clarity are, if traced back, philosophical in origin. Such is the case, for example, with the ideas of motion, matter and energy, of atoms, of continuity and discreteness. But it must not be understood from this statement that philosophy has some inherent sovereignty over science. It means in fact that the division between philosophy and natural science is often arbitrary. What actually exists is a certain division of labor, in which the more speculative and hypothetical phase of intellectual activity is distinguished as philosophical and the more detailed and specifically verified part as scientific. The distinction that is made, ex post facto, is of temporal aspects of development rather than of something intrinsic. While it is true, as Lewes and some of the positivists have contended, that what was once philosophy is now science, the conclusion that philosophy is bound ultimately to disappear in science does not hold, at least not unless significant advance in science is to come to an end. For it is equally true that the generative ideas of future science will appear first in a speculative or philosophical form.

The intrinsic need of scientific progress for free speculation is reenforced by a cause which is moral or psychological in character. The human mind is subject, in its higher as well as in its more casual and directly practical activities, to the principle of habit and inertia. When scientific investigation gets definitely launched in a given direction, depending upon certain guiding ideas, it tends to move in grooves. Even when difficulties are encountered, the tendency is to follow the line of least resistance and to make some minor adaptation in the directive concept instead of trying some other principle. The use of epicycles in Ptolemaic astronomy is an example of a principle not confined to astronomy. All scientific theories tend to assume at some stage an epicyclical form. Thus it often happens that a philosopher, approaching the matter from a different point of view from that which obtains in current science and breaking loose from concepts that have become conventional through use, will initiate a fruitful line of inquiry. Even ignorance or lack of specialized knowledge may be an aid in freeing imagination and permitting the generation of ideas that give a new direction to interest and attention.

It is not claimed of course that this particular role of philosophy with respect to science has always been beneficial. Sometimes positive inquiry has been either started off or else confirmed in lines that lead nowhere by philosophy. There has been an overproduction in philosophy of speculative hypotheses, especially with respect to those advanced as being proved by intuition or reason apart from experimental evidence. Nevertheless, the philosophic function is indispensable, and a certain amount of excess production and seeming waste is necessary in order to insure freedom and flexibility in scientific advance.

The cultural role of philosophy has been even more extensive in social and political theories and the practical movements connected with the latter than in the natural sciences. Indeed it would be difficult to find in the social disciplines an important idea whose origin cannot be traced to one or another historic system of philosophy. The thoroughness with which philosophic ideas have been wrenched loose from their original context and given a career of their own in jurisprudence, political science and economics is the chief reason why their origin in philosophy can so easily be ignored. The influence of Greek philosophy upon Roman law, partly through the stoics and partly by more indirect channels, has already been alluded to. The very concept of law was indeed philosophical in origin. The idea of the "law of nature" was central in the ethical and political theories of the scholastic thinkers, and the organizing principle of all jurisprudence. It was given a new interpretation in the sixteenth and seventeenth centuries and became at the hands of Grotius the generating, directive idea of international law as regulative of war and peace. It is almost superfluous to point out the practical influence of the conception of natural rights in the seventeenth and eighteenth centuries and its effect upon the formation of political constitutions as well as upon court decisions far into the nineteenth century—nor is its power exhausted even now. Yet the idea originated not in legislative or judicial halls but in abstract theory.

The concept of sovereignty, which has had such an enormous role in political organization and practise, was quickly taken up by statesmen and made the basis and justification of their activities. But for the most part the idea received reasoned formulation at the hands of philosophers, in its extreme form by Hobbes and Spinoza and in its limited, or "liberal," form by John Locke. John Austin could not be classed as a philosopher in the technical sense of that term, but he (like Jeremy Bentham, who was specifically a moral and political philosopher) is not explicable historically apart from a philosophical tradition that includes Hobbes and also a thinker very different from Hobbes, namely David Hume. The entire conception of what Bentham called the "omnicompetence" of the legislature is strictly philosophical in origin.

As in the case of the natural sciences, many of the ideas borrowed by political theory and taken over into practical political
life have had unfortunate consequences. This is particularly true
because as a rule these ideas and their rational support have been
set forth as if possessed of universal validity, instead of as directive intellectual instrumentalities for particular periods. Hence
they have often had their greatest influence in a sense opposite to
that entertained by their original promulgators. The use made in
the nineteenth century of the doctrine of natural rights, or of liberty of contract, to protect property in a privileged position is a
case in point, for in its early phase it was a weapon of attack
upon the class then having legal and political control. Nevertheless, the role of philosophy is indispensable if political activity is
to rise above rule of thumb procedure. Only leading ideas, not
themselves verified at the time or indeed verifiable in a strict
positivistic sense, can bind together the mass of empirical details
of political practise into an organized whole and thus canalize
aspiration and endeavor toward definite ends.

What is true of law and politics is equally true of economics. In
Plato and Aristotle economics is definitely subordinated to politics; and politics is a branch, the most important branch, of ethical theory. Upon the whole this conception remained dominant
into the seventeenth century. The rise of the natural sciences
produced in the eighteenth century a new conception of nature
and of natural law, now distinguished not from positive law but
from artificial, man made regulations. Social phenomena were
regarded as expressions of human nature in a definite technical
sense whereby "nature" was set over against deliberate and conscious arrangement and control, the latter being artificial. The
consequence was that economic relations like that of supply and
demand were treated as "natural" laws, and political relations as
artificial and secondary. The philosophical psychology associated with classic political and legal theory had set up ideas and
reason as the ruling factors in man. The theory of human nature
which the philosophy of economics brought forward treated
wants as fundamental and ideas as subordinate. "Reason" was
merely the power of calculating the means by which desires could
be satisfied economically and effectively. This mode of theorizing
coincided with the growth of industry following the industrial
revolution and was used as a weapon to free commerce from

regulations adapted to feudal agrarianism but now operating to shackle human activity. The alleged "scientific" form of the psychology that was employed disguised the strictly philosophic character of the basic ideas of the new economics and of the whole laissez faire economy and politics.

There is an obvious reason why the affiliation of philosophy is more intimate in the case of the social sciences than in that of the physical. The former are more directly connected with problems of policy, and problems of policy all involve ends and purposes, and hence judgments of value. This fact is peculiarly conspicuous in the career of philosophy as matrix of educational theory and practise. Every important movement in education having conscious direction, that is, every one that does not follow tradition and custom, has been initiated by some philosophic development. The basic educational import of Plato's philosophy is clearly brought out in his *Republic*; and while it had no practical effect in its own day, its conception of the relation of education and social reform has since inspired members of different schools of thought. The fact that the philosophers of the mediaeval period are known as the schoolmen and that the philosophy of the period has the name of scholasticism is sufficient evidence of the close union of philosophy and education during that period. John Locke wrote specifically upon education of the young and his theories played a decided role in shaping Rousseau's *Émile*. It is probable also that the influence of his essay on human understanding and his treatise on civil government in formulating the intellectual creed of liberalism had an even more marked effect upon subsequent educational ideas than his express writings on the subject. The conception of the omnipotence of education in forming mind and character, presented most explicitly by Helvétius, was a direct outcome of Locke's theory of the receptivity of the mind to impressions from without.

The two leading directions of educational thought in Germany in the early nineteenth century were set by philosophy. The dominant theories of method in instruction and discipline were derived from the thought of Herbart. The conception of education as an expression of national culture and a means of maintaining its vitality came from the idealistic school. While the most striking single manifestation of this fact is the influence of Fichte in promoting a moral revival after the Napoleonic defeat, the influ-

ence of the Hegelian philosophy of history and the state perme-
ated far beyond the bounds of strictly Hegelian circles. In Great
Britain John Stuart Mill and Herbert Spencer carried over into
education the influence of the opposed empirical school, Spencer
in particular constituting himself the champion of the claims of
natural science.

In addition to the definite services of philosophy in generating
ideas that inspire and direct thinking in the physical and social
fields, philosophy exercises a third and rather indirect and vague
function. Although few philosophers have found a significant
aesthetic form of expression for their ideas, when expression is
judged by the criterion of literature, nevertheless philosophy performs for some exactly the same office that the fine arts perform
for others. There is a kind of music of ideas that appeals, apart
from any question of empirical verification, to the minds of
thinkers, who derive an emotional satisfaction from an imaginative play synthesis of ideas obtainable by them in no other
way. The objective side of this phenomenon is the role of philosophy in bringing to a focus of unity and clarity the ideas that are
at work in a given period more or less independently of one another, in separate cultural streams. Much of the culture characteristic of the eighteenth century is summed up for all subsequent
history in the Enlightenment, and the Enlightenment is definitely
a philosophical synthesis. The same is true of the romanticism of
the nineteenth century, especially in Germany. It applies also to
the vogue, during the latter part of the nineteenth century, of the
idea of universal evolution. The significance of such synthesizing
ideas is more or less independent of the question of verifiability.
The human mind, taken collectively, experiences the need of
holding itself together, and during periods of rapid influx of new
materials and the inception of new and diverging tendencies, accomplishes this task by means of comprehensive speculative ideas.

On the other hand, the failure from the standpoint of verifiability of these adventures in synthesis is one cause, and a rather
large cause, of the comparative eclipse of philosophy in recent
days. If such ventures were frankly offered as imaginative, without claiming objective truth, it is probable that the reaction
against philosophy provoked by them (and largely in proportion
to their previous vogue) would not occur. The positive cause
which accounts for the recent comparative decline of the prestige

of philosophy is found, however, in the tremendous multiplication of specialized knowledge and in the irreconcilable diver-
gences among social tendencies characteristic of the present
time. Uncertainty in the position of religion, due to its affiliation
with a supernaturalism that is discredited from the standpoint of
natural science; the enormous mass of specialized detail in science; sharp conflicts between movements in politics and economic life, between tradition and innovation, have often forced
philosophy into either taking sides and becoming the intellectual
partisan of a particular movement, or else withdrawing completely from the field of vital common experience and becoming
itself another technical mode of specialization. The recent general revival of formalism in philosophical thought is probably to
be accounted for on this basis. Judging from past history, this divided and crippled state of philosophy is a transitional phenomenon, preliminary to the appearance of comprehensive even if
rival formulations, as subject matter is better digested and the
lines of cleavage in social movements become more articulate.
From the standpoint of culture philosophy is a perennial adventure of the human spirit.

See: RELIGION; ETHICS; SCIENCE; LOGIC; METHOD, SCIENTIFIC; IDEAL-
ISM; MATERIALISM; RATIONALISM; REALISM; NATURALISM; PRAGMA-
TISM; POSITIVISM; EDUCATION; POLITICAL SCIENCE; SOCIOLOGY; VALUES.

Consult: Paulsen, Friedrich, *Einleitung in die Philosophie* (24th ed. Stuttgart
1912), tr. from 3rd German ed. by Frank Thilly (2nd ed. New York 1898);
Varisco, Bernardino, *I massimi problemi* (2nd ed. Milan 1914), tr. by R. C. Lodge
(London 1914); Santayana, George, *The Life of Reason*, 5 vols. (New York
1922); Dewey, John, *Reconstruction in Philosophy* (New York 1920), and *Philosophy and Civilization* (New York 1931); Dilthey, Wilhelm, "Über das Studium der
Geschichte der Wissenschaften vom Menschen, der Gesellschaft und dem Staat,"
and "Das Wesen der Philosophie" in his *Gesammelte Schriften*, 8 vols. (Leipsic
1921–31) vol. v, p. 31–73, 339–416; Groethuysen, Bernhard, "Philosophische
Anthropologie," and Dempf, Alois, "Kulturphilosophie" in *Handbuch der Philosophie*, ed. by Alfred Baeumler and Manfred Schroeter, pt. iii, nos. 21, 32–33,
and pt. iv, nos. 35–36 (Munich 1927–34); Brunschvicg, Léon, *Le progrès de la
conscience dans la philosophie occidentale*, 2 vols. (Paris 1927).

Contributions to
The Educational Frontier

The Social-Economic Situation
and Education

I

The confusions and conflicts which have just been dealt with grow out of the very conditions of American life. They exist in educational thought because they are traits of national opinion and conduct. For the same reason, the new educational emphasis which is asked for must grow out of forces actually at work in American life. We therefore now take up the discussion of the American social situation, past and present, and of educational theory and concepts, in their relation to one another.

Up to about the turn of the century, the most generally accepted statement of the aim of education was couched in terms of the individual: the complete and harmonious development of all the powers of the individual, physical, intellectual, moral. Then there occurred a significant shift. Increased emphasis was put in theory upon social aims and upon social forces and factors as means of realizing these aims. Education was presented as a process of transmission and reconstruction of culture; the dependence of the individual upon the resources, material and spiritual, of the collective heritage was stressed. The need for enabling individuals to take part in the task of a constantly changing society was put in the foreground of educational philosophy. The idea that the school should be itself a form of community life, and that this principle should be applied in discipline, instruction, and the conduct of the recitation, gained appreciable though far from universal recognition.[1]

1. Emphasis on the earlier concept of the individual, though often in an enriched and emancipated form, is characteristic of much of our prevailing philosophy of education, especially in scientific and progressive education circles, this em-

[Written with John L. Childs; first published as chapter 2 in *The Educational Frontier*, ed. William H. Kilpatrick (New York and London: Century Co., 1933), pp. 32–72.]

This change in the underlying concepts of education gave promise of a type of educational philosophy which would have closer contact with the realities of present-day life than was possessed by the older theory. It contained within itself the seed of efforts to bring about a definite integration of activities within the school with the activities going on in the larger community beyond the school walls. The promise has not been realized in any substantial degree. Translation of the theory into effective practice has been attempted in other countries on a much larger scale than in our own. Emphasis upon the creative activity of individuals as a necessary *part* of the wider office of social reconstruction has been the element in the theory which has affected practice in this country in a serious way. In this form it has entered into the continuance of individualistic concepts, which is dealt with in the next chapter. What was the cause of this check and change? Why, even when the social concepts were retained in theory, were they treated in a way which left them mainly only a nominal force, their transforming effect on practice being evaded? Why were they so often used merely to justify and to supply a terminology for traditional practices? The reason which lies on the surface is that an abstract and formal conception of society was substituted for the earlier formal concept of the individual. General ideas like transmission and critical remaking of social values, reconstruction of experience, receive acceptance in words, but are often merely plastered on to existing practices, being used to provide a new vocabulary for old practices and a new means for justifying them.

Any social conception remains formal and abstract which is not applied to some particular society existing at a definite time and place. Factors of time and place do not receive recognition as long as nominal social conceptions of education are not connected with the concrete facts of family, industry, business, politics, church, science, in this country. If we are not to be content with formal generalities (which are of value only as an introduction of a new point of view), they must be translated into descriptions and interpretations of the life which actually goes on in the

---

phasis being marked since the close of the war. This tendency is discussed and criticized in the next chapter. Accordingly this chapter is limited to consideration of the socialized strand in educational philosophy.

United States to-day for the purpose of dealing with the forces which influence and shape it.

Failure to accomplish this task results in an unconscious but deplorable lack of sincerity in prevalent educational philosophies. Theory made much of the need of participation in social activities and interests through breaking down the isolation of school from life. Actually pupils have been protected from too intimate contact with the realities of the institutions of family, industry, business, as they exist to-day. Just as schools have been led by actual conditions to be non-sectarian in religion, and thus have been forced to evade important questions about the bearings of contemporary science and historical knowledge upon traditional religious beliefs, so they have tended to become colorless, because neutral, in most of the vital social issues of the day. The practical result is an indiscriminate complacency about actual conditions.

The evil goes much deeper than the production of a split between theory and practice and the creating of a corresponding unreality in theory. Our educational undertakings are left without unified direction and without the ardor and enthusiasm that are generated when educational activities are organically connected with dominant social purpose and conviction. Lacking direction by definite social ideals, these undertakings become the victim of special pressure groups, the subject of contending special interests, the sport of passing intellectual fashions, the toys of dominant personalities who impress for a time their special opinions, the passive tools of antiquated traditions. They supply students with technical instrumentalities for realizing such purposes as outside conditions breed in them. They accomplish little in forming the basic desires and purposes which determine social activities.

The deeper and more enduring education, that which shapes disposition, directs action, and conditions experience, comes not from formal educational agencies but out of the very structure and operation of institutions and social conditions. During the earlier—the pioneer—period of American life, these social forces were for the most part unified, and they operated quite directly upon individuals. The school specialized in providing what life in general failed to furnish in an adequate way: namely, the instrumentalities of learning. Schools, in spite of their seeming remoteness from life about them, actually supplemented that life in an admirable way.

The causes which brought about the confused diversification of the earlier simplified and unified office of the school also explain why the social concepts of education were relegated to a formal plane and were not applied in the special conditions of our place and time. Social life has been too confused and divided to encourage this translation. On the one side, the influential forces at work in industrial and business activities, so influential as to be dominant upon the whole, are directly antagonistic to the social ideals professed in educational philosophy. On the other side, the lag in school practice due to inertia and to maintenance of older conceptions of the cultivated gentleman prevents the adequate recognition within the school of the part played by science and technology in modifying, even revolutionizing, conduct and belief outside the school.

It is our conviction, accordingly, that (1) any educational philosophy which is to be significant for American education at the present time must be the expression of a social philosophy and that (2) the social and educational theories and conceptions must be developed with definite reference to the needs and issues which mark and divide our domestic, economic, and political life in the generation of which we are a part.

The demand upon educational theory has both a critical and a constructive side. Theory must face present realities in their discords, defects, and perversions. But it must also face them with an eye to detect the new forces which are operative, the new patterns which are forming. With respect to individuality, it will not only recognize that individuals now find their lives disintegrated because of absence of defined and unifying objects of loyalty, but it will also consider the ends now forming which may bring unity and order into belief and action. It must search out, in other words, the forces and patterns which, if they were promoted, would on the one hand remake society and on the other enable individuals to find themselves as they find a place within a society which is in process of forming.

The demand for a philosophy of education which shall grow out of intelligent acknowledgment of both the conflicts and the new-forming patterns of social life did not find its origin in the present crisis. But one aspect of it is illustrated by a breakdown so great as to compel consideration of needs and problems that were more easily covered from view in days of complacent "prosperity." An example of what is meant may be drawn from one aspect of present economic society. The crisis has affected untold numbers of teachers very directly. They face a demand to use their income for relief of relatives and friends, for general relief of the unemployed, at the very time when their salaries may be in arrears or seriously cut. These facts might be dismissed as part of a general situation which concerns teachers only as it concerns all other citizens as constituent parts of an interdependent community. But there is another phase of the matter which surely has direct educational significance.

The general burden of taxation is so directly felt that there is widespread demand for drastic curtailment of educational services. There is an actual, not merely theoretical, danger that the most significant expansions of the last forty years in school activities will be seriously impaired. In some cities they are already undermined and eliminated. Under the plea of economy, there is already going on a reversion to the curriculum of the three R's. This is a question which affects education as education and not merely the fortunes of teachers and administrators within the school system.

Here assuredly is an illustration of the way in which economic conditions have such obvious impact upon the work of education that educators as educators need to become acquainted with the workings of our industrial and financial system; to discover what is wrong and why; and to be interested from the standpoint of their own calling in methods of social action that will improve conditions. As far as the depression tends to undermine, through its effect on the experience and development of millions of future citizens, what teachers are striving to accomplish; as far as it is a symbol of conditions which are hostile to the realization of educational aims, it is a definitely educational force which teachers have both the right and the duty to face and to reckon with. There is, however, danger that the very obviousness of the illustration just used will narrow our apprehension of the point illustrated. Change the instance from the time of *depression* to times when economic forces are working inequitably even when there is no marked depression, and from conditions which present themselves in the school to conditions which affect the life of children and youth out of school, and the principle still holds.

The illustration is taken from conditions which militate against the realization of educational aims. But the extension of the social philosophy of education into the realities of contemporary life should not be restricted to negative conditions. It is a commonplace that our country has an abundance of natural riches, that it has an extraordinary equipment of machinery, of skilled engineers and trained workers. It is well known that we have both the material and the human resources to give to all that degree of security and reasonable comfort in life which afford the physical basis for cultural development. Technically speaking, the crisis which is attacking the enriched curriculum is needless. The educator, then, as educator, not merely as human being and citizen, has a direct concern with all the positive agencies by which the work of education may be protected from adverse influence and rendered constructively effective. The philosophy of education must discover and ally itself with the social forces which promote educational aims, as well as uncover and oppose the vested interests which nullify ideals and reduce them to mere flourishes or to phrases on paper.

Only by such an extension of the intellectual and moral horizon of educational theory can the demands of the social conception of education be saved from unreality. Only in this way can those who consciously take on themselves the responsibility for transmitting and remaking social values carry their work forward. Only in this way can they experience the great emotional drive which is implicit in their function but which is now dulled by convention and dissipated by inner confusion and conflict.

It is for this reason that we are impelled to begin our exposition of educational philosophy with an account of the social institutions and arrangements which condition the work of education. Since these conditions exercise the greatest and most enduring educative (including miseducative) effect on the life experience and on the culture which prevails, any serious theory of education must begin with them rather than with the school system as such. Since the field is broad and complex, we shall approach it through an historical survey of the social scene. The object will be to elicit the essential elements in our national democratic tradition; to disclose the changes in our industrial life which have worked against them and have deprived them of vitality; and to indicate the potential forces which can be employed to give our historic social heritage new meaning and force under present changed conditions. In this way we shall arrive at a conception of the intrinsic nature of a democratic society educationally considered, and of the implications of the aims and values of such a society for the profession of education and the work of the American public school.

II

Human history records no expansion like that which has occurred in the United States in the less than 150 years of its existence. From the quantitative point of view the expansion is unparalleled. We have grown from a group of colonies on the Atlantic seaboard to continental size, from a few million to almost fifty times the original number. The qualitative change in the habits, occupations, interests, and values of the people is even more significant. The growth of the nation has coincided in time with the change known as the industrial revolution. Not only have the two been contemporaneous, but the United States has contributed more to effecting the transformation than has any other people, and it has experienced the consequences more fully. It is *the* industrialized nation, *par excellence*, of the world. In the past forty years the transformation has gone on at an accelerated pace, so that from an agrarian nation we have become a manufacturing and distributing people with the centre of gravity transferred from open country to the congested city.

In the early days of our existence, the remoteness of the American continent from Great Britain contributed to a spirit of political independence which was intensified by commercial conditions and was consummated in the formation of an independent nation. Both negative and positive conditions favored the development of a philosophy of free and representative government, a conception which at that time was new in the world. By sheer force of conditions the democratic idea grew to include much more than a republican form of government. It became a social ideal, asserting the right of all individuals to equality of opportunity and to the widest possible sphere of freedom of personal action unhampered by external interference and control. The belief that social welfare and progress were best served by allowing every individual a wide area of personal choice, initiative, and action was fostered by both internal and external conditions. A century ago the population was sparse; land, with fertile fields, with forest and minerals, was abundant and unappropriated. Enormous natural resources invited human exploitation; individual energy was stimulated even to the point of reckless waste. A continent needed conquest, and the need excited and rewarded the ambition of all but the congenitally lazy and apathetic. Nature seemed to make equal opportunity for all a reality; it was easy to suppose that, barring illness and accident, individuals won or lost in the industrial race according to their own industry and ability. Individual success and satisfaction of social need bore a close relation to each other. Because of the abundance of unused natural wealth, the economic struggle of individuals was not so much against one another as with nature itself. In fact, individual initiative and enterprise, directed toward subduing a continent, had moral significance. The men and women who did their part in clearing away the forest, making roads, building habitations, churches, and schools, cultivating the soil, were rightfully sustained by a sense of social value. Personal success was not merely private. It was also a contribution to the improvement of community life. Outwardly, early American life seemed often lost in materialistic activity, but at that time this materialism was at least the basis for a possible new civilization in which all should share the goods of life more freely and more fully than in any prior state of society.

As long as life was predominantly rural, democratic ideals were readily embodied on the political side of community life. The old town meeting, as is often pointed out, was as close an approximation to political democracy as the world has ever seen. Neighbors who knew one another, who were judges of one another's characters and achievements, met to confer about matters of common interest: their own roads, their schools, their taxes. Public interests, being so largely local, were genuinely public; they were open, not concealed nor masked; they were close by, not remote; substantial, not shadowy. Problems might be difficult, but at least they came to citizens in terms of conditions which were familiar because they touched the lives of all citizens.

It was natural to think of government as a cooperative effort of individuals to preserve initiative from being interfered with and to protect the fruits of private industry and skill. The subordination of political action and ends was a natural, an inevitable, product of the situation.

External conditions operated in exactly the same direction. The citizens of a country which had just won its independence by revolt against established government were inclined to look with jealous eyes upon all political authority. It was something to be watched, as having an inherent tendency to swell and to assume despotic power. Freedom was thought to be identical with limitation of powers of government. The conceptions of rights inhering in individuals as individuals prior to any social order, rights which set fixed limits to the sphere of government and for the sake of protecting which governments were called into being, awakened a natural response. In like fashion, the doctrine of *laissez faire* in economic matters seemed to express the actual conditions of American life and to set forth the conditions under which life might continue to prosper. From every point of view, individualism was the philosophy which set forth the intrinsic conditions and aspirations of American life in its early period.

Yet the original formulation and acceptance were also affected by the temporary factors growing out of conditions which were not eternal but which belonged to American life as it was lived on the large and as yet unutilized and unappropriated soil of the United States. Reckless abuse and waste of natural resources was bred; constant change developed into love for the excitement of aimless mobility; ruthlessness was not confined to dealings with physical nature but was carried over into dealings with fellowmen; wild speculation was always likely to encroach upon slow-going and patient industry. Complacency and undue optimism were the fruits of the comparatively easy success made possible by abundant gifts of nature. We have always been prone to attribute to the excellence of our chosen institutions and our own virtues of character results which for the most part should be attributed in fact to the circumstances in which our national life went on. The constant lure of new opportunities has rendered self-criticism an unwelcome diversion and a source of irritation.

In spite of all limitations, however, the earlier conceptions contained the core of that democratic idea which forms the distinctive ethical tradition of the United States. It includes the political aspect of democracy; this was definitely limited in the first part of the history of the republic but broadened out later to include the right and duty of every mature citizen of the country to participate in the government of his locality, state, and nation, on the ground that such participation both made the individual a better citizen and helped ensure that government would serve the public good. The democratic idea included also broader moral ideas, such as the equal right of every individual for opportunity to make his own career and develop his own personal being; moral individualism, which asserted the right of all to personal freedom of development without allowing fixed classes and castes to develop; faith in the possibility of an abundant life for all, not only materially but culturally; belief that government is an affair of voluntary organization for the common good, so that the people have the right to change their institutions when they find that they are failing to meet the common need, Jefferson and Lincoln agreeing that this right extends even to revolutionary action; faith in individual inventiveness and adaptability; an attitude which welcomes change as an omen of future good rather than resists it as a sign of degeneration from a superior past.

Such beliefs as these are integral in the national democratic tradition. They are denied by some who are skeptical about the soundness of democracy as a moral ideal; by some who appeal to biology as authority for the belief that a division of classes is inherent in human nature; by some on the ground that history has demonstrated that the ideas are unworkable; by others on the ground that experience shows that such ideas can be realized only in primitive, agrarian conditions, and that when society becomes complex and large fortunes are established, there must follow either anarchy or else a strong centralized oligarchy consisting of the economically successful members of society. Still others hold that the ideals can be realized only by a complete and violent revolution which will put total power in the hands of the proletariat. We are not concerned here to defend the democratic faith against either Fascist or Bolshevist attack. Not till we have turned our backs upon what is most significant and distinctive in the tradition of American life will these ideas be abandoned by the American people. But educators must concern themselves with forces which undermine and contract the essential elements of the democratic faith, which in the end may cause them to be destroyed in fact even when retained in name.

Our dominant individualism, in both its sterling and its less desirable aspects, found expression in the development of our public school system: in administration, in subject-matter, in methods, and in ideals. Even a brief consideration must note at least such factors as the following in the educational philosophy which, even when unformulated, operated in our schools and gave their dominant tone.

In the first place, remoteness from the sources of our inherited culture, distance from Europe, produced dependence upon special agencies for maintaining culture. Old-world culture was not deeply embodied in the customary indigenous arrangements of our daily life. It did not transmit itself vitally and unconsciously as it had done in the Old World where it originated and was at home. Hence there was a great, almost a superstitious, faith in schools as the special and almost exclusive organs for keeping intact the borrowed culture. Just as our excessive dependence upon law-making is the correlative of absence of stability in our exceedingly mobile community life, so our dependence upon schools has been the reflex of the precarious state of traditional culture.

But since, nevertheless, life was still going on and actual habits were being shaped by the occupations and interests which employed the time, energy, and serious efforts of men and women, there resulted a split between life and traditional culture. The schools, devoting themselves to mastery of distinctively intellectual tools, operated through the medium of a reverence for books, while life outside shaped character. Of course, something of this work is characteristic of school education wherever it exists. But the peculiar conditions of American life rendered attachment to the bookish tradition and to the importance of mere mastery of the linguistic tools of culture both thinner and firmer than it was elsewhere. Life in the open, in the neighborhood and local community, through participation in the duties of the home and the farm, through contact with industries still carried on by hand tools in the home and neighborhood and demanding individual skill acquired in actual apprenticeship, was the force which shaped character and which counted in the development of personality and power. The school had a precious but relatively specialized office to fulfill: to teach the three R's and to equip youth with the technical intellectual arms which life, especially under the conditions of pioneer life, failed to provide. A similar division of labor, amounting to dualism, was found in method. Life outside the school stimulated individual energy and ambition, possibly to an exaggerated extent. School was a place for passive acquisition. The chief business of the school was to help pupils absorb what they did not come in effectual contact with either at home or in the local community.

In the third place, the dominant purpose of school education was to prepare individuals for successful achievement, for getting on, in the struggle of life. Preparation for success, help in the struggle to "rise," was almost inevitably the function of the school in pioneer days. Parents made great sacrifices to send their children to school and keep them there in order that their children might have a "better chance in life" than they had had. It was everywhere taught that diligence and faithfulness in learning school lessons was the surest road to success in adult life. We laugh now at the legend that school-children were once taught that each one who did his work properly had a chance to become the President of the United States. But the legend is genuinely significant of two traits that once marked American life: belief in unrestricted opportunity for all and belief that the school afforded the best and surest means for converting opportunity for personal success into a fact. The counterbalancing "social" factor was the belief that the literate person made a better citizen as a matter of course, since ignorance (identified with illiteracy) was admitted to be the source of poverty, crime, and other social defects.

At the same time, belief in the right of every individual to start equal in the race of life with other individuals, unhampered by conditions of birth or the economic status of parents, was a marked force in the spread of a universal and unified system of common schools, in the constant increase upward of provision of school facilities, and in making schools free, supported by public taxes, not by payment of fees. In the Western States, which were created after the establishment of national independence, the same idea operated powerfully in the institution of the educational ladder with the tax-supported State university at its apex. The social conception that the republican form of government required universal literacy and the conception of the moral claims of individuality united to create the ardent faith which has prevailed in the United States in the possibility and the necessity of state-supported education on a wide scale. In the region of education the idea of inherent limitation of governmental functions has not been permitted to interfere with collective action.

III

In contrast with the facts and forces of our earlier agrarian culture stand the transforming forces which came in with machine industrialization. The revolution in industrial affairs developed in this country at an extraordinary rate of speed. The new agencies which it provided for mass production, for the utilization of unused natural resources, and for the quick distribution of persons, materials, and commodities over a vast territory, answered so completely to the felt and obvious needs of the time that the advance of industrialization took on all the marks of an unplanned and inevitable advance of natural forces. Certainly no one foresaw, much less planned, its ulterior social consequences. Every one was busy in turning the new forces to immediate account in fulfilment of some immediate need.

Nevertheless—more correctly, all the more on this account—the industrial and financial transformation has affected every phase of social life. It has doomed many of our earlier habits and attendant aspirations and beliefs to extinction as surely as great geological changes have extinguished so many of the earlier forms of animal life. It has nullified our original democratic ideals *in the form* in which they were originally stated and held. It has introduced and caused to prevail forces which are totally alien to the practices and the beliefs of our old agrarian culture. It has created a multitude of problems which have to be solved by new methods of thought and action if the American tradition of equal opportunity and free development of all potentialities is to be kept from becoming a mere phrase. It has tended to limit the earlier individualism to the strictly economic sphere, substituting material gain for development of personal character, conceiving initiative, energy, and independence in terms of material success only, and distorting the struggle of man with nature into a competitive struggle against other individuals in which those who lose in the race are put on the level of physical means of production and distribution.

Much recent indoctrination from highly placed sources has identified the doctrine of American individualism with strictly economic activity of a competitive kind, and has taught that success in obtaining wealth is the natural measure and criterion of moral qualities. In many respects American youth have been taught to regard the men who acquire unusual material substance and the men who contribute to the production of wealth by new inventions and the like as the characteristically American personages to be admired and emulated. All that was conceived necessary to justify such teaching was that the persons in question were born poor or handicapped, instead of with silver spoons in their mouths, and made their way or "got ahead" by their own efforts. Probably nowhere in the world at any time has there been so much teaching of an intimate relation between moral qualities and material reward as in this country.

So effectually has the idea of intrinsic moral stamina been identified with individual effort in the economic area that the more privileged elements of society have constantly resisted all efforts at social insurance of workers, prevention of child labor, old-age pensions, etc., not primarily on the obvious ground that these measures might lessen profits, nor on the legal ground that they violated freedom of contract (an idea bound up with the natural rights conception), but always principally on the moral ground that they would weaken the moral fiber of sturdiness and independence of character. Even organized labor has opposed social legislation on the ground that it is better for workers to win benefits from their employers in a direct way than to have them conferred by "paternalistic" legislation, as they have chosen to call it. Meantime, however, employers did not permit their moral ideals to interfere with securing from government favors in tariffs and franchises, etc., while even these were justified on the ground that they provided more opportunities for laborers to work and to rise in the social scale.

The development of machine industry necessarily brought about concentration. This tendency is reflected in the growth of cities, and within the cities in the congestion of population in crowded quarters, only the especially well-to-do living in habitations exclusively possessed by themselves. This concentration is further seen in the shift of production of goods from small shops, where men worked together in close companionship, to huge factories with their impersonal character and with subordination of the mass of "hands" to superintendents and bosses, and to the general adoption of a semi-military discipline. It is exhibited in all the phenomena of standardized mass production. It has led to the concentration of wealth in corporate forms in order to secure the capital needed to carry on mass production on a large scale and to relieve individual investors of undue personal risks. There has followed in turn the concentration of great wealth in the hands of the few, with an accompanying concentration there of effective power in the direction of social affairs, the setting of standards, the moulding of public opinion.

In spite of this practical transformation of social conditions, amounting to a revolution, the theories, watchwords, and slogans of the earlier agrarian period have been maintained and cherished. The industrial and commercial class which made use of governmental power for franchises and special favors had definite reasons for gaining control of governmental agencies. Corruption followed, inevitably. The *theory* of *laissez faire* has been constantly combined with the *practice* of "pork-barrel" government. Sometimes a considerable measure of public benefit resulted, as in the Homestead Acts which followed the Civil War. A frequent outcome has been an inextricable mixture of idealistic and materialistic motives and results. Thus the unrestricted policy of immigration was supported in part by genuine belief in the country as a refuge for the oppressed of all nations, the land of opportunity for those who had not had a chance, and in part by a desire for factory-fodder, for cheap and docile labor. The instance illustrates the peculiar union of general social planlessness and definite planning and control within limited private areas which has characterized much of American life.

In multitudes of respects, of which the matters cited are sample instances, the earlier national ideals have under the impact of the new industrialism, been maintained in verbal form and in accompanying sentiment, often intense, while departed from or distorted in fact. In consequence they tend to become mere holdovers having a strong emotional appeal which can be aroused and manipulated for special purposes, but do not give guidance in thinking and action chosen and directed by personal insight. These ideals need now to be reinterpreted in the light of changed and changing conditions.

We need to realize, in the first place, the nature and extent of the change effected by the industrialization of the country. The change has taken place so rapidly and in many ways so unconsciously and so unintentionally as far as the mass of persons are concerned (who have passively experienced its effects rather than actively directed its course) that almost all, including educators, retain intact old convictions and watchwords as if they were still applicable. Hence we are confused in the face of any emergency which social realities present to us. In our ideas and sentiments we live in the past, while we are compelled to act in the present. There is such disparity between the two that we are necessarily torn and divided without knowing what is the source of our difficulties. The conflict is especially marked in the case of those who profess liberalism; for their hopes and aspirations, being generous, make them concerned with the development of a better and more human future. But their intellectual tools and weapons, their conceptions of liberty and equality, of democracy and individualism, are derived from past conditions which have been destroyed by the industrialization of the country. Cynics and pessimists may argue that the basic conceptions are mere illusions. Those who have faith in the national tradition of democracy will desire to slough off whatever social changes have rendered inapplicable and to reinterpret the essential ideas in terms of present life. This work cannot be done apart from educational agencies.

There are, however, various ways of accepting the social conception of education in name and denying it in fact. One way is that of the academic intellectualist. He is sufficiently impressed with the vogue of the social concept to desire to attach himself to it; but in substance he remains a traditionalist. So he calls attention to the fact—and it is a fact—that number, linguistic forms, words, history, etc., the material of the accepted curriculum, are social tools, such important social instrumentalities that social life could not be carried on without them. Every other consideration and subject is, upon this educational philosophy, an "extra"; the school may be obliged to take it up, but that is only because some other institution is failing in its duty, not because it belongs in school. In principle the school is a fenced-off sanctuary devoted exclusively to "teaching" and "learning" the great intellectual means by which civilized society is maintained. Of course society would relapse into barbarism without the transmission of the arts, skills, and understandings which make up the traditional curriculum. The essential point of a social conception of education, however, is that these subjects be taught *in* and with definite reference to their social context and use; taken out of their social bearing, they cease to have a social meaning, they become wholly technical and abstract. It is then a mere matter of accident for what ends they are used outside of the conscious educational system. There is nothing to protect them from being tools of private advantage and material success, or even being put to anti-social use. Moreover, apart from reference to their place and function in social life, the educator has no guide to help decide what parts and aspects of the great complex of intellectual subject-matter shall be selected nor any guide in choosing the methods of instruction and discipline which build up attitudes in the pupils. The inevitable effect is conformity to and duplication of the existent order with all its limitations and evils.

Another method of avoiding the practical implications of the social conception consists in failure to take account of the changes which are going on in the concrete institutions of society and of the causes of these changes. Or, putting the matter positively, those who accept the idea that education is a social operation must, if their acceptance is sincere, consider how family life, the church, the production and distribution of goods, agriculture, the means and modes of amusement and recreation, ends and means in politics, have been affected by the development of science and technology, these being the two great causal forces at work. They must ask how far the changes which are taking place are themselves the inherent product of these forces, and how far they are the effects of beliefs and attitudes which are themselves the result of prior education of human nature and which therefore are capable of modification by change in educational aims and methods. In short, they must definitely orient the work of education, both critically and constructively, to the concrete social situation in its needs, defects, conflicts, and problems as well as in its positive achievements. The first step in the accomplishment of this task, without the performance of which education in the schools will remain aimless and confused, is a better under-

standing by the teaching profession of social issues with intellectual courage to face them.

This is not, of course, the place to consider in detail the nature
of the modifications going on in family life and sex relations, in
the church, business, commerce, finance, the press, the theater,
and organized sport, government and politics, because of the impact of science and technology. And yet the substantial material
and effective method of teaching must be determined on this
basis. Otherwise a philosophy of education employing social
concepts will inevitably become formal and tend to be an affair
of phraseology without specific bearing on the conduct of the
educational system. Science and machinery have affected the traditional doctrines of the church; they have profoundly modified
family life in all urban communities; they have made child labor
in factories sufficiently remunerative to call children away from
school; they have taken multitudes of women from the home;
they have left millions of children no place to play except the
street; they have encouraged as a by-product the organization of
gangs that easily become criminal; they have through physiology
and psychology modified sex and parental relations; they have,
in connection with the dominant motive of private profit, introduced on a large scale alluring forms of commercialized amusement that leave children and youth passive but excited at the time
when they are also deprived of normal outlets for action. Close
and vital contact with the realities of nature have been eliminated
for youth in the cities and much reduced for those in the country,
as standardized finished products of mechanical work constantly
gain in distribution. Inventiveness in technical things, tools and
machines, has been stimulated to a great degree, but inventiveness in social forms and methods has been discouraged rather
than promoted. A certain degree of literacy has become a necessity, and so universal and compulsory instruction has been favored. But, at the same time, a premium has been put on control
of reading matter and publicity devices by those who would gain
the management of public sentiment and opinion. The public
which is literate in use of linguistic tools but which is not educated in social information and understanding becomes a ready
victim of those who use, for their own private economic and political ends, the public press. Direct pecuniary profit at the same

time causes the public to be the recipient of an incalculable amount of trash and trivialities, esthetically if not morally degrading.

IV

These are casual illustrations of the immediate effect of the forces of science and technology upon basic customs and institutions of society. We cannot extend them here nor go into any detailed analysis. But it is necessary to consider some of the outstanding *mis*educative results which have attended the diversion of the earlier agricultural individualism into the competitive economic individualism of present society. For the school system has to reckon with the consequences both negatively and positively: negatively, since its own work is conditioned by them; constructively, since without a knowledge of them it cannot see clearly its own place and function in the making of a society whose institutions will have a better effect on the experience and the attitudes of its members.

1. They—science and technology—have helped form a society in which chronic insecurity is such a factor in the lives of the majority of men and women that the insecurity and the fear it engenders have come to be counted as the chief motives which drive men to work, achievement, and thrift. Under the very conditions in which stability and security are imperative needs of the masses, there has thus developed positive antagonism even to schemes of social insurance which might mitigate insecurity.

2. They have created a popular mentality which regards acquisitive motives as the normal ones in human nature and which correspondingly depresses activity that is moved by direct interest in work itself for its own sake, productive activity as such. Appeal to pecuniary profit is so universal and seemingly so necessary in a society like ours that other potential forces of human action are slighted and shoved out. The greater number of persons taking part in productive activity engage in it under such conditions that labor in itself is regarded as an evil to be endured for the sake of ultimate external reward. Even the laboring classes do not regard it as the purpose of their organizations to achieve control of the conditions and plans of industry but merely to get

increased pecuniary reward and reduced hours of labor, and if possible to bring it about that their offspring become members of the possessing and employing class.

The counterpart of this conception of productive activity as something to be undergone for reasons outside itself is that countless thousands believe that the real satisfactions and enjoyments of life are to be found in "leisure" which is thought of as a period of amusement and idle relaxation if not dissipation. It is but a short step from this attitude to the psychology of the racketeer and gangster whose motto is "get by the shortest possible course, the one which involves the minimum work and the maximum excitement."

3. Emphasis upon acquisition has intensified the motives which oppose to the greatest extent the tenor of all deliberate religious and moral teaching and create a state of ethical confusion and conflict. It has also exaggerated the significance of business and money, materialistic in comparison with cultural aims and values. It is not too much to say that the official and the popular views of human psychology have been seriously corrupted. Habits and attitudes which in fact are the product of social conditions interacting with native tendencies have been treated as if they were innate in the human make-up and incapable of modification. It is constantly repeated, and finally generally believed, that most men would not engage in productive effort unless driven by hope of personal gain or the pressure of imminent loss and disaster. The failure of Soviet Russia was, for example, predicted on the purely *a priori* ground that any system which tries to eliminate the profit motive *must* fail.

The extension of this theory of human motives was distinctly unfavorable to higher culture. Science came to be prized mainly because of its use in money-making applications and was correspondingly disregarded in its contribution to an enrichment of experience and to the method to be adopted in all matters subject to intellectual inquiry and test. Art tends to be pushed to one side as an extraneous adornment, valuable as an evidence of polish and of ability to engage in display and "conspicuous consumption." In other cases, art is deliberately cultivated simply as a means of escape from hard realities which overwhelm sensitive spirits. It is a matter of common notice that as a nation we are laggards in interest in ideas as ideas. Such interest as does exist is likely to be specialized and thin even when intense, or else is employed as a self-conscious emblem of superiority to the common herd. Interest in seeing ideas applied is of course an added value when the application is in the humane interests of life, but usually "application" is limited to economic matters, and the entire meaning of the "practical" is degraded by the limitation.

4. Emphasis upon individualism as primarily economic in character and as having value in other respects only in dependence upon the economic has induced apathy and incapacity of thought in collective matters. In spite of talk about regimentation and suppression of ideas, there was never a time in our history when as many persons had concern for intellectual things and strove to be critical in their thinking as now. But this thinking rarely takes social effect. Indeed, many intellectuals pride themselves upon keeping their thinking "pure" by keeping it remote from social problems and needs. In consequence, there is relatively little ability to think effectively upon collective matters to a collective effect. There is a painful contrast between personal culture and culture that is socially grounded and effective. In consequence, no small part of our present crisis is due to the fact that social belief and thought are dominated by convention and outworn tradition and by notions that are deliberately put in circulation by publicity agents of the dominant pecuniary group. Our literature is marked by the growth of a critical and discontented spirit, but one which has contributed little to the integration of a new social culture.

5. Competitive tendencies in human nature are stimulated to an excessive degree. While the individuals may find their operation in conflict with official religious teachings as to the proper attitude to be taken toward one's fellows, the official intellectual apologists for our economic order teach that the whole social welfare is best promoted when every individual looks out for himself.

6. The whole tendency of the *laissez-faire* system, as this works in our industrial and financial life, leads to distrust of the effectiveness of planned endeavor to control social conditions. Substantial and active faith in intelligence is undermined by this distrust. A defeatist psychology comes to prevail as to the possibility of securing and maintaining social values by organized collective effort, while extreme phantasies are created as to the prospects of

private and material success for the individual. The same psychology of intelligence which forms inventiveness has been stimulated in physical matters by our social arrangements. In the making of tools and mechanical devices we have been prominent, but there has been comparatively little inventiveness in social affairs. Here we have been largely content to depend upon tradition and accident. Nothing like as much creativeness has gone into the formation of ends and purposes as into mechanical means for ends externally determined. Since foresight and planning of consequences are conditions of a recognition of responsibility for results, an indirect outcome of the absence of systematic social planning is absence of any conviction of personal responsibility. When things go wrong on a large scale, the blame is put on uncontrollable natural and social forces, and the same forces are depended upon to bring a turn in the wheel of fortune. Because the individual does not participate in collective projects of social planning and control, he feels himself submerged and paralyzed by forces too large and blind, apparently, for any control. The final result is a spirit of fatalism combined with one of reckless speculation.

7. Finally, there is generated a growing pessimism about the possibility and the value of democracy not only as a form of government but as a principle of social relations and organization. When industry and finance are managed autocratically and for private pecuniary gain rather than as cooperative enterprises for mutual service, political democracy, in a society so dominated by industry and finance as is our own, is inevitably degraded to something formal, external, more or less mechanical, and hence comparatively easily manipulated by those who have material prosperity as their goal. In their relative helplessness under the conditions of power conferred by concentrated wealth and consequent control of the machinery of production and exchange, the masses "rationalize" the decay of democracy on the theory that the small number of industrial captains in control will know how to spread the blessings of prosperity to others. Political democracy thus tends to become a shell. The old ideal endures in the form of a pathetic hope that under the régime of "equal opportunity" one's children at least will become members of the economically governing class. Non-participation in the direction of

the work done by men and women breeds indifferent, routine, and passive minds.

V

The picture just drawn has been intentionally sharpened to bring out the darker side. Many qualifying and offsetting conditions have been omitted. This course has been taken not only because of limited space, but because the brighter features of the situation are constantly brought to our attention and are even used to cover up the blacker traits of our social organization and life. It might have been stated, in what has just been said about the effect of our economic system upon mental and moral dispositions and beliefs, that the breeding of an uncritical optimism is essential to the perpetuation of the system. Even statistically and in so-called prosperous times, the proportion of economic failures to successes is at least ten to one, and it requires a continual stream of propaganda of success stories to prevent the rise of widespread doubts as to the soundness of the system. The schools have repeated and represented the existing system with faithfulness, so that the great need in the development of a directive educational philosophy is a clearer recognition of the needs and problems which call for educational readjustment in connection with social and industrial reconstruction.

An honest facing of the defects, needs, and unsolved problems of the situation will not, however, breed pessimistic hopelessness as to the possibilities of a rebirth of our original native ideals in a form consonant with present conditions. It will not create despair as to the possibility of active participation of the educational system in creating a better social order. For it will reveal that the evils noted are not the intrinsic products of the two great forces which are operating, namely, science and technology, but of certain inherited customs, legalized institutions, and generally unquestioned traditions which developed before the rise of modern industrial society. The evils centre about the principle of private labor for private gain, a principle which was natural and on the whole probably more beneficial than harmful under the conditions of the origin, but which has taken on a malign form when linked up with the tremendous expansion and centralization of power effected by technological industry.

Science in itself is method: a method of inquiry, discovery, testing. Yet to most persons it seems something apart, isolated, peculiar, esoteric. To very many it seems to be a combination of the miraculous and the merely curious and strange, so that the "popular science" of the Sunday newspaper is often a mass of absurdities concocted for a supposed sensational value, and swallowed with avidity, to be displaced in a short time by other trivialities and "wonders." In its application, to be considered shortly in the discussion of technology, it has had a revolutionary effect on daily life. But in itself as a method of observation and reasoning, of investigation and verification, it remains the possession of a comparatively small number of specialists. It has not become the organ of everyday ways of thinking in formation of beliefs. It is not a part of the popular mind. The ways of thought of the latter remain much as they were before the rise of science. Some of the important conclusions of science have, of course, dispelled from popular belief many things held to be true before its rise. In some matters of religion and a few of moral belief this effect has been important enough to be disturbing and to call for a certain amount of reorientation. But conclusions of science are accepted for the most part on authority and not because of personal command of the method by which the conclusions were reached.

The cause for this enduring remoteness of science as method is a matter for most searching thought, especially since, after a long period of resistance from ultraconservatives, the teaching of various sciences has obtained a foothold in the schools. The reason which reflection directly suggests is that science has been limited to things remote from human life, so that its results touch human life only through the medium of some mechanical application rather than directly. In consequence science in itself assumes a purely technical—that is, compartmentalized—aspect. That the physical sciences should develop and should obtain prestige prior to those dealing with man and society was so much in the nature of the case as to cause no surprise. But it should be a matter of surprise that the idea of the possibility and desirability of impartial and cooperative methods of inquiry should hardly have made an impression on the public mind. It should be a matter of surprise that, while it is assumed as a matter of course that beliefs regarding physical things should be reached through a skilled technique of investigation and testing, the great mass, including even scientific men eminent in their special fields, should rest content with moral and political beliefs which express tradition, dogma, emotional appeal, and the vested interests of classes. It should be a matter of surprise that, whereas it is taken for granted in the physical field that planned invention and control of natural conditions should follow from discovery of facts and relations, the very idea of inventiveness and planned control in the social area is ignored or recognized only to be frowned upon as dangerous radicalism.

The difference of attitudes points to some deep-seated source of resistance on the social side. The dead inertia of custom and habituation counts for much. But resistance is active and often aggressive. These facts point to class interests which fear the free play of critical inquiry and constructive invention in social institutions. Otherwise a universal organ of observation and thinking would not have been changed from an instrumentality into an end in itself and given almost superstitious reverence as something apart, while it is opposed as the method to be used in the institutions and arrangements of society.

The conclusion is that education possesses in scientific method a potential agency for ridding the present situation of its confusions and conflicts and for making the transition to a society which will be emancipated from many of the undesirable traits of present life that have been indicated. To make this potential actual and operative, the method must be simplified and generalized. This will take place when *experimentalism* is realized to be the heart of science as method of discovery and test. Experimentalism is the cause of the victories won by science in the physical field, while the social field is kept as a preserve sacred from the free use of experimental procedure. The result is unbalance, distortion, and misuse of the physical fruits of science. Those who hold the remaking of institutions and traditions is as much the office of conscious education as is the transmission of values attained in the past will not see their ideal realized even in a fragmentary way until the formation of an experimental attitude of mind becomes the unified and unifying goal of education in its intellectual phase.

The vested interest which most definitely and actively blocks emancipation of method and prevents the experimental attitude from becoming universal is business as an institution carried on for profit. This welcomes "science" as long as it produces discoveries which can be utilized in ways that will show on the credit side of the financial ledger. It stimulates—and appropriates—invention within the same limits. But the publicity, the cooperativeness, the common and gratuitous sharing which are inherent in the scientific method of inquiry and verification are hostile to this end of private and competitive gain and so are resisted as subversive of law and order.

The factors which have brought society to its present pass and impasse contain forces which, when released and constructively utilized, form the positive basis of an educational philosophy and practice that will recover and will develop our original national ideals. The basic principle in that philosophy and practice is that we should use that method of experimental action called natural science to form a disposition which puts a supreme faith in the experimental use of intelligence in all situations of life.

A second basic principle is the use of technology for social ends. Modern machine industry is, of course, the product of technology, and this in turn is the result of application of the findings of scientific method. There are those who personify the machine much as our savage ancestors personified the forces of nature, and thus surrender their minds to a new form of mythological animism. In itself, the machine is of course but the effective supplementation of the energy of human muscle and nerve by the inanimate energies of heat, electricity, chemical reaction. The only basis on which the machine can be condemned logically is that of a passive and pessimistic philosophy which regards all exercise of energy as intrinsically evil. The present widespread blame of the machine for our present evils is a projection of the unwillingness of human beings to blame themselves for permitting the development and growth of legal and political institutions which make machine-industry the fountain head of widespread insecurity, poverty, fear, physical and mental crippling, with subjection of the many to the privileged power of the few.

Inherently the new technology is simply skilled control on a wide scale of the energies of nature. It contains within itself the possibility of not merely doing away with the evils which result from our present economic régime but of ushering in an order of unprecedented security and abundant comfort as the material basis for a high culture in which all and not merely the few shall share. It is as certain as any fact can be that we have within our power the means, including technical and managerial skill, by which the natural resources of the earth may be used to save all from dire want, from paralyzing insecurity, and to guarantee the essential conditions of a life devoted to higher things than the mere struggle to escape destitution for one's self and one's dependents.

It is not necessary to recite here all the evidence that the man-made legal and political system under which technological industry operates is the cause of our troubles rather than machine-industry itself. On the negative side the evidence is overwhelming that material success is not the attendant of superior character and that poverty and unemployment are not the results of inferior character. The sole alternative is that the social system is at fault. There have been times when it was utopian to indulge in a belief in a state of society in which all dire want and its attendant evils would be abolished. Our present technology brings the hope wholly within the region of possibility. The educational profession has therefore a direct concern in all that concerns the use of technological resources for the formation of a more secure and more humane order. Because of conditions which have been indicated, our professed and professional educational aims are fated to impotency with respect to both social advance and the systematic development of personal character unless the power inherent in science and technology is utilized for ends which are not controlled by economic institutions where competition for pecuniary gain is supreme.

The net conclusion of the discussion is:

An identity, an equation, exists between the urgent social need of the present and that of education. Society, in order to solve its own problems and remedy its own ills, needs to employ science and technology for social instead of merely private ends. This need for a society in which experimental inquiry and planning for social ends are organically contained is also the need for a new education. In one case as in the other, there is supplied a new dynamic in conduct and there is required the cooperative use of intelligence on a social scale in behalf of social values.

In this conception there is neither an explicit nor a lurking assumption of an opposition between individuality and social ends and values. The opposition is between the public and shared on one side and the private and isolated on the other. This opposition works to the detriment equally of individuality and society. An extension of activity on behalf of public community interests by the organization of collective social agencies is necessary under present conditions for developing and sustaining mature, intelligent, unified personalities.

We have stated that present conditions need not be a source of permanent depression and pessimism. Since science and technology have equipped us with the means of establishing a sound material basis for our civilization, our problem shifts from a material one to a moral one: the challenge is now to good-will, intelligence, and courage. Conditions present us with a magnificent opportunity: that of forming a society wherein continuous experimental planning with respect to our abundant resources and material and technical skill further a democratic faith to full life and action, while nothing else will do so. It has been pointed out, particularly by Dr. Counts, that our original democratic institutions were furthered by a happy conjunction of circumstances. The circumstances have changed. We can no longer depend upon external conditions. Our continued democracy of life will depend upon our own power of character and intelligence in using the resources at hand for a society which is not so much plann*ed* as plann*ing*—a society in which the constructive use of experimental method is completely naturalized. In such a national life, society itself would be a function of education, and the actual educative effect of all institutions would be in harmony with the professed aims of the special educational institution.

A society in which science and technology are employed under social direction for social ends will emancipate "individualism" from the alien forces which have gathered about it. It will restore its original moral significance. Individuals find, as we have said, their lives broken and confused because of the absence of clear and coherent objects of allegiance. They are torn between the ethical and religious principles which instill regard for the common and public good, and conditions of economic life which compel exclusive regard for private good. A community wherein cooperative intelligence is steadily used in behalf of promotion of a shared culture will eliminate this deep division in life. It will also render unnecessary that escape to special and isolated realms of science and art which is now the sole recourse of many who put culture above material values, since it would integrate these values with the purposes of the common life. Faith in promotion of shared values and devotion to a constantly growing and varied method of experimentation will supply the void which now exists in the life of so many individuals because of collapse of those objects of traditional loyalty which once held men together and once supplied meaning to individual life.

In opening new avenues to trained intelligence, such a community would fill the gap which now exists between theory and practice, between the intellectual and the executive type, and thereby also promote the integration of the individual. At present those concerned with social science and philosophy confine themselves to specialized fact-finding and isolated theorizing, with no responsibility for the execution or even the formulation of policies of action. On the other hand, the practical executives in business and government are largely concerned with immediate accommodations and manipulations, adherence to catchwords and worn-out traditions, unillumined by generous and informed thought. A unified individuality is hard to maintain where intelligence which is public by nature cannot operate effectually for public results, and where the ever-urgent demands of practice compel compromise, evasion, and conformity to ideals that do not command spontaneous loyalty.

If education were to awaken to a sense of its identity with the cause of a community which employs science and technology for experimental planning and action in the common interest, the effect upon it would be equally sound and integrating. Direction would be given to an aimless situation; unity would grow in a system now distracted by a multiplicity of special movements that are not held together by any single purpose; simplifying order would appear in a congested situation; definiteness and continuity would accrue to efforts that are now wavering and oft interrupted.

Harmony would be effected between actual practice and professed theory. Our present philosophy extols education through participation in community life, the winning of insight and understanding through direct taking part in the realities of life. But under existing economic conditions, it often seems the part of humanity to protect children and youth from too close contact with surrounding realities. For the defense of the young we maintain the school in isolation from life even while we proclaim that the isolation must be broken down. In a society which continuously planned its activities for the common good, educational theory would of necessity be carried into operation.

The change would affect also the subject-matter of instruction. In spite of all educational endeavors, there are many subjects in our schools which remain academic and aloof and which are pursued in a pedantic spirit, or from the traditional identification of culture with a polish belonging to the few in distinction from the mass. On the other hand, so-called practical and vocational subjects and courses are introduced which lack depth and intellectual substance. They are not used to contribute to an understanding of society or to recognition of the scientific foundation of callings that are socially important in the modern world. Instead, they are used for the superficial purpose of enabling individuals to "adjust" themselves externally to a profit-seeking civilization. In a planning society, the plans and methods of maintaining and furthering the life of the community would form the natural core of the course of study. The split between personal culture and the vocational would disappear.

These are examples of ways in which programs of social and educational reconstruction meet and correspond. Each must develop in intellectual reference to the other and as far as possible in practical connection with the other. The first step in clarification of philosophy is to see the entire educational enterprise in the perspective of that form of social life which is needed to save us from present evils and is required by forces which already exist. Such a vision is preliminary to action which will develop the new society. The detailed development of an outlook and program of this kind demands the combined thought and effort of all educators in connection with students of social affairs. But certain conditions stand out which map the field and define the problem. Intellectual and practical reconstruction will be compelled to take account of the following factors in our society.

1. Society has become in fact corporate. Its interests and activities are so tied together that human beings have become dependent upon one another, for good or for harm, to an unprecedented degree. This is a statement of fact, whether the fact be

welcomed or deplored. This interdependence is increasing, not lessening. It must be taken into account by education. We must not only educate individuals to live in a world where social conditions beyond the reach of any one individual's will affect his security, his work, his achievements, but we must (and for educational reasons) take account of the total incapacity of the doctrine of competitive individualism to work anything but harm in the state of interdependence in which we live.

2. Not merely the material welfare of the people, but the cultural and moral values, which are the express concern of the educational profession, demand a reorganization of the economic system, a reconstruction in which education has a great part to play.

3. The crucial problem is no longer one of stimulating production, but one of organization of distribution with reference to the function of consumption and use, so as to secure a stable basis of living for all, with provision against the hazards of occupation, old age, maternity, unemployment, etc., in order that an abundant cultural development for all may be a reality.

4. Strictly speaking, the idea of *laissez faire* has not been carried out for a long time. Monopolistic ownership of land and of values socially created, privileged control of the machinery of production and of the power given by control of financial credit, has created control by a class, namely, control over production, exchange, and distribution. Hence general and public repudiation of the doctrine of *laissez faire* in behalf of the principle and practice of general social control is necessary. Education has a responsibility for training individuals to share in this social control instead of merely equipping them with ability to make their private way in isolation and competition. The ability and the desire to think collectively, to engage in social planning conceived and conducted experimentally for the good of all, is a requirement of good citizenship under existing conditions. Educators can ignore it only at the risk of evasion and futility.

5. The interdependence spoken of has developed on a world-wide scale. Isolated and excessive nationalism renders international interdependence, now existing as a fact, a source of fear, suspicion, antagonism, potential war. In order that interdependence may become a benefit instead of a dread evil and possible world-wide catastrophe, educators must revise the conception of

patriotism and good citizenship so that it will accord with the imperative demands of world-wide association and interaction.

6. We are in possession of a method of controlled experimental action which waits to be extended from limited and compartmentalized fields of operation and value to the wider social field. In the use of this method there lies the assurance not only of continued planning and inventive discovery, but also of continued reconstruction of experience and of outlook. The expanded and generalized use of this method signifies the possibility of a social order which is continuous by self-repairing, a society which does not wait for periodic breakdowns in order to amend its machinery and which therefore forestalls the breakdowns that are now as much parts of social activity as storms of nature are of the physical order.

The fact that all the changes which we have spoken of are connected with whole-hearted loyalty to the method of intelligent experimentation saves us equally from external and dogmatic inculcation and from colorless neutrality in the face of issues so crucial that the very values of civilization are at stake. Intelligent experimentation is based upon possession of working hypotheses. These hypotheses are themselves the fruit of careful study of actual conditions, a study conducted as honestly and impartially as is possible to human beings. The convictions which we set forth are arrived at in consequence of our own survey and analysis of conditions; they are offered not as dogmas which must be accepted but as hypotheses to be thought out and to be tested by their reasonableness, by their connection with actual facts and their fruits in action as far as they are adopted. The alternative to them is neither abstinence from all conviction, under the name of amiable but aimless impartiality, nor the assertion of something else as an absolute truth. Rather is the alternative a resurvey of the facts to show that these have been misinterpreted, that important considerations have been neglected, or that the conceded facts point to other working convictions than those which have been advanced. In this spirit we invite the cooperation of the profession even though the outcome of that cooperative work be a modification of the principles herein advanced.

Professor Rex Tugwell has said: "If we know as educators that society is likely to work coöperatively, that it is to create its future by a constant use of planning and shaping activities, and if it is to

press continually for amelioration, we can revolutionize education—and perhaps in time society—by preparing our students
for the tasks involved. We prepare them not by insisting upon
conformity, but by resisting its encroachments, by free consideration of alternatives, by generalizing vocationalism, by opening
their minds to the consideration of social materials. What we want
is to have them learn to approach and manipulate the factors involved, how to look forward, fitting things together, how to aspire
and how to reach toward their aspirations, how actually to manipulate the new mechanisms which are coming into being."[2]

If to prepare individuals to take part intelligently in the management of conditions under which they will live, to bring them
to an understanding of the forces which are moving, to equip
them with the intellectual and practical tools by which they can
themselves enter into direction of these forces, is indoctrination,
then the philosophy of education which we have in mind may be
adjudged to be an instrument of indoctrination. Otherwise, not.

We too easily forget that at present there is an immense deal of
actual indoctrination, partly overt and even more covert, in our
schools. The outworn and irrelevant ideas of competitive private
individualism, of *laissez faire*, of isolated competitive nationalism
are all strenuously inculcated. We are demanding the abolition of
all such indoctrination, on the ground that it is injurious equally
to the health and growth of genuine individuality and to that of
collective public order. We are not proposing that other doctrines should be arbitrarily imposed in their place. We are proposing that those materials and activities which enter into a philosophy of education and which find their place in the schools
shall represent the realities of present, not of past, social life, and
we are asking that there be freedom of intelligence in teaching
and study so that the subject-matter of study and school activity
may be followed out into the conclusions toward which this material itself points. If the method we have recommended leads
teachers and students to better conclusions than those which we
have reached—as it surely will if widely and honestly adopted—
so much the better. We have done what we can to see and note
the facts and to point out whither they lead in the way of plans
and directions. This fact is an invitation to others to pursue the

2. Unpublished ms.

same course further. Instead of recommending an imposed in-doctrination, we are striving to challenge all the indoctrinations of conscious dogma and of the unconscious bias of tradition and vested interest which already exist.

Upon one thing we take our stand. We frankly accept the democratic tradition in its moral and human import. That is our premise and we are concerned to find out and state its implica-tions for present life under present conditions, in order that we may know what it entails for theory and practice of public educa-tion. Events often move rapidly. The alternatives to such a philos-ophy as is here projected (and sketched in further detail in what follows) is likely to be a society planned and controlled on some other than the democratic basis. Russia and Italy both present us with patterns of planned societies. We believe profoundly that so-ciety requires planning; that planning is the alternative to chaos, disorder, and insecurity. But there is a difference between a so-ciety which is plann*ed* and a society which is continuously plan-n*ing*—namely, the difference between autocracy and democracy, between dogma and intelligence in operation, between suppres-sion of individuality and that release and utilization of individu-ality which will bring it to full maturity.

The Underlying Philosophy of Education

In previous chapters a philosophy of education has been presented. The presentation has been in terms of application and operation, not in the abstract. In this concluding chapter we wish to draw out the distinctively theoretical implications of the discussion and give them definite formulation. In so doing we shall try neither to present new material nor yet merely to summarize what has already been said. We shall endeavor to make explicit the ideas and principles which implicitly form the framework of our entire discussion.

In the first place there is not implied any pretension to offer *the* philosophy of education. We do not believe that there is any such thing—not in a world in which men act for opposed ends and follow divergent paths. We believe that a treatment which claims to be the exclusive and all comprehensive theory of education leads unconsciously but necessarily to a kind of insincerity; for it tends to cover up the conflicts that are highly important in practice. The statements thus far are negative. But they rest upon a positive basis.

For all education is an affair of action. Call before your mental eye any schoolroom and you see in imagination something going on, something being done. Even the schoolrooms in which silence and physical immobility are most insisted upon are still doing something. They are imposing these things as parts of a policy of action adapted to reach the ends which are prized. Instruction and discipline are modes of action. Now all truly human action involves preference. It signifies working for one end rather than for another in situations where alternatives exist. The chosen policy may be adopted on the basis of imitation and obe-

[Written with John L. Childs; first published as chapter 9 in *The Educational Frontier*, ed. William H. Kilpatrick (New York and London: Century Co., 1933), pp. 287–319.]

dience to tradition, or it may be thought through and adopted on the basis of a clear view and decided choice of the ends and consequences which the policy serves. But preference for one kind of end and value is always there, because one kind of outcome rather than another is brought about as a consequence of action.

It is the business of a philosophy of education to make clear what is involved in the action which is carried on within the educational field, to transform a preference which is blind, based on custom rather than thought, into an intelligent choice—one made, that is, with consciousness of what is aimed at, the reasons why it is preferred, and the fitness of the means used. Nevertheless intelligent choice is still choice. It still involves preference for one kind of end rather than another one which might have been worked for. It involves a conviction that such and such an end is valuable, worth while, rather than another. Sincerity demands a maximum of impartiality in seeking and stating the reasons for the aims and the values which are chosen and rejected. But the scheme of education itself cannot be impartial in the sense of not involving a preference for some values over others. The obligation to be impartial is the obligation to state as clearly as possible what is chosen and why it is chosen. We have attempted to meet this obligation. We have set forth the values we believe education should strive to achieve in our own day in our own country, and we have stated the grounds of our choice. We believe that it will be helpful if those who disagree in practice, in the courses of action they are following, will also clarify and expose the grounds for their policies: in short, develop and formulate *their* philosophies of education.

So much in general. The point which most specifically follows is that some philosophy is implied in every educational measure and recommendation made as to every method of teaching and discipline. There is no possible opposition therefore between that which is termed "science" and that which is termed "philosophy" in education. For as soon as a science is actually *used*, as soon as action based upon it occurs, then values, consequences, enter in. Choice operates and produces consequences. There are, then, philosophical implications, since philosophy is a theory of values to be achieved and to be rejected. But a conflict of *philosophies*, between a philosophy and what purports to be a science, is both possible and actual. For example, the presupposition of much of the work done in the name of science is that there is no need for philosophy itself. This view itself involves a decided philosophy. It does so in at least three ways and directions. In the first place, since the only thing to which factual science *can* be applied is something already in existence, there is a virtual assumption that educational direction and progress rest upon analysis of existing practices with a view to rendering them more efficient. The underlying philosophy is that it is the function of education to transmit and reproduce existing institutions—only making them more efficient. This philosophy we deny.

In the second place, the assumption implicit in the method of much of the work referred to is that processes and functions with which education deals are isolable, because they are independent of one another. This involves the philosophical notion that character, mental life, experience, and the methods of dealing with them, are composed of separable parts and that there is no whole, no integralness in them; that what seems to be a unity is in reality nothing but an aggregate of parts. This philosophy once dominated physical science. In physics and biology its inadequacy from a scientific point of view is now realized. Yet it has been taken over by that school of educational "science" which denies the importance of a philosophy in conducting education. The ends and values which we regard as the proper ends of choice in action are consistent only with a philosophy which recognizes the basic importance of organization and patterns of integration.

The work done in the name of science (in the third place) during the recent period has been largely in connection with the *impersonal* phase of education, and has reduced personality as far as possible to impersonal terms. These terms do lend themselves most readily to factual and statistical treatment—but a nonsocial philosophy is implied. When it is acted upon, the implication becomes practically anti-social. It takes the individual out of the medium of associations and contexts in which he lives. It ignores social connections and bearings, and, in ignoring them, it invites that kind of educational policy which is in line with an outworn philosophy of individualism. Our philosophy, while accepting the results of authenticated scientific work, builds upon the idea that organisms, selves, characters, minds, are so intimately connected with their environments, that they can be studied and understood only in relation to them. The emphasis which is found in the previous pages upon the culture of a time and a community is, for example, one phase of this general philosophy.

We now come to the main content of our philosophy as far as that can be set forth in a brief number of explicit propositions.

I

Our position implies that a philosophy of education is a branch of social philosophy and, like every social philosophy, since it requires a choice of one type of character, experience, and social institutions, involves a *moral* outlook. Education, as we conceive it, is a process of social interaction carried on in behalf of consequences which are themselves social—that is, it involves interactions between persons and includes shared values. A frequent objection to this view rests upon a misunderstanding. It asserts that this conception fails to grasp the basic value of individuality. The reverse is the case. *Social* cannot be opposed in fact or in idea to *individual*. Society *is* individuals-in-their-relations. An individual apart from social relations is a myth—or a monstrosity. If we deal with actual individuals, and not with a conceptual abstraction, our position can be also formulated in these terms: Education is the process of realization of integrated individualities. For integration can occur only in and through a medium of association. Associations are many and diverse, and some of them are hostile to the realization of a full personality, they interfere with it and prevent it. Hence *for the sake of individual development*, education must promote some forms of association and community life and must work against others. Admit that education is concerned with a development of individual potentialities and you are committed to the conclusion that education cannot be neutral and indifferent as to the kind of social organization which exists. Individuals develop not in a remote entity called "society" at large but in connection *with one another*. The conditions of their association with one another, of their participation and communication, of their cooperation and competition, are set by legal, political, and economic arrangements. In the interest, therefore, of education—not of any pre-conceived "ism" or code—the fact is emphasized that education must operate in view of a deliberately preferred social order.

The criticisms made in previous pages of an individualistic philosophy do not imply depreciation of the value of individuality. On the contrary they assert that the form which the historic individualism of the eighteenth and the nineteenth centuries took is now adverse to the realization of individuality in and for *all*. It favors and supports legal and economic institutions which encourage an exaggerated and one-sided development of egoistic individuality in a privileged few, while militating against a full and fair opportunity for a normal individuality in the many.

It was implied in our introductory survey of the social demands made upon education to-day that the democratic way of life is that in which the identity of interest of the individual and the social is best realized. The democratic faith is individual in that it asserts the claims of every individual to the opportunity for realization of potentialities unhampered by birth, family status, unequal legal restrictions, and external authority. By the same token it has been social in character. It has recognized that this end for individuals cannot be attained save through a particular type of political and legal institutions. Historically, conditions emphasized at first the negative phase of this principle: the overthrow of institutions that were autocratic. It is now seen that the positive side of the principle needs attention: namely, the extension of democracy to the creation of the kind of institutions that will effectively and constructively serve the development of *all* individuals. It is at once obvious that this extension affects economic, as well as legal and political, institutions.

Social arrangements are to be judged ultimately by their educative effect, by what they do in the way of liberating, organizing, integrating the capacities of men and women, boys and girls. These capacities include esthetic factors, those which lie at the basis of music, literature, painting, architecture in both production and appreciation; intellectual and scientific power and taste; capacities for friendship; and capacities for appropriation and control of natural materials and energies. It is the function of education to see to it that individuals are so trained as to be capable of entering into the heritage of these values which already exist, trained also in sensitiveness to the defects of what already exists and in ability to recreate and improve. But neither of these ends can be adequately accomplished unless people are trained to grasp and be concerned about the effect of social institutions upon individual capacities, and this not just in general but in discriminating detail.

Philosophy has two definite factual bases, one individual, the other institutional. Each base is susceptible of scientific study. Psychology can study the matter from the side of the individual, asking how this and that environmental condition, especially in the human environment, affects the powers of this and that person; how it calls out, strengthens, furthers, or weakens and retards this and that potentiality. Since education is a process of human interactions, while physiology and other subjects may supply material, adequate educational psychology must be a *social* psychology, not an impersonal one. Also are institutions and social arrangements to be studied factually and scientifically. The study becomes *educationally* significant only when it is extended to include how this and that social condition works causally to modify the experience and affect the character and capacity of individuals who come under its influence.

II

While choice cannot be eliminated nor preference reduced to intellectual and logical entities, nevertheless concrete, positive material of experience affords the basis for making choice intelligent. The difference between intelligent and arbitrary choice is between a preference which does not know what it is about, which has not considered the meaning of what it prefers, namely, the consequences which will result from action, and one based on the preference which surveys conditions and probable results of the choice made. The social analyses and interpretations which are included in previous chapters set forth the rationale of the choice which determines our educational philosophy. We believe the reasonableness and validity of a choice can be judged by such tests as the following: (1) Does the choice depend upon a survey and interpretation which discloses existing social conditions and trends? Does it, in short, rest upon genuine and thorough observation of the moving forces of a given state of social culture? (2) Does it sense and formulate the deeper and more intangible aspirations, purposes and values, for our own educational philosophy, in our own American scene and life?[1]

In holding that the values which should determine the direction of education can be dug out of life-experience itself, we are denying by implication the position taken by some opposed types of philosophical theory. We affirm that genuine values and tenable ends and ideals are to be derived from what is found within the movement of experience. Hence we deny the views which assert that philosophy can derive them out of itself by excogitation, or that they can be derived from authority, human or supernatural, or from any transcendent source. Our analyses of social forces are made because of the bearing of these forces upon the choice of values and the institution of purposes.

The position we take can be maintained only by recognizing that any existing society is marked by both negative and positive values. Were there no values already experienced, there would be no material out of which to frame ends and ideals. But an end and ideal also imply something to be striven for, something therefore which is as yet non-existent. The aspect of an end which goes contrary to what exists does not come however out of the blue, or out of anything remote from actual experience. A man makes health an end because he has enjoyed it enough to know what it means and what it is to enjoy it. But he also has experienced lack of health and is aware that health is not automatic, that it has foes, and that it must therefore be pursued and cultivated. Values as they exist are often both obscure and conflicting. They neither lie on the surface nor constitute a self-coherent whole. If they did, education would be infinitely simpler than it is. The most urgent problems of current educational theory and practice grow out of the extraordinarily confused and conflicting state of values at the present time.

The conflict is practical; it involves clashes of individuals, of groups and classes. It can be resolved only where it exists, namely, in action. But action needs to be intelligent as to the values con-

1. Criticism of the philosophy we advance is likely, therefore, to be effective according as it centres upon, first, the criteria we employ, and, second, the correctness and adequacy of the use we have made of them in interpreting and recording the social situation in which we live.

cerned, values negative and positive. Otherwise it will be more wasteful and destructive than it needs to be. Philosophy is the operation of studying the values at stake, of clearing up the understanding of them, of forming them in idea into a new integration, in which social forces will realize values in individual lives more broadly and equitably than at present. The formation of such a philosophy is instrumental rather than final. That is to say, it observes, criticizes, and integrates values in thought in order to determine and guide the action which will integrate them in fact.[2] A philosophy based upon actual experience is so framed, in other words, as to react, through the plan of action which it projects, back into an experience which is directly realized and not merely conceived. Moreover, it is not implied that philosophy comes to completion as a preliminary and that then action takes place afterwards. There is a continuing interaction. The intellectual formulation develops from the vague to the definite through the action which it suggests and directs, and there is no end to this process. Philosophy develops as society does. It does not provide a substitute for the values which life contributes, but it does enter—vitally, if it performs its proper function—into the very social process in which values are generated and realized. A philosophy of education may thus be truly said to be general philosophy formulated with particular reference to its social office.

III

A goal cannot be intelligently set forth apart from the path which leads to it. Ends cannot be conceived as operative ends, as directors of action, apart from consideration of conditions which obstruct and means which promote them. If stated at large, apart from means, ends are empty. Ends may begin as the plan and purpose in the rough. This is useful if it leads to search for and discovery of means. So the otherwise bare idea of building a house may be the first stage in thinking out detailed plans and specifications for its erection, and thus be translated over into a statement of means.

The necessary relation between means and ends explains the

2. The relation between thought and action receives explicit attention below.

attention we have given to the economic phase of society. Our emphasis does not imply that economic values are superior as *values*. But economic forces are at the present time superior to others in causal power. They condition what people can do and how they can develop more than do other forces. Moreover, the habit of separating economic interests from ideal interests affords a typical instance of the too common separation of means and ends, with the result that ideals become empty and impotent, while means, left to themselves in isolation from service to ends, produce brutal and unjust consequences. The emphasis laid upon the economic is not due therefore to any *a priori* theory of its necessary importance but is due to the power of economic factors in contemporary culture. Because of the organic relation of ends and means and because the economic is so potent both as potential means for values and as a retarding and distorting force, and because it is the means most susceptible of modification by concerted effort, it is, strategically, the key at present to other values.

There are many grounds on which people associate together and there are many ends for which they associate. We do not imply in our emphasis upon the economic side of present social life that economic ends are the only things which bring people together. More particularly the American people have shown that they are peculiarly apt at entering into association; they are given to organizing and joining social groups, quite independent of direct economic aims. But we find that this ability is arrested and deflected into wrong channels by an economy in which a system of mass production and distribution is subordinated to gaining pecuniary profit. This particular example may serve as an illustration of a whole group of cases in which forms of social cooperation and participation are shunted aside and deformed by a predominant economic force.

One case is, however, so striking that it will be singled out for especial remark. Attention was called earlier to the way in which scientific values are restricted and kept down by subordination to pecuniary values. The case of art and esthetic value is even more significant. No one can doubt that art and appreciation are among the values which preeminently enrich experience and make life worth living. So true is this that no question probes deeper into any culture than inquiry as to how it stands with reference to the creative arts and esthetic enjoyment. But here again values are vacuous and impotent as ends in the degree in which they lack means for expansion.

It is customary, for example, to refer the relatively low level of esthetic use of leisure time in this country, as reflected in the movie, radio, and amusement generally, to an inherently low grade of taste. This explanation leaves out of account the commercialization which uses these things to make money instead of to serve the values involved. As long as the conditioning means remain unchanged, there is little benefit likely to accrue from eulogizing fine art no matter how ecstatic the admiration. When conditions confine the development of taste to a privileged few, its status in the community will be that of a contrast effect with the things of ordinary life. Popular art will then be a rebound to stimulation and excitement from those activities of working hours which lack freedom and meaning. Art will be a widespread enhancement of the joy and significance of living only when economic barriers do not switch it off to the esoteric for the few and the sensational for the many. The humanizing of the economic system will detract from the power of the acquisitive and add to that of the creative aspect of life. It will surely prove more efficacious in extending the scope of the arts than any amount of praise of them uttered in the face of forces which keep persons aloof from their enjoyment, and which induce disregard of the ugly as long as it is not shown to be pecuniarily unprofitable. Thus in the case of two things as far apart seemingly as the poles, material economy and ideal art, the connection of means with values that are ends is strikingly demonstrated. The liberation of individual creative activity and elevation of esthetic taste which would follow the reconstruction of the economic system is moreover an illustration of the position we have taken as to the relation of individual and social.

IV

The problem of the relation of knowledge and action equals in importance that of the individual and the social. For we live in a world wherein we have to act, where action is imperative and unescapable but where knowledge is conditional, dependent upon ourselves. And the consequences of action, that is, what comes from it and remains as a permanent deposit, depend—within limits at least—upon whether or not action is informed with knowledge and is guided by adequate intelligence. Even the will to refrain from acting, to withdraw from the scene of action, is itself, in the end, but one policy and mode of action.

Because the necessity for action is unescapable, there is one question of supreme importance: What is its dominating method and spirit? A survey of the field shows that in fact there are many methods used to regulate action. There is the method of external authority dictating conformity to its requirements under penalty of suffering. There is the method of custom, of walking by precedents of the past. There is the method of routine, of persisting automatically, without asking for a reason, in paths worn deep, smooth, and easy by long repetition. There is the method of self-interest of individuals or of a class dressed up to look like public service. There is the method of trial by force to see which is stronger in cannon and gunpowder, or in command of money and credit.

History shows that all of these methods have been more widely used and more influential in the life of humanity than has the method of knowledge and intelligence. Speaking in general terms, life is characterized by a gap between knowledge and conduct, by separation between theory and practice. This divorce between the two is "rationalized" in the philosophies which have hitherto been most influential in thought. These have glorified knowledge as an end in itself, something divine, superior to the vicissitudes of experience, while at the same time they have depreciated the importance of action, connecting it with a realm of existence which is transitory, related to the body and material interests rather than to mind and ideal things, connected with mundane affairs instead of with pure truth. On the other hand, a so-called practical people have condemned theory as an idle and impotent luxury. They have put their trust in superior force and covert stratagem.

Some separation between intelligence and action is unavoidable in a world wherein action often cannot wait, and where it plunges ahead into the novel. But professed theorist and professed practical man have deliberately widened the gap. Thinkers have not seen channels by which their ideas could be translated into effective action. They have, by way of compensation, proclaimed that ideas are too fine and pure to be sullied by contact with the baser conditions of practice. "Practical" people have been content to take thinkers at their word. They have borrowed what they wanted of what thinkers have found out, and turned it to their own account in managing affairs to their own advantage.

The gulf between thought and conduct, knowledge and action, was not originated by philosophers, though they have celebrated it hitherto as a good. It began in primitive days when there was no knowledge in existence competent to control affairs outside a small area of immediate necessities. Methods which grew up under those conditions, compounded of magic, authority backed by force, and a rule-of-thumb empiricism, persisted because of the inertia of custom and because these methods could be laid hold of to maintain privilege and vested interest. They subtly displayed their power by patronizing philosophy, art, science, and religion as long as these remained practically innocuous.

The schools as special instrumentalities of education have upon the whole adopted the principle of the divorce of knowledge and practice and have conformed to it. In so doing they have maintained the division and widened the rift. "Practice" has consisted in repetition of actions in which more emphasis is placed on mechanical accuracy than on understanding. Acquisition of automatic skill has been aimed at apart from conscious purpose in the minds of those performing the exercises. It was supposed that skill would then be ready for use when some reason for its use developed later in life. "Efficiency" in doing has been made a goal irrespective of *what* efficiency is for.

Knowledge, on the other hand, has been treated as accumulation of information with little reference to perceived bearing of what is acquired. The criterion for the selection of particular bodies of information taught has been some standard of the past regarding culture or utility, rather than connection with the values of the active present. The emphasis on information apart from purposed bearing and application has affected the governing concepts of learning and its methods. The former has been thought of as something stored in books and the heads of learned men, and the latter as transmission by a kind of scholastic pipe-line into the minds of pupils whose business is to absorb what is transmitted.

Aside from being a definite illustration in a particular case of what is involved in the separation of theory and practice, the instance cited is of importance because of its social effect. Many of those who have had their habits formed on the basis of repetitions designed to give specific skills, carry away a permanent division in their make-up. They are habituated on one side to routine activity; they fall into lines of conduct the reason for which they do not see and the purpose of which is fixed by others. They are not used to judging for themselves and forming purposes on their own account. They thus readily become later in life passive instruments in execution of the plans and desires of others, perpetuating one of the evil features of our economic system. They become factory-fodder, as in militaristic autocracies individuals are trained to be cannon-fodder. Mass production of this type of mentality compromises in advance the success of political democracy.

On the other side, the important phases of conduct cannot be reduced to acquisition of specific skills. The most significant factors in conduct are general patterns of desire and appreciation. These are not touched by routine exercises. Here too comes into play the fallacy of psychologies which try to build a whole out of an aggregation of specific but isolated parts. Basic appetites are left undisciplined even though the motto of this type of school practice is "discipline." The deeper and more inclusive drives and moving forces are not cultivated and hence find accidental and unregulated outlet. The social effect is that youth having an unusual amount of untrained energy to dispose of fall readily into careers of revolt and potential crime; those with more moderate equipment become a ready prey to external stimulations. They grow into seekers after dissipation and excitement in order to obtain a simulation of a fulfilment of themselves which is denied them in the monotony of routine occupations.

From many angles, the separation of intelligence and practice tends to maintain the *status quo*. Change which is inevitable in any case is left to accident and external pressure. Instead of having a process of continuous self-repair on the part of society, corresponding to a continuous reconstruction of experience in the individual, we have periods of undue conservatism alternating

with shorter periods of unregulated change. Only the acknowledgment, first in idea and then in practical fact, of the intimate
union of theory and practice, knowledge and action, can create a
society having foresight and the capacity to plan so as to regulate
the inevitable processes of change.

The significant fact is that it is now possible, perhaps for the
first time in human history, honestly to develop and act upon the
conception of the union, instead of the separation, of thought
and practice. So far as the past is concerned, the philosophies
that assumed a separation were honest intellectual reports of the
actual situation. Social institutions were so governed by authority, tradition, and precedent, along with possession of power
by a small class, that such an ideal (as Plato for example advanced) of control of social action by understanding and insight
was purely utopian. Nor did the fault lie exclusively on the side
of practical conditions. The pursuit of knowledge and the state of
thought did not permit the development of techniques for their
effective operation in action. Intellectual activity was so driven
back upon itself that it is not surprising that thinkers who were
preeminently occupied with it produced by way of compensation
the theory of its intrinsic superiority to practice and the need for
keeping it "pure"—that is, aloof—in order that its superior value
might not be tarnished and diluted.

For reasons which will be stated below, this situation has now
changed both from the side of social conditions and from the
side of the pursuit of knowledge. On the economic side, an advanced industrial country such as the United States is passing
from a deficit to a surplus economy. So intellectually we are passing from an epoch in which knowledge and understanding were
the precarious possession of a small class, and had to be guarded
and cherished lest the flame die out, into an era in which scientific knowledge breaks through into control of actual conditions
in the technological field, while there are at hand techniques by
which a similar control can be developed and applied in other
and broader fields.

A small class devoted to distinctively intellectual pursuits—in
science and philosophy—have always found the cultivation of
thought and extension of knowledge of priceless value. To those
who enjoy these things, no other enjoyments offer comparable

values. To them, thought and learning are in a very genuine sense ends in themselves. No theory of the intimate connection of thought and action can deprive such persons of this legitimate and precious good. But a value cannot be converted on the ground of private appreciation into a theory of the structure, nature, and function of thought and knowledge. Logically, such a conversion is on a par with the conduct of those who enjoying lower, more sensual goods make their personal satisfaction in these things a measure of the status and purpose of values in the structure of the universe. The intrinsic structure and function of knowledge cannot be fixed from the side of personal appreciation, but only from an examination of thought and knowledge themselves. Moreover, in the past only a few have been so constituted by temperament and so placed by circumstances that they could enjoy distinctively intellectual values. Even from the side of personal appreciation, then, there is responsibility for a change of conditions that will enable many more to share in the enjoyment.

Action, we repeat, goes on anyway. It will continue as long as life endures. The only way to arrest it is to destroy human life itself. Upon action of one sort or another depend all consequences in the way of realization of values, and of their prevention and depreciation. There is no genuine alternative between action and withdrawal from action. The only alternatives are between different methods of action. He would be a bold person who would deny that, were it possible, knowledge and thought offer a better method for directing action than do external authority, self-interest and the vested interest of a privileged class, reliance on imitation and precedent, or violent force and so on. Few would deny, I think, that *if* intelligence could be raised to the position of the controlling method of action, it would change social life to an extent not short of revolutionary. Few would deny that if and when intelligence were once installed in this role, the conservation and extension of its function would become an object of supreme consideration.

The basic question is, then, one of fact. Is it possible for intelligence informed by knowledge to be a fundamentally significant method of projecting and directing action, individual and collective? Certain objections and misunderstandings will be considered later. At this point we shall consider some reasons why the possibility is within the bounds of reasonable endeavor at the present time. The consideration of these reasons will also disclose the nature of intelligence conceived as method of action.

V

The development of the natural sciences since the seventeenth century has demonstrated the falsity of the idea that reason and thought apart from action can issue in valid knowledge. The primary bond of union of thought with existence or "reality" is action. These statements do not rest upon opinion but upon the observed fact that the progress of natural knowledge has been made constant and secure only by the adoption of the experimental method. Thought *suggests* a course and way of acting so as to effect a change of conditions. The execution of the procedure which is suggested effects consequences which enable the validity of the idea to be judged and which bring about its further development. In this way thought is converted into authentic knowledge. The process by its very nature is self-continuing. Ideas must be framed in a form which will indicate acts to be performed and the interpretation to be put upon their consequences. Here is the criterion which controls the operations of thinking and the development of ideas. Consideration of their applicability to action in the two ways just mentioned gives the criterion for selection and rejection among the multitude of suggestions and fancies which vegetate and come to birth in mind. Think in terms of action and in terms of *those* acts whose consequences will expand, revise, test, your ideas and theories. This is the first commandment of the experimental method. It is by observation of this commandment that thinking, inquiry, observation, and interpretation have been rendered fruitful in progressive knowledge of nature.

On the other hand, action, doing, when directed by ideas, brings new facts to light and thus ensures the progress of thought and the generation of new knowledge. Before and apart from the use of experimental method, new facts were merely stumbled upon. Their disclosure was a matter of accident. And what is even more important, they did not find their proper place in a larger system. They remained isolated or else they were forced by thought into some merely intellectual scheme and system. Facts which are discovered by the use of experimental observation, on the other hand, either fall naturally into place because the ideas instigating the experiment of which they are the fruit supply their natural context; or, if what is discovered is unexpected and inconsistent with those ideas, new ideas are suggested that lead to new experiments. In either case, they do not remain a surd and perplexity but they help define a problem for further inquiry.

This revolutionary change in thought and knowledge, this complete shift from aloofness from action over to adoption of action into the very structure and procedure of thought and knowledge, makes necessary a reconsideration of all beliefs and traditions based on the assumption that the gulf between knowledge and action is intrinsic and final. We can go further than this statement. As a matter of fact, in certain limited but important fields it is demonstrated that intelligence and action can be effectively wedded, and control of conditions brought about. In these fields, we have not the possibility but the accomplished actuality of knowledge being the authorized method of action.

Reference is here made, of course, to the field of inventions which have taken place as a direct product of the advance in natural knowledge that is due to the experimental method. The telephone, telegraph, radio, steam locomotive, electric light, dynamo, internal combustion engine, automobile, and airplane are, for example, so many exhibits testifying to the reality, already effected, of knowledge as instrumentality of action. Our entire machine age and its technology is the same testimony written large.

This situation of accomplished fact suggests, and in an emphatic way, the possibility of extension of the same union to the wider social field. If we can effect the use of intelligence as method of control in the physical and mechanical field, why should we not strive to develop it in the field of human relations? Moreover, the social effects of the limited and more technical control that has been effected do more than suggest the possibility of a wider and deeper moral application. They create an urgent need, a necessity, that it be done. The contrast which exists between insight, foresight, and direction in the physical and in the human territories has become a commonplace. It is almost equally a commonplace that because of this contrast, it is not yet decided whether the control that has been effected in the physical field is to be a blessing or a curse: whether, in other words, the machine and its technology are to be the servants or the masters of mankind. What is not so generally recognized is that the heart of the problem is whether the experimental method can be made as fundamental in social knowledge and action as it now is in physical. If it cannot, the split between mere drift in human affairs and mastery in material things is bound to widen, and possibly to result in the destruction of civilization.

Just what is the experimental method which has brought forth such fruit and such continued possibility of fruit-bearing in the physical sciences? If experiment means simply trying, there is nothing new about it. Life itself is an experiment; everything we undertake is experimental in one way or another. When the most assured dogmatist starts out to act in conformity with his dogma, he may have some private and subjective certainty as to the rightness and beneficence of his course. He may deem it absolutely warranted by the assured truths which he assumes that he possesses. But actually he is *trying* something. He cannot absolutely guarantee the consequences of what he does. His dogma will not guarantee them in fact. It will only blind his eyes to many bad results of his action and prevent his learning anything from what he does. The outsider, when he looks at what is going on in another country, say Russia or Italy, spontaneously speaks of them as experiments, as trials. Even though they may seem to be something else to some of those engaged in them, that is what they are. In a world where there is as much complexity and contingency as there is in our world, it is true both that action is necessary and that action must be experimental, a trying.

Experimental method, in the sense in which we have referred to it, is then something different from the bare fact of the omnipresence of uncertain trial in all action. The difference is that between experiment which is aware of what it is about and experiment which ignores conditions and consequences. Empirical action in the sense in which *empirical* is applied to the practice of a physician who is guided by custom, by accumulation of particular past experiences rather than by scientific insight, is experimental in a sense, but distinctly *not* that of experimental *method*.

Experimental method is the universal and inescapable fact of *experimentation become conscious of itself and so directing action by this consciousness.* It is opposed to dogmatism, to empiricism as the rule of custom, to authoritarianism, to personal egoism, etc. But also it has a positive content of its own.

In the first place, every experimentation which is not aware that it is a trial operates in a world of unknowns, of contingencies and uncertainties, without taking that fact into account. Or if it does take it into account it deals with it through magic—which includes for our present purpose every ritual and formula blindly adhered to. Experimental method takes honest account of the fact of contingency by consciously propounding and defining a *problem* as the base from which action proceeds. Experimental method converts the conditions which bring about uncertainty into terms of a definite question to be asked, a definite problem to be resolved. It recognizes that uncertainty is inevitable and then turns it to positive account. For it searches for data which will first enable us to pose a question, and then to think of a course of action which will help us find the answer to the question. Experimental method thus teaches us how to deal with doubt. We do not cover it up and deny its existence. We are to cultivate it. But we are not to cherish it, as ancient skeptics did, as an end in itself. It then tends to paralyze action. We are to cherish doubt as but the first stage in the development of a question so put that it will direct action to the discovery of facts which will answer the question.

In the second place, experimentation which is so conscious as to take proper account of itself operates on the basis of an idea. This idea is used as an *hypothesis.* That is, it is employed as directive of action for the sake of the consequences which action produces, and which when produced indicate how to proceed next. Experimental method is fatal to dogmatism because it shows that all ideas, conceptions, theories, however extensive and self-consistent and esthetically attractive they may be, are to be entertained provisionally until they have been tested by acting upon them. To state the fact in its full force, ideas prior to active test are intellectually significant only as guides and as plans of *possible actions.* The actions when undertaken produce consequences which test, expand, and modify the ideas previously tentatively entertained. The experimental method is thus opposed once and for all to all methods which claim to be sure-fire.

Persons of natural energy are urged on by their very energy to action. This urge to direct action, to doing something right away, is a chief psychological cause of inclination to dogmatic belief. Uncertainty is a hindrance; it defers overt action. Curiosity, inquiry, reflection, examination, all postpone it. So a person having strong bent toward doing things is impatient of thought. He tends to lay hold of any belief or theory which will justify him in going ahead full steam. Now the experimental method does not sickly over this determination to action by the pale cast of thought. It rather would utilize it, while giving it a new temper through enforcing upon it recognition of need for keeping track of the consequences of what is done, and modifying the further progress of action accordingly. It does not propose thought as a substitute for action, but rather the introduction of thought into action as its directive principle.

Finally, a marked trait of experimental method is its introduction of the principle of degree and measure. It puts probability in place of what claims to be the absolute, and endeavors to measure degrees of probability. It recognizes the extent to which different and alternative possibilities enter into action. In pursuing the chosen one, it does not slam the door in the face of others. It renders action more alert and wary. For before thought passes into action a number of alternative hypotheses are considered and practice is thus rendered flexible and readaptable when need for change of direction shows itself. Firmness is required in order that the consequences of action may be adequately instructive, but firmness is not allowed to become so rigid that it moves fatalistically to an uncriticized end.

VI

The meaning of experimental method may be further developed by considering certain objections and misunderstandings which are more or less current. Almost all of these have a common source. Old ideas that are deeply embedded have a kind of inertia and momentum of their own. They are not only difficult to displace by newer ideas, but they are employed to interpret new ideas even when the latter are intended to replace them. Most of the objections we are about to consider spring, ironically enough, from reading into the new conception of intelligence, reached by connecting it with action, the old conception of reason and intellect whose meaning was formed by keeping them separate from action. The new conception of intelligence is treated as if it were the old "intellect" with merely a new function added. Of course defects and contradictions are then found in it.

First, there is the radical misconception which assumes that the method makes action just as action an end in itself. The previous discussion should have rendered this mistake so obvious that it may briefly be disposed of. It is action informed by knowledge and guided by an operative idea or working hypothesis which is commended, and such action is instrumental to the disclosure of new facts for new observation and enjoyment, and to the evocation of more significant ideas. Both *knowing and acting* as such are ultimately instrumental to the protection, expansion, and installation of values to be directly experienced.

The second misunderstanding is of an opposite nature, though sometimes both are joined in the same person. The operational theory of knowledge and action holds, as we have seen, that ends and ideals must not be sought in the blue; that they are to be reached through inquiry into existing conditions taken both as obstacles and as potential means. This intellectual acknowledgment of the existent state of things is conceived by some critics to be a commendation of a policy of conformity and servile acceptance. This conclusion would follow naturally from the conception of thought as something isolated from action. But in experimental philosophy this intellectual acknowledgment is a preliminary stage in the formation of a method of action which will bring about *change* in the existing state of affairs. To form relevant and effective ideals we must first be acquainted with and take notice of actual conditions. Otherwise our ideals become vacuous or else filled with a content drawn from Utopia. Existent conditions do not determine the end and purpose. They determine the *problem* with which a purpose has to deal. In forming the purpose, there is room for all the imagination and all the adventure which any mind can bring to the situation. Indeed, there is a positive demand for imagination, and no limits are set to its flight except that its product be capable of application in action to bring about a changed state of affairs. Even this limitation permits objects of other flights to remain for private esthetic enjoyment. But it protects ideals in this aspect from being confused with ends that are valid to intelligence. Thus it prevents action from being itself so confused as to invite deception and insincerity.

The third point is so similar that it needs only brief mention. The experimental theory connects thought biologically with attempts at adaptation which are characteristic of all animal life. The statement of the theory was accompanied by pointing to the radical difference between the kind of adaptation which takes place through the medium of thought and that which takes place without thought through mere habituation. Yet the experimental theory is charged with teaching the doctrine of accommodation to whatever exists in any potent degree. Actually the experimental philosophy signifies (as was pointed out in its first statement) that genuine experimental action effects an adjustment *of* conditions, not *to* them: a remaking of existing conditions, not a mere remaking of self and mind to fit into them. Intelligent adaptation is always a *re*adjustment, a re-construction of what exists.

In the fourth place, as already indicated, the adoption of intelligence as the very heart of a philosophy of action does not exclude firmness of conviction nor daring. It rather affirms that convictions must be firm *enough* to evoke and justify action, while also they are to be held in a way which permits the individual to learn from his further experience. It implies that every sound conviction will be confirmed, in the degree of its soundness, by subsequent experience. It trusts to convictions which are firm because con-firmed in experience rather than those which are intense mainly because of immaturity. At the same time it recognizes that maturity often leads to the limitations of rigid fixation, and that inexperience and ignorance when animated by sincerity are often capable of thoughts and adventures of which a mind closed in by habit and indurated by past experiences is incapable.

Fifth, the philosophy is not one of opportunism. As opportunism is usually understood, it implies that only small situations are recognized and dealt with in thought and action, small in the sense of being rather narrowly limited in place and of short span in time. Experimentalism recognizes that extent, like depth, is a function of the situation dealt with. There exists a whole nest of situations varying in inclusiveness and scope. Continuity is a chief trait of situations which demand intelligent action. Conse-

quences abide and are cumulative. Hypotheses of great comprehensiveness and long-time span are therefore imperatively needed.
They form the larger policies and define the more enduring ends
of conduct. All that is demanded by the logic of the experimental
philosophy is that whether the situation be small or great, and
the guiding idea of near-by or far-off application, the spirit of hypothesis and experiment enter into the procedure for managing it.

Sixth, the method is not identical with a sweet reasonableness
in which sweetness in the sense of weak compromise is more evident than reasonableness. The kind of measure to be undertaken
in any particular situation is a function of *that* situation. It cannot be derived from the general concept of method. Just because
the experimental method has *not* been operative to any great extent in the past in social affairs, social situations are marked by
conflicts of interest in which force, open and underhand, is used
by those occupying privileged positions. The method of intelligence requires that we open our eyes instead of shutting them to
these conflicts, for they are an inexorable part of the conditions
to be acknowledged intellectually and dealt with practically. The
method of action employed in such situations cannot, if it is the
method of intelligence, be identical in detail with that which will
be followed when intelligence has already obtained a greater
foothold. For example, experience shows that the method of violent action has usually been so wasteful that the antecedent presumption is against it. But an experimental philosophy as such
cannot absolutely prejudge this case any more than it can any
other. As far as experience and reflection indicate that pacific
measures are most likely to be effective, the philosophy is paci-
fist; where the reverse is indicated by the best available knowledge of actual conditions, it is revolutionary. All that the method
intrinsically calls for is that neither extreme be made so absolute
a doctrine that it obstructs inquiry and pushes the plan of action
in advance into prejudged channels. Both absolute pacificism
and absolute progress reached only through class struggle suffer
from the same disease. Neither of them is consistent with experimentalism. Even those persons who hold with either of them
usually have certain exceptional cases in reserve at the back of
their minds.

Finally, it is not true that the method is intellectualistic or that
it exaggerates the place of thought, inquiry, observation at the ex-

pense of emotion, desire, and impulse. This misunderstanding is perhaps the best illustration to be found of the effect of carrying over into experimental philosophy a conception of intellect framed on the basis of separation from action. Were there such a thing as intellect or reason all by itself, then a method based upon it would be fatally exposed to this objection. There is no doubt that careful discrimination and acute criticism, that clarification of ideas and integration of them into a coherent whole, follow from the experimental method. But what equally follows (but is overlooked by the objection) is that these exist only as they operate with and in the material which demands action. Since they have no existence by themselves but only *in* the material of the concrete situation, they are colored throughout by the quality of that material. If that calls out ardor and enthusiasm, repulsion and disgust, then thinking is impregnated with these emotions. The very idea of the method implies *interest* in the situation and its constituents, whether positive or negative, desire or aversion. All that the method demands of emotion is that it be not permitted to swamp and suppress thought and observation; or, stated positively, that emotion be employed to intensify and stimulate the intellectual as well as the overt phase of the action undertaken.

The idea that people have ever been emotionally indifferent in the degree in which they are intellectually aroused is contradicted by the facts of all productive intellectual activity. The contrary idea is probably due to traditional philosophies and psychologies that have cherished a conception of intellect as something outside the situation in which action is to occur, and to the correct inference that *such* an intellect would necessarily be "cold": intellectual and nothing but intellectual. Since intelligence as the method of action is what it is as the method, the how, *of* a particular scene of action, it will share in all the excitement involved in the active situation. It may be passionate to any degree—provided it be intelligent passion.

VII

If method could be separated from the subject-matter in which it operates, then experimental method would be neutral as respects any particular type and condition of social life and equally applicable in any and every one of them. As a matter of fact, a complete and adequate operation of the method is consistent only with certain types of society, because method and subject-matter stand in one-to-one correspondence with each other. A *truncated, one-sided* application of the method may be found, it is true, in any situation; it may be used even in behalf of anti-social measures. The children of darkness are often wiser than the children of light, and a predatory character may use the experimental method in a *limited* field more effectually than a would-be benevolent person in a wider field. But only when intelligence is not accepted as the *central* virtue can we stop short with a particular limited use of it. The choice of intelligence as the preferred method of action implies, like every choice, a definite *moral* outlook. The scope of this choice is so inclusive that the moral implication outlines, when followed out, an entire ethical and social philosophy. In our philosophy of education, its two main constituents, the relationships of the social and the individual and of knowledge and action, coalesce in this conclusion.

In the first place, the experimental method cannot be made an effective reality in its full adequacy except in a certain kind of society. A society which includes warring class interests will always fight against its application outside of a particular limited field. Sinister class interests flourish better in the dark. If the free play of intelligence were not intrinsically a foe of their schemes, they would not fear it as they do, and they would not attempt by continuous propaganda to palm off substitutes for it. The social implication of the philosophy of intelligence may be judged from the fact that its opposite is obscurantism, while obscurantism is the chief ally of social abuses, corruptions, and iniquities. The objective precondition of the complete and free use of the method of intelligence is a society in which class interests that recoil from social experimentation are abolished. It is incompatible with every social and political philosophy and activity and with every economic system which accepts the class organization and vested class interest of present society.

The positive side of this statement is that life based on experimental intelligence provides the only possible opportunity for *all* to develop rich and diversified experience, while also securing continuous cooperative give and take and intercommunication.

The method cannot be fully established in life unless the right of every person to realization of his potential capacities is effectively recognized. For without this condition the full material for judgment of values in action will be absent. Every bar to free communication from one to another has precisely the same limiting effect. There are marked differences between the experimental method in physical and in human matters. But one phase of physical science is significant for our purposes. Science progresses because a discovery made by one inquirer is at once made available for all workers in the field. Without constant exchange and mutual reinforcement, the science of nature would still be in a rudimentary state. Free communication on one side signifies power to receive and to participate in values on the other side. The great problem of society is to combine a maximum of different values, achieved by giving free play to individual taste and capacity, with a minimum of friction and conflict. The experimental method solves this problem as no other method can.

The experimental method is the only one compatible with the democratic way of life, as we understand it. Every extension of intelligence as the method of action enlarges the area of common understanding. Understanding may not ensure complete agreement, but it gives the only sound basis for enduring agreement. In any case where there is a difference, it will conduce to agreement to differ, to mutual tolerance and sympathy, pending the time when more adequate knowledge and better methods of judging are at hand. It is impossible to estimate the full import of the method on the basis of present conditions. The present economic organization stimulates the use of experiment in one-sided ways restricted to technical fields: those of machinery in the service of profit. This economic organization will itself be modified by extension of the method. Every accomplished extension will extend the variety and scope of human experience; it will liberate and intensify the processes of cooperative exchange and sharing of values. The adequate installation of the method in life would result in such an identification of the method with the values which it ensures that its own value would then be a matter of sight and not, as now, of faith and idea.

It is possible to put the processes of social change and of education in opposition to one another, and then debate whether desirable social change would follow education, or whether radical social change must come before marked improvements in education can take place. We hold that the two are correlative and interactive. No social modification, slight or revolutionary, can endure except as it enters into the action of a people through their desires and purposes. This introduction and perpetuation are effected by education. But every improvement in the social structure and its operations releases the educative resources of mankind and gives them a better opportunity to enter into normal social processes so that the latter become themselves more truly educative.

The process of interaction is circular and never-ending. We plead for a better, a more just, a more open and straightforward, a more public, society, in which free and all-round communication and participation occur as a matter of course in order that education may be bettered. We plead for an improved and enlarged education in order that there may be brought into existence a society all of whose operations shall be more genuinely educative, conducive to the development of desire, judgment, and character. The desired education cannot occur within the four walls of a school shut off from life. Education must itself assume an increasing responsibility for participation in projecting ideas of social change and taking part in their execution in order to be educative. The great problem of American education is the discovery of methods and techniques by which this more direct and vital participation may be brought about. We have conceived that the office of a philosophy of education at the present time is to indicate this pressing need and to sketch the lines on which alone, in our conception, it can be met. The method of experimental intelligence as the method of action cannot be established as a constant and operative habit of mind and character apart from education. But it cannot be established *within* education except as the activities of the latter are founded on a clear idea of the active social forces of the day, of what they are doing, of their effect, for good and harm, upon values, and except as this idea and ideal are acted upon to direct experimentation in the currents of social life that run outside the school and that condition the effect and determine the educational meaning of whatever the school does.

How We Think

A Restatement of the Relation of Reflective
Thinking to the Educative Process

Preface to the New Edition

To say that a text is "revised" may signify slight verbal changes or an extensive rewriting. The new edition of *How We Think*, which is presented herewith, is a revision of the latter sort. It is, as its subtitle indicates, a "restatement" of *How We Think*.

In the first place, although some material found in the original edition has been excised, there has been considerable expansion. The present book contains nearly a quarter more than did the older account.

In the second place, the revision has been made with a view to increased definiteness and clearness of statement. Scrupulous pains have been taken to restate all ideas that were found by teachers to give undue trouble in understanding. The changes in this respect apply both to matters of phrasing, where a multitude of minor alterations have been made in the interests of greater sureness of comprehension, and also to the development of major ideas. The latter changes are most numerous and complete in Part II, the theoretical section of the book. There the whole logical analysis of reflection has been rewritten and, it is believed, very considerably simplified in statement. At the same time, the basic ideas, those that gave the original work its distinctive character, have not only been retained but have also been enriched and developed further. In the interests of clearness more illustrative material has been added, and some rearrangement of the position of entire chapters has been made.

In the third place, changes will be evident in the parts devoted to teaching. These changes reflect the large changes that have taken place in schools, especially in the management of teaching and studying, since 1910, when the book first appeared. Some methods that were criticized because of their currency at that time have now practically disappeared from the better schools.

New topics have come to the fore. Adjustments have accordingly been made in the text; for example, the present chapter on "The Recitation" is practically all new.

In conclusion, it is a great pleasure to express my thanks to the many teachers whose experience in using the older book has been freely put at my disposal in preparing the new and, I venture to hope, improved version.

JOHN DEWEY

New York City, May, 1933.

Preface to the First Edition

Our schools are troubled with a multiplication of studies, each in turn having its own multiplication of materials and principles. Our teachers find their tasks made heavier in that they have come to deal with pupils individually and not merely in mass. Unless these steps in advance are to end in distraction, some clew of unity, some principle that makes for simplification, must be found. This book represents the conviction that the needed steadying and centralizing factor is found in adopting as the end of endeavor that attitude of mind, that habit of thought, which we call scientific. This scientific attitude of mind might, conceivably, be quite irrelevant to teaching children and youth. But this book also represents the conviction that such is not the case; that the native and unspoiled attitude of childhood, marked by ardent curiosity, fertile imagination, and love of experimental inquiry, is near, very near, to the attitude of the scientific mind. If these pages assist any to appreciate this kinship and to consider seriously how its recognition in educational practice would make for individual happiness and the reduction of social waste, the book will amply have served its purpose.

It is hardly necessary to enumerate the authors to whom I am indebted. My fundamental indebtedness is to my wife, by whom the ideas of this book were inspired, and through whose work in connection with the Laboratory School, existing in Chicago between 1896 and 1903, the ideas attained such concreteness as comes from embodiment and testing in practice. It is a pleasure, also, to acknowledge indebtedness to the intelligence and sympathy of those who cooperated as teachers and supervisors in the conduct of that school, and especially to Mrs. Ella Flagg Young, then a colleague in the University, and now Superintendent of the Schools of Chicago.

JOHN DEWEY

New York City, December, 1909.

Part One

The Problem of Training Thought

1. What Is Thinking?

I. Different Meanings of Thought

THE BEST WAY OF THINKING

No one can tell another person in any definite way how he *should* think, any more than how he ought to breathe or to have his blood circulate. But the various ways in which men *do* think can be told and can be described in their general features. Some of these ways are better than others; the reasons why they are better can be set forth. The person who understands what the better ways of thinking are and why they are better can, if he will, change his own personal ways until they become more effective; until, that is to say, they do better the work that thinking can do and that other mental operations cannot do so well. The better way of thinking that is to be considered in this book is called reflective thinking: the kind of thinking that consists in turning a subject over in the mind and giving it serious and consecutive consideration. Before we take up this main theme, we shall, however, first take note briefly of some other mental processes to which the name *thought* is sometimes given.

THE "STREAM OF CONSCIOUSNESS"

All the time we are awake and sometimes when we are asleep, something is, as we say, going through our heads. When we are asleep we call that kind of sequence "dreaming." We also have daydreams, reveries, castles built in the air, and mental streams that are even more idle and chaotic. To this uncontrolled coursing of ideas through our heads the name of "thinking" is sometimes given. It is automatic and unregulated. Many a child has attempted to see whether he could not "stop thinking"—that is, stop this procession of mental states through his mind—and in vain. More of our waking life than most of us would care to admit is whiled away in this inconsequential trifling with mental pictures, random recollections, pleasant but unfounded hopes, flitting, half-developed impressions. Hence it is that he who offers "a penny for your thoughts" does not expect to drive any great bargain if his offer is taken; he will only find out what happens to be "going through the mind" and what "goes" in this fashion rarely leaves much that is worth while behind.

REFLECTIVE THOUGHT IS A CHAIN

In this sense, silly folk and dullards *think*. The story is told of a man in slight repute for intelligence, who, desiring to be chosen selectman in his New England town, addressed a knot of neighbors in this wise: "I hear you don't believe I know enough to hold office. I wish you to understand that I am thinking about something or other most of the time." Now, reflective thought is like this random coursing of things through the mind in that it consists of a succession of things thought of, but it is unlike in that the mere chance occurrence of any chance "something or other" in an irregular sequence does not suffice. Reflection involves not simply a sequence of ideas, but a *con*-sequence— a consecutive ordering in such a way that each determines the next as its proper outcome, while each outcome in turn leans back on, or refers to, its predecessors. The successive portions of a reflective thought grow out of one another and support one another; they do not come and go in a medley. Each phase is a step from something to something—technically speaking, it is a *term* of thought. Each term leaves a deposit that is utilized in the next term. The stream or flow becomes a train or chain. There are in any reflective thought definite units that are linked together so that there is a sustained movement to a common end.

THINKING USUALLY RESTRICTED TO THINGS NOT DIRECTLY PERCEIVED

The second meaning of thinking limits it to things not sensed or directly perceived, to things *not* seen, heard, touched, smelt, or tasted. We ask the man telling a story if he saw a certain

incident happen, and his reply may be, "No, I only thought of it."
A note of invention, as distinct from faithful record of observation, is present. Most important in this class are successions of
imaginative incidents and episodes that have a certain coherence,
hang together on a continuous thread, and thus lie between ka-
leidoscopic flights of fancy and considerations deliberately employed to establish a conclusion. The imaginative stories poured
forth by children possess all degrees of internal congruity; some
are disjointed, some are articulated. When connected, they simu-
late reflective thought; indeed, they usually occur in minds of
logical capacity. These imaginative enterprises often precede
thinking of the close-knit type and prepare the way for it. In this
sense, a thought or idea is a mental picture of something not actually present, and thinking is the succession of such pictures.

REFLECTIVE THINKING AIMS AT
A CONCLUSION

In contrast, reflective thinking has a purpose beyond
the entertainment afforded by the train of agreeable mental inventions and pictures. The train must lead somewhere; it must
tend to a conclusion that can be substantiated outside the
course of the images. A story of a giant may satisfy merely because of the story itself; a reflective conclusion that a giant
lived at a certain date and place on the earth would have to
have some justification outside of the chain of ideas in order to
be a valid or sound conclusion. This contrasting element is
probably best conveyed in the ordinary saying: "Think it *out*."
The phrase suggests an entanglement to be straightened out,
something obscure to be cleared up through the application of
thought. There is a goal to be reached, and this end sets a task
that controls the sequence of ideas.

THINKING AS PRACTICALLY SYNONYMOUS
WITH BELIEVING

A third meaning of thought is practically synonymous
with *belief*. "I think it is going to be colder tomorrow," or "I
think Hungary is larger than Jugo-Slavia" is equivalent to "I
believe so-and-so." When we say, "Men used to think the world

was flat," we obviously refer to a belief that was held by our ancestors. This meaning of thought is narrower than those previously mentioned. A belief refers to something beyond itself by which its value is tested; it makes an assertion about some matter of fact or some principle or law. It means that a specified state of fact or law is accepted or rejected, that it is something proper to be affirmed or at least acquiesced in. It is hardly necessary to lay stress upon the importance of belief. It covers all the matters of which we have no sure knowledge and yet which we are sufficiently confident of to act upon and also the matters that we now accept as certainly true, as knowledge, but which nevertheless may be questioned in the future—just as much that passed as knowledge in the past has now passed into the limbo of mere opinion or of error.

There is nothing in the mere fact of thought as identical with belief that reveals whether the belief is well founded or not. Two different men say, "I believe the world is spherical." One man, if challenged, could produce little or no evidence for thinking as he does. It is an idea that he has picked up from others and that he accepts because the idea is generally current, not because he has examined into the matter and not because his own mind has taken any active part in reaching and framing the belief.

Such "thoughts" grow up unconsciously. They are picked up—we know not how. From obscure sources and by unnoticed channels they insinuate themselves into the mind and become unconsciously a part of our mental furniture. Tradition, instruction, imitation—all of which depend upon authority in some form, or appeal to our own advantage, or fall in with a strong passion—are responsible for them. Such thoughts are prejudices; that is, prejudgments, not conclusions reached as the result of personal mental activity, such as observing, collecting, and examining evidence. Even when they happen to be correct, their correctness is a matter of accident as far as the person who entertains them is concerned.

REFLECTIVE THINKING IMPELS TO INQUIRY

Thus we are brought again, by way of contrast, to the particular kind of thinking that we are to study in this volume, *reflective thinking*. Thought, in the two first senses mentioned, may be harmful to the mind because it distracts attention from the real world, and because it may be a waste of time. On the other hand, if indulged in judiciously these thoughts may afford genuine enjoyment and also be a source of needed recreation. But in either case they can make no claim to truth; they cannot hold themselves up as something that the mind should accept, assert, and be willing to act upon. They may involve a kind of emotional commitment, but not intellectual and practical commitment. Beliefs, on the other hand, do involve precisely this commitment and consequently sooner or later they demand our investigation to find out upon what grounds they rest. To think of a cloud as a whale or a camel—in the sense of to "fancy"—does not commit one to the conclusion that the person having the idea would ride the camel or extract oil from the whale. But when Columbus "thought" the world was round, in the sense of "believed it to be so," he and his followers were thereby committed to a series of other beliefs and actions: to beliefs about routes to India, about what would happen if ships traveled far westward on the Atlantic, etc., precisely as thinking that the world was flat had committed those who held it to belief in the impossibility of circumnavigation, and in the limitation of the earth to regions in the small civilized part of it Europeans were already acquainted with, etc.

The earlier thought, belief in the flatness of the earth, had some foundation in evidence; it rested upon what men could see easily within the limits of their vision. But this evidence was not further looked into; it was not checked by considering other evidence; there was no search for new evidence. Ultimately the belief rested on laziness, inertia, custom, absence of courage and energy in investigation. The later belief rests upon careful and extensive study, upon purposeful widening of the area of observation, upon reasoning out the conclusions of alternative conceptions to see what would follow in case one or the other were adopted for belief. As distinct from the first kind of thinking there was an orderly chain of ideas; as distinct from the second, there was a controlling purpose and end; as distinct from the third, there was personal examination, scrutiny, inquiry.

Because Columbus did not accept unhesitatingly the current traditional theory, because he doubted and inquired, he arrived at his thought. Skeptical of what, from long habit, seemed most certain, and credulous of what seemed impossible, he went on thinking until he could produce evidence for both his confidence and his disbelief. Even if his conclusion had finally turned out wrong, it would have been a different sort of belief from those it antagonized, because it was reached by a different method. *Active, persistent, and careful consideration of any belief or supposed form of knowledge in the light of the grounds that support it and the further conclusions to which it tends* constitutes reflective thought. Any one of the first three kinds of thought may elicit this type; but once begun, it includes a conscious and voluntary effort to establish belief upon a firm basis of evidence and rationality.

II. The Central Factor in Thinking

THE SUGGESTION OF SOMETHING NOT OBSERVED

There are, however, no sharp lines of demarcation between the various operations just outlined. The problem of attaining correct habits of reflection would be much easier than it is, did not the different modes of thinking blend insensibly into one another. So far, we have considered rather extreme instances of each kind in order to get the field clearly before us. Let us now reverse this operation; let us consider a rudimentary case of thinking, lying between careful examination of evidence and a mere irresponsible stream of fancies. A man is walking on a warm day. The sky was clear the last time he observed it; but presently he notes, while occupied primarily with other things, that the air is cooler. It occurs to him that it is probably going to rain; looking up, he sees a dark cloud between him and the sun, and he then quickens his steps. What, if anything, in such a situation can be called thought? Neither the act of walking nor the noting of the cold is a thought. Walking is one direction of activity; looking and noting are other modes of activity. The likelihood that it will rain is, however, something *suggested*. The pedestrian *feels* the cold; first he *thinks* of clouds, then he looks and perceives them, and then he thinks of something he does not see: a storm. This *suggested possibility* is the idea, the thought. If it is believed in as a genuine possibility which may occur, it is the kind of thought which falls within the scope of knowledge and which requires reflective consideration.

Up to a certain point there is the same sort of situation as when one who looks at a cloud is reminded of a human figure and face. Thinking in both of these cases (the cases of belief and of fancy) involves noting or perceiving a fact, followed by something else that is not observed but that is brought to mind, suggested by the thing seen. One thing reminds us, as we say, of the other. Side by side, however, with this factor of agreement in the two cases of suggestion is a factor of marked disagreement. We do not *believe* in the face suggested by the cloud; we do not consider at all the probability of its being a fact. There is no *reflective* thought. The danger of rain, on the contrary, presents itself to us as a genuine possibility—a fact of the same nature as the observed coolness. Put differently, we do not regard the cloud as meaning or indicating a face, but merely as suggesting it, while we do consider that the coolness may *mean* rain. In the first case, on seeing an object, we just happen, as we say, to think of something else; in the second, we consider the *possibility and nature of the connection between the object seen and the object suggested*. The seen thing is regarded as in some way *the ground or basis of belief* in the suggested thing; it possesses the quality of *evidence*.

THE FUNCTION OF SIGNIFYING

This function whereby one thing signifies or indicates another, thus leading us to consider how far the one may be regarded as warrant for belief in the other, is, then, the central factor in all reflective or distinctively intellectual thinking. By calling up various situations to which such terms as *signifies* and *indicates* apply, the student will realize for himself the actual facts denoted. Synonyms for these terms are: points to, tells of, betokens, prognosticates, represents, stands for, implies.[1] We also say one thing portends another, is ominous of another, or a

1. *Implies* is more often used when a principle or general truth brings about belief in some other truth; the other phrases are more frequently used to denote the cases in which a fact or event leads us to believe in some other fact or in a law.

symptom of it, or a key to it, or (if the connection is quite obscure) that it gives a hint, clue, or intimation. Reflection is not identical with the mere fact that one thing indicates, means, another thing. It commences when we begin to inquire into the reliability, the worth, of any particular indication; when we try to test its value and see what guarantee there is that the existing data *really* point to the idea that is suggested in such a way as to *justify* acceptance of the latter.

REFLECTION IMPLIES BELIEF ON EVIDENCE

Reflection thus implies that something is believed in (or disbelieved in), not on its own direct account, but through something else which stands as witness, evidence, proof, voucher, warrant; that is, as *ground of belief*. At one time, rain is actually felt or directly experienced; at another time, we *infer* that it has rained from the appearance of the grass and trees, or that it is going to rain because of the condition of the air or the state of the barometer. At one time, we see a man (or suppose we do) without any intermediary fact; at another time, we are not quite sure what we see, and hunt for accompanying facts that will serve as signs, indications, tokens of what we are to believe.

Thinking, for the purposes of this inquiry, is accordingly defined as *that operation in which present facts suggest other facts (or truths) in such a way as to induce belief in what is suggested on the ground of real relation in the things themselves*, a relation between what suggests and what is suggested. A cloud *suggests* a weasel or a whale; it does not *mean* the latter, because there is no tie, or bond, in the things themselves between what is seen and what is suggested. Ashes not merely suggest a previous fire, but they signify there has been a fire, because ashes are produced by combustion and, if they are genuine ashes, only by combustion. It is an objective connection, the link in actual things, that makes one thing the ground, warrant, evidence, for believing in something else.

III. Phases of Reflective Thinking

We may carry our account further by noting that *reflective* thinking, in distinction from other operations to which we apply the name of thought, involves (1) a state of doubt, hesitation, perplexity, mental difficulty, in which thinking originates, and (2) an act of searching, hunting, inquiring, to find material that will resolve the doubt, settle and dispose of the perplexity.

THE IMPORTANCE OF UNCERTAINTY AND OF INQUIRY

In our illustration, the shock of coolness generated confusion and suspended belief, at least momentarily. Because it was unexpected, it was a shock or an interruption needing to be accounted for, identified, or placed. To say that the abrupt occurrence of the change of temperature constitutes a problem may sound forced and artificial; but if we are willing to extend the meaning of the word *problem* to whatever—no matter how slight and commonplace in character—perplexes and challenges the mind so that it makes belief at all uncertain, there is a genuine problem, or question, involved in an experience of sudden change.

The turning of the head, the lifting of the eyes, the scanning of the heavens, are activities adapted to bring to recognition facts that will answer the question presented by the sudden coolness. The facts as they first presented themselves were perplexing; they suggested, however, clouds. The act of looking was an act to discover whether this suggested explanation held good. It may again seem forced to speak of this looking, almost automatic, as an act of research, or inquiry. But once more, if we are willing to generalize our conceptions of our mental operations to include the trivial and ordinary as well as the technical and recondite, there is no good reason for refusing to give this title to the act of looking. For the result of the act is to bring facts before the mind that enable a person to reach a conclusion on the basis of evidence. In so far, then, as the act of looking was deliberate, was performed with the intention of getting an external basis on which to rest a belief, it exemplifies in an elementary way the operation of hunting, searching, inquiring, involved in any reflective operation.

Another instance, commonplace also, yet not quite so trivial, may enforce this lesson. A man traveling in an unfamiliar region comes to a branching of the road. Having no sure knowledge to fall back upon, he is brought to a standstill of hesitation and suspense. Which road is right? And how shall his perplexity be resolved? There are but two alternatives: he must either blindly and arbitrarily take his course, trusting to luck for the outcome, or he must discover grounds for the conclusion that a given road is right. Any attempt to decide the matter by thinking will involve inquiring into other facts, whether brought to mind by memory, or by further observation, or by both. The perplexed wayfarer must carefully scrutinize what is before him and he must cudgel his memory. He looks for evidence that will support belief in favor of either of the roads—for evidence that will weight down one suggestion. He may climb a tree; he may go first in this direction, then in that, looking, in either case, for signs, clues, indications. He wants something in the nature of a signboard or a map, and *his reflection is aimed at the discovery of facts that will serve this purpose.*

The foregoing illustration may be generalized. Thinking begins in what may fairly enough be called a *forked-road* situation, a situation that is ambiguous, that presents a dilemma, that proposes alternatives. As long as our activity glides smoothly along from one thing to another, or as long as we permit our imagination to entertain fancies at pleasure, there is no call for reflection. Difficulty or obstruction in the way of reaching a belief brings us, however, to a pause. In the suspense of uncertainty, we metaphorically climb a tree; we try to find some standpoint from which we may survey additional facts and, getting a more commanding view of the situation, decide how the facts stand related to one another.

THE REGULATION OF THINKING
BY ITS PURPOSE

Demand for the solution of a perplexity is the steadying and guiding factor in the entire process of reflection. Where there is no question of a problem to be solved or a difficulty to be surmounted, the course of suggestions flows on at random; we have the first type of thought described. If the stream of suggestions is controlled simply by their emotional congruity, their fitting agreeably into a single picture or story, we have the second type. But a question to be answered, an ambiguity to be resolved, sets up an end and holds the current of ideas to a definite channel. Every suggested conclusion is tested by its reference to this regulating end, by its pertinence to the problem in hand. This need of straightening out a perplexity also controls the kind of inquiry undertaken. A traveler whose end is the most beautiful path will look for other signs and will test suggestions on another basis than if he wishes to discover the way to a given city. *The nature of the problem fixes the end of thought,* and *the end controls the process of thinking.*

IV. Summary

We may recapitulate by saying that the origin of thinking is some perplexity, confusion, or doubt. Thinking is not a case of spontaneous combustion; it does not occur just on "general principles." There is something that occasions and evokes it. General appeals to a child (or to a grown-up) to think, irrespective of the existence in his own experience of some difficulty that troubles him and disturbs his equilibrium, are as futile as advice to lift himself by his boot-straps.

Given a difficulty, the next step is suggestion of some way out—the formation of some tentative plan or project, the entertaining of some theory that will account for the peculiarities in question, the consideration of some solution for the problem. The data at hand cannot supply the solution; they can only suggest it. What, then, are the sources of the suggestion? Clearly, past experience and a fund of relevant knowledge at one's command. If the person has had some acquaintance with similar situations, if he has dealt with material of the same sort before, suggestions more or less apt and helpful will arise. But unless there has been some analogous experience, confusion remains mere confusion. Even when a child (or a grown-up) has a problem, it is wholly futile to urge him to think when he has no prior experiences that involve some of the same conditions.

There may, however, be a state of perplexity and also previous experience out of which suggestions emerge, and yet thinking need not be reflective. For the person may not be sufficiently *critical* about the ideas that occur to him. He may jump at a conclusion without weighing the grounds on which it rests; he may forego or unduly shorten the act of hunting, inquiring; he may take the first "answer," or solution, that comes to him because of mental sloth, torpor, impatience to get something settled. One can think reflectively only when one is willing to endure suspense and to undergo the trouble of searching. To many persons both suspense of judgment and intellectual search are disagreeable; they want to get them ended as soon as possible. They cultivate an over-positive and dogmatic habit of mind, or feel perhaps that a condition of doubt will be regarded as evidence of mental inferiority. It is at the point where examination and test enter into investigation that the difference between reflective thought and bad thinking comes in. To be genuinely thoughtful, we must be willing to sustain and protract that state of doubt which is the stimulus to thorough inquiry, so as not to accept an idea or make positive assertion of a belief until justifying reasons have been found.

2. Why Reflective Thinking Must Be an Educational Aim

I. The Values of Thinking

IT MAKES POSSIBLE ACTION WITH A CONSCIOUS AIM

We all acknowledge, in words at least, that ability to think is highly important; it is regarded as the distinguishing power that marks man off from the lower animals. But since our ordinary notions of how and why thinking is important are vague, it is worth while to state explicitly the values possessed by reflective thought. In the first place, it emancipates us from merely impulsive and merely routine activity. Put in positive terms, thinking enables us to direct our activities with foresight and to plan according to ends-in-view, or purposes of which we are aware. It enables us to act in deliberate and intentional fashion to attain future objects or to come into command of what is now distant and lacking. By putting the consequences of different ways and lines of action before the mind, it enables us to *know what we are about* when we act. *It converts action that is merely appetitive, blind, and impulsive into intelligent action.* A brute animal, as far as we know, is pushed on from behind; it is moved in accordance with its present physiological state by some present external stimulus. The being who can think is moved by remote considerations, by results that can be attained perhaps only after a lapse of years—as when a young person sets out to gain a professional education to fit himself for a career in years to come.

For example, an animal without thought will go into its hole when rain threatens, because of some immediate stimulus to its organism. But a thinking being will perceive that certain given facts are probable signs of a future rain and will take steps in the light of this anticipated future. To plant seeds, to cultivate the soil, to harvest grain, are intentional acts, possible only to a being who has learned to subordinate the immediately felt elements of an experience to those values which these elements hint at and prophesy. Philosophers have made much of the phrases "book of nature," "language of nature." Well, it is in virtue of thought that given things are significant of absent things and that nature speaks a language which may be interpreted. To a being who thinks, things are records of their past, as fossils tell of the prior history of the earth, and are prophetic of their future, as from the present positions of heavenly bodies remote eclipses are foretold. Shakespeare's "tongues in trees, books in the running brooks," expresses literally enough the power superadded to existences when they are used by a thinking being. Only when things about us have meaning for us, only when they signify consequences that can be reached by using them in certain ways, is any such thing as intentional, deliberate control of them possible.

IT MAKES POSSIBLE SYSTEMATIC PREPARATIONS AND INVENTIONS

By thought man also develops and arranges artificial signs to remind him in advance of consequences and of ways of securing and avoiding them. As the trait just mentioned makes the difference between savage man and brute, so this trait makes the difference between civilized man and savage. A savage who has been shipwrecked on a river may note certain things that serve him as signs of danger in the future. But civilized man deliberately *makes* such signs; he sets up in advance of any particular shipwreck warning buoys, and builds lighthouses where he sees signs that such an event may occur. A savage reads weather signs with great expertness; civilized man institutes a weather service by which signs are artificially secured and information is distributed in advance of the appearance of any signs that could be detected without special methods. A savage finds his way skillfully through a wilderness by reading certain obscure indications; civilized man builds a highway that shows the road to all. The savage learns to detect the signs of fire and thereby to invent methods of producing flame; civilized man discovers illuminating gas and oils, and invents lamps, electric lights, stoves, furnaces, central heating plants, etc. The very essence of civilized culture is that we deliberately erect monuments and memorials, lest we forget; and deliberately institute, in advance of the happening of various contingencies and emergencies of life, devices for detecting their approach and registering their nature, for warding off what is unfavorable, or at least for protecting ourselves from its full impact and for making more secure and extensive what is favorable. All forms of artificial apparatus are intentional modifications of natural things so designed that they may serve better than in their natural estate to indicate the hidden, the absent, and the remote.

IT ENRICHES THINGS WITH MEANINGS

Finally, thought confers upon physical events and objects a very different status and value from those which they possess to a being that does not reflect. These words are mere scratches, curious variations of light and shade, to one to whom they are not linguistic signs. To him for whom they are signs of other things, the collection of marks stands for some idea or object. We are so used to the fact that things have meaning for us, that they are not mere excitations of sense organs, that we fail to recognize that they are charged with the significance they have only because in the past absent things have been suggested to us by what is present and these suggestions have been confirmed in subsequent experience. If we stumble against something in the dark, we may react to it and get out of the way to save ourselves a bruise or a tumble without recognizing what particular *object* it is. We react almost automatically to many stimuli; they have no meaning for us or are not definite individual objects. For an *object* is more than a mere *thing*; it is a thing having a definite significance.

The distinction we are making can be most readily understood if the reader will call to mind things and events that are strange to him and compare them with the same things and events as they appear to persons having expert knowledge of them; or if he will compare a thing or event as it is *before*, with what it is *after*, he has obtained intellectual mastery over it. To a layman a particular body of water may signify only something to wash with or to drink; to another person it may stand for a union of two chemical elements, themselves not liquids but gases; or it may signify something that should *not* be drunk because of danger of typhoid fever. To a baby things are at first only patterns of color and light, sources of sound; they acquire meaning only as they become signs of possible, but not yet present and actual, experiences. To the learned scientific man, the range of meanings possessed by ordinary things is much widened. A stone is not merely a stone; it is a stone of a given mineralogical type, from a particular geological stratum, etc. It tells him something about what happened millions of years ago, and helps paint the picture of the earth's history.

CONTROL AND ENRICHED VALUE

The first two values mentioned are of a practical sort; they give increased power of *control*. The value just mentioned is an enrichment of meaning apart from added control—a certain event in the heavens cannot be warded off just because we know it is an eclipse and how it is produced, but it does have a significance for us that it did not have before. We may not need to do any thinking now when some event occurs, but if we have thought about it before, the outcome of that thinking is funded as a directly added and deepened meaning of the event. The great reward of exercising the power of thinking is that there are no limits to the possibility of carrying over into the objects and events of life, meanings originally acquired by thoughtful examination, and hence no limit to the continual growth of meaning in human life. A child to-day may see meanings in things that were hidden from Ptolemy and Copernicus because of the results of reflective investigations that have occurred in the meantime.

Various values of the power of thought are summed up in the following quotation from John Stuart Mill.

To draw inferences has been said to be the great business of life. Every one has daily, hourly, and momentary need of ascertaining facts which he has not directly observed: not from any general purpose of adding to his stock of knowledge, but because the facts themselves are of importance to his interests or to his occupations. The business of the magistrate, of the military commander, of the navigator, of the physician, of the agriculturist, *is merely to judge of evidence and to act accordingly.* . . . As they do this well or ill, so they discharge well or ill the duties of their several callings. *It is the only occupation in which the mind never ceases to be engaged.*[1]

TWO REASONS FOR TRAINING THOUGHT

These three values, in their cumulative effect, make the difference between a truly human and rational life and the existence lived by those animals that are immersed in sensation and appetite. Beyond a somewhat narrow limit, enforced by the necessities of life, the values that have been described do not, however, automatically realize themselves. For anything approaching their adequate realization, thought needs careful and attentive educational direction. Nor is that the whole story. Thinking may develop in positively wrong ways and lead to false and harmful beliefs. The need of systematic training would be less than it is if the only danger to be feared were lack of any development; the evil of the wrong kind of development is even greater.

An earlier writer than Mill, John Locke (1632–1704), brings out the importance of thought for life and the need of training so that its best and not its worst possibilities will be realized, in the following words:

No man ever sets himself about any thing but upon some view or other, which serves him for a reason for what he does; and whatsoever faculties he employs, the understanding with such light as it has, well or ill informed, constantly leads; and by that light, true or false, all his operative powers are directed. . . . Temples have their sacred images, and we see what influence they have always had over a great part of mankind. But in truth the ideas and images in men's minds are the invisible powers that constantly govern them, and to these they all, universally, pay a ready submission. It is therefore of the highest concernment that great care should be taken of the understanding, to conduct it aright in the search of knowledge and in judgments it makes.[2]

1. Mill, *System of Logic*, Introduction, sec. 5.
2. Locke, *The Conduct of the Understanding*, first paragraph.

While the power of thought, then, frees us from servile subjection to instinct, appetite, and routine, it also brings with it the occasion and possibility of error and mistake. In elevating us above the brute, it opens the possibility of failures to which the animal, limited to instinct, cannot sink.

II. Tendencies Needing Constant Regulation

PHYSICAL AND SOCIAL SANCTIONS OF CORRECT THINKING

Up to a certain point, the necessities of life enforce a fundamental and persistent discipline of thought for which the most cunningly devised artifices would be ineffective substitutes. The burnt child dreads the fire; a painful consequence emphasizes the need of correct inference much more than would learned discourses on the properties of heat. Social conditions also put a premium on correct inference in matters where action based on valid thought is socially important. These sanctions of proper thinking may affect life itself, or at least a life reasonably free from perpetual discomfort. The signs of enemies, of shelter, of food, of the main social conditions, have to be correctly apprehended.

But this disciplinary training, efficacious as it is within certain limits, does not carry us far. Logical attainment in one direction is no bar to extravagant conclusions in another. A savage who is expert in judging the movements and location of the animals that he hunts will accept and gravely narrate the most preposterous yarns concerning the origin of their habits and peculiarities of structure. When there is no direct appreciable reaction of the inference upon the security and prosperity of life, there are no natural checks to the acceptance of wrong beliefs. Conclusions may be accepted merely because the suggestions are vivid and interesting, while a large accumulation of dependable data may fail to suggest a proper conclusion because of opposition from existing customs. Then there is a "primitive credulity," a natural tendency to believe anything that is suggested unless there is overpowering evidence to the contrary. It sometimes seems, upon surveying the history of thought, that men exhausted pretty much all wrong forms of belief before they hit upon the right conceptions. The history of scientific beliefs also shows that when a wrong theory once gets general acceptance, men will expend ingenuity of thought in buttressing it with additional errors rather than surrender it and start in a new direction: witness for example the elaborate pains taken to preserve the Ptolemaic theory of the solar system. Even to-day correct beliefs about the constitution of nature are held by the great multitude merely because they are current and popular rather than because the multitude understands the reasons upon which they rest.

SUPERSTITION IS AS NATURAL AS SCIENCE

As to the mere function of suggestion, there is no difference between the power of a column of mercury to portend rain and that of the entrails of an animal or the flight of birds to foretell the fortunes of war. For all anybody can tell in advance, the spilling of salt is as likely to import bad luck as the bite of a mosquito to import malaria. Only systematic regulation of the conditions under which observations are made and severe discipline of the habits of entertaining suggestions can secure a decision that one type of belief is vicious and the other sound. The substitution of scientific for superstitious habits of inference has not been brought about by any improvement in the acuteness of the senses or in the natural workings of the function of suggestion. It is the result of regulation *of the conditions* under which observation and inference take place. When such regulation is absent, dreams, the position of stars, the lines of the hand, are regarded as valuable signs, and the fall of cards as an inevitable omen, while natural events of the most crucial significance go disregarded. Hence beliefs in portents of various kinds, now mere nook-and-cranny superstitions, were once universal. A long discipline in exact science was required for their conquest.

THE GENERAL CAUSES OF BAD THINKING: BACON'S "IDOLS"

It is instructive to note some of the attempts that have been made to classify the main sources of error in reaching beliefs. Francis Bacon, for example, at the beginning of modern scientific inquiry, enumerated four such classes, under the somewhat fantastic title of "idols" (Gr. εἴδωλα, images), spectral forms that allure the mind into false paths. These he called the idols, or phantoms, of (*a*) the tribe, (*b*) the market place, (*c*) the cave or den, and (*d*) the theatre; or, less metaphorically, (*a*) standing erroneous methods (or at least temptations to error) that have their roots in human nature generally, (*b*) those that come from intercourse and language, (*c*) those that are due to causes peculiar to a specific individual, and finally, (*d*) those that have their sources in the fashion or general current of a period. Classifying these causes of fallacious belief somewhat differently, we may say that two are intrinsic and two are extrinsic. Of the intrinsic, one is common to all men alike (such as the universal tendency to notice instances that corroborate a favorite belief more readily than those that contradict it), while the other resides in the specific temperament and habits of the given individual. Of the extrinsic, one proceeds from generic social conditions—like the tendency to suppose that there is a fact wherever there is a word, and no fact where there is no linguistic term—while the other proceeds from local and temporary social currents.

LOCKE ON TYPICAL FORMS OF WRONG BELIEF

Locke's method of dealing with typical forms of wrong belief is less formal and may be more enlightening. We can hardly do better than quote his forcible and quaint language, when, enumerating different classes of men, he shows different ways in which thought goes wrong:

(*a*) The first is of those who seldom reason at all, but do and think according to the example of others, whether parents, neighbours, ministers, or who else they are pleased to make choice of to have an implicit faith in, for the saving of themselves the pains and troubles of thinking and examining for themselves.
(*b*) This kind is of those who put passion in the place of reason, and being resolved that shall govern their actions and arguments, neither use their own, nor hearken to

other people's reason, any farther than it suits their
humour, interest, or party.[3]

(c) The third sort is of those who readily and sincerely
follow reason, but for want of having that which one may
call large, sound, round-about sense, have not a full view
of all that relates to the question. . . . They converse but
with one sort of men, they read but one sort of books,
they will not come in the hearing but of one sort of notions. . . . They have a pretty traffick with known corre-
spondents in some little creek . . . but will not venture out
into the great ocean of knowledge. [Men of originally equal
natural parts may finally arrive at very different stores of
knowledge and truth] when all the odds between them has
been the different scope that has been given to their understandings to range in, for the gathering up of information
and furnishing their heads with ideas and notions and observations, whereon to employ their mind.[4]

In another portion of his writings,[5] Locke states the same ideas
in slightly different form.

1. That which is inconsistent with our *principles* is so
far from passing for probable with us that it will not be
allowed possible. The reverence borne to these principles is
so great, and their authority so paramount to all other,
that the testimony, not only of other men, but the evidence
of our own senses are often rejected, when they offer to
vouch any thing contrary to these *established rules.* . . .
There is nothing more ordinary than children's receiving
into their minds propositions . . . from their parents,
nurses, or those about them; which being insinuated in
their unwary as well as unbiassed understandings, and fas-

---

3. In another place Locke says: "Men's prejudices and inclinations impose often
upon themselves. . . . Inclination suggests and slides into discourse favourable
terms, which introduce favourable ideas; till at last by this means that is concluded clear and evident, thus dressed up, which, taken in its native state, by
making use of none but precise determined ideas, would find no admittance
at all."
4. *The Conduct of the Understanding*, sec. 3.
5. *Essay concerning Human Understanding*, Bk. IV, Ch. XX, "Of Wrong Assent,
or Error."

tened by degrees, are at last (and this whether true or false) riveted there by long custom and education, beyond all possibility of being pulled out again. For men, when they are grown up, reflecting upon their opinions and finding those of this sort to be as ancient in their minds as their very memories, not having observed their early insinuation, nor by what means they got them, they are apt to reverence them as sacred things, and not to suffer them to be profaned, touched, or questioned. [They take them as standards] to be the great and unerring deciders of truth and falsehood, and the judges to which they are to appeal in all manner of controversies.

2. Secondly, next to these are men whose understandings are cast into a mould, and fashioned just to the size of a received hypothesis. [Such men, while not denying the existence of facts and evidence, cannot be convinced even by the evidence that would decide them if their minds were not so closed by adherence to fixed belief.]

3. Predominant Passions. Thirdly, probabilities which cross men's appetites and prevailing passions run the same fate. Let ever so much probability hang on one side of a covetous man's reasoning, and money on the other, it is easy to foresee which will outweigh. Earthly minds, like mud walls, resist the strongest batteries.

4. Authority. The fourth and last wrong measure of probability I shall take notice of, and which keeps in ignorance or error more people than all the others together, is the giving up our assent to the common received opinions, either of our friends or party, neighbourhood or country.

IMPORTANCE OF ATTITUDES

We have quoted from influential thinkers of the past. But the facts to which they refer are familiar in our everyday experience. Any observant person can note any day, both in himself and in others, the tendency to believe that which is in harmony with desire. We take that to be true which we should like to have so, and ideas that go contrary to our hopes and wishes have difficulty in getting lodgment. We all jump to conclusions; we all fail to examine and test our ideas because of our personal attitudes.

When we generalize, we tend to make sweeping assertions; that is, from one or only a few facts we make a generalization covering a wide field. Observation also reveals the powerful influence wielded by social influences that have actually nothing to do with the truth or falsity of what is asserted and denied. Some of the dispositions that give these irrelevant influences power to limit and mislead thought are good in themselves, a fact that renders the need of training the more important. Reverence for parents and regard for those placed in authority are in the abstract surely valuable traits. Yet, as Locke points out, they are among the chief forces that determine beliefs apart from and even contrary to the operations of intelligent thought. The desire to be in harmony with others is in itself a desirable trait. But it may lead a person too readily to fall in with the prejudices of others and may weaken his independence of judgment. It even leads to an extreme partisanship that regards it as disloyal to question the beliefs of a group to which one belongs.

Because of the importance of attitudes, ability to train thought is not achieved merely by knowledge of the best forms of thought. Possession of this information is no guarantee for ability to think well. Moreover, there are no set exercises in correct thinking whose repeated performance will cause one to be a good thinker. The information and the exercises are both of value. But no individual realizes their value except as he is personally animated by certain dominant attitudes in his own character. It was once almost universally believed that the mind had faculties, like memory and attention, that could be developed by repeated exercise, as gymnastic exercises are supposed to develop the muscles. This belief is now generally discredited in the large sense in which it was once held. Similarly it is highly questionable whether the practice of thinking in accordance with some logical formula results in creation of a general habit of thinking; namely, one applicable over a wide range of subjects. It is a matter of common notice that men who are expert thinkers in their own special fields adopt views on other matters without doing the inquiring that they know to be necessary for substantiating simpler facts that fall within their own specialities.

THE UNION OF ATTITUDE AND
SKILLED METHOD

What can be done, however, is to cultivate those *attitudes* that are favorable to the use of the best methods of inquiry and testing. Knowledge of the methods alone will not suffice; there must be the desire, the will, to employ them. This desire is an affair of personal disposition. But on the other hand the disposition alone will not suffice. There must also be understanding of the forms and techniques that are the channels through which these attitudes operate to the best advantage. Since these forms and techniques will be taken up for discussion later, we shall here mention the attitudes that need to be cultivated in order to secure their adoption and use.

a. Open-mindedness. This attitude may be defined as freedom from prejudice, partisanship, and such other habits as close the mind and make it unwilling to consider new problems and entertain new ideas. But it is something more active and positive than these words suggest. It is very different from empty-mindedness. While it *is* hospitality to new themes, facts, ideas, questions, it is not the kind of hospitality that would be indicated by hanging out a sign: "Come right in; there is nobody at home." It includes an active desire to listen to more sides than one; to give heed to facts from whatever source they come; to give full attention to alternative possibilities; to recognize the possibility of error even in the beliefs that are dearest to us. Mental sluggishness is one great factor in closing the mind to new ideas. The path of least resistance and least trouble is a mental rut already made. It requires troublesome work to undertake the alteration of old beliefs. Self-conceit often regards it as a sign of weakness to admit that a belief to which we have once committed ourselves is wrong. We get so identified with an idea that it is literally a "pet" notion and we rise to its defense and stop our mental eyes and ears to anything different. Unconscious fears also drive us into purely defensive attitudes that operate like a coat of armor not only to shut out new conceptions but even to prevent us from making a new observation. The cumulative effect of these forces is to shut in the mind, and to create a withdrawal from new intellectual contacts that are needed for learning. They can best be fought by cultivating that alert curiosity and spontaneous outreaching for the new which is the essence of the open mind. The mind that is open merely in the sense that it passively permits things to trickle in and through will not be able to resist the factors that make for mental closure.

b. *Whole-heartedness.* When anyone is thoroughly interested in some object and cause, he throws himself into it; he does so, as we say, "heartily," or with a whole heart. The importance of this attitude or disposition is generally recognized in practical and moral affairs. But it is equally important in intellectual development. There is no greater enemy of effective thinking than divided interest. This division unfortunately is often produced in school. A pupil gives an external, perfunctory attention to the teacher and to his book and lesson while his inmost thoughts are concerned with matters more attractive to him. He pays attention with ear or eye, but his brain is occupied with affairs that make an immediate appeal. He feels obliged to study because he has to recite, to pass an examination, to make a grade, or because he wishes to please his teacher or his parents. But the material does not hold him by its own power. His approach is not straightforward and single-minded. This point may in some cases seem trivial. But in others it may be very serious. It then contributes to the formation of a general habit or attitude that is most unfavorable to good thinking.

When a person is absorbed, the subject carries him on. Questions occur to him spontaneously; a flood of suggestions pour in on him; further inquiries and readings are indicated and followed; instead of having to use his energy to hold his mind to the subject (thereby lessening that which is available for the subject, itself, and creating a divided state of mind), the material holds and buoys his mind up and gives an onward impetus to thinking. A genuine enthusiasm is an attitude that operates as an intellectual force. A teacher who arouses such an enthusiasm in his pupils has done something that no amount of formalized method, no matter how correct, can accomplish.

c. *Responsibility.* Like sincerity or whole-heartedness, responsibility is usually conceived as a moral trait rather than as an intellectual resource. But it is an attitude that is necessary to win the adequate support of desire for new points of view and new ideas and of enthusiasm for and capacity for absorption in subject matter. These gifts may run wild, or at least they may lead the mind to spread out too far. They do not of themselves ensure that centralization, that unity, which is essential to good thinking. To be intellectually responsible is to consider the consequences of a projected step; it means to be willing to adopt these consequences when they follow reasonably from any position already taken. Intellectual responsibility secures integrity; that is to say, consistency and harmony in belief. It is not uncommon to see persons continue to accept beliefs whose logical consequences they refuse to acknowledge. They profess certain beliefs but are unwilling to commit themselves to the consequences that flow from them. The result is mental confusion. The "split" inevitably reacts upon the mind to blur its insight and weaken its firmness of grasp; no one can use two inconsistent mental standards without losing some of his mental grip. When pupils study subjects that are too remote from their experience, that arouse no active curiosity, and that are beyond their power of understanding, they begin to use a measure of value and of reality for school subjects different from the measure they employ for affairs of life that make a vital appeal. They tend to become intellectually irresponsible; they do not ask for the *meaning* of what they learn, in the sense of what difference it makes to the rest of their beliefs and to their actions.

The same thing happens when such a multitude of subjects or disconnected facts is forced upon the mind that the student does not have time and opportunity to weigh their meaning. He fancies he is accepting them, is believing them, when in fact his belief is of a totally different kind and implies a different measure of reality from that which operates in his life and action out of school. He then becomes mentally mixed; mixed not only about particular things but also about the basic reasons that make things worthy of belief. Fewer subjects and fewer facts and more responsibility for thinking the material of those subjects and facts through to realize what they involve would give better results. To carry something through to completion is the real meaning of thoroughness, and power to carry a thing through to its end or conclusion is dependent upon the existence of the attitude of intellectual responsibility.

THE BEARING OF THESE PERSONAL
ATTITUDES UPON READINESS TO THINK

The three attitudes that have been mentioned, open-mindedness, whole-hearted or absorbed interest, responsibility in facing consequences, are of themselves personal qualities, traits of character. They are not the only attitudes that are important in order that the *habit* of thinking in a reflective way may be developed. But the other attitudes that might be set forth are also traits of character, attitudes that, in the proper sense of the word, are *moral*, since they are traits of personal character that have to be cultivated. Any person thinks at times on particular subjects that arouse him. Other persons have habits of thinking quite persistently in special fields of interest; on matters, for example, that are their professional concern. A thoroughgoing habit of thinking is, however, more extended in its scope. No one can think about everything, to be sure; no one can think about *anything* without experience and information about it. Nevertheless, there is such a thing as *readiness* to consider in a thoughtful way the subjects that do come within the range of experience—a readiness that contrasts strongly with the disposition to pass judgment on the basis of mere custom, tradition, prejudice, etc., and thus shun the task of thinking. The personal attitudes that have been named are essential constituents of this general readiness.

If we were compelled to make a choice between these personal attitudes and knowledge about the principles of logical reasoning together with some degree of technical skill in manipulating special logical processes, we should decide for the former. Fortunately no such choice has to be made, because there is no opposition between personal attitudes and logical processes. We only need to bear in mind that, with respect to the aims of education, no separation can be made between impersonal, abstract principles of logic and moral qualities of character. What is needed is to weave them into unity.

3.   Native Resources in Training Thought

We have just discussed the values to be obtained by edu-
cating the mind in habits of thought and some of the obstacles
that lie in the way of its development. But nothing can grow except from germs, from potentialities that tend to some development of themselves. There must be a native stock, or capital, of
resources; we cannot force the power to think upon any creature
that does not first think spontaneously, "naturally," as we say. But
while we cannot learn or be taught to think, we do have to learn
how to think well, especially *how* to acquire the general *habit* of
reflecting. Since this habit grows out of original native tendencies, the teacher needs to know something about the nature of
the primary capital stock that constitutes the germs out of which
alone the habit is to be developed. Unless we know what there is
to be laid hold of and used, we work in the dark and waste time
and energy. We shall probably do something even worse, striving
to impose some unnatural habit from without instead of directing native tendencies toward their own best fruition.

Teaching may be compared to selling commodities. No one can
sell unless someone buys. We should ridicule a merchant who
said that he had sold a great many goods although no one had
bought any. But perhaps there are teachers who think that they
have done a good day's teaching irrespective of what pupils have
learned. There is the same exact equation between teaching and
learning that there is between selling and buying. The only way
to increase the learning of pupils is to augment the quantity and
quality of real teaching. Since learning is something that the
pupil has to do himself and for himself, the initiative lies with the
learner. The teacher is a guide and director; he steers the boat,
but the energy that propels it must come from those who are
learning. The more a teacher is aware of the past experiences of
students, of their hopes, desires, chief interests, the better will he

understand the forces at work that need to be directed and utilized for the formation of reflective habits. The number and
quality of these factors vary from person to person. They cannot
therefore be categorically enumerated in a book. But there are
some tendencies and forces that operate in every normal individual, forces that must be appealed to and utilized if the best methods for the development of good habits of thought are to be
employed.

I. Curiosity

Every living creature, while it is awake, is in constant interaction with its surroundings. It is engaged in a process of give
and take, of doing something to objects around it and receiving
back something from them—impressions, stimuli. This process
of interacting constitutes the framework of experience. We are fitted out with devices that help us ward off destructive influences,
devices that intercept harmful influences and protect us from
them. But we also have tendencies that are forward-reaching and
out-reaching, that go out to make new contacts, that seek new
objects, that strive to vary old objects, that revel, as it were, in
experiences for their own sake and so are ceaselessly active in
enlarging the range of experience. These various tendencies are
summed up in curiosity. Wordsworth's saying applies particularly
to childhood:

> The eye—it cannot choose but see;
>   We cannot bid the ear be still;
> Our bodies feel, where'er they be,
>   Against or with our will.

All our sense and motor organs are, when we are awake, acting and being acted upon by something in the environment.
With adults many of these contacts have been made; grown-ups
permit themselves to become stale; they fall into ruts of experience and are contented with what happens in these ruts. To children the whole world is new; there is something thrilling to the
healthy being in every new contact and it is eagerly sought for,
not merely passively awaited and endured. There is no single faculty called "curiosity"; every normal organ of sense and of motor

activity is on the *qui vive*. It wants a chance to be active, and it needs some object in order to act. The sum total of these outgoing tendencies constitutes curiosity. It is the basic factor in enlargement of experience and therefore a prime ingredient in the germs that are to be developed into reflective thinking.

THREE STAGES, OR LEVELS, OF CURIOSITY

1. In the first manifestations, curiosity is far removed from thinking. It is a vital overflow, an expression of an abundant organic energy. A physiological uneasiness leads a child to get "into everything,"—to be reaching, poking, pounding, prying. Observers of animals have noted what one author calls "their inveterate tendency to fool." "Rats run about, smell, dig, or gnaw, without real reference to the business in hand. In the same way Jack [a dog] scrabbles and jumps, the kitten wanders and picks, the otter slips about everywhere like ground lightning, the elephant fumbles ceaselessly, the monkey pulls things about." [1] The most casual observation of the activities of a young child reveals a ceaseless display of exploring and testing activity. Objects are sucked, fingered, and thumped; drawn and pushed; handled and thrown; in short, they are experimented with until they cease to yield new qualities. Such activities are hardly intellectual, and yet without them intellectual activity would be feeble and intermittent through lack of stuff for its operations.

2. A higher stage of curiosity develops under the influence of social stimuli. When the child learns that he can appeal to others to eke out his store of experiences, so that, if objects fail to respond interestingly to his experiments, he may call upon persons to provide interesting material, a new epoch sets in. "What is that?" "Why?" become the unfailing signs of a child's presence. At first this questioning is hardly more than a projection into social relations of the physical overflow that earlier kept the child pushing and pulling, opening and shutting. He asks in succession what holds up the house, what holds up the soil that holds the house, what holds up the earth that holds the soil; but his questions are not evidence of any genuine consciousness of rational connections. His *why* is not a demand for scientific explanation;

---

1. Hobhouse, *Mind in Evolution*, p. 195.

the motive behind it is simply eagerness for a larger acquaintance with the mysterious world in which he is placed. The search is not for a law or principle, but only for another, a bigger fact. Yet there is more than a desire to accumulate just information or heap up disconnected items—although sometimes the interrogating habit threatens to degenerate into a mere disease of language. In the feeling, however dim, that the facts which directly meet the senses are not the whole story, that there is more behind them and more to come from them, lies the germ of *intellectual* curiosity.

3. Curiosity rises above the organic and the social level and becomes intellectual in the degree in which it is transformed into interest in finding out for oneself the answers to questions that are aroused by contact with persons and things. In what was just called the "social" stage, children are often more interested in the mere process of asking a question than they are in giving heed to the answer. At all events no particular question is attended to for very long; one asking succeeds another so fast that none is developed into a train of thought. Immediate asking and answering discharges curiosity. The crucial problem for the educator, whether parent or school teacher, is to utilize for *intellectual* purposes the organic curiosity of physical exploration and linguistic interrogation. This can be accomplished by attaching them to ends that are more remote, that require finding and inserting intermediate acts, objects, and ideas. To the degree that a distant end controls a sequence of inquiries and observations and binds them together as means to an end, just to that degree does curiosity assume a definitely intellectual character.

HOW CURIOSITY IS LOST

Unless transition to an intellectual plane is effected, curiosity degenerates or evaporates. Bacon's saying that we must become as little children in order to enter the kingdom of science is at once a reminder of the open-minded and flexible wonder of childhood and of the ease with which this endowment is lost. Some lose it in indifference or carelessness; others in a frivolous flippancy; many escape these evils only to become incased in a hard dogmatism that is equally fatal to the spirit of wonder. Some are so taken up with routine as to be inaccessible to new facts and problems. Others retain curiosity only with reference to what concerns their personal advantage in their chosen career. With many, curiosity is arrested on the plane of interest in local gossip and in the fortunes of their neighbors; indeed, so usual is this result that very often the first association with the word *curiosity* is a prying inquisitiveness into other people's business. With respect, then, to curiosity, the teacher has usually more to learn than to teach. Rarely can he aspire to the office of kindling or even of increasing it; his province is rather to provide the materials and the conditions by which organic curiosity will be directed into investigations that have an aim and that produce results in the way of increase of knowledge, and by which social inquisitiveness will be converted into ability to find out things known to others, an ability to ask questions of books as well as of persons. The teacher has to protect the growing person from those conditions which occasion a mere succession of excitements which have no cumulative effect, and which, therefore, make an individual either a lover of sensations and sensationalism or leave him blasé and uninterested. He has to avoid all dogmatism in instruction, for such a course gradually but surely creates the impression that everything important is already settled and nothing remains to be found out. He has to know how to give information when curiosity has created an appetite that seeks to be fed, and how to abstain from giving information when, because of lack of a questioning attitude, it would be a burden and would dull the sharp edge of the inquiring spirit.

II. Suggestion

IDEAS OCCUR SPONTANEOUSLY

Many a child, as noted earlier, has tried to see whether he could not stop "thinking," whether he could not arrest the flow of ideas passing through his head. But "thoughts," of this rudimentary and uncontrolled sort, spring into being quite as surely as "our bodies feel, where'er they be, against or with our will." We cannot make ourselves have ideas or not have them any more than we can directly make ourselves have sensations from things. In the one case as in the other, we can put ourselves or be put by others into situations where we are likely to have sensations and ideas in worth-while ways, in ways that lead on to something else and so insure that the person be developed and recreated by them and not be exhausted by the mere having of them.

WHAT A SUGGESTION IS

Ideas, in this primitive and spontaneous sense, are *suggestions*. Nothing in experience is absolutely simple, single, and isolated. Everything experienced comes to us along with some other object, quality, or event. Some object is focal and most distinct, but it shades off into other things. A child may be absorbed in watching a bird; for the bright centre of his consciousness there is nothing but the bird there. But of course it is somewhere—on the ground, in a tree. And the actual experience includes much more. The bird also is doing something—flying, pecking, feeding, singing, etc. And the experience of the bird is itself complex, not a single sensation; there are numbers of related qualities included within it. This highly elementary illustration indicates why it is that the next time a child sees a bird, he will "think" of something else that is not then present. That is to say, that portion of his present experience which is like that of prior experience will call up or *suggest* some thing or quality connected with it which was present in the total previous experience; that thing or quality in turn may suggest something connected with itself; it not only *may* do so, but it *will* do so unless some new object of perception starts another train of suggestions going. In this primary sense, then, the having of ideas is not so much something we do, as it is something that happens to us. Just as, when we open our eyes, we see what is there; so, when suggestions occur to us, they come to us as functions of our past experience and not of our present will and intention. So far as thoughts in this particular meaning are concerned, it is true to say "it thinks" (as we say "it rains"), rather than "I think." Only when a person tries to get control of the *conditions* that determine the occurrence of a suggestion, and only when he accepts responsibility for using the suggestion to see what follows from it, is it significant to introduce the "I" as the agent and source of thought.

THE DIMENSIONS OF SUGGESTION

Suggestion has a variety of aspects (or "dimensions," as we may term them), varying in different persons, both in themselves and in their mode of combination. These dimensions are (*a*) ease, or promptness; (*b*) range, or variety; and (*c*) depth, or profundity.

a. Ease, or Promptness. The common classification of persons into the dull and the bright is made primarily on the basis of the readiness or facility with which suggestions follow upon the presentation of objects and upon the happening of events. As the metaphor of "dull" and "bright" implies, some minds are impervious, or else they absorb passively. Everything presented is lost in a drab monotony that gives nothing back. But others reflect, or give back in varied lights, all that strikes upon them. The dull make no response; the bright flash back the fact with an added quality. An inert or stupid mind requires a heavy jolt or an intense shock to move it to suggestion; the bright mind is quick, is alert, to react with interpretation and suggestion of consequences to follow.

Yet the teacher is not entitled to assume stupidity or even dullness merely because of unresponsiveness to school subjects or to a lesson as presented by textbook or teacher. The pupil labeled "hopeless" may react in quick and lively fashion when the thing-in-hand seems to him worth while, as some out-of-school sport or social affair. Indeed, even the school subject might move him, were it set in a different context and treated by a different method. A boy dull in geometry may prove quick enough when he takes up the subject in connection with manual training; the girl who seems inaccessible to historical facts may respond promptly when it is a question of judging the character and deeds of people of her acquaintance or of fiction. Barring physical defect or impaired health, slowness and dullness in *all* directions are comparatively rare. Moreover, slowness of response is not necessarily dullness; a thoughtful person waits to think things over.

b. Range, or Variety. Irrespective of the difference in persons as to the ease and promptness with which they respond to facts, there is a difference in the number or range of the suggestions that occur. We speak truly, in some cases, of the "flood" of suggestions; in others, there is but a slender "trickle." Occasionally, slowness of outward response is due to a great variety of suggestions that check one another and lead to hesitation and suspense, while a lively and prompt suggestion may take such possession of the mind as to preclude the development of others. Too few suggestions indicate a dry and meagre mental habit; when this is joined to great learning, the result is a pedant or a Gradgrind. Such a person's mind rings hard; he is likely to bore others with mere bulk of information. He contrasts with the person whom we call "ripe," "juicy," and "mellow."

A conclusion reached after consideration of a few alternatives may be formally correct, but it will not possess the fullness and richness of meaning of one arrived at after comparison of a greater variety of alternative suggestions. On the other hand, suggestions may be too numerous and too varied to secure the best discipline and development of mental habit. So many suggestions arise that the person is at a loss to select among them. He finds it difficult to reach any definite conclusion and wanders more or less helplessly among them. So much suggests itself *pro* and *con*, one thing leads on to another so naturally, that he finds it difficult to decide in practical affairs or to conclude in matters of theory. There is such a thing as too much thinking, as when action is paralyzed by the multiplicity of views suggested by a situation. Or again, the very number of suggestions may be hostile to tracing logical sequences among them, for it may tempt the mind away from the necessary but trying task of search for real connections, into the more congenial occupation of embroidering upon the given facts a tissue of agreeable fancies. The best mental habit involves a balance between paucity and superfluity of suggestions.

c. Depth, or Profundity. We distinguish between people not only upon the basis of the quickness and variety of their intellectual response, but also with respect to the plane upon which these occur—the intrinsic quality of their response.

One man's thought is profound, while another's is superficial; one goes to the roots of the matter, and another touches lightly its most external aspects. This phase of thinking is perhaps the most untaught of all, and the least amenable to external influence whether for improvement or harm. Nevertheless, the conditions of the pupil's contact with subject matter may be such that he is compelled to come to quarters with its more significant features or such that he is encouraged to deal with it upon the basis of what is trivial. The common assumptions that, if the pupil only thinks, one thought is just as good for his mental discipline as another, and that the end of study is the amassing of information—both of them tend to foster superficial, at the expense of significant, thought. Pupils who in matters of practical experience have a ready and acute perception of the difference between the significant and the meaningless often reach in school subjects a point where all things seem equally important or equally unimportant; where one thing is just as likely to be true as another; and where intellectual effort is expended, not in discriminating between things, but in trying to make verbal connections between words.

Depth and Slowness. Sometimes slowness and depth of response are intimately connected. Time is required in order to digest impressions, and translate them into substantial ideas. "Brightness" may be but a flash in the pan. The "slow but sure" person, whether man or child, is one in whom impressions sink and accumulate, so that thinking is done at a deeper level of value than by those with a lighter load. Many a child is rebuked for slowness, for not answering promptly, when his forces are taking time to gather themselves together to deal effectively with the problem at hand. In such cases, failure to afford time and leisure encourages, if it does not actually create, habits of speedy, but snapshot and superficial, judgment. The depth to which a sense of the problem, of the difficulty, sinks, determines the quality of the thinking that follows; and any habit of teaching that encourages the pupil for the sake of a successful recitation or of a display of memorized information to glide over the thin ice of genuine problems reverses the true method of mind-training.

It is profitable to study the lives of men and women who achieve in adult life fine things in their respective callings, but who were called dull in their school days. Sometimes the early wrong judgment was due mainly to the fact that the direction in which the child showed his ability was not one recognized by the good old standards in use, as in the case of Darwin's interest in beetles, snakes, and frogs. Sometimes it was due to the fact that the child dwelt habitually on a deeper plane of reflection than other pupils—or than his teachers—and so did not show to advantage when prompt answers of the usual sort were expected. Sometimes it was due to the fact that the pupil's natural mode of approach clashed habitually with that of the text or teacher, and the methods of the latter were assumed to be the absolute basis of estimate.

THINKING IS SPECIFIC AND ANY SUBJECT MAY BE INTELLECTUAL

In any event, it is desirable that the teacher should rid himself of the notion that "thinking" is a single, unalterable faculty; that he should recognize that it is a term denoting the various ways in which things acquire significance for the individual; and that individuals differ. It is desirable to expel also the kindred notion that some subjects are inherently "intellectual," and hence possessed of an almost magical power to train the faculty of thought. Thinking is specific, not a machinelike, ready-made apparatus to be turned indifferently and at will upon all subjects, as a lantern throws its light as may happen upon horses, streets, gardens, trees, or river. Thinking is specific, in that different things suggest their own appropriate meanings, tell their own unique stories, and do this in very different ways with different persons. As the growth of the body is through the assimilation of food, so the growth of the mind is through the logical organization of subject matter. Thinking is not like a sausage machine that reduces all materials indifferently to one stereotyped, marketable commodity, but is the power of following up and linking together the specific suggestions that specific things arouse. Accordingly, any subject, from Greek to cooking, and from drawing to mathematics, is intellectual, if intellectual at all, not in its fixed inner structure, but in its function—in its power to start and direct significant inquiry and reflection. What geometry does for one, the manipulation of laboratory apparatus, the mastery of a musical composition, or the conduct of a business affair, does for another.

III. Orderliness

REFLECTIVE THINKING IMPLIES
CONSECUTIVENESS, CONTINUITY, OR
ORDERING OF SUGGESTIONS

The mere occurrence of ideas or suggestions constitutes thinking, but not reflective thinking, not observation and thought directed to an acceptable conclusion—that is, to a conclusion which it is reasonable to believe because of the grounds on which it rests and the evidence which supports it. Ideas merely as such, apart from their orderly sequence, just "pop into our heads." "I just *happened* to think of something" is often a perfectly accurate statement. Another dimension is needed, accordingly, to transform suggestions into reflective thinking—the property of order, of consecutiveness. There is no thinking without what is called "association of ideas," or a train of suggestions. But such a train, of itself, does not constitute reflection. Only when the succession is so controlled that it is an orderly sequence leading up to a conclusion that contains the intellectual force of the preceding ideas, do we have reflective thought. And by "intellectual force" is signified force in making some idea worthy of belief; in making it *trust*worthy.

When the factors of facility, of fertility, and of depth are properly balanced or proportioned, we get as the outcome continuity of thought. We desire neither the slow mind nor yet the hasty. We wish neither random diffuseness nor fixed rigidity. Consecutiveness means flexibility and variety of materials, conjoined with singleness and definiteness of direction. It is opposed both to a mechanical routine uniformity and to a grasshopper-like movement. Of one kind of bright children, teachers often say that "they might do anything, if only they settled down," so quick and apt are they in a variety of responses. But, alas, they do not always settle.

On the other hand, it is not enough *not* to be diverted. A deadly and fanatic consistency is not our goal. Concentration does not mean fixity, or a cramped arrest or paralysis of the flow of suggestion. It means variety and change of ideas combined into a *single steady trend moving toward a unified conclusion.* Thoughts are concentrated, not by being kept still and quiescent, but by being kept moving toward an object, as a general marshals his troops for attack or defense. Holding the mind to a subject is like holding a ship to its course; it implies constant change of position combined with unity of direction. Consistent and orderly thinking is precisely the achieving of such a change *within* a given subject matter. Consistency is no more the mere absence of contradiction than concentration is the mere absence of diversion—which exists in dull routine or in a person "fast asleep." All kinds of varied and incompatible suggestions may sprout and be followed in their growth, and yet thinking be consistent and orderly, provided each one of the suggestions is viewed in relation to the main topic and the main end to be attained.

ORDERING OF THOUGHT OFTEN THE INDIRECT CONCOMITANT OF ORDERING OF ACTION

In the main, for most persons, the primary resource in the development of orderly habits of thought is indirect, not direct. Intellectual organization originates and for a time grows as an accompaniment of the organization of the means required to realize an end, not as the result of a direct appeal to thinking power. The need of thinking to accomplish something beyond thinking is more potent than thinking for its own sake. All people at the outset, and the majority of people probably all their lives, attain to some ordering of thought through ordering of action. Adults normally carry on some occupation, profession, pursuit; and this furnishes the stabilizing axis about which their knowledge, their beliefs, and their habits of reaching and testing conclusions are organized. Observations that have to do with the efficient performance of their calling are extended and rendered precise. Information related to it is not merely amassed and then left in a heap; it is classified and subdivided so as to be available as needed. Inferences are made by most men not from purely speculative motives, but because they are necessary for the efficient performance of the duties involved in their several callings. Thus their inferences are constantly tested by results achieved; futile and scattering methods tend to be discounted; orderly arrangements have a premium put upon them. The event, the issue, stands as a constant check on the thinking that has led up to it;

and this discipline by efficiency in action is the chief sanction, in practically all who are not scientific specialists, of orderliness of thought—provided always that action remains intelligent and does not become routine.

Such a resource—the main prop of disciplined thinking in adult life—is not to be despised in training the young in right intellectual habits. From an early age, children have to select acts and objects as means for reaching ends. With selection go arrangement and adaptation. These operations demand *judgment*. Suitable conditions work unconsciously to build up an attitude favorable to reflective operations. There are, however, profound differences between the immature and the adult with respect to the organized character of their activities—differences that must be taken seriously into account in any educational use of activities: (1) the external achievement resulting from activity is a more urgent necessity with the adult, and hence is with him a more effective means of disciplining the mind than with the child; (2) the ends of adult activity are more specialized than those of child activity.

1. The selection and arrangement of appropriate lines of action is a much more difficult problem with youth than it is in the case of adults. With the latter, the main lines are more or less settled by circumstances. The social status of the adult—the fact that he is a citizen, a householder, a parent, one occupied in some regular industrial or professional calling—prescribes the chief features of the acts to be performed, and secures, almost automatically as it were, appropriate and related modes of thinking. But with the child there is no such fixity of status and pursuit. There is almost nothing to dictate that such and such a consecutive line of action, rather than another, shall be followed; while the will of others, his own caprice, and circumstances about him tend to produce an isolated momentary act. The absence of continued motivation cooperates with the inner plasticity of the immature to increase the importance of educational training and at the same time magnifies the difficulties in the way of finding consecutive modes of activities that may do for child

and youth what serious vocations and functions do for the adult. In the case of children the choice is so peculiarly exposed to arbitrary factors, to mere school traditions, to waves of pedagogical fad and fancy, to fluctuating social cross currents, that sometimes, in sheer disgust at the inadequacy of results, a reaction occurs in favor of abandoning altogether the use of overt activity as an educational factor, and recourse is had to purely theoretical subjects and methods.

2. This very difficulty, however, points to the fact that the *opportunity for selecting truly educative activities* is indefinitely greater in child life than in adult. The factor of external pressure is so strong with most adults that the educative value of the pursuit—its reflex influence upon intelligence and character—however genuine, is incidental, and frequently almost accidental. The problem and the opportunity with the young is selection of orderly and continuous modes of occupation, which, while they lead up to and prepare for the indispensable activities of adult life, have their own *sufficient justification in their present reflex influence upon the formation of habits of thought.*

EXTREME VIEWS ABOUT OVERT ACTIVITIES IN EDUCATION

Educational practice shows a continual tendency to oscillate between two extremes with respect to overt and exertive activities.

One extreme is to neglect them almost entirely, on the ground that they are chaotic and fluctuating, mere diversions appealing to the transitory unformed taste and caprice of immature minds; or if they avoid this evil, are objectionable copies of the highly specialized, and more or less commercial, activities of adult life. If activities are admitted at all into the school, the admission is a grudging concession to the necessity of having occasional relief from the strain of constant intellectual work or to the clamor of outside utilitarian demands upon the school.

The other extreme is an enthusiastic belief in the almost magical educative efficacy of any kind of activity, granted it is an activity and not a passive absorption of academic and theoretic material. The conceptions of play, of self-expression, of natural growth, are appealed to almost as if they meant that almost any kind of spontaneous activity inevitably secures the desired or desirable training of mental power; or a mythological brain physiology is appealed to as proof that any exercise of the muscles trains power of thought.

THE REAL PROBLEM: DISCOVERING
THE VALUABLE OCCUPATIONS

While we vibrate from one of these extremes to the other, the most serious of all problems is ignored: the problem, namely, of discovering and arranging the occupations (*a*) that are most congenial, best adapted, to the immature stage of development; (*b*) that have the most ulterior promise as preparation for the social responsibilities of adult life; and (*c*) that, *at the same time*, have the maximum of influence in forming habits of acute observation and of consecutive inference. As curiosity is related to the acquisition of material of thought, as suggestion is related to flexibility and force of thought, so the ordering of activities, not themselves primarily intellectual, is related to the forming of intellectual powers of consecutiveness.

IV. Some Educational Conclusions

The wisest of the Greeks said that wonder was the author of science and philosophy. Wonder is not identical with curiosity; it is, however, the same as curiosity when the latter reaches the intellectual plane. External monotony and internal routine are the worst enemies of wonder. Surprise, the unexpected, novelty, stimulate it. Everyone knows that a moving object catches and holds the eye more readily than one at rest, and the more mobile parts of the body have the greater capacity for making tactile discriminations than those that are more fixed. Yet under the name of discipline and good order, school conditions are often made to approximate as nearly as possible to monotony and uniformity. Desks and chairs are in set positions; pupils are regimented with military precision. The same textbook is thumbed for a long period to the exclusion of other reading. All topics are barred from the recitation except those taken up in the text; "system" in the conduct of the recitation is so emphasized that spontaneity is excluded and likewise novelty and variety. These instances may seem exaggerated with respect to the administration of the better schools. But in schools where the chief aim is to establish mechanical habit and instill uniformity of conduct, the conditions that stimulate wonder and keep it energetic and vital are necessarily ruled out.

Unfortunately, reaction against this mechanical administration of education is often *merely* a reaction. Novelty is treated as if it were an end in itself, when in fact it is simply a stimulating occasion for the exercise of observation and inquiry. Variety is carried to the point where it is incompatible with that continuity that is essential for good thinking. Because order has been associated with external uniformity, the kind of order that promotes effective intellectual action is also slighted. Again, most enterprises in school are of too short a span to allow for that unfolding and leading of one thing into another without which good habits of reflection cannot be developed. In the desire for accuracy in remembering details, large and comprehensive views are shut out. The acquisition of information is identified with the amassing of isolated items, and not with assimilating mental food that is to be organized into thought if it is to have any value. It is an old saying that unity in variety marks every work of genuine art. Certainly the art of teaching bears out the saying. If one recalls his contacts with teachers who left a permanent intellectual impress, one will find that, although they may have violated in their teaching many of the set rules of pedagogy, they were persons who could maintain continuity of thought and effort even when admitting what seemed to be diversions and forays into side fields; that they were persons who introduced novelty and variety to keep attention alert and taut, but who also utilized these factors to contribute to the building up of the main problem and the enrichment of the main theme.

4.   School Conditions and the Training of Thought

I. Introductory: Methods and Conditions

FORMAL DISCIPLINE *VERSUS* REAL THINKING

The so-called "faculty psychology" went hand in hand with the vogue of the formal-discipline idea in education. If thought is a distinct piece of mental machinery, separate from observation, memory, imagination, and common-sense judgments of persons and things, then thought should be trained by special exercises designed for the purpose, as one might devise special exercises for developing the biceps muscles. Certain subjects are then to be regarded as intellectual or logical subjects *par excellence*, possessed of a predestined fitness to exercise the thought faculty, just as certain machines are better than others for developing arm power. With these three notions goes the fourth, that method consists of a set of operations by which the machinery of thought is set going and kept at work upon any subject matter.

We have tried to make it clear in the previous chapters that there is no single and uniform power of thought, but a multitude of different ways in which specific things—things observed, remembered, heard of, read about—evoke suggestions or ideas that are pertinent to a problem or question and that carry the mind forward to a justifiable conclusion. Training is that development of curiosity, suggestion, and habits of exploring and testing, which increases sensitiveness to questions and love of inquiry into the puzzling and unknown; which enhances the fitness of suggestions that spring up in the mind, and controls their succession in a developing and cumulative order; which makes more acute the sense of the force, the *proving* power, of every fact observed and suggestion employed. Thinking is not a separate mental process; it is an affair of the *way* in which the vast multitude of objects that are observed and suggested are employed, the way they run together and are *made* to run together, the way they are handled. Consequently any subject, topic, question, is intellectual not *per se* but because of the part it is made to play in directing thought in the life of any particular person.

THE TRAINING OF THOUGHT IS INDIRECT

For these reasons, the problem of *method* in forming habits of reflective thought is the problem of establishing *conditions* that will arouse and guide *curiosity*; of setting up the connections in things experienced that will on later occasions promote the flow of *suggestions*, create problems and purposes that will favor *consecutiveness* in the succession of ideas. These topics will be considered more at length later, but an illustration or two drawn from failure to secure proper conditions will indicate more clearly what is meant. Children are hushed up when they ask questions; their exploring and investigating activities are inconvenient and hence they are treated like nuisances; pupils are taught to memorize things so that merely one-track verbal associations are set up instead of varied and flexible connections with things themselves; no plans and projects are provided that compel the student to look ahead and foresee and in the execution of which the accomplishment of one thing sets up new questions and suggests new undertakings. The teacher may devise special exercises intended to train thinking directly, but when these wrong conditions exist, special exercises are doomed to be futile. The training of thought can be attained only by regulating the causes that evoke and guide it.

With respect to the training of habits of thought, the teacher's problem is thus twofold. On the one side, he needs (as we saw in the last chapter) to be a student of individual traits and habits; on the other side, he needs to be a student of the conditions that modify for better or worse the directions in which individual powers habitually express themselves. He needs to recognize that method covers not only what he intentionally devises and employs for the purpose of mental training, but also what he does without any conscious reference to it—anything in the atmosphere and conduct of the school that reacts in any way upon the curiosity, the responsiveness, and the orderly activity of children.

The teacher who is an intelligent student both of individual mental operations and of the effects of school conditions upon those operations can largely be trusted to select for himself methods of instruction in their narrower and more technical sense—those best adapted to achieve results in particular subjects, such as reading, geography, or algebra. In the hands of one who is not intelligently aware of individual capacities and of the influence unconsciously exerted upon them by the entire environment, even the best of technical methods are likely to get an immediate result at the expense of forming deep-seated and persistent *bad* habits.

GENERIC AND SPECIFIC CONDITIONS

There is always a temptation for the teacher to keep attention fixed upon a limited field of the pupil's activity. Is the student progressing in the particular topic in arithmetic, history, geography, etc., that is under consideration? When the teacher fixes his attention exclusively on such matters as these, the process of forming underlying and permanent habits, attitudes, and interests is overlooked. Yet the formation of the latter is the more important for the future. The other side of this fact is that the teacher, while fixing attention upon the *specific* conditions that seem to affect learning of the immediate lesson before the class, ignores the more general conditions that influence the creation of permanent attitudes, especially the traits of character, open-mindedness, whole-heartedness, and responsibility, mentioned in an earlier chapter. Postponing consideration of special points, we shall, accordingly, in the present chapter take up some of the more generic conditions of the schoolroom that affect the development of effective mental habits.

II. The Influence of the Habits of Others

Bare reference to the imitativeness of human nature is enough to suggest how profoundly the mental habits of others affect the attitude of the one being trained. Example is more potent than precept, and a teacher's best conscious efforts may be more than counteracted by the influence of personal traits that he is unaware of or that he regards as unimportant. Methods of instruction and discipline that are technically faulty may be rendered practically innocuous by the inspiration of the personal method that lies back of them.

THE TEACHER A STIMULUS TO RESPONSE IN INTELLECTUAL MATTERS

To confine, however, the conditioning influence of the educator, whether parent or teacher, to imitation is to get a very superficial view of the intellectual influence of others. Imitation is but one case of a deeper principle—that of stimulus and response. *Everything the teacher does, as well as the manner in which he does it, incites the child to respond in some way or other, and each response tends to set the child's attitude in some way or other.* Even the inattention of the child to the adult is often a response that is the result of unconscious training.[1] The teacher is rarely (and even then never entirely) a transparent medium of the access of another mind to a subject. With the young, the influence of the teacher's personality is intimately fused with that of the subject; the child does not separate or even distinguish the two. And as the child's response is *toward* or *away from* anything presented, he keeps up a running commentary, of which he himself is hardly distinctly aware, of like and dislike, of sympathy and aversion, not merely upon the acts of the teacher, but also upon the subject with which the teacher is occupied.

The extent and power of this influence upon morals and manners, upon character, upon habits of speech and social bearing, are almost universally recognized. But the tendency to conceive of thought as an isolated faculty often blinds teachers to the fact that this influence is just as real and pervasive in intellectual concerns. Teachers, as well as children, stick more or less to the main points, have more or less wooden and rigid methods of response, and display more or less intellectual curiosity about matters that come up. And every trait of this kind is an inevitable part of the teacher's method of teaching. Merely to accept without notice slipshod habits of speech, slovenly inferences, unimaginative and

---

1. A child of four or five who had been repeatedly called to the house by his mother with no apparent response on his own part, was asked if he did not hear her. He replied quite judicially, "Oh, yes, but she doesn't call very mad yet."

literal response, is to indorse these tendencies and to ratify them
into habits—and so it goes throughout the whole range of contact between teacher and student. In this complex and intricate
field, two or three points may well be singled out for special
notice.

a. Judging Others by Ourselves. Most persons are quite unaware of the distinguishing peculiarities of their own mental habits. They take their own mental operations for granted and unconsciously make them the standard for judging the mental
processes of others.[2] Hence there is a tendency to encourage
whatever in the pupil agrees with this attitude and to neglect or
fail to understand whatever is incongruous with it. The prevalent
overestimation of the value, for mind training, of *theoretic* subjects as compared with practical pursuits, is doubtless due partly
to the fact that the teacher's calling tends to select those persons
in whom the theoretic interest is specially strong and to repel
those in whom executive abilities are marked. Teachers sifted out
on this basis judge pupils and subjects by a like standard, encouraging an intellectual one-sidedness in those to whom it is
naturally congenial, and repelling from study those in whom
practical instincts are more urgent.

b. Undue Reliance upon Personal Influence. Teachers—and
this holds especially of the stronger and better teachers—tend to
rely upon their personal strong points to hold a child to his work,
and thereby to substitute their personal influence for that of subject matter as a motive for study. The teacher finds by experience
that his own personality is often effective where the power of the
subject to command attention is almost nil; then he utilizes the
former more and more, until the pupil's relation to the teacher
almost takes the place of his relation to the subject. In this way
the teacher's personality may become for the pupil a source of
personal dependence and weakness, an influence that renders the
pupil indifferent to the value of the subject for its own sake.

c. Satisfying the Teacher instead of the Problem. The operation of the teacher's own mental habit tends, unless carefully
watched and guided, to make the child a student of the teacher's

2. People who have *number-forms*—i.e., who project number series into space
and see them arranged in certain shapes—when asked why they have not mentioned the fact before, often reply that it never occurred to them; they supposed that everybody had the same habit.

peculiarities rather than of the subjects that he is supposed to study. His chief concern is to accommodate himself to what the teacher expects of him, rather than to devote himself energetically to the problems of subject matter. "Is this right?" comes to mean "Will this answer or this process satisfy the teacher?"— instead of meaning "Does it satisfy the inherent conditions of the problem?" It would be folly to deny the legitimacy or the value of the study of human nature that children carry on in school, but it is obviously undesirable that their chief intellectual problem should be to produce the answer approved by the teacher, and that their standard of success should be successful adaptation to the requirements of another person.

III. The Influence of the Nature of Studies

Studies are conventionally and conveniently grouped under these heads: (1) those especially involving the acquisition of skill in performance—the school arts, such as reading, writing, figuring, and music; (2) those mainly concerned with acquiring knowledge—"informational" studies, such as geography and history; and (3) those in which skill in doing and bulk of information are relatively less important, and appeal to abstract thinking, to "reasoning," is most marked—"disciplinary" studies, such as arithmetic and formal grammar.[3] Each of these groups of subjects has its own special pitfalls.

DISCIPLINARY STUDIES LIABLE TO LOSE CONTACT WITH THE PRACTICAL

In the case of the so-called disciplinary or preeminently logical studies, there is danger of the isolation of intellectual activity from the ordinary affairs of life. Teacher and student alike tend to set up a chasm between logical thought, as something abstract and remote, and the specific and concrete demands of everyday events. The abstract tends to become so aloof, so far away from application, as to be cut loose from practical and

3. Of course, any one subject has all three aspects; e.g., in arithmetic, counting, reading and writing numbers, rapid adding, etc., are cases of skill in doing; the tables of weights and measures are a matter of information, etc.

moral bearing. The gullibility of specialized scholars when out of their own lines, their extravagant habits of inference and speech, their ineptness in reaching conclusions in practical matters, their egotistical engrossment in their own subjects, are extreme examples of the bad effects of severing studies completely from their ordinary connections in life.

SKILL STUDIES LIABLE TO BECOME PURELY MECHANICAL

The danger in those studies where the main emphasis is upon acquisition of skill is just the reverse. The tendency is to take the shortest cuts possible to gain the required end. This makes the subjects *mechanical*, and thus restrictive of intellectual power. In the mastery of reading, writing, drawing, laboratory technique, etc., the need for economy of time and material, of neatness and accuracy, for promptness and uniformity, is so great that these things tend to become ends in themselves, irrespective of their influence upon general mental attitude. Sheer imitation, dictation of steps to be taken, mechanical drill, may give results most quickly and yet strengthen traits likely to be fatal to reflective power. The pupil is enjoined to do this and that specific thing, with no knowledge of any reason except that by so doing he gets his result most speedily; his mistakes are pointed out and corrected for him; he is kept at pure repetition of certain acts till they become automatic. Later, teachers wonder why the pupil reads with so little expression, and figures with so little intelligent consideration of the terms of his problem. In some educational dogmas and practices, the very idea of training the mind seems to be hopelessly confused with that of a drill which hardly touches *mind* at all—or touches it for the worse—since it is wholly taken up with training skill in external execution. This method reduces the "training" of human beings to the level of animal training. Practical skill, modes of effective technique, can be intelligently, non-mechanically *used* only when intelligence has played a part in their *acquisition*.

INFORMATIONAL STUDIES MAY FAIL
TO DEVELOP WISDOM

A false opposition is often set up also, especially in higher education, between information and understanding. One party insists that the acquisition of scholarship must come first, since intelligence can operate only on the basis of actual subject matter that is under control. The other party holds that scholarship for and by itself is at best an end only for the specialist, the graduate student, etc., and that the development of power to think is the chief thing. The real desideratum is getting command of scholarship—or skill—under conditions that *at the same time* exercise thought. The distinction between information and wisdom is old, and yet requires constantly to be redrawn. Information is knowledge that is merely acquired and stored up; wisdom is knowledge operating in the direction of powers to the better living of life. Information, merely as information, implies no special training of intellectual capacity; wisdom is the finest fruit of that training. In school, amassing information always tends to escape from the ideal of wisdom or good judgment. The aim often seems to be—especially in such a subject as geography—to make the pupil what has been called a "cyclopedia of useless information." "Covering the ground" is the primary necessity; the nurture of mind a bad second. Thinking cannot, of course, go on in a vacuum; suggestions and inferences can occur only to a mind that possesses information as to matters of fact.

But there is all the difference in the world whether the acquisition of information is treated as an end in itself, or is made an integral portion of the training of thought. The assumption that information that has been accumulated apart from use in the recognition and solution of a problem may later on be, at will, freely employed by thought is quite false. The skill at the ready command of intelligence is the skill acquired with the aid of intelligence; the only information which, otherwise than by accident, can be put to logical use is that acquired in the course of thinking. Because their knowledge has been achieved in connection with the needs of specific situations, men of little book-learning are often able to put to effective use every ounce of knowledge they possess; while men of vast erudition are often swamped by the mere bulk of their learning, because memory, rather than thinking, has been operative in obtaining it.

IV. The Influence of Current Aims and Ideals

It is, of course, impossible to separate this somewhat intangible condition from the points just dealt with; for automatic skill and quantity of information are educational ideals that pervade the whole school. We may distinguish, however, certain tendencies, such as that of judging education from the standpoint of external results, instead of from that of the development of personal attitudes and habits. The ideal of the *product*, as against that of the mental *process* by which the product is attained, shows itself both in instruction and in moral discipline.

THE EXALTATION OF EXTERNAL STANDARDS

a. In Instruction. In instruction, the external standard manifests itself in the importance attached to the "correct answer." No one other thing, probably, works so fatally against focussing the attention of teachers upon the training of mind as the domination of *their* minds by the idea that the chief thing is to get pupils to recite their lessons correctly. As long as this end is uppermost (whether consciously or unconsciously), training of mind remains an incidental and secondary consideration. There is no great difficulty in understanding why this ideal has such vogue. The large number of pupils to be dealt with and the tendency of parents and school authorities to demand speedy and tangible evidence of progress conspire to give it authority. Knowledge of subject matter—not of children—is alone exacted of teachers by this aim; and moreover, knowledge of subject matter only in portions definitely prescribed and laid out, and hence mastered with comparative ease. Education that takes as its standard the improvement of the intellectual attitude and method of students demands more serious preparatory training, for it exacts sympathetic and intelligent insight into the workings of individual minds and a very wide and flexible command of subject matter—so as to be able to select and apply just what is needed when it is needed. Finally, the securing of external results is an

aim that lends itself naturally to the mechanics of school administration—to examinations, marks, gradings, promotions, and
so on.

b. In Behavior. With reference to behavior also, the external
ideal has a great influence. Conformity of acts to precepts and
rules is the easiest, because most mechanical, standard to employ.
It is no part of our present task to tell just how far dogmatic instruction, or strict adherence to custom, convention, and the
commands of a social superior, should extend in moral training;
but since problems of conduct are the deepest and most common
of all the problems of life, the ways in which they are met have an
influence that radiates into every other mental attitude, even
those far remote from any direct or conscious moral consideration. Indeed, the *deepest plane of the mental attitude of everyone
is fixed by the way in which problems of behavior are treated.* If
the function of thought, of serious inquiry and reflection, is reduced to a minimum in dealing with them, it is not reasonable to
expect habits of thought to exercise great influence in less important matters. On the other hand, habits of active inquiry and
careful deliberation in the significant and vital problems of conduct afford the best guarantee that the general structure of mind
will be reasonable.

IS THERE TRANSFER OF TRAINING IN THINKING?

The point just made leads to the question that is sometimes raised as to whether the rejection of the idea of special faculties that can be trained by formal exercises does not demand
the rejection also of the possibility of training thought. The question has been partly answered in the conception of the nature of
thinking that has been set forth (that it is not a "faculty," but an
organization of materials and activities) and its relation to objective conditions. But there is another aspect of the question that is
suggested by the term "transfer." The question is asked whether
the ability to think gained in dealing with one situation or subject will prove itself equally efficient in dealing with another subject and situation; that it does not do so necessarily is indicated
by the fact that a scientific specialist may be a child in practical
affairs of business; that he may violate in matters of politics or

religious belief every principle that he scrupulously observes in his special field of inquiry. It is now generally recognized that common elements are the basis of so-called "transfer." That is, the carrying over of skill and understanding from one experience to another is dependent upon the existence of like elements in both experiences. The simplest sort of example is found in the extended application given by children to ideas and words. A young child whose acquaintance with quadrupeds is limited to a dog will tend to call any four-footed animal of a similar size "doggie." Similar qualities are always the bridge over which the mind passes in going from a former experience to a new one. Now thinking, as we shall see later in detail, is a process of *grasping in a conscious way* the common elements. It thus adds greatly to the availability of common elements for purposes of transfer. Unless these elements are seized and held by the mind (as they are in a rudimentary way by the symbol "dog"), any transfer occurs only blindly, by sheer accident. The first answer to the objection that the building up of a general habit of thinking is impossible is, therefore, that thinking is precisely the factor that makes transfer possible and that brings it under control.

The more technical a subject, the fewer common elements it provides for thinking to work with. In fact, we might almost set up this test for the technical nature of any subject, theme, or undertaking: in what degree is it isolated from the material of everyday experiences because of absence of elements common to both? To the person just beginning algebra and physics, the ideas of "exponent" and "atom" are technical; they stand alone. He is not aware of these meanings in connection with the objects and acts of his ordinary experience; they do not seem to be contained in even the materials of his school experience. To the mature scientist, on the contrary, the ideas are much less technical because they enter into so many experiences that have become familiar to him as a scientific inquirer. During the early stages of experience and for the greater part of *all* experience, save that of specialists, the common elements are the *human* elements, those connected with the relations of persons to one another and to groups. The most important things to a child are his connections with father and mother, brother and sister. Elements connected with them recur in most of the experiences he has. They saturate the greater number of his experiences and supply them with their meaning.

These human and social factors are accordingly those that carry over and can be carried over most readily from one experience to another. They furnish the material best suited for developing generalized abilities of thinking. One reason why much of elementary schooling is so useless for the development of reflective attitudes is that, on entering school life, a break is suddenly made in the life of the child, a break with those of his experiences that are saturated with social values and qualities. Schooling is then technical because of its isolation, and the child's thinking cannot operate because school has nothing in common with his earlier experiences.

Part Two

Logical Considerations

5. The Process and Product of Reflective Activity: Psychological Process and Logical Form

I. Thinking as a Formal and as an Actual Occurrence

THE LOGIC OF THE TEXTBOOKS

When you look into a treatise on Logic, you find in it a classification of terms, such as particular, general, denotative, connotative, etc.; of propositions, such as positive, negative, universal, particular; and of arguments in the form of syllogisms. A familiar example of the latter is: All men are mortal; Socrates is a man; therefore, Socrates is mortal. It is characteristic of a formal statement that particular specific objects may be eliminated and a blank substituted which may be filled in with any material. The form of the syllogism just cited is: All M (human beings in this case) is P; all S is M; therefore, all S is P. In this formulation S stands for the subject of the conclusion, P for its predicate, and M for the *middle* term. The middle term appears in both premises and is the connecting link by which S and P, otherwise logically disconnected, are locked into unity. It is the ground and justification of the assertion at the close that S is P. In invalid reasonings the middle term fails to bind together tightly and exclusively the subject and predicate of the conclusion. It is possible to state a number of rules setting forth the forms in which syllogisms, positive and negative, are valid, and ruling out incorrect forms.

HOW ACTUAL THINKING DIFFERS FROM FORMAL LOGIC

Inspection shows important differences between formal reasoning and thinking as it actually goes on in the mind of any

person. (1) The subject matter of formal logic is strictly impersonal, as much so as the formulae of algebra. The forms are thus
independent of the attitude taken by the thinker, of his desire and
intention. Thought carried on by anyone depends, on the other
hand, as we have already seen, upon his habits. It is likely to be
good when he has attitudes of carefulness, thoroughness, etc.,
and bad in the degree in which he is headlong, unobservant, lazy,
moved by strong passion, tending to favor himself, etc. (2) The
forms of logic are constant, unchanging, indifferent to the subject matter with which they are filled. They exclude change as
much as does the fact that 2 plus 2 equals 4. Actual thinking is a
process; it occurs, goes on; in short, it is in continual change as
long as a person thinks. It has at every step to take account of
subject matter; for parts of the material dealt with offer obstacles,
pose problems and perplexities, while other portions indicate solutions and make the road out of intellectual difficulties. (3) Because forms are uniform and hospitable to any subject matter
whatever, they pay no attention to context. Actual thinking, on
the other hand, always has reference to some context. It occurs,
as we have seen, because of some unsettled situation that itself
lies outside of thinking. We may compare the formal syllogism
about Socrates with the state of mind of his disciples when they
were considering at the time of his trial the prospects of Socrates'
continuing to live.

THOUGHT AS LOGICAL FORM, OR PRODUCT, AND AS PSYCHOLOGICAL PROCESS

It follows from these contrasts that thought is looked at
from two different points of view. These two points of view are
indicated in the title of this chapter. We call them product and
process; logical form and existent, or psychological, process.
They may also be termed the historical, or chronological, and the
timeless. Forms are constant; thinking takes time. It is evident
that education is primarily concerned with thinking as it actually
takes place in individual human beings. It is concerned to create
attitudes favorable to effective thought, and it has to select and
arrange subject matter and the activities dealing with subject
matter so as to promote these attitudes.

It does not follow, however, that formal treatment lacks all
value for education. It has value, provided it is put and kept in its

place. That place is suggested by giving it the name "product." It sets forth forms into which the result of actual thinking is thrown in order to help test its worth. Consider, as an analogy, the relation that a map sustains to the explorations and surveys of which it is the outcome. The latter correspond to processes. The map is the product. *After* it is constructed, it can be used without any reference to the journeys and expeditions of which it is the fruit, although it would not exist if it had not been for them. When you look at a map of the United States, you do not have, in order to use it, to think of Columbus, Champlain, Lewis and Clark, and the thousands of others whose trials and labors are embodied in it.

Now the map is all there before you at once. It may with propriety be called the *form* of all the special journeyings from place to place that can be undertaken by any number of persons. Moreover, when a person is traveling, it serves, if he knows how to use it, as a check on his position and a guide to his movements. But it does not tell him where to go; his own desires and plans determine his goal, as his own past determines where he is now and where he must start from.

LOGICAL FORMS NOT USED IN ACTUAL THINKING, BUT TO SET FORTH RESULTS OF THINKING

Logical forms such as one finds in a logical treatise do not pretend to tell *how* we think or even how we *should* think. No one ever arrived at the idea that Socrates, or any other creature, was mortal by following the form of the syllogism. If, however, one who has arrived at that notion by gathering and interpreting evidence wishes to expound to another person the *grounds* of his belief, he might use the syllogistic form and would do so if he wished to state the proof in its most compact form. A lawyer, for example, who knows in advance what he wants to prove, who has a conclusion already formed in his mind, and who wishes to impress others with it, is quite likely to put his reasonings into syllogistic form.

In short, these forms apply not to *reaching* conclusions, not to *arriving* at beliefs and knowledge, but to the most effective way in which to set forth what has already been concluded, so as to convince others (or oneself if one wishes to recall to mind its

grounds) of the soundness of the result. In the thinking by which
a conclusion is actually reached, observations are made that turn
out to be aside from the point; false clues are followed; fruitless
suggestions are entertained; superfluous moves are made. Just
because you do not know the solution of your problem, you have
to grope toward it and grope in the dark or at least in an obscure
light; you start on lines of inquiry that in the end you give up.
When you are only seeking the truth and of necessity seeking
somewhat blindly, you are in a radically different position from
the one you are in when you are already in possession of truth.

The logical forms that characterize conclusions reached and
adopted cannot therefore prescribe the way in which we should
attempt to arrive at a conclusion when we are still in a condition
of doubt and inquiry. Yet partial conclusions emerge during the
course of reflection. There are temporary stopping places, land-
ings of past thought that are also stations of departure for subsequent thought. We do not reach *the* conclusion at a single jump.
At every such landing stage it is useful to retrace the processes
gone through and to state to oneself how much and how little of
the material previously thought about really bears on the conclusion reached and *how* it bears. Thus premises and conclusions
are formulated at the same time in definite relation to one another, and *forms* belong to such formulations.

ACTUAL THINKING HAS ITS OWN LOGIC; IT IS ORDERLY, REASONABLE, REFLECTIVE

The distinction between process and product of reflective inquiry is thus not fixed and absolute. In calling the process
"psychological" and the product "logical," we do not mean that
only the final outcome is logical or that the activity that goes in a
series of steps in time and that involves personal desire and purpose is not logical. Rather, we must distinguish between the logical *form*, which applies to the product, and the logical *method*,
which may and should belong to the process.

We speak of the "logic" of history; that is, of the orderly movement of events to a concluding climax. We say that one person
acts or talks "logically," another person "illogically." We do not
mean that the first person acts, thinks, or talks in syllogisms, but
that there is *order*, consecutiveness, in what he says and does;
that the means he uses are well calculated to reach the end he has

in mind. "Logically" in such cases is a synonym for "reasonably."
The illogical person wanders aimlessly; he shifts his topic without being aware of it; he skips about at random; he not only
jumps to a conclusion (all of us have to do that at some point),
but he fails to retrace his steps to see whether the conclusion to
which he has jumped is supported by evidence; he makes contradictory, inconsistent statements without being sensitive to what
he is doing.

A person, on the other hand, thinks logically when he is careful in the conduct of his thinking, when he takes pains to make
sure he has evidence to go upon, and when, after reaching a conclusion, he checks it by the evidence he can offer in its support. In
short, "logical," as applied to the process of thinking, signifies
that the course of thoughts is carried on *reflectively*, in the sense
in which reflection was discriminated from other kinds of thinking. A bungler can make a box, but the joints will not fit exactly;
the edges will not be even. A skilled person will do the work in a
way that does not waste time or material, and the result is firm
and neat. So it is with thinking.

When we say a person is *thoughtful*, we mean something more
than that he merely indulges in thoughts. To be really thoughtful
is to be logical. Thoughtful persons are heedful, not rash; they
look about, are circumspect instead of going ahead blindly. They
weigh, ponder, deliberate—terms that imply a careful comparing
and balancing of evidence and suggestions, a process of evaluat-
ing what occurs to them in order to decide upon its force and
weight for their problem. Moreover, the thoughtful person looks
into matters; he scrutinizes, inspects, examines. He does not, in
other words, take observations at their face value, but probes
them to see whether they are what they seem to be. "Skim milk
masquerades as cream"; a fungus looks like an edible mush-
room, but is poisonous; "fool's gold" seems like gold, but is only
iron pyrites. There are comparatively few cases in which we can
accept without questioning the so-called "evidence of the senses";
the sun does not really travel around the earth; the moon does
not actually change its own form, and so on. The logical person
inspects to make sure of his data. Finally, the thoughtful person
"puts two and two together." He reckons, calculates, casts up an
account. The word "reason" is connected etymologically with
the word "ratio." The underlying idea here is *exactness of relationship*. All reflective thinking is a process of detecting rela-

tions; the terms just used indicate that *good* thinking is not contented with finding "any old kind" of relation but searches until a relation is found that is as accurately defined as conditions permit.

IN SUMMARY

The "psychological," as we use the term, is not, then, opposed to the "logical." As far as an actual process of thought is truly reflective, it is alert, careful, thorough, definite, and accurate, pursuing an orderly course. In short, it is then logical. When we use the term "logical" in distinction from the actual process (when the latter is controlled), we have in mind the *formal* arrangement of the final *product* of a particular process of thinking, the arrangement being such as to sum up the net conclusion and to extract the exact grounds on which that conclusion rests. Loose thought leaves the result hanging in the air, with only a vague sense of just what has been proved or arrived at. A genuinely reflective activity terminates in declaring just what the outcome is. By formulating that outcome as definitely as possible, it is converted into a true *conclusion*. Reflective activity also makes a survey, a review, of the material upon which *alone* this conclusion rests, and thus formulates the *premises* upon which it rests. A geometrical demonstration, for example, always states at its close just what has been proved; and if the reasoning is understood and not merely memorized, the mind grasps the demonstrated proposition as a conclusion; it is aware of the prior points that prove it.

II. Education in Relation to Form

LEARNING IS LEARNING TO THINK

From what has been said, however, it is evident that education, *upon its intellectual side*, is vitally concerned with cultivating the attitude of reflective thinking, preserving it where it already exists, and changing looser methods of thought into stricter ones whenever possible. Of course, education is not exhausted in its intellectual aspect; there are practical attitudes of efficiency to be formed, moral dispositions to be strengthened and developed, esthetic appreciations to be cultivated. But in all these things there is at least an element of conscious meaning and hence of thought. Otherwise, practical activity is mechanical and routine, morals are blind and arbitrary, and esthetic appreciation is sentimental gush. In what follows we shall confine ourselves, however, to the intellectual side. We state emphatically that, *upon its intellectual side education consists in the formation of wide-awake, careful, thorough habits of thinking.*

Of course intellectual learning includes the amassing and retention of information. But information is an undigested burden unless it is understood. It is *knowledge* only as its material is *comprehended.* And understanding, comprehension, means that the various parts of the information acquired are grasped in their relations to one another—a result that is attained only when acquisition is accompanied by constant reflection upon the meaning of what is studied. There is an important distinction between verbal, mechanical memory and what older writers called "judicious memory." The latter seizes the *bearings* of what is retained and recalled; it can, therefore, use the material in new situations where verbal memory would be completely at a loss.

What we have called "psychological thinking" is just the actual process that takes place. This, in particular cases, may be random and disorderly or else a mere play of fantasy. But if it were *always* nothing but that, not only would thinking be of no use, but life could hardly be even maintained. If thought had nothing to do with real conditions and if it did not move logically from these conditions to the thought of ends to be reached, we should never invent, or plan, or know how to get out of any trouble or predicament. As we have already noted, there are both intrinsic elements and pressure of circumstances that introduce into thinking genuinely logical or reflective qualities.

THE CONNECTION BETWEEN PROCESS AND PRODUCT OF THINKING OVERLOOKED BY TWO EDUCATIONAL SCHOOLS

Curiously enough, the internal and necessary connection between the actual process of thinking and its intellectual product is overlooked by two opposite educational schools.

One of these schools thinks that the mind is naturally so illogical in its processes that logical form must be impressed upon it from without. It assumes that logical quality belongs only to organized knowledge and that the operations of the mind become logical only through absorption of logically formulated, ready-made material. In this case, the logical formulations are not the outcome of any process of thinking that is personally undertaken and carried out; the formulation has been made by another mind and is presented in a finished form, apart from the processes by which it was arrived at. Then it is assumed that by some magic its logical character will be transferred into the minds of pupils.

An illustration or two will make clear what is meant by the foregoing statements. Suppose the subject is geography. The first thing is to give its definition, marking it off from every other subject. Then the various abstract terms upon which depends the scientific development of the science are stated and defined one by one—pole, equator, ecliptic, zone—from the simpler units to the more complex that are formed out of them; then the more concrete elements are taken in similar series—continent, island, coast, promontory, cape, isthmus, peninsula, ocean, lake, coast, gulf, bay, and so on. In acquiring this material the pupil's mind is supposed not only to gain important information, but, by accommodating itself to ready-made logical definitions, generalizations, and classifications, gradually also to acquire logical habits.

This type of method has been applied to every subject taught in the schools—reading, writing, music, physics, grammar, arithmetic. Drawing, for example, has been taught on the theory that, since all pictorial representation is a matter of combining straight and curved lines, the simplest procedure is to have the pupil acquire the ability first to draw straight lines in various positions (horizontal, perpendicular, diagonals at various angles), then typical curves; and finally, to combine straight and curved lines in various permutations to construct actual pictures. This seemed to give the ideal "logical" method, beginning with analysis into elements, and then proceeding in regular order to more and more complex syntheses, each element being defined when used, and thereby clearly understood.

Even when this method in its extreme form is not followed, few schools (especially of the middle or upper elementary grades)

are free from an exaggerated attention to forms supposedly necessary for the pupil to use if he is to get his result logically. It is
held that there are certain steps, arranged in a certain order, that
express preeminently an understanding of the subject, and the
pupil is made to "analyze" his procedure into these steps; *i.e.*, to
learn a certain routine formula of statement. While this method
is usually at its height in grammar and arithmetic, it invades also
history and even literature, which are then reduced, under plea of
intellectual training, to outlines, diagrams, and other schemes of
division and subdivision. In memorizing this simulated cut-and-
dried copy of the logic of an adult, the child is generally made to
stultify his own vital logical movement. The adoption by teachers of this misconception of logical method has probably done
more than anything else to bring pedagogy into disrepute, for to
many persons "pedagogy" means precisely a set of mechanical,
self-conscious devices for replacing by some cast-iron external
scheme the personal mental movement of the individual.

It is evident from these examples that in such a scheme of instruction, the logical is identified exclusively with certain formal
properties of subject matter; with subject matter defined, refined,
subdivided, classified, organized according to certain principles
of connection that have been worked out by persons who are expert in that particular field. It conceives the method of instruction to be the devices by which similar traits are imported into
the mind by careful reproduction of the given material in arithmetic, geography, grammar, physics, biology, or whatnot. The
natural operations of the mind are supposed to be indifferent or
even averse to all logical achievement. Hence the mottoes of this
school are "discipline," "restraint," "conscious effort," "the necessity of tasks," and so on. From this point of view studies,
rather than attitudes and habits, embody the logical factor in
education. The mind becomes logical only by learning to con-
form to an external subject matter. To produce this conformity,
the study should first be analyzed (by textbook or teacher) into
its logical elements; then each of these elements should be defined; finally, all the elements should be arranged in series or
classes according to logical formulae or general principles. Then
the pupil learns the definitions one by one and, progressively
adding one to another, builds up the logical system, and thereby
is himself gradually imbued, from without, with logical quality.

A reaction inevitably occurs from the poor results that accrue from these professedly "logical" methods. Lack of interest in study, habits of inattention and procrastination, positive aversion to intellectual application, dependence upon sheer memorizing and mechanical routine with only a modicum of understanding by the pupil of what he is about, show that the theory of logical definition, division, gradation, and system does not work out practically as it is theoretically supposed to do. The consequent disposition—as in every reaction—is to go to the opposite extreme. The "logical" is thought to be wholly artificial and extraneous; teacher and pupil alike are to turn their backs upon it, and to give free rein to the expression of existing aptitudes and tastes. Emphasis upon natural tendencies and powers as the only possible starting point of development is indeed wholesome. But the reaction is false, and hence misleading, in what it ignores and denies: the presence of genuinely intellectual factors in existing powers and interests.

The other type of school really accepts the underlying premise of the opposite educational theory. It also assumes that the mind is naturally averse to logical form; it grounds this conviction upon the fact that many minds *are* rebellious to the particular logical forms in which a certain type of textbook presents its material. From this fact it is inferred that logical order is so foreign to the natural operations of the mind that it is of slight importance in education, at least in that of the young, and that the main thing is just to give free play to impulses and desires without regard to any definitely *intellectual* growth. Hence the mottoes of this school are "freedom," "self-expression," "individuality," "spontaneity," "play," "interest," "natural unfolding," and so on. In its emphasis upon individual attitude and activity, it sets slight store upon organized subject matter. It conceives *method* to consist of various devices for stimulating and evoking, in their natural order of growth, the native potentialities of individuals.

THE BASIC ERROR OF THE TWO SCHOOLS IS THE SAME

Thus the basic error of the two schools is the same. Both ignore and virtually deny the fact that tendencies toward a reflective and truly logical activity are native to the mind, and that they show themselves at an early period, since they are demanded by outer conditions and stimulated by native curiosity. There is an innate disposition to draw inferences, and an inherent desire to experiment and test. The mind at every stage of growth has its own logic. It entertains suggestions, tests them by observation of objects and events, reaches conclusions, tries them in action, finds them confirmed or in need of correction or rejection. A baby, even at a comparatively early period, makes inferences in the way of expectations from what is observed, interpreting what it sees as a sign or evidence of something it does not observe with the senses. The school of so-called "free self-expression" thus fails to note that one thing that is urgent for expression in the spontaneous activity of the young is *intellectual* in character. Since this factor is predominantly the *educative* one, as far as instruction is concerned, other aspects of activity should be made means to its effective operation.

Any teacher who is alive to the modes of thought operative in the natural experience of the normal child will have no difficulty in avoiding the identification of the logical with a ready-made organization of subject matter, as well as the notion that the way to escape this error is to pay no attention to logical considerations. Such a teacher will have no difficulty in seeing that the real problem of intellectual education is the *transformation* of natural powers into expert, tested powers: the transformation of more or less casual curiosity and sporadic suggestion into attitudes of alert, cautious, and thorough inquiry. He will see that the *psychological* and the *logical*, instead of being opposed to each other (or even independent of each other), are connected as the earlier and the terminal, or concluding, stages of the same process. He will recognize, moreover, that the kind of logical arrangement that marks subject matter at the stage of maturity is not the only kind possible; that the kind found in scientifically organized material is actually undesirable until the mind has reached a point of maturity where it is capable of understanding just *why* this form, rather than some other, is adopted.

That which is strictly logical from the standpoint of subject matter really represents the conclusions of an expert, trained mind. The definitions, divisions, and classifications of the conventional text represent these conclusions boiled down. The only

way in which a person can reach ability to make accurate definitions, penetrating classifications, and comprehensive generalizations is by thinking alertly and carefully on his own *present* level.
Some kind of intellectual organization must be required, or else
habits of vagueness, disorder, and incoherent "thinking" will be
formed. But the organization need not be that which would satisfy the mature expert. For the immature mind is still in process
of gaining the intellectual skill that the latter has already achieved.
It is absurd to suppose that the beginner can commence where
the adept stops. But the beginner should be trained to demand
from himself careful examination, consecutiveness, and some
sort of summary and formulation of *his* conclusions, together
with a statement of the reasons for them.

IN SUMMARY

We may summarize by saying that "logical" has at least
three different meanings. In its widest sense, any thinking that is
intended to reach a conclusion that is to be accepted and believed
in is logical, even though the actual operations are *il*-logical. In
the narrowest sense, "logical" signifies that which is demonstrated, according to certain approved forms, to follow from
premises the terms of which have clear and definite meanings; it
signifies *proof of a stringent character.* Between the two lies the
meaning, which is educationally vital: systematic care to safeguard the processes of thinking so that it is truly reflective. In this
connection, "logical" signifies the *regulation* of natural and
spontaneous processes of observation, suggestion, and testing;
that is, thinking as an *art.*

III. Discipline and Freedom

THE CONCEPTION OF DISCIPLINE

It was remarked in the foregoing discussion that two
schools of educational thought have opposing mottoes, or slogans. One of them makes *discipline* primary; the other, *freedom.*
The position we have taken implies, however, that each school
has a wrong notion of the meaning of its own professed prin-

ciple. If the natural, or "psychological," processes are lacking in all inherent logical quality, so that the latter has to be imposed from without, then discipline must be something negative. It will be a painfully disagreeable forcing of mind away from channels congenial to it into channels of constraint, a process grievous at the time but necessary as preparation for a more or less remote future. Discipline is then generally identified with drill; and drill is conceived after the mechanical analogy of driving, by unremitting blows, a foreign substance into a resistant material; or is imaged after the analogy of the mechanical routine by which raw recruits are trained to a soldierly bearing and habits that are naturally wholly foreign to their possessors. Training of this latter sort, whether it be called "discipline" or not, is not *mental* discipline. Its aim and result are not *habits* of thinking, but uniform *external modes of action.* By failing to ask what he means by discipline, many a teacher is misled into supposing that he is engaged in disciplining the mind of pupils, when in reality he is creating an aversion to study and a belief that using the mind is a disagreeable, instead of a delightful, operation.

In truth, discipline is positive and constructive. It is power, power of control of the means necessary to achieve ends and also power to value and test ends. A painter is disciplined in his art in the degree in which he can manage and use effectively all the elements that enter into his art—externally, canvas, colors, and brush; internally, his power of vision and imagination. Practice, exercise, are involved in the acquisition of power, but they do not take the form of meaningless drill, but of practising the *art.* They occur as part of the operation of attaining a desired end, and they are not mere repetition. Discipline is a product, an outcome, an achievement, not something applied from without. All genuine education *terminates* in discipline, but it *proceeds* by engaging the mind in activities worth while for their own sake.

THE CONCEPTION OF FREEDOM

This fact enables us to see the error in the conception of freedom held by the opposite school of educational theory. The discipline that is identical with trained power is also identical with *freedom.* For freedom is power to act and to execute independent of external tutelage. It signifies mastery capable of independent exercise, emancipated from the leading strings of others, not mere unhindered external operation. When spontaneity or naturalness is identified with more or less casual discharge of transitory impulses, the tendency of the educator is to supply a multitude of stimuli in order that spontaneous activity may be kept up. All sorts of interesting materials, equipments, tools, modes of activity, are provided in order that there may be no flagging of free self-expression. This method overlooks some of the essential conditions of the attainment of genuine freedom.

FREEDOM IS ACHIEVED BY CONQUERING OBSTACLES

Direct immediate discharge or expression of an impulsive tendency is fatal to thinking. Only when the impulse is to some extent checked and thrown back upon itself does reflection ensue. It is, indeed, a stupid error to suppose that arbitrary tasks must be imposed from without in order to furnish the factor of perplexity and difficulty that is the necessary cue to thought. Every vital activity of any depth and range inevitably meets obstacles in the course of its effort to realize itself—a fact that renders the search for artificial or external problems quite superfluous. The difficulties that present themselves within the development of an experience are, however, to be cherished by the educator, not minimized, for they are the natural stimuli to reflective inquiry. Freedom does not consist in keeping up an uninterrupted and unimpeded external activity, but is something achieved through conquering, by personal reflection, the difficulties that prevent immediate overflow into action and spontaneous success.

THINKING DEMANDS A NATURAL DEVELOPMENT FROM EARLY CHILDHOOD

A method that emphasizes the psychological and natural, yet fails to see what an important part of natural tendencies is constituted at every period of growth by curiosity, inference, and the desire to test, cannot secure a *natural development*. In natural growth each successive stage of activity prepares unconsciously, but thoroughly, the conditions for the manifestation of the next stage—as in the cycle of a plant's growth. There is no ground for assuming that thinking is a special, isolated natural tendency that will bloom inevitably in due season simply because various sense and motor activities have been freely manifested before; or because observation, memory, imagination, and manual skill have been previously exercised without thought. Only when thinking is constantly employed in using the senses and muscles for the guidance and application of observations and movements is the way prepared for subsequent higher types of thinking.

At present, the notion is current that childhood is almost entirely unreflective—a period of mere sensory, motor, and memory development, while adolescence suddenly brings the manifestation of thought and reason.

Adolescence is not, however, a synonym for magic. Doubtless youth should bring with it an enlargement of the horizon of childhood, a susceptibility to larger concerns and issues, a more generous and a more general standpoint toward nature and social life. This development affords an opportunity for thinking of a more comprehensive and abstract type than has previously obtained. But thinking itself remains just what it has been all the time, a matter of following up and testing the conclusions suggested by the facts and events of life. Thinking begins as soon as the baby who has lost the ball that he is playing with begins to foresee the possibility of something not yet existing—its recovery—and begins to forecast steps toward the realization of this possibility, and, by experimentation, to guide his acts by his ideas and thereby also test the ideas. Only by making the most of the thought factor already active in the experiences of childhood, is there any promise or warrant for the emergence of superior reflective power at adolescence or at any later period.

MENTAL HABITS, WHETHER GOOD OR BAD, ARE CERTAIN TO BE FORMED

In any case *positive habits are being formed*: if not habits of careful looking into things, then habits of hasty, heedless, impatient glancing over the surface; if not habits of consecutively following up the suggestions that occur, then habits of haphazard, grasshopper-like guessing; if not habits of suspending judgment till inferences have been tested by the examination of evidence, then habits of credulity alternating with flippant incredulity, belief or unbelief being based, in either case, upon whim, emotion, or accidental circumstances. The only way to achieve traits of carefulness, thoroughness, and continuity (traits that are, as we have seen, the elements of the "logical") is by exercising these traits from the beginning, and by seeing to it that conditions call for their exercise.

GENUINE FREEDOM IS INTELLECTUAL

Genuine freedom, in short, is intellectual; it rests in the trained *power of thought*, in ability to "turn things over," to look at matters deliberately, to judge whether the amount and kind of evidence requisite for decision is at hand, and if not, to tell where and how to seek such evidence. If a man's actions are not guided by thoughtful conclusions, then they are guided by inconsiderate impulse, unbalanced appetite, caprice, or the circumstances of the moment. To cultivate unhindered, unreflective external activity is to foster enslavement, for it leaves the person at the mercy of appetite, sense, and circumstance.

6. Examples of Inference and Testing

We have in previous chapters given an outline account of the nature of reflective thinking. We have stated some reasons why it is necessary to use educational means to secure its development and have considered the intrinsic resources, the difficulties, and ulterior purpose of its educational training—the formation of disciplined logical ability to think. We come now to some descriptions of simple genuine cases of thinking, selected from the class papers of students.

I. Illustrations of Reflective Activity

We have had repeated occasion to notice that there are both external and internal circumstances that call out and that guide, to some extent, thought of the reflective kind. Practical needs in connection with existing conditions, natural and social, evoke and direct thought. We begin with an instance of that sort. We have noted also that curiosity is a strong drive from within, and accordingly our second example is drawn from that field. Finally, a mind that is already exercised in scientific subjects will have inquiry aroused by intellectual problems, and our third instance is of that type.

A CASE OF PRACTICAL DELIBERATION

The other day, when I was down town on 16th Street, a clock caught my eye. I saw that the hands pointed to 12:20. This suggested that I had an engagement at 124th Street, at one o'clock. I reasoned that as it had taken me an hour to come down on a surface car, I should probably be twenty minutes late if I returned the same way. I might save twenty minutes by a subway express. But was there a station near? If not, I might lose more than twenty minutes in looking for one. Then I thought of the elevated, and I saw there was such a line within two blocks. But where was the station? If it were several blocks above or below the street I was on, I should lose time instead of gaining it. My mind went back to the subway express as quicker than the elevated; furthermore, I remembered that it went nearer than the elevated to the part of 124th Street I wished to reach, so that time would be saved at the end of the journey. I concluded in favor of the subway, and reached my destination by one o'clock.

A CASE OF REFLECTION UPON AN OBSERVATION

Projecting nearly horizontally from the upper deck of the ferryboat on which I daily cross the river is a long white pole, bearing a gilded ball at its tip. It suggested a flagpole when I first saw it; its color, shape, and gilded ball agreed with this idea, and these reasons seemed to justify me in this belief. But soon difficulties presented themselves. The pole was nearly horizontal, an unusual position for a flagpole; in the next place, there was no pulley, ring, or cord by which to attach a flag; finally, there were elsewhere two vertical staffs from which flags were occasionally flown. It seemed probable that the pole was not there for flag-flying.

I then tried to imagine all possible purposes of such a pole, and to consider for which of these it was best suited: (*a*) Possibly it was an ornament. But as all the ferryboats and even the tugboats carried poles, this hypothesis was rejected. (*b*) Possibly it was the terminal of a wireless telegraph. But the same considerations made this improbable. Besides, the more natural place for such a terminal would be the highest part of the boat, on top of the pilot house. (*c*) Its purpose might be to point out the direction in which the boat is moving.

In support of this conclusion, I discovered that the pole was lower than the pilot house, so that the steersman could easily see it. Moreover, the tip was enough higher than the base, so that, from the pilot's position, it must appear to project far out in front of the boat. Moreover, the pilot being near the front of the boat, he would need some such guide as to its direction. Tugboats would also need poles for such a purpose. This hypothesis was so much more probable than the others that I accepted it. I formed the conclusion that the pole was set up for the purpose of showing the pilot the direction in which the boat pointed, to enable him to steer correctly.

A CASE OF REFLECTION INVOLVING EXPERIMENT

In washing tumblers in hot soapsuds and placing them mouth downward on a plate, I noticed that bubbles appeared on the outside of the mouth of the tumblers and then went inside. Why? The presence of bubbles suggests air, which I note must come from inside the tumbler. I see that the soapy water on the plate prevents escape of the air save as it may be caught in bubbles. But why should air leave the tumbler? There was no substance entering to force it out. It must have expanded. It expands by increase of heat or by increase of pressure, or by both. Could the air have become heated after the tumbler was taken from the hot suds? Clearly not the air that was already entangled in the water. If heated air was the cause, cold air must have entered in transferring the tumblers from the suds to the plate. I test to see whether this supposition is true by taking several more tumblers out. Some I shake so as to make sure of entrapping cold air in them. Some I take out, holding them mouth downward in order to prevent cold air from entering. Bubbles appear on the outside of every one of the former and on none of the latter. I must be right in my inference. Air from the outside must have been expanded by the heat of the tumbler, which explains the appearance of the bubbles on the outside.

But why do they then go inside? Cold contracts. The tumbler cooled and also the air inside it. Tension was removed, and hence bubbles appeared inside. To be sure of this, I test by placing a cap of ice on the tumbler while the bubbles are still forming outside. They soon reverse.

THESE THREE CASES FORM A SERIES

These three cases have been purposely selected so as to form a series from the more rudimentary to more complicated cases of reflection. The first illustrates the kind of thinking done by everyone during the day's business, in which neither the data nor the ways of dealing with them lie outside the limits of everyday experience. The last furnishes a case in which neither problem nor mode of solution would have occurred except to one with some prior scientific training. The second case forms a natural transition; its materials lie well within the bounds of everyday, unspecialized experience; but the problem, instead of being directly involved in the person's business, arises indirectly in connection with what he happened to be doing and appeals to a somewhat theoretic and impartial interest.

In the next chapter we shall give an analytic account of what the three instances exhibit in common. In what immediately follows we shall set forth, first, how they all illustrate the nature of that operation of *inference* which is the heart of all intelligent action, and second, how the aim and outcome of thinking in all cases is the transformation of a *dubious* and perplexing situation into a *settled*, or determinate, one.

II. Inference to the Unknown

NO THOUGHT WITHOUT INFERENCE

In every case of reflective activity, a person finds himself confronted with a given, present situation from which he has to arrive at, or conclude to, something else that is not present. This process of arriving at an idea of what is absent on the basis of what is at hand is *inference*. What is present *carries* or *bears* the mind over to the idea and ultimately the acceptance of something else. From the consideration of established facts of location and time of day, the person in the first case cited made an inference as to the best way to travel in order to keep an appointment, which is a future and, at first, uncertain event. From observed and remembered facts, the second person inferred the probable use of a long pole. From the presence under certain conditions of bubbles and from a knowledge of securely established physical facts and principles, the third person inferred the explanation or cause of a particular event, previously unknown;

namely, the movement of water in the form of bubbles from the outside to the inside of a tumbler.

INFERENCE INVOLVES A LEAP

Every inference, just because it goes beyond ascertained and known facts, which are given either by observation or by recollection of prior knowledge, involves a *jump from the known into the unknown*. It involves a leap beyond what is given and already established. As we have already noted,[1] the inference occurs via or through the suggestion that is aroused by what is seen and remembered. Now, while the suggestion pops into the mind, just *what* suggestion occurs depends first upon the experience of the person. This in turn is dependent upon the general state of culture of the time; suggestions, for example, that occur readily now could not possibly spring up in the mind of a savage. Second, suggestions depend upon the person's own preferences, desires, interests, or even his immediate state of passion. The inevitableness of suggestion, the lively force with which it springs before the mind, the natural tendency to accept it if it is plausible or not obviously contradicted by facts, indicate the necessity of controlling the suggestion which is made the basis of an inference that is to be believed.

PROVING IS TESTING

This control of inference prior to, and on behalf of, belief constitutes *proof*. To prove a thing means primarily to *test* it. The guest bidden to the wedding feast excused himself because he had to *prove* his oxen. Exceptions are said to prove a rule; *i.e.*, they furnish instances so extreme that they try in the severest fashion its applicability; if the rule will stand such a test, there is no good reason for further doubting it. Not until a thing has been tried—"tried out," in colloquial language—do we know its true worth. Till then it may be pretense, a bluff. But the thing that has come out victorious in a test or trial of strength carries its credentials with it; it is approved, be-

1. See pages 119 and 145.

cause it has been proved. Its value is clearly evinced, shown; *i.e.*, demonstrated. So it is with inferences. The mere fact that inference in general is an invaluable function does not guarantee, nor does it even help out, the correctness of any particular inference. Any inference may go astray; as we have seen, there are standing influences ever ready to instigate it to go wrong. *What is important is that every inference be a tested inference; or* (since often this is not possible) *that we discriminate between beliefs that rest upon tested evidence and those that do not, and be accordingly on our guard as to the kind and degree of assent or belief that is justified.*

TWO KINDS OF TESTING

All three instances manifest the presence of testing operations that transform what would otherwise have been loose thinking into reflective activity. Examination reveals that the testing is of two kinds. Suggested inferences are tested in *thought* to see whether different elements in the suggestion are coherent with one another. They are also tested, after one has been adopted, by *action* to see whether the consequences that are anticipated in *thought* occur in *fact*. A good example of this second kind of proving is found in the first case cited, where reasoning had led to the conclusion that the use of the subway would bring the person to the place of his appointment in time. He tried or tested the idea by acting upon it, and the result confirmed the idea by bringing what was inferred actually to pass.

In the second case, the test by action could occur only as the person *imagined* himself in the place of the pilot who was using the pole to steer by. The test of coherence or consistency is markedly in evidence. Suggestions of flagpole, ornament, wireless, were rejected because, as soon as they were reflected upon, it was seen that they did not fit into some elements of the observed facts; they were dropped because they failed to agree with these elements. The idea that the pole was used to show the direction of movement of the boat, on the contrary, was found to agree with a number of important elements, such as (*a*) the need of the pilot, (*b*) the height of the pole, (*c*) the relative locations of its base and tip.

In the third instance, both kinds of testing are employed. After the conclusion was reached, it was acted upon by a further experiment, undertaken not only in imagination but also in fact. A cap of ice was placed upon the tumbler, and the bubbles behaved as they should behave if the inference was the correct one. Hence it was borne out, corroborated, verified. Other testing acts occurred in the process by using different ways of taking tumblers out of the water. The testing of consistency in thought occurred by reflecting upon the nature of expansion in its relation to heat and by considering whether the observed phenomena agreed with the facts that would have to follow from this principle. Obviously the use of both methods of proving a proposed inference is better than one alone. The two methods do not differ, however, in kind. Testing in thought for consistency involves acting in *imagination*. The other mode carries the imagined act out overtly. True inference is defined first as involving a leap to a suggested conclusion, and second as *trying* the suggestion to determine its agreement with the requirements of the situation. The original pattern of reflective action is set by cases in which the need for doing something is urgent, and where the results of what is done test the value of thought. As intellectual curiosity develops, connection with overt action becomes indirect and incidental. Yet it persists even if only in imagination.

III. Thinking Moves from a Doubtful to a Settled Situation

IT ARISES FROM A DIRECTLY EXPERIENCED SITUATION

Examination of the instances will show that in each case thinking arises out of a directly experienced situation. Persons do not just think at large, nor do ideas arise out of nothing. In one case a student is busy in a certain part of a city and is reminded of an engagement at another place. In the second case a person is engaged in riding on a ferryboat and begins to wonder about something in the construction of the boat. In the third case a student with prior scientific training is busy washing dishes. In each case the nature of the situation as it is actually experienced arouses inquiry and calls out reflection.

There is nothing in this fact peculiar to these special instances. Go through your own experience and you will not find a case where thinking started up out of nothing. Sometimes the train of thoughts will have taken you so far away from the starting point that you will have difficulty in getting back to that prior something out of which the thinking arose, but follow the thread far enough and you will find some situation that is directly experienced, something undergone, done, enjoyed, or suffered, and not just thought of. Reflection is occasioned by the character of this primary situation. It does not merely *grow out* of it, but it *refers back* to it. Its aim and outcome are decided by the situation out of which it arose.

Probably the most frequent cause of failure in school to secure genuine thinking from students is the failure to insure the existence of an experienced situation of such a nature as to call out thinking in the way in which these out-of-school situations do. A teacher was troubled by the failure of pupils, when dealing with arithmetical problems in multiplication involving decimals, to place the decimal point correctly. The numerical figures would be correct, but the values all wrong. One student might, for example, say $320.16; another, $32.016; and a third, $3201.60. This result showed that, while the pupils could manipulate figures correctly, they did not *think*. For if they had used thought, they would not vary so arbitrarily in grasping the values involved. Accordingly he sent the pupils to a lumberyard to purchase boards for use in the manual-training shop, having arranged with the dealer to let *them* figure the cost of their purchases. The same numerical operations were involved as in the textbook problems. No mistakes at all were made in placing the decimal. The situation itself induced them to think and controlled their grasp of the values involved. The contrast between the textbook problem and the requirements of the actual purchase in the lumberyard provides an excellent example of the necessity of a situation in order to induce and direct thought.

IT MOVES TOWARD A SETTLED SITUATION

Examination of the three cases also shows that each situation is in some fashion uncertain, perplexed, troublesome, if only in offering to the mind an unresolved difficulty, an unsettled question. It shows in each case that the function of reflection is to bring about a new situation in which the difficulty is resolved, the confusion cleared away, the trouble smoothed out, the question it puts answered. Any particular process of thinking naturally comes to its close when the situation before the mind is settled, decided, orderly, clear, for then there is nothing to call out reflection until a new bothersome or doubtful situation arises.

The function of reflective thought is, therefore, to transform a situation in which there is experienced obscurity, doubt, conflict, disturbance of some sort, into a situation that is clear, coherent, settled, harmonious.

The *stated* conclusion, the conclusion that is set forth in a proposition, is not the *final* conclusion but is the key to its formation. For example, the first person reached the conclusion "the best way to 124th Street is the subway train." But that conclusion was only the *key* to reaching the ultimate conclusion; namely, the keeping of an engagement. Thinking was the means of developing the original, perplexed situation into an eventual, satisfactory one. You can readily make similar analyses in the case of the other two illustrations. One great difficulty with the "logical," the exclusively formal type of which we spoke in the previous chapter, is that it begins and ends with mere propositions instead of bringing before the imagination the two actual life-situations to which the propositions refer; the one, which contains the doubt or difficulty, and the other, which is the final desired outcome and which was brought about by means of reflection.

There is no better way to decide whether genuine inference has taken place than to ask whether it terminated in the substitution of a clear, orderly, and satisfactory situation for a perplexed, confused, and discordant one. Partial and ineffectual thinking ends in conclusions that are formally correct but that make no difference in what is personally and immediately experienced. Vital inference always leaves one who thinks with a world that is experienced as different in some respect, for some object in it has gained in clarity and orderly arrangement. Genuine thinking winds up, in short, with an appreciation of new values.

7. Analysis of Reflective Thinking

I. Facts and Ideas

When a situation arises containing a difficulty or perplexity, the person who finds himself in it may take one of a number of courses. He may dodge it, dropping the activity that brought it about, turning to something else. He may indulge in a flight of fancy, imagining himself powerful or wealthy, or in some other way in possession of the means that would enable him to deal with the difficulty. Or, finally, he may face the situation. In this case, he begins to reflect.

REFLECTION INCLUDES OBSERVATION

The moment he begins to reflect, he begins of necessity to observe in order to take stock of conditions. Some of these observations are made by direct use of the senses; others by recollecting observations previously made either by himself or by others. The person who had the engagement to keep, notes with his eyes his present location, recalls the place where he should arrive at one o'clock, and brings back to mind the means of transportation with which he is acquainted and their respective locations. In this way he gets as clear and distinct a recognition as possible of the nature of the situation with which he has to deal. Some of the conditions are obstacles and others are aids, resources. No matter whether these conditions come to him by direct perception or by memory, they form the "*facts* of the case." They are the things that are *there*, that have to be reckoned with. Like all facts, they are stubborn. They cannot be got out of the way by magic just because they are disagreeable. It is no use to *wish* they did not exist or were different. They must be taken for just what they are. Hence observation and recollection must be used to the full so as not to glide over or to mistake important features. Until the habit of thinking is well formed, facing the situation to discover the facts requires an effort. For the mind tends to dislike what is unpleasant and so to sheer off from an adequate notice of that which is especially annoying.

REFLECTION INCLUDES SUGGESTIONS

Along with noting the conditions that constitute the facts to be dealt with, suggestions arise of possible courses of action. Thus the person of our illustration[1] thinks of surface cars, elevated trains, and the subway. These alternative suggestions compete with one another. By comparison he judges which alternative is best, which one is the more likely to give a satisfactory solution. The comparison takes place indirectly. The moment one thinks of a possible solution and holds it in suspense, he turns back to the facts. He has now a point of view that leads him to new observations and recollections and to a reconsideration of observations already made in order to test the worth of the suggested way out. Unless he uses the suggestion so as to guide to new observations instead of exercising suspended judgment, he accepts it as soon as it presents itself. Then he falls short of truly reflective thought. The newly noted facts may (and in any complex situation surely will) cause new suggestions to spring up. These become clews to further investigation of conditions. The results of this survey test and correct the proposed inference or suggest a new one. This continuous interaction of the facts disclosed by observation and of the suggested proposals of solution and the suggested methods of dealing with conditions goes on till some suggested solution meets all the conditions of the case and does not run counter to any discoverable feature of it.[2]

DATA AND IDEAS ARE CORRELATIVE AND INDISPENSABLE FACTORS IN REFLECTION

A technical term for the observed facts is *data*. The data form the material that has to be interpreted, accounted

1. See page 187.
2. The statements just made should be tested and illustrated by reference to the three cases set forth in the previous chapter.

for, explained; or, in the case of deliberation as to what to do or how to do it, to be managed and utilized. The suggested solutions for the difficulties disclosed by observation form *ideas*. Data (facts) and ideas (suggestions, possible solutions) thus form the two indispensable and correlative factors of all reflective activity. The two factors are carried on by means respectively of *observation* (in which for convenience is included memory of prior observations of similar cases) and *inference*. The latter runs beyond what is actually noted, beyond what is found, upon careful examination, to be actually present. It relates, therefore, to what is *possible*, rather than to what is actual. It proceeds by anticipation, supposition, conjecture, imagination. All foresight, prediction, planning, as well as theorizing and speculation, are characterized by excursion from the actual into the possible. Hence (as we have already seen) what is inferred demands a double test: first, the process of forming the idea or supposed solution is checked by constant cross reference to the conditions observed to be actually present; secondly, the idea *after* it is formed is tested by *acting* upon it, overtly if possible, otherwise in imagination. The consequences of this action confirm, modify, or refute the idea.

We shall illustrate what has been said by a simple case. Suppose you are walking where there is no regular path. As long as everything goes smoothly, you do not have to think about your walking; your already formed habit takes care of it. Suddenly you find a ditch in your way. You think you will jump it (supposition, plan); but to make sure, you survey it with your eyes (observation), and you find that it is pretty wide and that the bank on the other side is slippery (facts, data). You then wonder if the ditch may not be narrower somewhere else (idea), and you look up and down the stream (observation) to see how matters stand (test of idea by observation). You do not find any good place and so are thrown back upon forming a new plan. As you are casting about, you discover a log (fact again). You ask yourself whether you could not haul that to the ditch and get it across the ditch to use as a bridge (idea again). You judge that idea is worth trying, and so you get the log and manage to put it in place and walk across (test and confirmation by overt action).

If the situation were more complicated, thinking would of course be more elaborate. You can imagine a case in which making a raft, constructing a pontoon bridge, or making a dugout would be the ideas that would finally come to mind and have to be checked by reference to conditions of action (facts). Simple or complicated, relating to what to do in a practical predicament or what to infer in a scientific or philosophic problem, there will always be the two sides: the conditions to be accounted for, dealt with, and the ideas that are plans for dealing with them or are suppositions for interpreting and explaining the phenomena.

In predicting an eclipse, for example, a multitude of observed facts regarding position and movements of earth, sun, and moon, comes in on one side, while on the other side the ideas employed to predict and explain involve extensive mathematical calculations. In a philosophic problem, the facts or data may be remote and not susceptible of direct observation by the senses. But still there will be data, perhaps of science, or of morals, art, or the conclusions of past thinkers, that supply the subject matter to be dealt with and by which theories are checked. On the other side, there are the speculations that come to mind and that lead to search for additional subject matter which will both develop the proposed theories as ideas and test their value. Mere facts or data are dead, as far as mind is concerned, unless they are used to suggest and test some idea, some way out of a difficulty. Ideas, on the other hand, are *mere* ideas, idle speculations, fantasies, dreams, unless they are used to guide new observations of, and reflections upon, actual situations, past, present, or future. Finally, they must be brought to some sort of check by actual given material or else remain ideas. Many ideas are of great value as material of poetry, fiction, or the drama, but not as the stuff of knowledge. However, ideas may be of intellectual use to a penetrating mind even when they do not find any immediate reference to actuality, provided they stay in the mind for use when new facts come to light.

II. The Essential Functions of Reflective Activity

We now have before us the material for the analysis of a complete act of reflective activity. In the preceding chapter we saw that the two limits of every unit of thinking are a perplexed, troubled, or confused situation at the beginning and a cleared-up, unified, resolved situation at the close. The first of these situations may be called *pre*-reflective. It sets the problem to be solved; out of it grows the question that reflection has to answer. In the final situation the doubt has been dispelled; the situation is *post*-reflective; there results a direct experience of mastery, satisfaction, enjoyment. Here, then, are the limits within which reflection falls.

FIVE PHASES, OR ASPECTS, OF REFLECTIVE THOUGHT

In between, as states of thinking, are (1) *suggestions*, in which the mind leaps forward to a possible solution; (2) an intellectualization of the difficulty or perplexity that has been *felt* (directly experienced) into a *problem* to be solved, a question for which the answer must be sought; (3) the use of one suggestion after another as a leading idea, or *hypothesis*, to initiate and guide observation and other operations in collection of factual material; (4) the mental elaboration of the idea or supposition as an idea or supposition (*reasoning*, in the sense in which reasoning is a part, not the whole, of inference); and (5) testing the hypothesis by overt or imaginative action.

We shall now take up the five phases, or functions, one by one.

THE FIRST PHASE, SUGGESTION

The most "natural" thing for anyone to do is to go ahead; that is to say, to *act* overtly. The disturbed and perplexed situation arrests such direct activity temporarily. The tendency to continue *acting* nevertheless persists. It is diverted and takes the form of an idea or a suggestion. The *idea* of what to do when we find ourselves "in a hole" is a substitute for direct action. It is a vicarious, anticipatory way of acting, a kind of dramatic rehearsal. Were there only one suggestion popping up, we should undoubtedly adopt it at once. But where there are two or more, they collide with one another, maintain the state of suspense, and produce further inquiry. The first suggestion in the instance recently cited was to jump the ditch, but the perception of conditions inhibited that suggestion and led to the occurrence of other ideas.

Some inhibition of *direct* action is necessary to the condition of hesitation and delay that is essential to thinking. Thought is, as it were, conduct turned in upon itself and examining its purpose and its conditions, its resources, aids, and difficulties and obstacles.

THE SECOND PHASE, INTELLECTUALIZATION

We have already noted that it is artificial, so far as thinking is concerned, to start with a ready-made problem, a problem made out of whole cloth or arising out of a vacuum. In reality such a "problem" is simply an assigned *task*. There is not at first a situation *and* a problem, much less just a problem and no situation. There is a troubled, perplexed, trying situation, where the difficulty is, as it were, spread throughout the entire situation, infecting it as a whole. If we knew just what the difficulty was and where it lay, the job of reflection would be much easier than it is. As the saying truly goes, a question well put is half answered. In fact, we know what the problem *exactly* is simultaneously with finding a way out and getting it resolved. Problem and solution stand out *completely* at the same time. Up to that point, our grasp of the problem has been more or less vague and tentative.

A blocked suggestion leads us to reinspect the conditions that confront us. Then our uneasiness, the shock of disturbed activity, gets stated in some degree on the basis of observed conditions, of objects. The width of the ditch, the slipperiness of the banks, not the mere presence of a ditch, is the trouble. The difficulty is getting located and defined; it is becoming a true problem, something intellectual, not just an annoyance at being held up in what we are doing. The person who is suddenly blocked and troubled in what he is doing by the thought of an engagement to keep at a time that is near and a place that is distant has the suggestion of getting there at once. But in order to carry this suggestion into effect, he has to find means of transportation. In order to find them he has to note his present position and its distance from the station, the present time, and the interval at his disposal. Thus the perplexity is more precisely located: just so much ground to cover, so much time to do it in.

The word "problem" often seems too elaborate and dignified

to denote what happens in minor cases of reflection. But in every case where reflective activity ensues, there is a process of *intellectualizing* what at first is merely an *emotional* quality of the whole situation. This conversion is effected by noting more definitely the conditions that constitute the trouble and cause the stoppage of action.

THE THIRD PHASE, THE GUIDING IDEA, HYPOTHESIS

The first suggestion occurs spontaneously; it comes to mind automatically; it *springs* up; it "pops," as we have said, "into the mind"; it flashes upon us. There is no direct control of its occurrence; the idea just comes or it does not come; that is all that can be said. There is nothing *intellectual* about its occurrence. The intellectual element consists in *what we do with it*, how we use it, *after* its sudden occurrence as an idea. A controlled use of it is made possible by the state of affairs just described. In the degree in which we define the difficulty (which is effected by stating it in terms of objects), we get a better idea of the kind of solution that is needed. The facts or data set the problem before us, and insight into the problem corrects, modifies, expands the suggestion that originally occurred. In this fashion the suggestion becomes a definite supposition or, stated more technically, a *hypothesis*.

Take the case of a physician examining a patient or a mechanic inspecting a piece of complicated machinery that does not behave properly. There is something wrong, so much is sure. But how to remedy it cannot be told until it is known *what* is wrong. An untrained person is likely to make a wild guess—the suggestion—and then proceed to act upon it in a random way, hoping that by good luck the right thing will be hit upon. So some medicine that appears to have worked before or that a neighbor has recommended is tried. Or the person fusses, monkeys, with the machine, poking here and hammering there on the chance of making the right move. The trained person proceeds in a very different fashion. He *observes* with unusual care, using the methods, the techniques, that the experience of physicians and expert mechanics in general, those familiar with the structure of the organism or the machine, have shown to be helpful in detecting trouble.

The idea of the solution is thus controlled by the diagnosis that has been made. But if the case is at all complicated, the physician or mechanic does not foreclose further thought by assuming that the suggested method of remedy is certainly right. He proceeds to act upon it tentatively rather than decisively. That is, he treats it as a guiding idea, a working hypothesis, and is led by it to make more observations, to collect more facts, so as to see if the *new* material is what the hypothesis calls for. He reasons that *if* the disease is typhoid, *then* certain phenomena will be found; and he looks particularly to see if *just* these conditions are present. Thus both the first and second operations are brought under control; the sense of the problem becomes more adequate and refined and the suggestion ceases to be a *mere* possibility, becoming a *tested* and, if possible, a *measured* probability.

THE FOURTH PHASE, REASONING
(IN THE NARROWER SENSE)

Observations pertain to what exists in nature. They constitute the facts, and these facts both regulate the formation of suggestions, ideas, hypotheses, and test their probable value as indications of solutions. The ideas, on the other hand, occur, as we say, in our heads, in our minds. They not only occur there, but are capable, as well, of great development there. Given a fertile suggestion occurring in an experienced, well-informed mind, that mind is capable of elaborating it until there results an idea that is quite different from the one with which the mind started.

For example, the idea of heat in the third instance in the earlier chapter[3] was linked up with what the person already knew about heat—in his case, its expansive force—and this in turn with the contractive tendency of cold, so that the idea of expansion could be used as an explanatory idea, though the mere idea of heat would not have been of any avail. Heat was quite directly suggested by the observed conditions; water was felt to be hot. But only a mind with some prior information about heat would have reasoned that heat meant expansion, and then used the idea of expansion as a working hypothesis. In more complex cases, there are long trains of reasoning in which one idea leads up to another

3. See page 189.

idea known by previous test to be related to it. The stretch of links brought to light by reasoning depends, of course, upon the store of knowledge that the mind is already in possession of. And this depends not only upon the prior experience and special education of the individual who is carrying on the inquiry, but also upon the state of culture and science of the age and place. Reasoning helps extend knowledge, while at the same time it depends upon what is already known and upon the facilities that exist for communicating knowledge and making it a public, open resource.

A physician to-day can develop, by reasoning from his knowledge, the implications of the disease that symptoms suggest to him as probable in a way that would have been impossible even a generation ago; just as, on the other hand, he can carry his observation of symptoms much farther because of improvement in clinical instruments and the technique of their use.

Reasoning has the same effect upon a suggested solution that more intimate and extensive observation has upon the original trouble. Acceptance of a suggestion in its first form is prevented by looking into it more thoroughly. Conjectures that seem plausible at first sight are often found unfit or even absurd when their full consequences are traced out. Even when reasoning out the bearings of a supposition does not lead to its rejection, it develops the idea into a form in which it is more apposite to the problem. Only when, for example, the conjecture that a pole was an index pole had been thought out in its implications could its particular applicability to the case in hand be judged. Suggestions at first seemingly remote and wild are frequently so transformed by being elaborated into what follows from them as to become apt and fruitful. The development of an idea through reasoning helps supply intervening or intermediate terms which link together into a consistent whole elements that at first seemingly conflict with each other, some leading the mind to one inference and others to an opposed one.

Mathematics as Typical Reasoning. Mathematics affords the typical example of how far can be carried the operation of relating ideas to one another, without having to depend upon the observations of the senses. In geometry we start with a few simple conceptions, line, angle, parallel, surfaces formed by lines meeting, etc., and a few principles defining equalities. Knowing something about the equality of angles made by parallel lines when they intersect a straight line, and knowing, by definition, that a perpendicular to a straight line forms two right angles, by means of a combination of these ideas we readily determine that the sum of the interior angles of a triangle is equal to two right angles. By continuing to trace the implications of theorems already demonstrated, the whole subject of plane figures is finally elaborated. The manipulation of algebraic symbols so as to establish a series of equations and other mathematical functions affords an even more striking example of what can be accomplished by developing the relation of ideas to one another.

When the hypothesis indicated by a series of scientific observations and experiments can be stated in mathematical form, that idea can be transformed to almost any extent, until it assumes a form in which a problem can be dealt with most expeditiously and effectively. Much of the accomplishment of physical science depends upon an intervening mathematical elaboration of ideas. It is not the mere presence of measurements in quantitative form that yields scientific knowledge, but that particular kind of mathematical statement which can be developed by reasoning into other and more fruitful forms—a consideration which is fatal to the claim to scientific standing of many educational measurements merely because they have a quantitative form.

THE FIFTH PHASE, TESTING THE HYPOTHESIS BY ACTION

The concluding phase is some kind of testing by overt action to give *experimental corroboration*, or *verification*, of the conjectural idea. Reasoning shows that *if* the *idea* be adopted, certain consequences follow. So far the conclusion is hypothetical or conditional. If when we look we find present all the conditions demanded by the theory, and if we find the characteristic traits called for by rival alternatives to be lacking, the tendency to believe, to accept, is almost irresistible. Sometimes direct observation furnishes corroboration, as in the case of the pole on the boat. In other cases, as in that of the bubbles, experiment is required; that is, *conditions are deliberately arranged in accord with the requirements of an idea or hypothesis to see whether the results theoretically indicated by the idea actually occur.* If it is found that the experimental results agree with the theoretical, or rationally deduced, results, and if there is reason to believe that *only* the conditions in question would yield such results, the confirmation is so strong as to induce a conclusion—at least until contrary facts shall indicate the advisability of its revision.

Of course, verification does not always follow. Sometimes consequences show failure to confirm instead of corroboration. The idea in question is refuted by the court of final appeal. But a great advantage of possession of the habit of reflective activity is that failure is not *mere* failure. It is instructive. The person who really thinks learns quite as much from his failures as from his successes. For a failure indicates to the person whose thinking has been involved in it, and who has not come to it by mere blind chance, what further observations should be made. It suggests to him what modifications should be introduced in the hypothesis upon which he has been operating. It either brings to light a new problem or helps to define and clarify the problem on which he has been engaged. Nothing shows the trained thinker better than the use he makes of his errors and mistakes. What merely annoys and discourages a person not accustomed to thinking, or what starts him out on a new course of aimless attack by mere cut-and-try methods, is a stimulus and a guide to the trained inquirer.

THE SEQUENCE OF THE FIVE PHASES IS NOT FIXED

The five phases, terminals, or functions of thought, that we have noted do not follow one another in a set order. On the contrary, each step in genuine thinking does something to perfect the formation of a suggestion and promote its change into a leading idea or directive hypothesis. It does something to promote the location and definition of the problem. Each improvement in the idea leads to new observations that yield new facts or data and help the mind judge more accurately the relevancy of facts already at hand. The elaboration of the hypothesis does not wait until the problem has been defined and adequate hypothesis has been arrived at; it may come in at any intermediate time. And as we have just seen, any particular overt test need not be final; it may be introductory to new observations and new suggestions, according to what happens in consequence of it.

There is, however, an important difference between test by overt action in practical deliberations and in scientific investigations. In the former the practical commitment involved in overt action is much more serious than in the latter. An astronomer or a chemist performs overt actions, but they are for the sake of knowledge; they serve to test and develop his conceptions and theories. In practical matters, the main result desired lies outside of knowledge. One of the great values of thinking, accordingly, is that it defers the commitment to action that is irretrievable, that, once made, cannot be revoked. Even in moral and other practical matters, therefore, a thoughtful person treats his overt deeds as experimental so far as possible; that is to say, while he cannot call them back and must stand their consequences, he gives alert attention to what they teach him about his conduct as well as to the non-intellectual consequences. He makes a problem out of consequences of conduct, looking into the causes from which they probably resulted, especially the causes that lie in his own habits and desires.

In conclusion, we point out that the five phases of reflection that have been described represent only in outline the indispensable traits of reflective thinking. In practice, two of them may telescope, some of them may be passed over hurriedly, and the burden of reaching a conclusion may fall mainly on a single phase, which will then require a seemingly disproportionate development. No set rules can be laid down on such matters. The way they are managed depends upon the intellectual tact and sensitiveness of the individual. When things have come out wrong, it is, however, a wise practice to review the methods by which the unwise decision was reached, and see where the misstep was made.

ONE PHASE MAY BE EXPANDED

In complicated cases some of the five phases are so extensive that they include definite subphases within themselves. In this case it is arbitrary whether the minor functions are regarded as parts or are listed as distinct phases. There is nothing especially sacred about the number five. For example, in matters of practical deliberation where the object is to decide what to do, it may be well to undertake a scrutiny of the underlying desires and motives that are operating; that is, instead of asking what ends and means will best satisfy one's wish, one may turn back to the attitudes of which the wish is the expression. It is a matter of indifference whether this search be listed as an independent problem, having its own phases, or as an additional phase in the original problem.

REFERENCE TO THE FUTURE AND TO THE PAST

Again, it has been suggested that reflective thinking involves a look into the future, a forecast, an anticipation, or a prediction, and that this should be listed as a sixth aspect, or phase. As a matter of fact, every intellectual suggestion or idea is anticipatory of some possible future experience, while the final solution gives a definite set toward the future. It is both a record of something accomplished and an assignment of a future method of operation. It helps set up an enduring habit of procedure. When a physician, for example, has diagnosed a case, he usually makes also a *prognosis*, a forecast, of the probable future course of the disease. And not only is his treatment a verification—or the reverse—of the idea or hypothesis about the disease upon which he has proceeded, but the result also affects his treatment of future patients. In some cases, the future reference may be so important as to require special elaboration. In this case, it may be presented as an added, distinct phase. Some of the investigations of an astronomical expedition to watch an eclipse of the sun may be directly intended, for example, to get material bearing on Einstein's theory. But the theory, itself, is so important that its confirmation or refutation will give a decided turn to the future of physical science, and this consideration is likely to be uppermost in the minds of scientists.

Of equal importance is the reference to the *past* involved in reflection. Of course, suggestions are dependent in any case upon one's past experience; they do not arise out of nothing. But while sometimes we go ahead with the suggestion without stopping to go back to the original experience of which it is the fruit, at other times we go consciously over the past experience in considerable detail as part of the process of testing the value of the suggestion.

For example, it occurs to a man to invest in real estate. Then he recalls that a previous investment of this kind turned out unfortunately. He goes over the former case, comparing it bit by bit with the present, to see how far the two cases are alike or unlike. Examination of the past may be the chief and decisive factor in thought. The most valuable reference to the past is likely, however, to come at the time the conclusion is reached. We noted earlier[4] the importance of a final survey to secure a net formulation of the exact result and of the premises upon which it logically depends. This is not only an important part of the process of *testing*, but, as was stated in the earlier discussion, is almost necessary if good habits are to be built up. Ability to *organize* knowledge consists very largely in the habit of reviewing previous facts and ideas and relating them to one another on a new basis; namely, that of the conclusion that has been reached. A certain amount of this operation is included in the testing phase that has been described. But its influence upon the attitude of students is so important that it may be well at times so to emphasize it that it becomes a definite function, or phase, on its own account.

4. See page 174.

8. The Place of Judgment in Reflective Activity

I. Three Factors in Judging

We have been dealing so far with the act of reflection as an entirety. There are subordinate unities within the process upon whose character the efficiency of the whole undertaking depends.

JUDGMENTS, THE CONSTITUENT UNITS OF THOUGHT

From one point of view the whole process of thinking consists of making a series of judgments that are so related as to support one another in leading to a final judgment—the conclusion. In spite of this fact, we have treated reflective activity as a whole, first, because judgments do not occur in isolation but in connection with the solution of a problem, the clearing away of something obscure and perplexing, the resolution of a difficulty; in short, as units in reflective activity. The purpose of solving a problem determines what kind of judgments should be made. If I were suddenly to announce that it would take twenty-two and a half yards of carpet to cover a certain floor, it might be a perfectly correct statement, but as a *judgment* it would be senseless if it did not bear upon some question that had come up. Judgments need to be *relevant* to an issue as well as correct. Judging is the act of selecting and weighing the bearing of facts and suggestions as they present themselves, as well as of deciding whether the alleged facts are really facts and whether the idea used is a sound idea or merely a fancy. We may say, for short, that a person of sound judgment is one who, in the idiomatic phrase, has "horse sense"; he is a good judge of *relative values*; he can estimate, appraise, evaluate, with tact and discernment.

It follows that the heart of a good habit of thought lies in the power to pass judgments *pertinently* and *discriminatingly*. We sometimes meet men with little schooling whose advice is greatly relied upon and who are spontaneously looked to when an emergency arises, men who are conspicuously successful in conducting vital affairs. They are the persons of sound judgment. A man of sound judgment in any set of affairs is an *educated* man as respects those affairs, whatever his schooling or academic standing. And if our schools turn out their pupils in that attitude of mind which is conducive to good judgment in any department of affairs in which the pupils are placed, they have done more than if they sent out their pupils possessed *merely* of vast stores of information or high degrees of skill in specialized branches.

THE FEATURES OF JUDGMENT

The significant traits of judgment may be gathered from a consideration of the operations to which the word *judgment* was originally applied; namely, the authoritative decision of matters in a legal controversy—the procedure of the *judge on the bench*. There are three such features: (1) a controversy, consisting of opposite claims regarding the same objective situation; (2) a process of defining and elaborating these claims and of sifting the facts adduced to support them; (3) a final decision, or sentence, closing the particular matter in dispute while also serving as a rule or principle for deciding future cases.

IT ARISES FROM DOUBT AND CONTROVERSY

1. Unless there is something doubtful, the situation is read off at a glance; it is taken in on sight; *i.e.*, there is merely perception, recognition, not judgment. If the matter is wholly doubtful, if it is dark and obscure throughout, there is a blind mystery and again no judgment occurs. But if it suggests, however vaguely, different meanings, rival possible interpretations, there is some *point at issue*, some *matter at stake*. Doubt takes the form of discussion, of controversy within the mind. Different sides compete for a conclusion in their favor. Cases brought to trial before a judge illustrate neatly and unambiguously this strife of alternative interpretations; but any attempt to clear up intellectually a doubtful situation exemplifies the same traits. A mov-

ing blur catches our eye in the distance; we ask ourselves: "What is it? Is it a cloud of whirling dust? a tree waving its branches? a man signaling to us?" Something in the total situation suggests each of these possible meanings. Only one of them can possibly be correct; perhaps none of them is appropriate; yet *some* meaning the thing in question surely has. Which of the alternative suggested meanings has the rightful claim? What does the perception really mean? How is it to be interpreted, estimated, appraised, placed? Every judgment proceeds from some such situation.

IT DEFINES THE ISSUE BY SELECTING EVIDENTIAL FACTS AND APPROPRIATE PRINCIPLES

2. The hearing of the controversy, the trial, the weighing of alternative claims, divides into two branches, either of which, in a given case, may be more conspicuous than the other. In the consideration of a legal dispute these two branches are sifting the evidence and selecting the rules that are applicable; they are "the facts" and "the law" of the case. In ordinary judgment they are (*a*) the determination of the data that are important in the given case, and (*b*) the elaboration of the conceptions or meanings suggested by the crude data.[1] They are concerned with the two questions: (*a*) What portions or aspects of the situation are significant in controlling the formation of the interpretation? (*b*) Just what is the full meaning and bearing of the idea used as a method of interpretation? These questions are strictly correlative; the answer to each depends upon the answer to the other. We may, however, for convenience, consider them separately.

a. Selecting the Facts. In every actual occurrence there are many details that are part of the total occurrence, but nevertheless are not significant in relation to the point at issue. All parts of an experience are equally present, but they are very far from being equally valuable as signs or as evidences. Nor is there any tag, or label, on any trait saying: "This is important" or "This is trivial." Nor is intensity, or vividness, or conspicuousness a safe measure of indicative and proving value. The glaring thing may be totally

---

1. Compare the fourth function in the analysis made in Chapter 7.

insignificant in this particular situation, and the key to the understanding of the whole matter may be modest or hidden. Features
that are not significant are distracting; they insist upon their
claim to be regarded as clews and cues to interpretation, while
traits that are really significant do not appear on the surface at
all. Hence, judgment is required *even in reference to the situation*
or event that is present to the senses; elimination or rejection,
selection, discovery, or bringing to light must take place. Till we
have reached a final conclusion, rejection and selection must be
tentative or conditional. We select the things that we hope or
trust are cues to meaning. But if they do not suggest a situation
that accepts and includes them, we reconstitute our data, the
facts of the case; for we mean, intellectually, by the facts of the
case *those traits that are used as evidence in reaching a conclusion or forming a decision.*

No hard and fast rules for this operation of selecting and re-
jecting, or fixing upon significant evidential facts, can be given. It
all comes back, as we say, to the good judgment, the good sense,
of the one judging. To be a good judge is to have a sense of the
relative indicative or signifying values of the various features of
the perplexing situation; to know what to let go as of no account; what to eliminate as irrelevant; what to retain as conducive to the outcome; what to emphasize as a clew to the difficulty.
This power in ordinary matters we call *knack, tact, cleverness*; in
more important affairs, *insight, discernment*. In part it is instinctive or inborn, but it also represents the funded outcome of long
familiarity with like operations in the past. Possession of this
ability to seize what is evidential or significant and to let the rest
go is the mark of the expert, the connoisseur, the *judge*, in any
matter.

Mill cites the following case, which is worth noting as an instance of the extreme delicacy and accuracy to which may be
developed this power of sizing up the significant factors of a
situation.

A Scotch manufacturer procured from England, at a high
rate of wages, a working dyer, famous for producing very fine
colors, with the view of teaching to his other workmen the
same skill. The workman came; but his method of propor-
tioning the ingredients, in which lay the secret of the effects
he produced, was by taking them up in handfuls, while the

common method was to weigh them. The manufacturer sought to make him turn his handling system into an equivalent weighing system, that the general principles of his peculiar mode of proceeding might be ascertained. This, however, the man found himself quite unable to do, and could therefore impart his own skill to nobody. He had, from individual cases of his own experience, established a connexion in his mind between fine effects of color and tactual perceptions in handling his dyeing materials; and from these perceptions he could, in any particular case, *infer the means to be employed* and the effects which would be produced.

Long brooding over conditions, intimate contact associated with keen interest, thorough absorption in a multiplicity of allied experiences, tend to bring about those judgments which we then call "intuitive"; but they are true judgments, because they are based on intelligent selection and estimation, with solution of a problem as the controlling standard. Possession of this capacity makes the difference between the artist and the intellectual bungler.

Such is ability to judge in its completest form. But in any case there is a certain feeling after the way to be followed; a tentative picking out of certain qualities to see what emphasis upon them would lead to; a willingness to hold final appraisal in suspense; willingness to reject the factors entirely or relegate them to a different position in the evidential scheme if other features yield more solvent suggestions. Alertness, flexibility, curiosity, are the essentials; dogmatism, rigidity, prejudice, caprice, arising from routine, passion, and flippancy, are fatal.

b. Selecting the Principles. This selection of data is, of course, for the sake of controlling the *development and elaboration of the suggested meaning in the light of which they are to be interpreted.*[2] Evolution of conceptions thus goes on simultaneously with determination of the facts; one possible meaning after another is held before the mind, considered in relation to the data to which it is applied, is developed into its more detailed bearings, is dropped or tentatively accepted and used. We do not approach any problem with a wholly naïve or virgin mind; we approach it with certain acquired habitual modes of under-

2. Cf. pages 197 and 202.

standing, with a certain store of previously evolved meanings or at least of experiences from which meanings may be educed.

If a habit is checked, and so inhibited from easy application, a possible meaning for the facts in question comes to the mind. No hard and fast rules decide whether a meaning suggested is the right and proper meaning to follow up. The individual's own good (or bad) judgment is the guide. There is no label, on any given idea or principle, that says automatically, "Use me in this situation"—as the magic cakes of Alice in Wonderland were inscribed "Eat me." The thinker has to decide, to choose; and there is always a risk, so that the prudent thinker selects warily—subject, that is, to confirmation or frustration by later events. If one is not able to estimate wisely what is relevant to the interpretation of a given perplexing or doubtful issue, it avails little that arduous learning has built up a large stock of concepts. For learning is not wisdom; information does not guarantee good judgment. Memory may provide a refrigerator in which to store a stock of meanings for future use, but judgment selects and adopts the one to be used in an emergency—and without an emergency (some crisis, slight or great) there is no call for judgment. No conception, even if it is carefully and firmly established in the abstract, can at first safely be more than a *candidate* for the office of interpreter. Only greater success than that of its rivals in clarifying dark spots, untying hard knots, reconciling discrepancies, can elect it and prove it to be a valid idea for the given situation. In short, thinking is a continual appraising of both data and ideas. Unless the pertinence and force of each seemingly evidential fact and seemingly explanatory idea is *judged*, appraised, the mind goes on a wild-goose chase.

IT TERMINATES IN A DECISION

3. The judgment when formed is a *decision*; it closes, or concludes, the question at issue. This determination not only settles that particular case, but it also helps fix a rule or method for deciding similar matters in the future; as the sentence of the judge on the bench both terminates that dispute and also forms a precedent for future decisions. If the interpretation settled upon is not controverted by subsequent events, a presumption is built up in favor of similar interpretation in other

cases where the features are not so obviously unlike as to make it inappropriate. In this way, principles of judging are gradually built up; a certain manner of interpretation gets weight, authority. In short, meanings get *standardized*; they become logical concepts.[3]

II. Analysis and Synthesis: The Two Functions of Judgment

Through judging, confused data are cleared up, and seemingly incoherent and disconnected facts are brought together. The clearing up is *analysis*. The bringing together, or unifying, is *synthesis*. Things may have a peculiar feeling for us; they may make a certain indescribable impression upon us: the thing may *feel* round (that is, present a quality which we afterwards define as "round"); an act may seem rude; yet this impression, this quality, may be lost, absorbed, blended in the total situation. Only as we need to use just that aspect of the original situation as a tool of grasping something perplexing or obscure in another situation, do we detach the quality so that it becomes individualized. Only because we need to characterize the shape of some new object or the moral quality of some new act, does the element of roundness or rudeness in the old experience detach itself and so stand out as a distinctive feature. If the element thus selected clears up what is otherwise obscure in the new experience, if it settles what is uncertain, it thereby gains in positiveness and definiteness of meaning. This point will meet us again in the following chapter; here we speak of the matter only as it bears upon the question of analysis and synthesis.

MENTAL ANALYSIS IS NOT LIKE PHYSICAL DIVISION

Even when it is definitely stated that intellectual and physical analyses are different sorts of operations, intellectual analysis is often treated after the analogy of physical, as if it were the breaking up of a whole into all its constituent parts

3. See page 236.

in the mind instead of in space. As nobody can possibly tell what breaking a whole into its parts in the mind means, this conception leads to the further notion that logical analysis is a mere enumeration and listing of all conceivable qualities and relations. The influence upon education of this conception has been very great.[4] Every subject in the curriculum has passed through—or still remains in—what may be called the phase of "anatomical" or "morphological" method: the stage in which understanding the subject is thought to consist of multiplying distinctions of quality, form, relation, and so on, and attaching some name to each distinguished element. In normal growth, specific properties are emphasized and so individualized only when they serve to clear up a present difficulty. Only as they are involved in judging some specific situation is there any motive or use for analyses, for emphasis upon some element or relation as peculiarly significant.

The same putting the cart before the horse, the product before the process, is found in that overconscious formulation of methods of procedure so current in elementary instruction. The method that is employed in discovery, in reflective inquiry, cannot possibly be identified with the method that emerges *after* the discovery is made.[5] In the genuine operation of inference, the mind is in the attitude of *search*, of *hunting*, of *projection*, of *trying this and that*; when the conclusion is reached, the search is at an end. The Greeks used to discuss: "How is learning (or inquiry) possible? For either we know already what we are after, and then we do not learn or inquire; or we do not know, and then we cannot inquire, for we do not know what to look for." The dilemma is at least suggestive, for it points to the true alternative: the use in inquiry of doubt, of tentative suggestion, of experimentation. After we have reached the conclusion, a reconsideration of the steps of the process to see what is helpful, what is harmful, what is merely useless, assists in dealing more promptly and efficaciously with analogous problems in the future. In this way the method of *organizing* thought is built up.[6]

---

4. Thus arise all those falsely analytic methods in geography, reading, writing, drawing, botany, arithmetic, which we have already considered in another connection. (See page 178.)
5. See pages 173–174.
6. Compare the discussion (pages 176–177) of the psychological and the logical.

CONSCIOUS METHOD AND UNCONSCIOUS LOGICAL ATTITUDE

The common assumption that, unless the pupil from the outset *consciously recognizes and explicitly states* the method logically implied in the result he is to reach, he will have *no* method and his mind will work confusedly or anarchically is fallacious. It is equally erroneous to believe that, if he accompanies his performance with conscious statement of some form of procedure (outline, topical analysis, list of headings and subheadings, uniform formula), his mind is safeguarded and strengthened. As a matter of fact, the gradual, largely unconscious, development of *logical attitude and habit* comes first. A conscious setting forth of the method logically adapted for reaching an end is possible only after the result has first been reached by unconscious and tentative methods. Such conscious setting forth of the method is valuable when a review of the method that achieved success in a given case will throw light upon a new similar case. The ability to fasten upon and single out (abstract, analyze) those features of one experience that are logically best is hindered by premature insistence upon their explicit formulation. Repeated use is what gives a *method* definiteness; given this definiteness, precipitation into formulated statement should follow naturally. But because teachers find that the things that they themselves best understand are marked off and defined in clear-cut ways, our schoolrooms are pervaded with the superstition that children are to *begin* with crystallized formulae of method.

As analysis is conceived to be a sort of picking to pieces, so synthesis is thought to be a sort of physical piecing together. When it is so imagined, it too becomes a mystery. In fact, synthesis takes place wherever we grasp the bearing of facts on a conclusion or of a principle on facts. As analysis is *emphasis*, so synthesis is *placing*; the one causes the emphasized fact or property to stand out as significant; the other puts what is selected in its *context*, its connection with what is signified. It unites it with some other meaning to give both increased significance. When quicksilver was linked to iron, tin, etc., as a *metal*, all these objects obtained new intellectual value. Every judgment is analytic in so far as it involves discernment, discrimination, marking off the trivial from the important, the irrelevant from what points to a conclusion; and it is synthetic in so far as it leaves the mind with an inclusive situation within which selected facts are placed.

ANALYSIS AND SYNTHESIS IN EDUCATIONAL PROCEDURE

Educational methods that pride themselves on being exclusively analytic or exclusively synthetic are (so far as they carry out their boasts) incompatible with normal operations of judgment. Discussions have taken place, for example, as to whether the teaching of geography should be analytic or synthetic. The synthetic method is supposed to begin with the partial, limited portion of the earth's surface already familiar to the pupil, and then gradually piece on adjacent regions (the county, the country, the continent, and so on) till an idea of the entire globe is reached, or of the solar system that includes the globe. The analytic method is supposed to begin with the physical whole, the solar system or globe, and to work down through its constituent portions till the immediate environment is reached. The underlying conceptions here deal with physical wholes and physical parts. As a matter of fact, we cannot assume that the portion of the earth already familiar to the child is such a definite object, mentally, that he can safely start with and from his present idea of it. His knowledge of it is misty and vague as well as incomplete. Accordingly, mental progress will involve analysis of *it*—emphasis of features that are significant till they will stand out clearly. Moreover, his own locality is not sharply marked off, neatly bounded, and measured. His experience of it is already an experience that involves sun, moon, and stars as parts of the scene he surveys; it involves a changing horizon line as he moves about. In short, even his more limited and local experience involves far-reaching factors that take his imagination out beyond his own street and village. Connection, relationship with a larger whole, is already involved. But understanding of these relations is inadequate, vague, incorrect. He needs to define the features of the local environment in order to clarify and enlarge his conceptions of the larger geographical scene to which they belong. At the same time, not till he has grasped the larger scene will many of even the commonest features of his local environment become intelligible. Analysis leads to synthesis, while synthesis perfects analysis. As the pupil grows in comprehension of the vast complicated earth in its setting in space, he also sees more definitely the meaning of familiar local details. This intimate interaction between selective emphasis and interpretation through a context of what is selected is found wherever reflection proceeds normally. Hence the folly of trying to set analysis and synthesis over against each other.

Whenever we appraise, we both select and emphasize a particular quality or feature, and we link together things that, from an intellectual point of view, were previously separate. In appraising the value of land, the appraiser not only causes its monetary property to stand out, but he also places it in a scale of the land values of the whole community. Something of this sort happens in all judgment.

9.   Understanding: Ideas and Meanings

I. Ideas as Suggestions and Conjectures

We see something moving, hear a sound unexpectedly, smell an unusual odor, and we ask: What is it? What does what we see, hear, smell, *mean*? When we have found out what it signifies, a squirrel running, two persons conversing, an explosion of gunpowder, we say that we *understand*. To understand is to grasp meaning. Until we understand, we are, if we have curiosity, troubled, baffled, and hence moved to inquire. After we understand, we are, comparatively at least, intellectually at home. There is a time during our investigation when meaning is only suggested; when we hold it in suspense as a possibility rather than accept it as an actuality. Then the meaning is an *idea*. An idea thus stands midway between assured understanding and mental confusion and bafflement. While a meaning is *conditionally* accepted, accepted for use and trial, it is an idea, a supposal. When it is *positively* accepted, some object or event is understood.

IDEAS ARE ELEMENTS IN JUDGMENTS, TOOLS OF INTERPRETATION

An idea is thus not a unity like judgment, but rather a unit element in forming a judgment. We may compare a complete reflection to a paragraph; then the judgment is like a sentence in the structure of the paragraph, and an idea is like a word in the sentence. That ideas are necessary constituents of inference, we have already seen. Positive inference can be deferred and kept in process of development and test only while a meaning is *not* asserted and believed in. Moreover, ideas are indispensable to inference because they direct observations and regulate the collection and inspection of data. Without a guiding idea, facts would be heaped up like grains of sand; they would not be organized into intellectual unity. In discussing ideas we are not, accordingly, introducing a new topic, but are, as in the discussion of judgment, going into detail regarding an element in the whole already considered.

Let us take the instance of a blur in motion at a distance. We wonder what the *thing is*; that is, what the *blur means*. A man waving his arms, a friend beckoning to us, are suggested as possibilities. To accept at once either alternative is to arrest judgment. But if we treat what is suggested as only a suggestion, a supposition, a possibility, it becomes an idea, having the following traits: (*a*) As merely a suggestion, it is a conjecture, a guess, which in cases of greater dignity we call a "hypothesis" or a "theory." That is to say, it is *a possible, but as yet doubtful, mode of interpretation*. (*b*) Even though doubtful, it has an office to perform; namely, that of directing inquiry and examination. If this blur means a friend beckoning, then careful observation should show certain other traits. If it is a man driving unruly cattle, certain other traits should be found. Let us look and see if these traits are found. Taken merely as a doubt, an idea would paralyze inquiry. Taken merely as a certainty, it would arrest inquiry. Taken as a doubtful possibility, it affords a standpoint, a platform, a method of inquiry.

Ideas, then, are not genuine ideas unless they are tools with which to search for material to solve a problem. Suppose it is desired that the pupil grasp *the idea* of the sphericity of the earth. This is different from teaching him its sphericity *as a fact*. He may be shown (or reminded of) a ball or a globe and be told that the earth is round like those things; he may then be made to repeat that statement day after day till the shape of the earth and the shape of the ball are welded together in his mind. But he has not thereby acquired an *idea* of the earth's sphericity; at most, he has had a certain image of a sphere and has finally managed to image the earth after the analogy of his ball image. To grasp "sphericity" as an idea, the pupil must first have realized certain confusing features in observed facts and have had the idea of spherical shape suggested to him as a possible way of accounting for such phenomena as tops of masts being seen at sea after the hulls have disappeared, the shape of shadows of the earth in an eclipse, etc. Only by use as a method of interpreting data so as to give them fuller meaning does sphericity become a genuine idea. There may be a vivid image and no idea; or there may be a fleeting, obscure image and yet an idea, if that image performs the function of instigating and directing the observation and relation of facts.

Logical ideas are like keys that are shaped with reference to opening a lock. Pike, separated by a glass partition from the fish upon which they ordinarily prey, will—so it is said—butt their heads against the glass until it is literally beaten into them that they cannot get at their food. Animals learn (when they learn at all) by a "cut-and-try" method, by doing at random first one thing then another thing and continuing the things that happen to succeed. This procedure is followed by human beings when they do not operate on the basis of ideas, when they "monkey," to use a term derived from the random activity of one of the most intelligent of the lower animals. Action directed consciously by ideas—by suggested meanings accepted for the sake of experimenting with them—is the sole alternative both to bull-headed stupidity and to learning bought from that dear teacher—chance experience.

It is significant that many words for intellience suggest the idea of circuitous, evasive activity—often with a sort of intimation of even moral obliquity. The bluff, hearty man goes straight (and stupidly, it is implied) at some work. The intelligent man is cunning, shrewd (crooked), wily, subtle, crafty, artful, designing—the idea of indirection is involved.[1] An idea is a method of evading, circumventing, or surmounting through reflection obstacles that otherwise would have to be attacked by brute force. But ideas may lose their intellectual quality because of habitual use. When a child was first learning to recognize, in some hesitating suspense, cats, dogs, houses, marbles, trees, shoes, and other objects, ideas—conscious and tentative meanings—intervened as methods of identification. Now, as a rule, the thing and the meaning are so completely fused that there is no idea proper, but only automatic recognition. On the other hand, things which are

---

1. See Ward, *Psychic Factors of Civilization*, p. 153.

so familiar, so known already, that they are recognized without an intervening idea may appear in an unusual context and give rise to a problem that necessitates intermediate ideas in order that the object be understood. For example, a person drawing a room will be compelled to form a new idea of the corner of the room formed by the meeting of two walls and the ceiling, since now that corner has to be represented on a plane surface. A child has practical familiarity with squares and spheres in the context of daily life, as shapes of toys and utensils. But when they present themselves in a definitely geometrical connection, he is obliged to use mental effort to form ideas of them.

IDEAS ARE LOGICAL INSTRUMENTS, NOT PSYCHIC COMPOUNDS

It will be noted that an idea in its logical significance is something quite different from ideas as they are often treated in psychological texts. An idea, logically speaking, is not a faded perception of an object, nor is it a compound of a number of sensations. You would not get the peculiar meaning that is attached to, say, "chair" by having a mental picture of one. A savage might be able to form an image of poles and wires, and a layman of a complex scientific diagram. But unless the savage knew something about telegraphy, he would have no idea, or at least no correct idea, of the poles and wires, while the most accurate mental reproduction of the diagram would leave the layman totally without understanding of its meaning, and hence without an idea of it, even though he could list all *its* qualities one by one. The fact is that an idea, intellectually, cannot be defined by its structure, but only by its function and use. Whatever in a doubtful situation or undecided issue helps us to form a judgment and to bring inference to a conclusion by means of anticipating a possible solution is an idea, and nothing else is. It is an idea because of what it *does* in clearing up a perplexity or in harmonizing what is otherwise fragmentary, not because of its psychical make-up.

II. Things and Meanings

An idea normally terminates in giving understanding, so that an event or thing acquires meaning. A thing understood, a thing with a meaning, is different from both an idea, which is a doubtful and still unattached meaning, and from a mere brute, physical thing. I can stumble against something in the dark and get hurt without any understanding of what the thing is. So far, it is *merely* a thing, a something or other. If I get a light and investigate, I learn that the thing is a stool, or a coalhod, or a log of firewood. Now it is a *known* object, a thing understood, a thing with a meaning—all three being synonymous expressions.

TO UNDERSTAND IS TO GRASP MEANING

If a person comes suddenly into your room and calls out "Paper," various alternatives are possible. If you do not understand the English language, there is simply a noise that may act as a physical stimulus or irritant. But the noise is not an intellectual object; it does not have intellectual value. It is the mere brute thing just spoken of. If, first, the cry is the usual accompaniment of the delivery of the morning paper, the sound will have meaning, intellectual content; you will understand it. Or if, second, you are eagerly awaiting the receipt of some important document, you may assume that the cry means an announcement of its arrival. If, third, you understand the English language, but no context suggests itself from your habits and expectations, the *word* has meaning, but not the whole event. You are then perplexed and incited to think out, to hunt for, some explanation of the apparently meaningless occurrence. If you find something that accounts for the performance, it gets meaning; you come to understand it. As intelligent beings, we presume the existence of meaning, and its absence is an anomaly. Hence, if it should turn out that the person merely meant to inform you that there was a scrap of paper on the sidewalk, or that paper existed somewhere in the universe, you would think him crazy or yourself the victim of a stupid joke. To grasp the meaning of a thing, an event, or a situation is to see it in its *relations* to other things: to note how it operates or functions, what consequences follow from it, what causes it, what uses it can be put to. In contrast, what we have called the brute thing, the thing without meaning to us, is something whose relations are not grasped.

Since all knowing, including all scientific inquiry, aims at clothing things and events with meaning—at understanding them,—it always proceeds by taking the thing inquired into out of its isolation. Search is continued until the thing is discovered to be a related part in some larger whole. Thus a piece of rock may be understood by referring it to a sedimentary stratum known to have been formed under certain conditions, or a suddenly appearing light in the heavens may be understood when identified as the return of Halley's comet. Suppose that the rock has peculiar markings on it. They may be contemplated purely esthetically, as curiosities. But they may arouse inquiry. If so, the resulting investigation will have for its purpose the removal of the apparent isolation, the non-connectedness, of the markings. Finally, they are explained as glacial scratches. They no longer stand alone. They have been brought into connection with a past era of the earth's history in which great masses of slow-moving ice descended into regions now temperate, carrying with them grit and rocks that ground and scratched other rocks imbedded in place.

INTERACTION OF TWO MODES OF UNDERSTANDING

In these illustrations two types of grasp of meaning have been exemplified. When the English language is understood, the person grasps at once the meaning of "paper." He may not, however, see any meaning or sense in the performance as a whole. Similarly, the person identifies the object on sight as a stone; there is no secret, no mystery, no perplexity, about that. But he does not understand the markings on it. They have some meaning, but what is it? In one case, owing to familiar acquaintance, the thing and its meaning, up to a certain point, are one; in the other, the thing and its meaning are, temporarily at least, sundered, and meaning has to be sought in order to understand the thing. In one case understanding is direct, prompt, immediate; in the other, it is roundabout and delayed.

Most languages have two sets of words to express these two modes of understanding; one for the direct taking in or grasp of meaning, the other for its circuitous apprehension, thus: γνῶναι and εἰδέναι in Greek; *noscere* and *scire* in Latin; *kennen* and *wissen* in German; *connaître* and *savoir* in French; while in English *to be acquainted with* and *to know of or about* have been suggested as equivalents.[2] Now, our intellectual life consists of a peculiar interaction between these two types of understanding. All judgment, all reflective inference, presupposes some lack of understanding, a partial absence of meaning. We reflect in order that we may get hold of the full and adequate significance of what happens. Nevertheless, *something* must be already understood, the mind must be in possession of some meaning that it has mastered, or else thinking is impossible. We think in order to grasp meaning, but none the less every extension of knowledge makes us aware of blind and opaque spots, where with less knowledge all had seemed obvious and natural. A scientist brought into a new district will find many things that he does not understand, while the native savage or rustic will be wholly oblivious to any meanings beyond those directly apparent. Some Indians brought to a large city remained stolid at the sight of mechanical wonders of bridge, trolley, and telephone, but were held spellbound by the sight of workmen climbing poles to repair wires. Increase of the store of meanings makes us conscious of new problems, while only through translation of the new perplexities into what is already familiar and plain do we understand or solve these problems. This is the constant spiral movement of knowledge.

INTELLECTUAL PROGRESS A RHYTHM

Our progress in genuine knowledge always consists *in part in the discovery of something not understood in what had previously been taken for granted as plain, obvious, matter-of-course, and in part in using meanings that are directly grasped as instruments for getting hold of obscure and doubtful meanings.* No object is so familiar, so obvious, so commonplace that it may

2. James, *Principles of Psychology*, vol. I, p. 221. To *know* and to *know that* are perhaps more precise equivalents; compare "I know him" and "I know *that* he has gone home." The former expresses a fact simply; for the latter, evidence might be demanded and supplied.

not unexpectedly present, in a novel situation, some problem, and thus arouse reflection in order to understand it. No object or principle is so strange, peculiar, or remote that it may not be dwelt upon till its meaning becomes familiar—taken in on sight without reflection. We may come to *see, perceive, recognize, grasp, seize, lay hold of* principles, laws, abstract truths—*i.e.*, to understand their meaning in an immediate fashion. Our intellectual progress consists, as has been said, in a rhythm of direct understanding—technically called *ap*prehension—with indirect, mediated understanding—technically called *com*prehension.

III. The Process by Which Things Acquire Meaning

The first problem that comes up in connection with direct understanding is how a store of directly recognized meanings is built up. How do we learn to view things on sight as significant members of a situation or as having, as a matter of course, specific meanings? Our chief difficulty in answering this question lies in the thoroughness with which the lesson of familiar things has been learned. Thought can more easily traverse an unexplored region than it can undo what has been so thoroughly done as to be ingrained in unconscious habit. We apprehend chairs, tables, books, trees, horses, clouds, stars, rain, so promptly and directly that it is hard to realize that once these objects were mere brute things, as alien to our understanding as the sounds of the Choctaw language would be if we now suddenly heard them.

VAGUE WHOLES ARE ANTECEDENT TO UNDERSTANDING

In an often quoted passage, Mr. James has said: "The baby, assailed by eyes, ears, nose, skin, and entrails at once, feels it all as one great blooming, buzzing confusion."[3] Mr. James is speaking of a baby's world taken as a whole; the description, however, is equally applicable to the way any new thing strikes an adult, so far as the thing is really new and

3. *Principles of Psychology*, vol. I, p. 488.

strange. To the traditional "cat in a strange garret," everything is blurred and confused; the usual marks that label things so as to separate them from one another are lacking. Foreign languages that we do not understand always seem jabberings, babblings, in which it is impossible to fix a definite, clear-cut, individualized group of sounds. The countryman in the crowded city street, the landlubber at sea, the ignoramus in sport at a contest between experts in a complicated game, are instances. Put an unexperienced man in a factory, and at first the work seems to him a meaningless medley. All strangers of another race proverbially look alike to the visiting foreigner. Only gross differences of size or color are perceived by an outsider in a flock of sheep, each of which is perfectly individualized to the shepherd. A diffusive blur and indiscriminate shifting characterize what we do not understand. The problem of the acquisition of meaning by things, or (stated in another way) of forming habits of simple apprehension, is thus the problem of introducing (*a*) *definiteness*, or *distinction* and (*b*) *consistency*, *coherence*, *constancy*, or *stability* of meaning into what is otherwise vague and wavering.

PRACTICAL RESPONSES CLARIFY THE VAGUE

The acquisition of definiteness and of consistency of meanings is derived primarily from practical activities. By rolling an object, the child makes its roundness appreciable; by bouncing it, he singles out its elasticity; by lifting it, he makes weight its conspicuous distinctive factor. Not through the senses, but by means of the reaction, the responsive adjustment, is an impression given a character marked off from qualities that call out unlike reactions. Children, for example, are usually quite slow in apprehending differences in color. Differences from the standpoint of the adult so glaring that it is impossible not to note them are recognized and recalled by the young with great difficulty. Doubtless colors do not all *feel* alike, but there is no intellectual recognition of what constitutes the difference. The redness or greenness or blueness of the object does not call out a reaction that is sufficiently peculiar to give prominence or distinction to the color trait. Gradually, however, certain characteristic habitual responses associate themselves with certain things; the white becomes the sign, say, of milk and sugar, to which the child reacts favorably; blue becomes the sign of a dress that the child likes to wear, and so on; and the distinctive reactions tend to single out color qualities from other things in which they had been submerged.

Take another example. We have little difficulty in distinguishing from one another rakes, hoes, plows and harrows, shovels and spades. Each has its own associated characteristic use and function. A student of botany or chemistry may have, however, great difficulty in recalling the difference between serrate and dentate, ovoid and obovoid, in the shapes and edges of leaves, or between acids in *ic* and in *ous*. There is some difference; but just what? Or, he knows what the difference is; but which is which? Variations in form, size, color, and arrangement of parts have much less to do, and the uses, purposes, and functions of things and of their parts much more to do, with distinctness of character and meaning than we should be likely to think. What misleads us is the fact that the qualities of form, size, color, and so on, are *now* so distinct that we fail to see that the problem is precisely to account for the way in which they originally obtained their definiteness and conspicuousness. As long as we sit passive before objects, they are not distinguished out of the vague blur that swallows them all. Differences in the pitch and intensity of sounds leave behind a different feeling, but until we assume different attitudes toward them, or *do* something special in reference to them, their vague difference cannot be *intellectually* gripped and retained.

ILLUSTRATIONS FROM DRAWING AND LANGUAGE

Children's drawings afford a further exemplification of the same principle. Perspective does not exist, for the child's interest is not in *pictorial representation*, but in the *values* of the things represented; and while perspective is essential to the former, it is no part of the characteristic use and function of the things themselves. The house is drawn with transparent walls, because the rooms, chairs, beds, people inside, are the important things in the house-meaning; smoke always comes out of the chimney—otherwise, why have a chimney at all? At Christmas time, the stockings may be drawn almost as large as the house or even so large that they have to be put outside of it—in any case, it is the scale of values in use that furnishes the scale for their qualities. The drawings are diagrammatic reminders of these values, not impartial records of physical and sensory qualities. One of the chief difficulties felt by most persons in learning the art of pictorial representation is that habitual uses and results of use have become so intimately read into the character of things that it is practically impossible to shut them out at will.

The acquiring of meaning by sounds, in virtue of which they become words, is perhaps the most striking illustration that can be found of the way in which mere sensory stimuli acquire definiteness and constancy of meaning and are thereby themselves defined and interconnected for purposes of recognition. Language is a specially good example because there are hundreds or even thousands of words in which meaning is now so thoroughly consolidated with physical qualities as to be directly understood. In the case of words it is easier to recognize that this connection has been gradually and laboriously acquired than in the case of physical objects, such as chairs, tables, buttons, trees, stones, hills, flowers, and so on, where it seems as if the union of intellectual meaning with physical fact were aboriginal. It now seems to be thrust upon us rather than acquired through active explorations. But in the case of the meaning of words, we see readily that it is by making sounds and noting the results that follow, by listening to the sounds of others and watching the activities that accompany them, that a given sound finally becomes the stable bearer of a meaning.

MEANING AND CONTEXT

In the case of the meaning of words, we are aware by watching children and by our own experience in learning French or German that happenings, like sounds, which originally were devoid of significance acquire meaning by use, and that this use always involves a *context*. With children just learning to understand and use speech, the context is largely that of objects and acts. A child associates *hat* with putting something on his head when he is going outdoors; *drawer* with pulling something out of a table, etc. Single words, because of the direct presence of a context of actions performed with objects, then have the force that complete sentences have to an older person. Gradually other words that originally gained meaning by use in a context of overt actions become capable of supplying the context, so that the mind can dispense with the context of things and deeds. Speaking in sentences marks obviously a *linguistic* gain. But the more important matter is that it shows a person has made a great *intellectual* advance. He can now think by putting together verbal signs of things that are not present to the senses and are not accompanied by any overt actions on his part. As he understands similar combinations made by others, he has a new resource that extends his otherwise narrow personal experience indefinitely. When he learns to read, arbitrary marks on paper acquire meaning for him, and he gains possession of the means of still further extending his experience so as to include what others, far remote from him in space and time, have experienced.

As was indicated a short time ago, it is not easy to grasp the fact that things had at first no significance in our experience, and that significance was acquired in their case, as in that of sounds, by entering into a context of use, by bringing help and enjoyment to us—articles of food, furniture, and wearing apparel,—or by bringing harm and suffering—like fire approached too closely, pins that scratch, hammers that hit fingers instead of nails.

Take, for example, a little spark of light appearing at night in the heavens, and compare the original mere sight of it with the discriminating and extensive knowledge of it that the expert astronomer has. He identifies it, say, as planet, asteroid, satellite, or fixed star that is the sun of some other system. Each one of these things carries an immense store of meanings with it—distance, rate of movement, chemical composition, indeed all the things that one finds in a bulky volume upon astronomy. The change from a mere spark to an immensely significant object illustrates the acquisition of meaning which has taken place in the case of everything that we understand or know. It illustrates also the fact that the acquisition of ability to understand (which is the same as the acquisition of significance by things) is immensely furthered by language and by elaboration of a series of meanings [4] and through reasoning. This latter process is itself dependent upon

4. See page 204.

possession of some kind of linguistic sign system—for we must remember that mathematical symbols are also a kind of language.

THE MEANS-CONSEQUENCE RELATION AND ITS EDUCATIONAL SIGNIFICANCE

We may sum up by stating that things gain meaning when they are used as *means to bring about consequences* (or as means to prevent the occurrence of undesired consequences), or as standing for *consequences* for which we have to discover *means*. The relation of *means-consequence* is the centre and heart of all understanding. The operations by which things become understood as chairs, tables, shoes, hats, food, illustrate the means-consequence relation from the "means" side. The relation beginning with the "consequence," or result-sought, side is illustrated in any invention. Edison thought of producing light by the use of electricity; he then had to discover the conditions of things and relations that would produce it—the means for it. The same obtained with Langley and the Wright brothers after they conceived the idea, as a desired end, of a machine to fly in the air. It is illustrated in all cases of ordinary planning. We think of something needful or desirable, and then we have to seek out materials and methods for bringing it to pass. Every time we have to solve a problem of this kind, things enter into the means-consequence relation and in doing so take on added meaning, just as carbon filaments obtained a new significance through the production of electric light, and as gasoline, once almost a waste by-product, secured new meaning when the internal-combustion engine was invented.

The educational bearing of this principle is almost too obvious for mention. One of the chief causes for failure in school to secure that gain in ability to understand that is a precious educational result is the neglecting to set up the conditions for active use as a means in bringing consequences to pass—the neglecting to provide projects that call out the inventiveness and ingenuity of pupils in proposing aims to realize, or finding means to realize, consequences already thought of. All routine and all externally dictated activity fail to develop ability to understand, even though they promote skill in external doing. Too many so-called "problems," in reality assigned tasks, call at best simply for a kind of mechanical dexterity in applying set rules and manipulating symbols. In short, there is a challenge to understanding only when there is either a desired consequence for which means have to be found by inquiry, or things (including symbols in the degree in which experience has matured) are presented under conditions where reflection is required to see what consequences can be effected by their use.

It is assumed too frequently that subject matter is understood when it has been stored in memory and can be reproduced upon demand. The net outcome of our discussion is that nothing is really known except in so far as it is understood.

10. Understanding: Conception and Definition

I. The Nature of Conceptions

In the preceding chapter we discussed meaning from two points of view, and we suggested a third aspect of it that we shall consider more fully in this chapter. The two aspects that were discussed were (1) meaning as doubtful, as a hypothetical possibility; in short as an *idea* (which, as was pointed out, is not a mere psychological complex but is an object or situation that has a status of being *supposed* instead of being accepted), and (2) meaning as a property of things and events. It was shown in that connection how things *acquire* meaning and how finally meaning is so consolidated with a thing that we do not dream of separating the thing from its significance.

THEY ARE ESTABLISHED MEANINGS

The aspect of meaning that was indicated in passing is the fact that an idea, after it has been used as a guide to observation and action, may be confirmed and so acquire an accepted status on its own behalf. Afterwards it is employed, not tentatively and conditionally, but with assurance as an instrumentality of understanding and explaining things that are still uncertain and perplexing. These established meanings, taken to be secure and warranted, are *conceptions*. They are means of judgment because they are *standards of reference*. They may be best described as "standardized meanings." Every common noun that is familiar and so well understood in itself that it can be used to judge other things expresses a concept. Table, stone, sunset, grass, animal, moon, and on through the list of common nouns that are solid and dependable, are concepts in their meaning. We see an object that looks strange; we are told that it is the kind of bed used by a certain folk. The thing in question is no longer unfamiliar in meaning; to us its significance is settled.

THEY ENABLE US TO GENERALIZE

Concepts enable us to *generalize*, to extend and carry over our understanding from one thing to another. If we know what "bed" means in general, we at least can tell what *kind* or what *sort* of thing the individual thing is. It is plain that conceptions, since they represent the whole class or set of things, economize our intellectual efforts tremendously. Sometimes of course we are especially interested in the peculiar traits of an object, in what is unique about it, what makes it an *individual*. But for practical purposes it is often enough to know what *kind* of thing it is; knowing that fact, we can bring into play the habits of thought and behavior that belong to every member of the entire class. The concept calls into play whatever is appropriate to a large number of cases previously known, thus freeing thought from preoccupation with finding out what *this* is.

THEY STANDARDIZE OUR KNOWLEDGE

Conceptions *standardize* our knowledge. They introduce solidity into what would otherwise be formless, and *permanence* into what would otherwise be shifting. If pounds arbitrarily changed their weight and foot rules their length while we were using them, weighing and measuring would, obviously, amount to nothing. What would it signify to say that a piece of cloth was a yard and a half wide, or that a bulk of sugar weighed twenty pounds? The standard of reference must remain the same to be of any use. The concept signifies that a meaning has been stabilized and remains the same in different contexts. Sometimes when persons are discussing a controversial matter, the argument gets confused and the debaters misled because, as they go along, they unconsciously shift the meanings of the terms they use. Reflection and new discoveries may, to be sure, change the meaning of an old concept, just as people may change from the foot-pound system of measurement to the metric system. But they should know what they are about and deliberately note that they are using a changed meaning unless they are to get hopelessly mixed up.

When persons are said to have come to an understanding with each other, it is meant that they have arrived at an *agreement* or *settlement* of some affair or issue that has been under discussion between them. This fact indicates that standardized and stable meanings are a condition of effective communication. When two persons speak languages that are not mutually understood, they can still communicate to some extent, provided there are gestures which have *identical meanings for both parties*. Indeed, the social necessity of meanings that are the same for two persons in spite of differences in their experiences and their conditions of life is one of the chief forces in standardizing meanings. After they are socially stabilized, an individual has the ability to keep his own thinking steady because some of his thoughts remain constant in what they refer to; "chair" always signifies the same; so do "sun," "water," "earth," etc. Each of our entire list of common nouns always refers to the same objects, in spite of differences of place, time, and other conditions of experience.

THEY HELP IDENTIFY THE UNKNOWN AND SUPPLEMENT THE SENSIBLY PRESENT

Stating the matter somewhat differently, conceptions, or standard meanings, are instruments of (*a*) identification, (*b*) supplementation, and (*c*) placing an object in a system. Suppose a little speck of light hitherto unseen is detected in the heavens. Unless there is a store of meanings to fall back upon in reasoning, that speck of light will remain just what it is to the senses—a mere speck of light. For all that it leads to intellectually, it might as well be a mere irritation of the optic nerve. Given, however, the stock of meanings built up in prior experience, this speck of light is mentally attacked by means of appropriate concepts. Does it indicate asteroid, or comet, or a new-forming sun, or a nebula resulting from some cosmic collision or disintegration? Each of these conceptions has its own specific and differentiating characters, which are then sought for by minute and persistent inquiry. As a result, then, the speck is identified, we will say, as a comet. Through a standard meaning it gets identity and stability of character. Supplementation then takes place. All the known qualities of comets are read into this particular thing, even though they have not been as yet observed. All that the astronomers of the past have learned about the paths and structure of comets becomes available capital with which to interpret the speck of light. Finally, this comet-meaning is, itself, not isolated; it is a related portion of the whole system of astronomic knowledge. Suns, planets, satellites, nebulae, comets, meteors, star dust—all these conceptions have a certain mutuality of reference and interaction, and when the speck of light is identified as meaning a comet, it is at once adopted as a full member in this vast kingdom of beliefs.

Darwin, in an autobiographical sketch, says that when a youth he told the geologist, Sedgwick, of finding a tropical shell in a certain gravel pit. Thereupon Sedgwick said it must have been thrown there by some person, adding: "But if it were really embedded there, it would be the greatest misfortune to geology, because it would overthrow all that we know about the superficial deposits of the Midland Counties"—since these were glacial. And then Darwin adds: "I was then utterly astonished at Sedgwick not being delighted at so wonderful a fact as a tropical shell being found near the surface in the middle of England. Nothing before had made me thoroughly realise *that science consists in grouping facts so that general laws or conclusions may be drawn from them.*" This instance (which might, of course, be duplicated from any branch of science) indicates how scientific notions make explicit the systematizing tendency involved in all use of concepts.

THE EDUCATIONAL SIGNIFICANCE OF CONCEPTS

It follows that it would be impossible to overestimate the educational importance of arriving at conceptions: that is, of meanings that are *general* because applicable in a great variety of different instances in spite of their difference; that are constant, uniform, or self-identical in what they refer to, and that are standardized, known points of reference by which to get our bearings when we are plunged into the strange and unknown.

Young children cannot of course acquire and employ the same conceptions that persons of riper experience use. But at *every* stage of development, each lesson, in order to be educative, should lead up to a certain amount of conceptualizing of impressions and ideas. Without this conceptualizing or intellectualizing, nothing is gained that can be carried over to the better understanding of new experiences. The *deposit* is what counts, educationally speaking. No amount of transient interest, however absorbing and exciting it may be, can compensate for failure to achieve an intellectual deposit.

The very importance of concepts has led, however, to great mistakes in the conduct of teaching. What we earlier termed the false use of the "logical"[1] had its roots in the belief that somehow definite and general meanings, or concepts, can be presented to pupils and absorbed by them *ready-made*, thus promoting the rapidity and efficiency of acquisition of knowledge. In consequence, failure to observe the conditions that are essential for the formation of conceptions left most pupils with only *verbal* formulae. Concepts were often presented that were so remote from the understanding and experience of students as to be positively confusing in their artificiality.

The reaction of education in experimental schools against the arbitrary imposition of indigestible material has often, however, been a reaction to the opposite extreme. A variety of worthwhile experiences and activities with real materials is introduced, but pains are not taken to make sure that the activities terminate in that which makes them *educationally* worth while, as distinct from an agreeable passing of the time—namely, the achievement of a fairly definite *intellectualization* of the experience. This intellectualization is the deposit of an *idea* that is both definite and general. Education in its intellectual aspect and getting an idea from what is experienced are synonymous. What does having an experience amount to unless, as it ceases to exist, it leaves behind an increment of meaning, a better understanding of something, a clearer future plan and purpose of action: in

1. See page 178.

short, an idea? With respect to teaching there is no more important topic than the question of the way in which genuine concepts are formed. To that question we now turn.

II. How Conceptions Arise

THEY ARE NOT FORMED BY EXTRACTING COMMON TRAITS FROM READY-MADE OBJECTS

It is convenient in discussing this question to begin with the negative side, with the mistaken character of some current beliefs about the way in which conceptions come into existence. They are *not* derived by taking a number of things, each of which is already well understood and definite in meaning, and then comparing them one with another, point by point, till all different qualities are excluded and there remains a core of what is common to all. The origin of concepts is sometimes described to be as if a child began with a lot of different particular things, say particular dogs: his own Fido, his neighbor's Carlo, his cousin's Tray. Having all these different objects before him, he analyzes them into a lot of different qualities, say (*a*) color, (*b*) size, (*c*) shape, (*d*) number of legs, (*e*) quantity and quality of hair, (*f*) foods eaten, and so on; and then strikes out all the unlike qualities (such as color, size, shape, hair), retaining traits, such as quadruped and domesticated, which they all have in common.

THEY BEGIN WITH EXPERIENCES

As a matter of fact, the child begins with whatever significance he has got out of some one dog he has seen, heard, and played with. He carries over from his experience of this one object to his subsequent experiences expectations of characteristic modes of behavior: he expects them before they show themselves. He assumes this attitude of anticipation whenever an object gives him any excuse for it. Thus he may call cats "little dogs" or horses "big dogs." But finding that other expected traits and modes of behavior are not fulfilled, he is forced to throw out certain traits from the dog-meaning, while by contrast some other traits are selected and emphasized. As he further applies the meaning to other animals, the dog-meaning gets still further defined and refined. He does not begin with a lot of ready-made objects from which he extracts a common meaning; he tries to apply in every new experience whatever result of his old experience will help him understand and deal with it.

THEY BECOME MORE DEFINITE WITH USE

It is not true that the child's idea of each individual dog is clear and definite to begin with, and that his own dog is perceived by him with its full equipment of distinct qualities. Rather his original idea of Fido is vague and pulpy, wavering, as long as Fido is the only dog (and much more so if the only animal) he knows. By observing the family cat, he is led to discriminate the particular qualities that characterize each of them. As he makes acquaintance with other animals, the horse, pig, etc., the definite properties that belong to a dog are still further demarcated. Thus, even without much comparison with other *dogs*, a dog concept is gradually built up. In just the extent to which he is aware of the qualities that make his Fido a *dog*, rather than a cat, horse, or any other animal, he has a standardized point of reference for assimilating and sorting out other animals as he makes acquaintance with them. During the whole process he has been trying to fit his idea, vague or definite according to his stage of experience, on all animals that are at all similar to dogs, applying it when he can, becoming aware of differences whenever it won't fit. By these processes, his idea gets body, steadiness, distinction; it becomes a concept.

THEY BECOME GENERAL WITH USE

By the same processes, a vague, more or less formless idea acquires *generality*. Conceptions, that is to say, are general because of use and application, not because of their ingredients. The view that a conception originates in an impossible sort of analysis has its counterpart in the idea that it is made up out of all the like elements that remain after dissection of a number of individuals. Not so; the moment a meaning is gained, it is a working tool of further apprehensions, an instrument of understanding other things. Thereby the meaning is *extended* as well as defined. Generality resides in application to the comprehension of new cases, not in the constituent parts of a notion. A collection of traits left as the common residuum, the *caput mortuum*, of a million objects, would be merely a collection, an inventory or aggregate, not a *general idea.* Any striking trait emphasized in an experience that afterward serves as an aid in understanding some other experience becomes, in virtue of that application, in so far general.

What has just been said may be compared with the earlier statements about analysis and synthesis.[2] The analysis that results in giving an idea the solidity and definiteness of a concept is simply emphasis upon that which gives a clew for dealing with some uncertainty. If a child identifies a dog seen at a distance by the way in which the animal wags its tail, then that particular trait, which may never have been *consciously* singled out before, becomes distinct—it is analyzed out of its vague submergence in the animal as a whole. The only difference between such a case and the analysis effected by a scientific inquirer in chemistry or botany is that the latter is alert for clews that will serve for the purpose of sure identification in the *widest possible area* of cases; he wants to find the signs by which he can identify an object as one of a definite kind or class even should it present itself under very unusual circumstances and in an obscure and disguised form. The idea that the selected trait is already plain to the mind and then is merely isolated from other traits equally definite puts the cart before the horse. It is selection as evidence or as a clew that gives a trait distinctness it did not possess before.

Synthesis is the operation that gives extension and generality to an idea, as analysis makes the meaning distinct. Synthesis is correlative to analysis. As soon as any quality is definitely discriminated and given a special meaning of its own, the mind at once looks around for other cases to which that meaning may be applied. As it is applied, cases that were previously separated in meaning become assimilated, identified, in their significance. They now belong to the same *kind* of thing. Even a young child,

2. See pages 216–218.

as soon as he masters the meaning of a word, tries to find occasion to use it; if he gets the idea of a cylinder, he sees cylinders in stove pipes, logs, etc. In principle this is not different from Newton's procedure in the story about the origin in his mind of the concept of gravitation. Having the idea suggested by the falling of an apple, he at once extended it in imagination to the moon as something also tending to fall towards the earth, and then to the movements of the planets in relation to the sun, to the movement of the ocean in the tides, etc. In consequence of this application of an idea that was discriminated, made definite in some one case, to other events, a large number of phenomena that previously were believed to be disconnected from one another were integrated into a consistent system. In other words, there was a comprehensive synthesis.

It would be a great mistake, however, as just indicated, to confine the idea of synthesis to important cases like Newton's generalization. On the contrary, when any one carries over any meaning from one object to another object that had previously seemed to be of a different kind, synthesis occurs. It is synthesis when a lad associates the gurgling that takes place when water is poured into what he had thought was an empty bottle with the existence and pressure of air; when he learns to interpret the siphoning of water and the sailing of a boat in connection with the same fact. It is synthesis when things themselves as different as clouds, meadow, brook, and rocks are so brought together as to be composed into a picture. It is synthesis when iron, tin, and mercury are conceived to be of the same kind in spite of individual differences.

III. Definition and Organization of Meanings

THE HARMFUL CONSEQUENCES OF VAGUENESS

A being that cannot understand at all is at least protected from *mis*-understandings. But beings that get knowledge by means of inferring and interpreting, by judging what things signify in relation to one another, are constantly exposed to the danger of *mis*-apprehension, *mis*-understanding, *mis*-taking—taking of a thing amiss. A constant source of mis-understanding and mistake is indefiniteness of meaning. Because of vagueness of meaning we misunderstand other people, things, and ourselves; because of ambiguity we distort and pervert. Conscious distortion of meaning may be enjoyed as nonsense; erroneous meanings, if clear-cut, may be followed up and got rid of. But vague meanings are too gelatinous to offer matter for analysis and too pulpy to afford support to other beliefs. They evade testing and responsibility. Vagueness disguises the unconscious mixing together of different meanings, and facilitates the substitution of one meaning for another, and covers up the failure to have any precise meaning at all. It is the ab-original logical sin—the source from which flow most bad intellectual consequences. Totally to eliminate indefiniteness is impossible; to reduce it in extent and in force requires sincerity and vigor.

MEANING AS INTENSION AND AS EXTENSION

To be clear or perspicuous, a meaning must be detached, single, self-contained, homogeneous as it were, throughout. The technical name for any meaning that is thus individualized is *intension*. The process of arriving at such units of meaning (and of stating them when reached) is *definition*. The intension of the terms "man," "river," "honesty," "supreme court," is the meaning that *exclusively* and *characteristically* attaches to those terms. This meaning is set forth in *definition* of these units of meaning.

The test of the distinctness of a meaning is that it successfully marks off a group of things that exemplify the meaning from other groups, especially from those objects that convey nearly allied meanings. The river-meaning (or character) must serve to *designate* the Rhone, the Rhine, the Mississippi, the Hudson, the Wabash, in spite of their varieties of place, length, quality of water; and must be such as *not* to suggest ocean currents, ponds, or brooks. This use of a meaning to mark off and group together a variety of distinct existences constitutes its *extension*.

As definition sets forth intension, so division (or the reverse process, classification) expounds extension. Intension and extension, definition and division, are clearly correlative; in language previously used, *intension* is meaning as a principle of identifying particulars; extension is the group of particulars identified and distinguished. Meaning, as extension, would be wholly in the air or unreal, did it not point to some object or group of objects; while objects would be as isolated and independent intellectually as they seem to be spatially, were they not bound into groups or classes on the basis of characteristic meanings they suggest and exemplify in a uniform way.

Together, definition and division put us in possession of definite meanings and also indicate the group of objects to which they refer, the *kind* of things indicated and its various subclasses. They typify the fixation and the organization of meanings. In the degree in which the meanings of any set of experiences are so cleared up as to serve as principles for grouping those experiences in relation to one another, that set of particulars becomes a science; *i.e.*, definition and classification are the marks of a science, as distinct from unrelated heaps of miscellaneous information and from habits that introduce coherence into our experience without our being aware of their operation.

THREE TYPES OF DEFINITIONS

Definitions are of three types, *denotative*, *expository*, *scientific*. Of these, the first and third are logically important, while the expository type is socially and pedagogically important as an intervening step.

a. Denotative. A blind man can never have an adequate understanding of the meaning of *color* and *red*; a seeing person can acquire the knowledge only by having certain things designated in such a way as to fix attention upon some of their qualities. This method of delimiting a meaning by calling out a certain attitude toward objects may be called *denotative*, or *indicative*. It is required for all sense qualities—sounds, tastes, colors—and equally for all emotional and moral qualities. The meanings of "honesty," "sympathy," "hatred," must be grasped by having them presented in an individual's first-hand experience. The reaction of educational reformers against linguistic and bookish training has always taken the form of demanding recourse to personal experience. However advanced the person is in knowledge and in scientific training, understanding of a new subject, or of a new aspect of an old subject, must always be through acts of experiencing directly or in imagination the existence of the quality in question.

b. Expository. Given a certain store of meanings that have been directly or denotatively marked out, language becomes a resource by which imaginative combinations and variations may be built up. A color may be defined to one who has not experienced it as lying between green and blue; a tiger may be defined (*i.e.*, the idea of it made more definite) by selecting some qualities from known members of the cat tribe and combining them with ideas of size and weight derived from other objects. Illustrations are of the nature of expository definitions; so are the accounts of meanings given in a dictionary. By taking better-known meanings and associating them, the attained store of meanings of the community in which one resides is put at one's disposal. But in themselves these definitions are second-hand and conventional; there is danger that instead of inciting one to effort after personal experiences that will exemplify and verify them, they will be accepted on authority as *substitutes* for direct observation and experiment.

c. Scientific. Even popular definitions serve as rules for identifying and classifying individuals, but the purpose of such identifications and classifications is mainly practical and social, not intellectual. To conceive the whale as a fish does not interfere with the success of whalers, nor does it prevent recognition of a whale when seen, while to conceive it not as a fish but as a mammal serves the practical end equally well, and also furnishes a much more valuable principle for scientific identification and classification. Popular definitions select certain fairly obvious traits as keys to classification. Scientific definitions select *conditions of causation, production, and generation* as their characteristic material. The traits used by the popular definition do not help us to understand why an object has its common meanings and qualities; they simply state the fact that it does have them. Causal and genetic definitions settle on the way an object is constructed as giving the key to its belonging to a certain *kind* of objects. They explain why it has its class or common traits on the basis of its manner of production.

If, for example, a layman of considerable practical experience were asked what he meant or understood by *metal*, he would probably reply in terms of the qualities useful in recognizing any given metal and in the arts. Smoothness, hardness, glossiness, and brilliancy, heavy weight for its size, would probably be included in his definition, because such traits enable us to identify specific things when we see and touch them; the serviceable properties of capacity for being hammered and pulled without breaking; of being softened by heat and hardened by cold, of retaining the shape and form given, of resistance to pressure and decay, would probably be included—whether or not such terms as "malleable" or "fusible" were used. Now a scientific conception, instead of using, even with additions, traits of this kind, determines meaning on a different basis. The present definition of metal is about like this: Metal means any chemical element that enters into combination with oxygen so as to form a base; *i.e.*, a compound that combines with an acid to form a salt. This scientific definition is founded, not on directly perceived qualities nor on directly useful properties, but on the *way in which certain things are causally related to other things*; *i.e.*, it denotes a relation. As chemical concepts become more and more those of relationships of interaction in constituting other substances, so physical concepts express more and more relations of operation: mathematical, functions of dependence and order of grouping; biological, relations of differentiation of descent, effected through adjustment of various environments; and so on through the sphere of the sciences. In short, our conceptions attain a maximum of definite individuality and of generality (or applicability) in the degree to which they show how things depend upon one another or influence one another, instead of expressing the qualities that objects possess statically. The ideal of a system of scientific conceptions is to attain continuity, freedom, and flexibility of transition in passing from any fact and meaning to any other; this demand is met in the degree in which we lay hold of the dynamic ties that hold things together in a continuously changing process—a principle that gives insight into mode of production or growth.

11. Systematic Method: Control of Data and Evidence

I. Method as Deliberate Testing of Facts and Ideas

Judgment, understanding, conception are all of them constituents of the reflective process in which a perplexing, confused, unsettled situation is transformed into one that is coherent, clear, and decided or settled. In discussing them we have introduced nothing new in principle but have amplified what was illustrated in the three cases set forth in Chapter 6 and analyzed in some detail in Chapter 7. We shall now return to the original account and utilize the added knowledge we have obtained to discuss the method of reflective activity when it is regulated in a technical and elaborate way. We saw in the first section of Chapter 7 that reflection is an operation in which facts on one side and meaning on the other are elicited through constant interaction with each other. Each newly discovered fact develops, tests, and modifies an idea, and every new idea and new shade of an idea lead to further inquiry, which brings to light new facts, modifying our understanding of facts previously observed.

The discussion in which we are now engaging accordingly has two sides. One side concerns method as it operates in gathering and testing the *data* that form the evidence upon which an inference must rest to be properly supported—method of control of observation and memory, which supply the facts upon which inference proceeds. The other side concerns the formation and development of method as it operates in arriving at the *ideas* that are used to interpret the data, to solve problems, and to elaborate and apply concepts. The two functions, as we have seen, accompany each other. The improved selection and discrimination of pertinent data gives a better clew to ideas that are fruitful when employed and to the tests to which they must be submitted. The improvement of ideas in turn stimulates the performance of new observations and the collection of new data.

THE NEED FOR SYSTEMATIZED METHOD

Method of a systematic sort is required in order to safeguard the operations by which we move from one to the other, from facts to ideas, and back again from ideas to the facts that will test them. Without adequate method a person grabs, as it were, at the first facts that offer themselves; he does not examine them to see whether they are truly facts or whether, even though they be real facts, they are relevant to the inference that needs to be made. On the other side, we are given to jumping at the first solution that occurs to us, accepting it as a conclusion without examination and test. We are given also to generalizing an idea far beyond support by evidence. We extend it to new cases without careful study to see whether these cases may not be so different as not to justify the generalization. Method is particularly needed in complex cases and cases of generalization, in order to safeguard us from falling into these errors.

We shall first give an illustration of the way in which the discovery of relevant facts on which to base, and by which to support and test, an inferred solution goes on in company with the formation and use of ideas to interpret the facts.

A man who has left his room in order finds it upon his return in a state of confusion, articles being scattered at random. Automatically, the notion comes to his mind that burglary would account for the disorder. He has not seen the burglars; their presence is not a fact of observation; it is a thought, an idea. The state of the room is a *fact*, certain, speaking for itself; the presence of burglars is a possibility that may explain the facts. Moreover, the man has no special burglar in mind. The state of his room is perceived and is particular, definite— exactly as it is; a burglar is inferred. But no particular individual is thought of; merely some indefinite, unspecified, member of a class.

The original fact, the room as it is first observed, does not by any means *prove* the fact of burglary. The latter conjecture may be correct, but evidence to justify accepting it positively is lacking. The total "fact" as given contains both too much and too little; too much, because there are many features in it that are irrelevant to inference, that are therefore *logically* superfluous. Too little, because the considerations that are crucial—that, if they were ascertained, would be decisive—do not appear on the surface. Thoughtful search for the *kind* of facts that are clews is therefore necessitated. If the illustration were followed out beyond the judgment as to whether there had been a burglary to the question of who the criminal was and how he was to be discovered and the crime brought home to him, the need for extensive and careful examination of the fact side of the case would be even clearer.

OBSERVATION VALUABLE WHEN GUIDED BY HYPOTHESES

This search needs guidance. If it is conducted purely at random a multitude of facts will be turned up, but they will be so unrelated that their very number will add to the difficulty of the case. It is quite possible for thinking to be swamped by the mere multiplicity and diversity of facts. The real problem is: What facts are *evidence* in this case? The search for evidential facts is best conducted when some suggested *possible* meaning is used as a guide in exploring facts, especially in instituting a hunt for some fact that would point conclusively to one explanation and exclude all others. So the person entertains various hypotheses. Besides burglary, there is the possibility that some member of the family had an urgent need to find some article and, being in a hurry, had not taken the time to put things in order again. There are children also in the family, and they are not above mischief on occasion. Each of these conjectured possibilities is developed to some extent. *If* it were a burglar, or an adult in a hurry, or mischief on the part of children, *then* certain features characteristic of each particular cause would be present. *If* it were a case of burglary, *then* articles of value would be missing. Guided by this idea, the person looks again, not any longer at the scene as a whole, but analytically, with reference to this one item. He finds jewelry gone; he finds that some silver articles have been twisted and bent, and left behind as merely plated wear. These data are incompatible with any hypothesis except burglary. Looking further, he finds data that are most naturally interpreted to mean that a window has been tampered with—a fact consistent only with the action of a burglar. Under any ordinary circumstances these data would give adequate evidence of the visit of a burglar; if the conditions were very unusual, there would be nothing but to continue thinking of further possibilities and looking for further facts as data by which to test them. The instance is taken from ordinary life. Scientific method represents the same sort of thing carried on with greater elaborateness, by means especially of instruments and apparatus devised for the purpose and of mathematical calculations.

II. The Importance of Method in Judging Data

From what has been said it is clear that the formation of the idea or hypothesis that is employed to interpret data and to unify them into a coherent situation is indirect. Fundamentally, suggestions just occur or do not occur, depending, as we have seen, on the state of culture and knowledge at the time; upon the discernment and experience and native genius of the individual; upon his recent activities; to some extent upon chance; for many of the most pregnant inventions and discoveries have come about almost accidentally, although these happy accidents never happen except to persons especially prepared by interest and prior thought. But while the original happening of a suggestion, whether it be brilliant or stupid, is not *directly* controlled, the acceptance and use of the suggestion is capable of control, given a person of a thoughtful habit of mind.

The primary method of control is that indicated in the illustration. The person who is confronted with the situation that has to be thought through returns upon, revises, extends, analyzes, and makes more precise and definite the facts of the case. He strives to convert them into just those data which will test the suggestions that occur to mind. This testing will take place, as in the burglary incident, by finding upon examination traits that are *incompatible* with some suggested possibility and consistent with some other. They are just what *should* be there in fact *if* that particular hypothesis is correct. The ideal of course is discovery of traits that could be present *only* upon a particular hypothesis.

This type of evidence can rarely be found in fact, but it is approximated by the methods of control of observation and collection of data that have been found to work well in scientific inquiry.

THE INTERRELATIONS OF OBSERVATION AND THOUGHT

It will be noted, then, that observation is not an operation that is opposed to thought or that is even independent of it. On the contrary, *thoughtful* observing is at least one half of thinking, the other half being the entertaining and elaboration of multiple hypotheses. Features that are glaringly conspicuous often need to be ignored; hidden traits need to be brought to light; obscure characteristics to be emphasized and cleared up.

Consider, for example, how a physician makes his diagnosis, his interpretation. If he is scientifically trained, he suspends—postpones—reaching a conclusion in order that he may not be led by superficial occurrences into a snap judgment. There are some facts that are given in an obvious way to his observation. But what is obvious may be, *when regarded as an evidential sign*, most misleading; the evidential facts, the real data, may show themselves only after a prolonged search involving artificial apparatus and a technique that expresses the methods found useful by a whole body of experts.

Conspicuous phenomena may forcibly suggest typhoid, but the physician avoids a conclusion or even any strong preference for this or that conclusion until he has both greatly *enlarged* the scope of his data and also rendered them more *minute*. He not only questions the patient as to his feelings and as to his acts prior to the disease, but by various manipulations with his hands (and with instruments made for the purpose) brings to light a large number of facts of which the patient is quite unaware. The state of temperature, respiration, and heart action is accurately noted, and their fluctuations from time to time are exactly recorded. Until this examination has worked *out* toward a wider collection and *in* toward a minuter scrutiny of details, inference is deferred.

REGULATIVE FEATURES OF
SCIENTIFIC METHOD

Scientific method includes, in short, *all the processes by which the observing and amassing of data are regulated with a view to facilitating the formation of explanatory conceptions and theories.* These devices are all directed toward selecting the precise facts to which weight and significance shall attach in forming suggestions or ideas. Specifically, this selective determination involves operations of (1) elimination by analysis of what is likely to be misleading and irrelevant, (2) emphasis of the important by collection and comparison of cases, and (3) deliberate construction of data by experimental variation.

ELIMINATION OF IRRELEVANT MEANINGS

1. It is a common saying that one must learn to discriminate between observed facts and judgments based upon them. Taken literally, such advice cannot be carried out; in every observed thing there is—if the thing have any meaning at all—some consolidation of meaning with what is sensibly and physically present, such that, if this were entirely excluded, what is left would have no sense. A says: "I saw my brother." The term *brother*, however, involves a relation that cannot be sensibly or physically observed; it is inferential in status. If A contents himself with saying, "I saw a man," the factor of classification, of intellectual reference, is less complex, but still exists. If, as a last resort, A were to say, "Anyway, I saw a colored object," some relationship, though more rudimentary and undefined, still subsists. Theoretically, it is possible that no object was there, only abnormal nerve stimulation. None the less, the advice to discriminate what is observed from what is inferred is sound practical advice. Its working import is that one should eliminate or exclude *those* inferences as to which experience has shown that there is greatest liability to error. This, of course, is a relative matter. Under ordinary circumstances no reasonable doubt would attach to the observation, "I see my brother"; it would be pedantic and silly to resolve this recognition back into a more elementary form. Under other circumstances it might be a per-

fectly genuine question as to whether A saw even a colored *thing*, or whether the color was due to a stimulation of the sensory optical apparatus (like "seeing stars" upon a blow) or to a disordered circulation. In general, the scientific man is one who knows that he is likely to be hurried to a conclusion and that part of this precipitancy is due to certain habits that tend to make him "read" certain meanings into the situation that confronts him, so that he must be on the lookout against errors arising from his interests, habits, and current preconceptions.

The technique of scientific inquiry thus consists in various processes that tend to exclude over-hasty "reading in" of meanings; devices that aim to give a purely "objective," unbiased rendering of the data to be interpreted. Flushed cheeks usually mean heightened temperature; paleness means lowered temperature. The clinical thermometer records automatically the actual temperature and hence checks up the habitual associations that might lead to error in a given case. All the instrumentalities of observation—the various -meters and -graphs and -scopes—fulfil a part of their scientific role in helping to eliminate meanings supplied because of habit, prejudice, the strong momentary preoccupation of excitement and anticipation, and by the vogue of existing theories. Photographs, phonographs, kymographs, actinographs, seismographs, plethysmographs, and the like, moreover, give records that are permanent, so that they can be employed by different persons, and by the same person in different states of mind; *i.e.*, under the influence of varying expectations and dominant beliefs. Thus purely personal prepossessions (due to habit, to desire, to after-effects of recent experience) may be largely eliminated. In ordinary language, the facts are *objectively*, rather than *subjectively*, determined. In this way tendencies to premature interpretation are held in check.

COLLECTION OF SUFFICIENT INSTANCES

2. Another important method of control consists in the multiplication of cases or instances. If I doubt whether a certain handful gives a fair sample or one representative, for purposes of judging value, of a whole carload of grain, I take a number of handfuls from various parts of the car and compare them. If they agree in quality, well and good; if they disagree, we try to get

enough samples so that when they are thoroughly mixed the result will be a fair basis for an evaluation. This illustration represents roughly the value of that aspect of scientific method that insists upon multiplying observations instead of basing the conclusion upon one or a few cases.

So prominent, indeed, is this aspect of method at a certain stage of its development that it is frequently treated as constituting induction. It is supposed that all controlled inference as to matters of fact is based upon collecting and comparing a number of like cases. Actually such comparison and collection is a secondary development within the process of securing a correct conclusion in some single case. If a man infers from one sample of grain as to the grade of wheat of the car as a whole, it is induction and, under certain circumstances, namely, if the entire bulk has been thoroughly mixed, it is a *sound* induction. Other cases are resorted to simply for the sake of rendering a suggested inference more guarded, and more probably correct. In like fashion, the reasoning that led up to the burglary idea in the instance already cited, the particulars upon which the general meaning (or relation) of burglary was grounded, were simply the sum total of the unlike items and qualities that made up the one case examined. Had this case presented very great obscurities and difficulties, recourse might *then* have been had to examination of a number of similar cases. But this comparison would not introduce scientific method into a process that was not previously of that character; it would only render inference more wary and adequate. *The object of bringing into consideration a multitude of cases is to facilitate the selection of the evidential or significant features upon which to base inference in some single case.*

UNLIKENESS AS IMPORTANT AS LIKENESS IN THESE INSTANCES

Accordingly, points of *unlikeness* are as important as points of *likeness* among the cases examined. *Comparison*, without *contrast*, does not amount to anything logically. In the degree in which other cases observed or remembered merely duplicate the case in question, we are no better off for purposes of inference than if we had permitted our single original fact to dictate a conclusion. In the case of various samples of grain, it is the fact that samples are *different*, at least as to the place of the car-load from which they are taken, that is important. Were it not for this difference, likeness in quality would be of no avail in control-ling inference.[1] If we are endeavoring to get a child to regulate his conclusions about the germination of a seed by taking into ac-count a number of instances, very little is gained if the conditions in all these instances closely approximate one another. But if one seed is placed in pure sand, another in loam, and another on blotting paper, and if in each case there are two conditions, one with and another without moisture, the unlike factors tend to throw into relief the factors that are significant (or "essential") for reaching a conclusion. Unless, in short, the observer takes care to have the differences in the observed cases as extreme as conditions allow, and unless he notes unlikenesses as carefully as likenesses, he has no way of determining the evidential force of the data that confront him.

Another way of bringing out this importance of unlikeness is the emphasis put by the scientist upon *negative* cases—upon in-stances that, it would seem, ought to fall into line but that, as a matter of fact, do not. Anomalies, exceptions, things that agree in most respects but disagree in some crucial point, are so impor-tant that many of the devices of scientific technique are designed purely to detect, record, and impress upon memory contrasting cases. Darwin remarked that, so easy is it to pass over cases that oppose a favorite generalization, he had made it a habit, not merely to hunt for contrary instances, but also to write down any exception he noted or thought of—as otherwise it was almost sure to be forgotten.

EXPERIMENTAL VARIATION OF CONDITIONS

3. We have already touched upon this factor of control of method, the one that is the most important of all wherever it is feasible. Theoretically, one sample case *of the right kind* will be as good a basis for an inference as a thousand cases; but cases of the right kind rarely turn up spontaneously. We have to search for them, and we may have to *make* them. If we take cases just as we

1. In terms of the phrases used in logical treatises, the so-called "methods of agreement" (comparison) and "difference" (contrast) must accompany each other or constitute a "joint method" in order to be of logical use.

find them—whether one case or many cases—they contain much that is irrelevant to the problem in hand, while much that is relevant is obscure, hidden. The object of experimentation is the *construction, by regular steps taken on the basis of a plan thought out in advance, of a typical, crucial case*, a case formed with express reference to throwing light on the difficulty in question. All methods on the fact side rest, as already stated,[2] upon regulation of the conditions of observation and memory; experiment is simply the most adequate regulation of these conditions that is possible. We try to make the observation such that every factor entering into it, together with the mode and the amount of its operation, may be open to recognition. Making observations open, overt, precise, constitutes experiment.

Three Advantages of Experiment. Such observations have many and obvious advantages over observations—no matter how extensive—with respect to which we simply wait for an event to happen or an object to present itself. Experiment overcomes defects due to (*a*) the *rarity*, (*b*) the *subtlety* and minuteness (or the violence), and (*c*) the rigid *fixity* of facts as we ordinarily experience them. The following quotations from Jevons's *Elementary Lessons in Logic* bring out all these points:

> We might have to wait years or centuries to meet accidentally with facts which we can readily produce at any moment in a laboratory; and it is probable that most of the chemical substances now known and many excessively useful products would never have been discovered at all by waiting till nature presented them spontaneously to our observation.

This quotation refers to the infrequency, or rarity, of certain facts of nature, even very important ones. The passage then goes on to speak of the minuteness of many phenomena that makes them escape ordinary experience:

> Electricity doubtless operates in every particle of matter, perhaps at every moment of time; and even the ancients could not but notice its action in the loadstone, in lightning, in the Aurora Borealis, or in a piece of rubbed amber. But in lightning electricity was too intense and dangerous; in the other cases it was too feeble to be properly understood. The

2. See page 199.

science of electricity and magnetism could only advance by getting regular supplies of electricity from the common electric machine or the galvanic battery and by making powerful electro-magnets. Most, if not all, the effects which electricity produces must go on in nature, but altogether too obscurely for observation.

Jevons then deals with the fact that, under ordinary conditions of experience, phenomena that can be understood only by seeing them under varying conditions are presented in a fixed and uniform way.

Thus carbonic acid is only met in the form of a gas, proceeding from the combustion of carbon; but when exposed to extreme pressure and cold, it is condensed into a liquid, and may even be converted into a snow-like solid substance. Many other gases have in like manner been liquefied or solidified, and there is reason to believe that every substance is capable of taking all three forms of solid, liquid, and gas, if only the conditions of temperature and pressure can be sufficiently varied. Mere observation of nature would have led us, on the contrary, to suppose that nearly all substances were fixed in one condition only, and could not be converted from solid into liquid and from liquid into gas.

Many volumes would be required to describe in detail all the methods that investigators have developed in various subjects for analyzing and restating the facts of ordinary experience so that we may escape from capricious and routine suggestions and may get the facts in such a form and in such a light (or context) that exact and far-reaching explanations may be suggested in place of vague and limited ones. But these various devices of inductive inquiry all have one goal in view: the indirect regulation of the function of suggestions, or formation of ideas; and, in the main, they will be found to reduce to some combination of the three types of selecting and arranging subject matter just described.

12. Systematic Method: Control of Reasoning and Concepts

I. The Value of Scientific Conceptions

We have already called attention to the fact that control of observation and memory so as to select and give proper weight to data as evidence depends upon the possession of a store of standardized meanings, or conceptions. If, in the case of the disordered room, the person did not have in hand fairly definite conceptions of burglary, mischief, etc., he would have been as much at a loss in interpreting the scene that met his eyes as a little child would have been. Conceptions are the intellectual instrumentalities that are brought to bear upon the material of sense perception and of recollection in order to clarify the obscure, to bring order into seeming conflict, and unity into the fragmentary. In the case of the physician's diagnosis, dependence upon the fund of already possessed knowledge is even more evident as well as complete. It is an old story that we know *with* what we already know or have mastered intellectually. And "achieved understanding," "established and solid meaning," and "conception" are synonymous terms. Hence the necessity for the regulated control of their formation.

THE BASIC IMPORTANCE OF SYSTEM IN CONCEPTS

We dealt previously with the way in which conceptions come into existence. We have now to consider the method by which a secure serial development of conceptions, one leading to another in regular sequence, is brought about. The important consideration here is the basic importance of relations between conceptions, of *system.*[1]

A concept may be excellent for the purpose of identifying events that frequently recur in our experience, even if it is not placed in a system or related body of concepts. Thus a person can identify a given four-legged animal as a dog, even though the concept of "dog" is not part of a system of concepts such as forms the science of zoology. But there are other problems of animal life that cannot possibly be solved by the everyday conception of "dog," problems that require a serial order of concepts: wolf-family, vertebrate, mammal, and a knowledge of the relations of mammal to birds, reptiles, etc.

The importance of the connections that bind concepts together into a whole is indicated by the words that we use to express the relation of premises and conclusions to each other. (1) The premises are called grounds, foundations, bases, and are said to underlie, uphold, support the conclusion. (2) We "descend" from the premises to the conclusion, and "ascend" in the opposite direction—as a river may be continuously traced from source to sea or *vice versa.* So the conclusion springs, flows, or is drawn from its premises. (3) The conclusion—as the word itself implies—closes, shuts in, locks up together the various factors stated in the premises. We say that the premises "contain" the conclusion, and that the conclusion "contains" the premises, thereby marking our sense of the inclusive and comprehensive unity in which the elements of reasoning are bound tightly together.

Popular concepts, like the ordinary one of a dog, are based on fairly obvious qualities, qualities that anyone having the normal use of his senses can readily perceive. But these popular concepts do not take us very far; they are extended or generalized to include cases outwardly different only with great risk. They are responsible for such generalizations as calling a bat a "bird," and a whale a "fish." They not only lead us astray, but they also stop far short of such generalizations as those that are basic and almost commonplace in science—electron, atom, molecule, mass, energy, etc. And it is this latter kind of concept that furthers discovery, invention, and the control of the forces of nature.

1. See page 204.

VALUE OF THE CONCEPTS OF QUANTITY

One of the great conquests of natural science has been effected by the development of mathematical concepts in a form applicable to observation and interpretation of natural events. Take for example the concepts of quantity and measurement. We can unite from the point of view of the popular concept such qualities as red, green, blue, etc., by bringing them together in the concept of color. But we can make much more exact and extensive inferences regarding color when we use the concept of rates of vibration. We can then relate color phenomena to other events apparently of a totally different kind—infra-red and ultra-violet, radio-active phenomena, sound, electro-magnetism, etc. Through the use of the concepts of quantity we can ignore the differences of quality which mark off things from one another and hence arrest inference. Consequently we can go from one fact to another to an almost indefinite extent if we treat them all as exhibiting measured differences of quantity.

DISTINCTIVE STANDARD CONCEPTS ESTABLISHED IN EACH SCIENCE

Every branch of science, geology, zoology, chemistry, physics, astronomy, as well as the different branches of mathematics, arithmetic, algebra, calculus, etc., aims at establishing its own specialized set of concepts that are keys to understanding the phenomena that are classified in each field. In this way there is provided for every typical branch of subject matter a set of meanings and principles so closely interknit that any one implies some other, according to definite conditions, that, under certain other conditions, implies another, and so on. In this way, substitutions of equivalent meanings are possible, and reasoning, without having recourse to specific observations, can trace out very remote consequences of any principle that is suggested. Definition, general formulae, and classification are the devices by which the fixation of a meaning and its elaboration into its ramifications are carried on. They are not ends in themselves—as they are frequently regarded even in elementary education—but instrumentalities for facilitating understanding, aids to the interpretation of the obscure and the explanation of the puzzling. Moreover, a conception that, in the form in which it first presents itself, is not applicable to the situation may have implied meanings that are readily applicable—as the rise of water or mercury in a vacuum is explained by developing the implications of weight and of the fact that air has weight. Again, the original concept may be quite limited in its application, while energy will be conserved if the implied ideas traced out by reasoning have wider application than the original idea had.

PLAYING WITH CONCEPTS

To the specialist, conceptual meanings become a subject matter of their own. It is an intellectual satisfaction to develop them in their logical relations of interdependence, of implication, without any reference at all to their immediate or even ulterior application to actual existence. To the trained mathematician, for example, nothing is more fascinating than to follow out the relations of concepts and, by discovering unexpected relations among them, see them unfold into a harmonious system whose contemplation gives great esthetic satisfaction. There is such a thing as *playing with ideas*.

It is possible for this form of sport to become much more absorbing than is playing games with things. No one, it is safe to say, has ever become distinguished as a thinker in any field of science or philosophy who did not have an absorbing interest in the relations of ideas for their own sake. Many children are much more capable of playing with ideas (provided they are within the range of their understanding) than is usually believed. Constraint arising from external imposition dulls this power and often turns into concealed daydreaming and fantasy-building what, under happier circumstances, would be an interest in connecting meanings with one another and a delight in coming upon unexpected combinations. One of the great values of creative work, as in writing, painting, or any art, is that it promotes a constructive, although unconscious, playing with meanings in their relations.

NEED OF FINAL TEST OF CONCEPTS

Although conceptions are capable of development without reference to direct observation, and although the habit of tracing their connection with one another as just ideas or meaning is absolutely indispensable to the growth of science and to high personal intellectual cultivation, yet the final test lies in the data furnished by experimental observation. Elaboration by reasoning may make a suggested idea very rich and very plausible, but it will not settle the validity of that idea. Only when facts are observed (by methods either of collection or of experimentation) that agree in detail and without exception with theoretical results, are we justified in accepting the rational conclusion as a conclusion that is valid for actual things. Thinking, in short, must end as well as begin in the domain of concrete observations if it is to be complete thinking. And the ultimate educative value of all deductive processes is measured by the degree to which they become working tools in the creation and development of new experiences.

II. Significant Applications to Education: Characteristic Inadequacies

Some of the points that have been made may be clinched by considering their bearing upon instruction and learning. We shall go back to the statement made earlier[2] about the correlative character of fact and meaning, observation and conception. For most of the educational mistakes about concepts, definition, and generalization result from making a false separation between facts and meanings. In this separation, "facts" become a dead weight of undigested, mechanical, largely verbal, so-called "information," while ideas become so remote from objects and acts of experience that they are empty. Instead of being means for better understanding, they become themselves incomprehensible mysteries, which for some unexplained reason haunt the schoolroom but do not belong anywhere else.

2. See pages 197–198.

ISOLATION OF FACTS FROM MEANING

In some school subjects and in many topics and lessons, pupils are immersed in mere details. Their minds are loaded with disconnected piecemeal items that are accepted on hearsay or authority. They may even be drawn from observation in so-called "object-lessons" if what is observed stands as an isolated thing, and no attempt is made to interpret it by placing it in relation to what it does, how it was caused, and what it stands for. It is not enough to load the memory with statement of facts and laws and then hope that later in life by some magic the mind will find a use for them. Even general principles, when merely memorized, stand on the same level as bare particular facts. Since they are not used either in understanding actual objects and events or in giving rise, through what they imply, to other conceptual meanings, they are, to the mind that memorizes them (falsely called *learning*), mere arbitrary items of information.

In laboratory instruction in higher education as well as in object lessons in elementary education, the subject is often so treated that the student fails to "see the forest on account of the trees." Things and their qualities are retailed and detailed, without reference to a more general character that they stand for and mean. In the laboratory the student becomes engrossed in the processes of manipulation, irrespective of the reason for their performance, without recognizing a typical problem for the solution of which they afford the appropriate method. Only deduction or reasoning brings out and emphasizes consecutive relationships, and only when *relationships* are held in view does learning become more than a miscellaneous scrap bag.

FAILURE TO FOLLOW UP BY REASONING

Again, the mind is allowed to hurry on to a vague notion of the whole of which the fragmentary facts are portions, without any attempt to become conscious of *how* they are bound together as parts of this whole. The student feels that "in a general way," as we say, the facts of the history or geography lesson are related thus and so; but "in a general way" here stands only for "in a vague way," somehow or other, with no clear recognition of just how.

The pupil may be encouraged to form, on the basis of the particular facts, a general notion, a conception of how they stand related, but no pains be taken to make the student follow up the notion, to elaborate it and see just what its bearings are upon the case in hand and upon similar cases. The inductive inference, the guess, is formed by the student; if it happens to be correct, it is at once accepted by the teacher; or if it is false, it is rejected. If any amplification of the idea occurs, it is quite likely carried through by the teacher, who thereby assumes the responsibility for its intellectual development. But a complete, an integral, act of thought requires that the person making the suggestion (the guess) be responsible also for reasoning out its bearings upon the problem in hand, for developing the suggestion enough at least to indicate the ways in which it applies to and accounts for the specific data of the case. Too often when a recitation does not consist in simply testing the ability of the student to display some form of technical skill or to repeat facts and principles accepted on authority, the teacher goes to the opposite extreme; and after calling out the spontaneous reflections of the pupils, their guesses or ideas about the matter, merely accepts or rejects them, assuming himself the responsibility for their elaboration. In this way, the function of suggestion and of interpretation is excited, but it is not directed and trained. Suggestion is stimulated but is not carried over into the *reasoning* phase necessary to complete it.

In other subjects and topics, the reasoning phase is isolated, and is treated as if it were complete in itself. This false isolation may show itself in either (and both) of two points; namely, at the beginning or at the end of the resort to general intellectual procedure.

ISOLATION OF DEDUCTION BY COMMENCING WITH IT

Beginning with definitions, rules, general principles, classifications, and the like, is a common form of the first error. This method has been such a uniform object of attack on the part of all educational reformers that it is not necessary to dwell upon it further than to note that the mistake is, logically, due to the attempt to introduce deductive considerations without first making acquaintance with the particular facts that create a need for

definition and generalization. Unfortunately, the reformer sometimes carries his objection too far or, rather, locates it in the
wrong place. He is led into a tirade against *all* definition, all systematization, all use of general principles, instead of confining
himself to pointing out their futility and their deadness when not
properly motivated by familiarity with concrete experiences.
Moreover, a flat statement of a general principle may properly
come at the beginning, provided it is used to challenge attention
and not to close inquiry.

ISOLATION OF CONCEPTIONS FROM DIRECTION OF NEW OBSERVATIONS

The isolation of general ideas is found at the other end
wherever there is failure to clinch and test the results of the general reasoning processes by application to new concrete cases.
The final point of the rational devices lies in their use in assimilating and comprehending individual cases. No one understands a
general principle fully—no matter how adequately he can dem-
onstrate it, to say nothing of repeating it—till he can employ it in
the mastery of new situations, which, if they *are* new, differ in
manifestation from the cases used in reaching the generalization.
Too often the student and teacher are contented with a series of
somewhat perfunctory examples and illustrations, and the student is not forced to carry the principle that he has formulated
over into further cases of his own experience. In so far, the principle is inert and dead; it does not move into new facts or ideas.

FAILURE TO PROVIDE FOR EXPERIMENTATION

It is only a variation upon this same theme to say that
every complete act of reflective inquiry makes provision for experimentation—for testing suggested and accepted principles
by employing them for the active construction of new cases, in
which new qualities emerge. Only slowly do our schools accommodate themselves to the general advance of scientific method.
From the scientific side, it is demonstrated that effective and integral thinking is possible only where the experimental method in
some form is used. Some recognition of this principle is evinced

in higher institutions of learning, colleges and high schools. But in elementary education, it is still assumed, for the most part, that the pupil's natural range of observations, supplemented by what he accepts on hearsay, is adequate for intellectual growth. Of course it is not necessary that laboratories shall be introduced under that name, much less that elaborate apparatus be secured; but the entire scientific history of humanity demonstrates that the conditions for complete mental activity do not exist unless adequate provision is made for carrying on activities that actually modify physical conditions, and that books, pictures, and even objects, that are passively observed but not manipulated do not furnish the required provision.

The counterpart error has already been touched upon. In some "progressive" schools, continual outward activity, even though of a somewhat random and disconnected character, is treated as if it were experimentation. In truth, every genuine experiment involves a problem in which something must be found out and where overt action must be guided by an idea used as a working hypothesis so as to give action purpose and point.

FAILURE TO SUMMARIZE NET ACCOMPLISHMENT

In such schools there is also a tendency to overlook the need of constant review, in the sense of looking back over what has been done and has been found out, so as to formulate the net outcome, thus getting mentally rid of débris, of all material and acts that do not sustain the outcome. Just because too explicit formulation and organization should *not* come at the beginning, it is so much the more necessary that the ongoing process of experience should be periodically arrested to make a survey of what has been going on and to secure a summary of its *net* accomplishment. Otherwise loose and disorderly habits are promoted.

13.   Empirical and Scientific Thought

I. What Is Meant by Empirical

Many of our ordinary inferences, in fact all of them that have not been regulated by scientific method, are empirical in character; that is to say, they are in effect habits of expectation based upon some regular conjunction or coincidence in the experience of the past. Whenever two things are associated together, like, say, thunder and lightning, there is a tendency on the part of the mind to expect that, when one occurs, the other will happen too. When the conjunction is frequently repeated, the tendency to expect becomes a positive belief that the things are so connected that it is safe to reason that when one happens, the other is sure, or almost sure, to accompany it.

For example, A says, "It will probably rain to-morrow." B asks, "Why do you think so?" and A replies, "Because the sky was lowering at sunset." When B asks, "What has that to do with it?" A responds, "I don't know, but it generally does rain after such a sunset." He does not know of any objective *connection* between the appearance of the sky and coming rain; he is not aware of any continuity in the facts themselves—any law or principle, as we usually say. From frequently recurring conjunctions of the two events, he has associated them so that, when he sees one, he thinks of the other. One *suggests* the other or is *associated* with it. A man may believe it will rain to-morrow because he has consulted the barometer; but if he has no conception how the height of the mercury column (or the position of an index moved by its rise and fall) is connected with variations of atmospheric pressure, and how these in turn are connected with a tendency toward precipitation, his belief in the likelihood of rain is purely empirical. When men lived in the open and got their living by hunting, fishing, or pasturing flocks, the detection of the signs and indications of weather changes was a matter of great importance. A body of proverbs and maxims, forming an extensive section of traditionary folklore, was developed. But as long as there was no understanding *why* or *how* certain events were signs, as long as foresight and weather shrewdness rested simply upon repeated conjunction among facts, beliefs about the weather were thoroughly empirical.

EMPIRICAL THINKING IS USEFUL
IN SOME MATTERS

In similar fashion wise men in the Orient learned to predict, with considerable accuracy, the recurrent positions of the planets, the sun, and the moon, and to foretell the time of eclipses, without understanding in any degree the laws of the movements of heavenly bodies—that is, without having a notion of the continuities existing among the facts themselves. They had learned from repeated observations that things happened in about such and such a fashion. Till a comparatively recent time, the truths of medicine were mainly in the same condition. Experience had shown that "upon the whole," "as a rule," "generally or usually speaking," certain results followed certain remedies, when certain symptoms were given. Most of our beliefs about human nature in individuals (psychology) and in masses (sociology) are still of a largely empirical sort. Even the science of geometry, now frequently reckoned a typical rational science, began, among the Egyptians, as an accumulation of recorded observations about methods of approximate mensuration of land surfaces and only gradually assumed, among the Greeks, scientific form.

IT HAS THREE OBVIOUS DISADVANTAGES

The *disadvantages* of purely empirical thinking are obvious. Attention may be called to three of them: (1) its tendency to lead to false beliefs, (2) its inability to cope with the novel, and (3) its tendency to engender mental inertia and dogmatism.

False Beliefs. First, while many empirical conclusions are, roughly speaking, correct; while they are exact enough to be of great help in practical life; while the presages of a weatherwise sailor or hunter may be more accurate, within a certain restricted range, than those of a scientist who relies wholly upon scientific observations and tests; while, indeed, empirical observations and records furnish the raw or crude material of scientific knowledge, yet the empirical method affords no way of discriminating between right and wrong conclusions. Hence it is responsible for a multitude of *false* beliefs. The technical designation for one of the commonest fallacies is *post hoc, ergo propter hoc*; the belief that because one thing comes *after* another, it comes *because* of the other. Now this weakness in method is the animating principle of empirical conclusions, even when they are correct—the correctness being almost as much a matter of luck as of method. That potatoes should be planted only during the crescent moon, that near the sea people are born at high tide and die at low tide, that a comet is an omen of danger, that bad luck follows the cracking of a mirror, that a patent medicine cures a disease— these and a thousand like notions are asseverated on the basis of empirical coincidence and conjunction.

The more numerous the experienced instances and the closer the watch kept upon them, the greater is the trustworthiness of constant conjunction as evidence of connection among the things themselves. Many of our most important beliefs still have only this sort of warrant. No one can yet tell, with certainty, the necessary cause of old age or of death, which are empirically the most certain of all expectations.

Confronting the Novel. Second, even the most reliable beliefs of this type fail when they confront the *novel*. Since they rest upon past uniformities, they are useless when further experience departs in any considerable measure from ancient incident and wonted precedent. Empirical inference follows the grooves and ruts that custom wears and has no track to follow when the groove disappears. So important is this aspect of the matter that Clifford found the difference between ordinary skill and scientific thought right here. "Skill enables a man to deal with the same circumstances that he has met before, scientific thought enables him to deal with different circumstances that he has never met before." And he goes so far as to define scientific thinking as "the application of old experience to new circumstances."

Mental Inertia and Dogmatism. Third, we have not yet made the acquaintance of the most harmful feature of the empirical method. Mental inertia, laziness, unjustifiable conservatism, are its probable accompaniments. Its general effect upon mental attitude is more serious than even the specific wrong conclusions in which it has landed. Wherever the chief dependence in forming inferences is upon the conjunctions observed in past experience, failures to agree with the usual order are slurred over, cases of successful confirmation are exaggerated. Since the mind naturally demands some principle of continuity, some connecting link between separate facts and causes, forces are arbitrarily invented for that purpose. Fantastic and mythological explanations are resorted to in order to supply missing links. The pump brings water because nature abhors a vacuum; opium makes men sleep because it has a dormitive potency; we recollect a past event because we have a faculty of memory. In the history of the progress of human knowledge, out-and-out myths accompany the first stage of empiricism, while hidden "essences" and occult "forces" mark its second stage. By their very nature these "causes" escape observation, so that their explanatory value can be neither confirmed nor refuted by further observation or experience. Hence belief in them becomes purely traditionary. They give rise to doctrines that, inculcated and handed down, become dogmas; subsequent inquiry and reflection are actually stifled.[1]

Certain men or classes of men come to be the accepted guardians and transmitters—instructors—of established doctrines. To question the beliefs is to question their authority; to accept the beliefs is evidence of loyalty to the powers that be, a proof of good citizenship. Passivity, docility, acquiescence, come to be primal intellectual virtues. Facts and events presenting novelty and variety are slighted or are sheared down till they fit into the Procrustean bed of habitual belief. Inquiry and doubt are silenced by citation of ancient laws or a multitude of miscellaneous and unsifted cases. This attitude of mind generates dislike of change, and the resulting aversion to novelty is fatal to progress. What will not fit into the established canons is outlawed; men who make new discoveries are objects of suspicion and even of persecution. Beliefs that perhaps originally were the products of fairly extensive and careful observation are stereotyped into fixed traditions and semi-sacred dogmas, accepted simply upon authority, and are mixed with fantastic conceptions that happen to have won the acceptance of authorities.

1. See pages 133–134.

II. Scientific Method

SCIENTIFIC METHOD EMPLOYS ANALYSIS

In contrast with the empirical method stands the scientific. Scientific method replaces the repeated conjunction or coincidence of separate facts by discovery of a single comprehensive fact, effecting this replacement by *breaking up the coarse or gross facts of observation into a number of minuter processes not directly accessible to perception.*

If a layman were asked why water rises from the cistern when an ordinary pump is worked, he would doubtless answer, "By suction." Suction is regarded as a force like heat or pressure. If such a person is confronted by the fact that water rises with a suction pump only about thirty-three feet, he easily disposes of the difficulty on the ground that all forces vary in their intensities and finally reach a limit at which they cease to operate. The variation with elevation above the sea level of the height to which water can be pumped is either unnoticed, or, if noted, is dismissed as one of the curious anomalies in which nature abounds.

Now the scientist advances by assuming that what seems to observation to be a single total fact is in truth complex. He attempts, therefore, to break up the single fact of water-rising-in-the-pipe into a number of lesser facts, in short, into data.[2] His method of proceeding is by *varying conditions one by one* so far as possible, and noting just what happens when each given condition is eliminated. In this way a fact too coarse and too extensive to be explained as a whole is resolved into a set of minor facts. Each minor fact is understood because it states a connection of cause and effect.

TWO METHODS OF VARYING CONDITIONS

There·are two methods of varying conditions.[3] The first is an extension of the empirical method of observation. It consists in comparing very carefully the results of a great number of observations that have occurred accidentally under *different* con-

2. See pages 197–198.
3. The next two paragraphs repeat, for purposes of the present discussion, what we have already noted in a different context. See page 257.

ditions. The difference in the rise of the water at different heights above the sea level and its total cessation when the distance to be lifted is, even at sea level, more than thirty-three feet, are emphasized, instead of being slurred over. The purpose is to find out what *special conditions* are present when the effect occurs and are absent when it fails to occur. These special conditions are then substituted for the gross fact. Some of these more definite and exact data will give the key to understanding the event.

The method of analysis by comparing cases is, however, badly handicapped; it can do nothing until a certain number of diversified cases happen to present themselves. And even when such cases are at hand, it will be questionable whether they vary in just these respects in which it is important that they should vary in order to throw light upon the question at issue. The method is passive and dependent upon external accidents. Hence the superiority of the active, or experimental, method. Even a small number of observations may suggest an explanation—a hypothesis, or theory. Working upon this suggestion, the scientist then *intentionally* varies conditions and notes what happens. If the empirical observations have suggested to him the possibility of a connection between air pressure on the water and the rising of the water in the tube where air pressure is absent, he deliberately empties the air out of the vessel in which the water is contained and notes that "suction" no longer works, or he intentionally increases atmospheric pressure on the water and notes the result. He institutes experiments to calculate the weight of air at the sea level and at various levels above and compares the results of reasoning based upon the pressure of air of these various weights upon a certain volume of water with the results actually obtained by observation. *Observations formed by variation of conditions on the basis of some idea or theory constitute experiment.* Experiment is the chief resource in scientific reasoning because it facilitates the picking out of significant elements in a gross, vague whole.

EXPERIMENT INVOLVES BOTH ANALYSIS AND SYNTHESIS

Experimental thinking, or scientific reasoning, is thus a conjoint process of *analysis and synthesis*, or, in less technical language, of discrimination and identification. The gross fact of water rising when the suction valve is worked is resolved or discriminated into a number of independent variables, some of which had never before been observed or even thought of in connection with the fact. One of these facts, the weight of the atmosphere, is then selectively seized upon as the key to the entire phenomenon. This disentangling constitutes *analysis*. But atmosphere and its pressure or weight is a fact not confined to this single instance. It is a fact familiar, or at least discoverable as operative, in a great number of other events. In fixing upon this imperceptible and minute fact as the essence or key to the elevation of water by the pump, the pump-fact has thus been assimilated to a whole group of ordinary facts from which it was previously isolated. This assimilation constitutes *synthesis*. Moreover, the fact of atmospheric pressure is itself a case of one of the commonest of all facts—weight, or gravitational force. Conclusions that apply to the common fact of weight are thus transferable to the consideration and interpretation of the *relatively* rare and exceptional case of the suction of water. The suction pump is seen to be a case of the same kind or sort as the siphon, the barometer, the rising of the balloon, and a multitude of other things with which at first sight it has no connection at all. This is another instance of the synthetic, or integrative, function of thinking.

If we revert to the advantages of scientific over empirical thinking, we find that we now have the clue to them.

Lessened Liability to Error. The increased security, the added factor of certainty or proof, is due to the substitution of the *detailed and specific fact* of atmospheric pressure for the gross and total and relatively miscellaneous fact of suction. The latter is complex, and its complexity is due to many unknown and unspecified factors; hence, any statement about it is more or less random and likely to be defeated by any unforeseen variation of circumstances. *Comparatively*, at least, the minute and detailed fact of air pressure is a measurable and definite fact—one that can be picked out and managed with assurance.

Ability to Manage the New. As analysis accounts for the added certainty, so synthesis accounts for ability to cope with the novel and variable. Weight is a much commoner fact than atmospheric weight, and this in turn is a much commoner fact than the workings of the suction pump. To be able to substitute the common and frequent fact for that which is relatively rare and peculiar is to reduce the seemingly novel and exceptional to cases of a general and familiar principle and thus to bring them under control for interpretation and prediction.

As Professor James says:

Think of heat as motion and whatever is true of motion will be true of heat; but we have a hundred experiences of motion for every one of heat. Think of rays passing through this lens as cases of bending towards the perpendicular, and you substitute for the comparatively unfamiliar lens the very familiar notion of a particular change in direction of a line, of which notion every day brings us countless examples.[4]

Interest in the Future. The change of attitude from conservative reliance upon the past, upon routine and custom, to faith in progress through the intelligent regulation of existing conditions is, of course, the reflex of the scientific method of experimentation. The empirical method inevitably magnifies the influences of the past; the experimental method throws into relief the possibilities of the future. The empirical method says, "*Wait* till there is a sufficient number of cases"; the experimental method says, "*Produce* the cases." The former depends upon nature's accidentally happening to present us with certain conjunctions of circumstances; the latter deliberately and intentionally endeavors to bring about the conjunction. By this method the notion of progress secures scientific warrant.

SCIENTIFIC THINKING IS FREED FROM CONSIDERATIONS OF THE IMMEDIATE AND THE FORCEFUL

Ordinary experience is controlled largely by the direct strength and intensity of various occurrences. What is bright, sudden, loud, secures notice and is given a conspicuous rating. What is dim, feeble, and continuous gets ignored, or is regarded as of slight importance. Customary experience tends to the control of thinking by considerations of *direct and immediate*

4. *Psychology*, vol. II, p. 342.

strength rather than by those of importance in the long run. Animals without the power of forecast and planning must, upon the whole, respond to the stimuli that are most urgent at the moment or cease to exist. These stimuli lose nothing of their direct urgency and clamorous insistency when the thinking power develops; and yet thinking demands the subordination of the immediate stimulus to the remote and distant. The feeble and the minute may be of much greater importance than the glaring and the big. The latter may be signs of a force that is already exhausting itself; the former may indicate the beginnings of a process in which the whole fortune of the individual is involved. The prime necessity for scientific thought is that the thinker be freed from the tyranny of sense stimuli and habit, and this emancipation is also the necessary condition of progress.

Consider the following quotation:

> When it first occurred to a reflecting mind that moving water had a property identical with human or brute force; namely, the property of setting other masses in motion, overcoming inertia and resistance,—when the sight of the stream suggested through this point of likeness the power of the animal,—a new addition was made to the class of prime movers; and when circumstances permitted, this power could become a substitute for the others. It may seem to the modern understanding, familiar with water wheels and drifting rafts, that the similarity here was an extremely obvious one. But if we put ourselves back into an early state of mind, when running water affected the mind *by its brilliancy, its roar and irregular devastation,* we may easily suppose that to identify this with animal muscular energy was by no means an obvious effort.[5]

THE VALUE OF ABSTRACTION

If we add to these obvious sensory features the various social customs and expectations that fix the attitude of the individual, the evil of the subjection of free and fertile suggestion to

5. Bain, *The Senses and Intellect*, third American ed., 1879, p. 492 (italics not in original).

empirical considerations—that is, to the *past* and to more or less uncontrolled experience—becomes evident.

Abstraction is an indispensable element in even ordinary thinking. It is found in all analysis, in all observation that detaches a quality from a vague blur in which it has been absorbed so as to give it distinctness. But scientific abstraction lays hold upon *relations* that could not in any case be perceived by sense. Its character is well brought out in the quotation just made from Bain. Some man got away from the almost overpowering conspicuous traits of running water to grasp a relation, that of carrying power.

A notion of abstraction is sometimes advanced that neglects this property and makes it intellectually insignificant. It is supposed to be simply the power of attending to some quality that an object is already known to possess to the exclusion of all other traits and features. But while this act is, under some circumstances, of practical value, the logical value of abstraction consists in seizing upon some quality or relation not previously grasped at all, making it stand out. It was an act of abstraction when the wing of a bird was seen to be identical, morphologically, with the forearm or foreleg, of other mammals; when the pod of peas and beans was seen to be a modified form of leaf and stem. Abstracting gets the mind emancipated from conspicuous familiar traits that hold it fixed by their very familiarity. Thereby it acquires ability to dig underneath the already known to some unfamiliar property or relation that is intellectually much more significant because it makes possible a more analytic and more extensive inference.

THE MEANING OF "EXPERIENCE"

The term *experience* may thus be interpreted with reference either to the *empirical* or to the *experimental* attitude of mind. Experience is not a rigid and closed thing; it is vital, and hence growing. When dominated by the past, by custom and routine, it is often opposed to the reasonable, the thoughtful. But experience also includes the reflection that sets us free from the limiting influence of sense, appetite, and tradition. Experience may welcome and assimilate all that the most exact and penetrating thought discovers. Indeed, the business of education might be defined as an emancipation and enlargement of experience. Education takes the individual while he is relatively plastic, before he has become so indurated by isolated experiences as to be rendered hopelessly empirical in his habit of mind. The attitude of childhood is naïve, wondering, experimental; the world of man and nature is new. Right methods of education preserve and perfect this attitude, and thereby short-circuit for the individual the slow progress of the race, eliminating the waste that comes from inert routine and lazy dependence on the past. Abstract thought is imagination seeing familiar objects in a new light and thus opening new vistas in experience. Experiment follows the road thus open and tests its permanent value.

Part Three

The Training of Thought

14. Activity and the Training of Thought

In this chapter we shall gather together and amplify considerations that have already been advanced, in various passages of the preceding pages, concerning the relation of *action to thought*. We shall follow, though not with exactness, the order of development in the unfolding of a human being.

I. The Early Stage of Activity

"WHAT IS THE BABY THINKING ABOUT?"

The sight of a baby often calls out the question: "What do you suppose he is thinking about?" By the nature of the case, the question is unanswerable in detail; but, also by the nature of the case, we may be sure about a baby's chief interest. His primary problem is mastery of his body as a tool of securing comfortable and effective adjustments to his surroundings, physical and social. The child has to learn to do almost everything: to see, to hear, to reach, to handle, to balance the body, to creep, to walk, and so on. Even if it be true that human beings have even more instinctive reactions than lower animals, it is also true that instinctive tendencies are much less perfect in men, and that most of them are of little use till they are intelligently combined and directed. A little chick just out of the shell will after a few trials peck at and grasp grains of food with its beak as well as at any later time. This involves a complicated coordination of the eye and the head. An infant does not even begin to reach definitely for things that the eye sees till he is several months old, and even then several weeks' practice is required before he learns the adjustment so as neither to overreach nor to underreach. It may not be literally true that the child will grasp for the moon, but it is true that he needs much practice before he can tell whether an object is within reach or not. The arm is thrust out instinctively in response to a stimulus from the eye, and this tendency is the origin of the ability to reach and grasp exactly and quickly; but nevertheless final mastery requires observing and selecting the successful movements and arranging them in view of an end. *These operations of conscious selection and arrangement constitute thinking*, though of a rudimentary type.

MASTERY OF THE BODY IS AN INTELLECTUAL PROBLEM

Since mastery of the bodily organs is necessary for all later developments, such problems are both interesting and important, and solving them supplies a very genuine training of thinking power. The joy the child shows in learning to use his limbs, to translate what he sees into what he handles, to connect sounds with sights, sights with taste and touch, and the rapidity with which intelligence grows in the first year and a half of life (the time during which the more fundamental problems of the use of the organism are mastered) are sufficient evidence that the development of physical control is not a physical, but an intellectual, achievement.

SOCIAL ADJUSTMENTS SOON BECOME IMPORTANT

Although in the early months the child is mainly occupied in learning to use his body to accommodate himself to physical conditions in a comfortable way and to use things skillfully and effectively, yet social adjustments are very important. In connection with parents, nurse, brother, and sister, the child learns the signs of satisfaction of hunger, of removal of discomfort, of the approach of agreeable light, color, sound, and so on. His contact with physical things is regulated by persons, and he soon distinguishes persons as the most important and interesting of all the objects with which he has to do.

Speech, the accurate adaptation of sounds heard to the movements of tongue and lips, is, however, the great instrument of social adaptation; and with the development of speech (usually in the second year) adaptation of the baby's activities to and with those of other persons gives the keynote of mental life. His range of possible activities is indefinitely widened as he watches what other persons do, and as he tries to understand and to do what they encourage him to attempt. The outline pattern of mental life is thus set in the first four or five years. Years, centuries, generations of invention and planning, may have gone to the development of the performances and occupations of the adults surrounding the child. Yet for him their activities are direct stimuli; they are part of his natural environment; they are carried on in physical terms that appeal to his eye, ear, and touch. He cannot, of course, appropriate their meaning directly through his senses; but they furnish stimuli to which he responds, so that his attention is focussed upon a higher order of materials and of problems. Were it not for this process by which the achievements of one generation form the stimuli that direct the activities of the next, the story of civilization would be writ in water, and each generation would have laboriously to make for itself, if it could, its way out of savagery. In learning to understand and make words, children learn a great deal more than the words themselves. They gain a habit that opens a new world to them.

THE ROLE OF IMITATION

Imitation is one, though only one,[1] of the means by which the activities of adults supply stimuli that are so interesting, so varied, so complex, and so novel as to occasion a rapid progress of thought. Mere imitation, however, would not give rise to thinking; if we could learn like parrots by simply copying the outward acts of others, we should never have to think; nor should we know, after we had mastered the copied act, what was the meaning of the thing we had done. Educators (and psychologists) have often assumed that acts that reproduce the behavior of others are acquired merely by imitation. But a child rarely learns by conscious imitation, and to say that his imitation is unconscious is to say that it is not, from his standpoint, imitation at all. The word, the gesture, the act, the occupation of another, falls in line with *some impulse already active* and suggests some

1. See pages 158–159.

satisfactory mode of expression, some end in which it may find fulfillment. Having this end of his own, the child then notes other persons, as he notes natural events, to get further suggestions as to means of its realization. He selects some of the means he observes, tries them on, finds them successful or unsuccessful, is confirmed or weakened in his belief in their value, and so continues selecting, arranging, adapting, testing, till he can accomplish what he wishes. The onlooker may then observe the resemblance of this act to some act of an adult and conclude that it was acquired by imitation, while as a matter of fact it was acquired by attention, observation, selection, experimentation, and confirmation by results. Only because this method is employed is there intellectual discipline and an educative result. The presence of adult activities plays an enormous role in the intellectual growth of the child because they add to the natural stimuli of the world new stimuli that are more exactly adapted to the needs of a human being, that are richer, better organized, more complex in range, permitting more flexible adaptations, and calling out novel reactions. But in utilizing these stimuli, the child follows the same methods that he uses when he is forced to think in order to master his body.

II. Play, Work, and Allied Forms of Activity

THE SIGNIFICANCE OF PLAY
AND OF PLAYFULNESS

When things become signs, when they gain a representative capacity as standing for other things, play is transformed from mere physical exuberance into an activity involving a mental factor. A little girl who had broken her doll was seen to perform with the leg of the doll all the operations of washing, putting to bed, and fondling, that she had been accustomed to perform with the entire doll. The part stood for the whole; she reacted, not to the stimulus sensibly present, but to the meaning suggested by the sense object. So children use a stone for a table, leaves for plates, acorns for cups. So they use their dolls, their trains, their blocks, their other toys. In manipulating them, they are living not with the physical things, but in the large world of meanings, natural and social, evoked by these things. So when children play horse, play store, play house or making calls, they are subordinating the physically present to the ideally signified. In this way, a world of meanings, a store of concepts (so fundamental in all intellectual achievement), is defined and built up.

Moreover, not only do meanings thus become familiar acquaintances, but they are organized, arranged in groups, made to cohere in connected ways. A play and a story blend insensibly into each other. The most fanciful plays of children rarely lose all touch with the mutual fitness and pertinency of various meanings to one another; the "freest" plays observe some principles of coherence and unification. They have a beginning, middle, and end. In games, rules of order run through various minor acts and bind them into a connected whole. The rhythm, the competition, and the cooperation involved in most plays and games also introduce organization. There is, then, nothing mysterious or mystical in the discovery made by Plato and remade by Froebel that play is the chief, almost the only, mode of education for the child in the years of later infancy.

Playfulness is a more important consideration than play. The former is an attitude of mind; the latter is a passing outward manifestation of this attitude. When things are treated simply as vehicles of suggestion, what is suggested overrides the thing. Hence the playful attitude is one of freedom. The person is not bound to the physical traits of things, nor does he care whether a thing really "means" what he takes it to represent. When the child plays horse with a broom and cars with chairs, the fact that the broom does not really represent a horse or a chair a locomotive is of no account. In order, then, that playfulness may not terminate in arbitrary fancifulness and in building up an imaginary world alongside the world of actual things, it is necessary that the play attitude should gradually pass into a work attitude.

THE SIGNIFICANCE OF WORK

What is work—work not as mere external performance, but as attitude of mind? In the natural course of growth, children come to find irresponsible, make-believe plays inadequate. A fiction is too easy a way out to afford contentment, not stimulus enough to call forth satisfactory mental response. When this point is reached, the ideas that things suggest are applied to the things with some regard to fitness. A small cart, resembling a "real" cart, with "real" wheels, tongue, and body, meets the mental demand better than merely making believe that anything that comes to hand is a cart. Occasionally to take part in setting a "real" table with "real" dishes brings more reward than forever to make believe a flat stone is a table and that leaves are dishes. The interest may still centre in the meanings; things may be of importance only as furthering a certain meaning. So far the attitude is one of play. But meaning becomes of such a character that it must find embodiment, or at least expression, in actual things.

The dictionary does not permit us to call such activities work. Nevertheless, they represent a passage of play into work. For work (as a mental attitude, not as mere external performance) *means interest in the adequate embodiment of a meaning* (a suggestion, purpose, aim) *in objective form through the use of appropriate materials and appliances.* Such an attitude takes advantage of the meanings aroused and built up in free play, but *controls their development by seeing to it that they are applied to things in ways consistent with the observable structure of things themselves.*

The word "work" is not very satisfactory. For it is often used to denote routine activity that accomplishes useful results with but a minimum of thoughtful selection of means, deliberate adjustment to produce desired consequences. We view work from the outside when we think of it as simply doing things that need to be done. But it may also be looked at from the inside; it must be so looked at when we are thinking of it in relation to education. Then work signifies activity directed by ends that thought sets before the person as something to be accomplished; it signifies ingenuity and inventiveness in selecting proper means and making plans, and thus, finally, signifies that expectations and ideas are tested by actual results.

A child, like an adult, may make or do something following the dictation of others, working mechanically from oral or printed instructions, or stereotyped blueprints. There is then next to no thought; his activity is not truly reflective. But as we have already noted, the means-consequence relation is the heart of all meaning. "Work," in the sense of *intelligent action*, is therefore highly educative, because it continually builds up meanings while at the same time it tests them by application to actual conditions. It is necessary, however, that the adult do not judge the value of such an activity on the part of the young by his familiar adult standards about the value of the *product*; if he does, the activity will usually seem to him to amount to little. He must judge from the standpoint of the planning, invention, ingenuity, observation, exercised by the young, remembering always that what is an old story to him may arouse emotion and thought in the child.

THE TRUE DISTINCTION BETWEEN PLAY AND WORK

The point of the distinction between play and work may be cleared up by comparing it with a more usual way of stating the difference. In play activity, it is said, the interest is in the activity for its own sake; in work, it is in the product or result in which the activity terminates. Hence the former is purely free, while the latter is tied down by the end to be achieved. When the difference is stated in this sharp fashion, there is almost always introduced a false, unnatural separation between process and product, between activity and its achieved outcome. The true distinction is not between an interest in activity for its own sake and interest in the external result of that activity, but between an interest in an activity just as it flows on from moment to moment, and an interest in an activity as tending to a culmination, to an outcome, and therefore possessing a thread of continuity binding together its successive stages. Both may equally exemplify interest in an activity "for its own sake"; but in the one case the activity in which the interest resides is more or less casual, following the accident of circumstance and whim, or of dictation; in the other, the activity is enriched by the sense that it leads somewhere, that it amounts to something.

Were it not that the false theory of the relation of the play and the work attitudes has been connected with unfortunate modes of school practice, insistence upon a truer view might seem an unnecessary refinement. But the sharp break that so often prevails between the kindergarten and the grades is evidence that the theoretical distinction has practical implications. Under the title of "play" the former is rendered unduly symbolic, fanciful, sentimental, and arbitrary; while under the antithetical caption of "work" the latter contains many *tasks externally assigned.* The former has no end; the latter an end so remote that only the educator, not the child, is aware that it is an end.

There comes a time when children must extend and make more exact their acquaintance with existing things, must conceive ends and consequences with sufficient definiteness to guide their actions by them, and must acquire some technical skill in selecting and arranging means to realize these ends. Unless these factors are gradually introduced in the earlier play period, they must later be introduced abruptly and arbitrarily, to the manifest disadvantage of both the earlier and the later stages.

CORRELATIVE FALSE NOTIONS OF IMAGINATION AND UTILITY

The sharp opposition of play and work is usually associated with false notions of utility and imagination. Activity that is directed upon matters of home and neighborhood interest is depreciated as merely utilitarian. To let the child wash dishes, set the table, engage in cooking, cut and·sew dolls' clothes, make boxes that will hold "real things," and construct his own playthings by using hammer and nails, excludes (so it is said) the aesthetic and appreciative factor, eliminates imagination, and subjects the child's development to material and practical concerns; while (so it is said) to reproduce symbolically the domestic relationships of birds and other animals, of human father and mother and child, of workman and tradesman, of knight, soldier, and magistrate, secures a liberal exercise of mind that is of great moral as well as intellectual value. It has even been stated that it is over-physical and utilitarian if a child plants seeds and takes care of growing plants in the kindergarten; whereas if he reproduces dramatically the operations of planting, cultivating, reaping, and so on, with no physical materials or with symbolic representatives, he educates imagination and his spiritual appreciation. Toy dolls, trains of cars, boats, and engines are rigidly excluded, but cubes, balls, and other symbols for representing his social activities are recommended. The more unfitted the physical object for its imagined purpose, such as a cube for a boat, the greater is the supposed appeal to the imagination.

There are several fallacies in this way of thinking.

First, the healthy imagination deals not with the unreal, but with the mental realization of what is suggested. Its exercise is not a flight into the purely fanciful and ideal, but a method of expanding and filling in what is real. To the child the homely activities going on about him are not utilitarian devices for accomplishing physical ends; they exemplify a wonderful world, the depths of which he has not sounded, a world full of the mystery and promise that attend all the doings of the grown-ups whom he admires. However prosaic this world may be to the adults who find its duties routine affairs, to the child it is fraught with social meaning. To engage in it is to exercise the imagination in constructing an experience of wider value than any the child has yet mastered.

Second, educators sometimes think children are reacting to a great moral or spiritual truth when the children's reactions are largely physical and sensational. Children have great powers of dramatic simulation, and their physical bearing may seem (to adults prepossessed with a philosophic theory) to indicate they have been impressed with some lesson of chivalry, devotion, or nobility when the children, themselves, are occupied only with transitory physical excitations. To symbolize great truths far beyond the child's range of actual experience is an impossibility, and to attempt it is to invite love of momentary stimulation.

Third, just as the opponents of play in education always conceive of play as mere amusement, so the opponents of direct and useful activities confuse occupation with labor. The adult is acquainted with responsible labor upon which serious financial results depend. Consequently he seeks relief, relaxation, amusement. Unless children have prematurely worked for hire, unless they have come under the blight of child labor, no such division exists for them. Whatever appeals to them at all appeals directly on its own account. There is no contrast between doing things for utility and for fun. Their life is more united and more wholesome. To suppose that activities customarily performed by adults only under the pressure of utility may not be done perfectly freely and joyously by children indicates a lack of imagination. Not the thing done, but the quality of mind that goes into the doing, settles what is utilitarian and what is unconstrained and creative.

III. Constructive Occupations

THE SCIENCES GREW OUT OF OCCUPATIONS

The history of culture shows that mankind's scientific knowledge and technical abilities have developed, especially in all their earlier stages, out of the fundamental problems of life. Anatomy and physiology grew out of the practical needs of keeping healthy and active; geometry and mechanics out of demands for measuring land, for building, and for making labor-saving machines; astronomy has been closely connected with navigation, keeping record of the passage of time; botany grew out of the requirements of medicine and of agronomy; chemistry has been associated with dyeing, metallurgy, and other industrial pursuits. In turn, modern industry is almost wholly a matter of applied science; year by year the domain of routine and crude empiricism is narrowed by the translation of scientific discovery into industrial invention. The trolley, the telephone, the electric light, the steam engine, with all their revolutionary consequences for social intercourse and control, are the fruits of science.

SCHOOL OCCUPATIONS OFFER
INTELLECTUAL POSSIBILITIES

These facts are full of educational significance. Most children are preeminently active in their tendencies. The schools have also taken on—largely from utilitarian, rather than from strictly educative, reasons—a large number of active pursuits commonly grouped under the head of manual training, including also school gardens, excursions, and various graphic arts. Perhaps the most pressing problem of education at the present moment is to organize and relate these subjects so that they will become instruments for forming alert, persistent, and fruitful *intellectual* habits. That they take hold of the more primary and native equipment of children (appealing to their desire to do) is generally recognized; that they afford great opportunity for training in self-reliant and efficient social service is gaining acknowledgment. But they may also be used for presenting *typical problems to be solved by personal reflection and experimentation and by acquiring definite bodies of knowledge leading later to more spe-*

cialized scientific knowledge. There is indeed no magic by which mere physical activity or deft manipulation will secure intellectual results.[2] Manual subjects may be taught by routine, by dictation, or by convention as readily as bookish subjects. But intelligent consecutive work in gardening, cooking, or weaving, or in elementary wood and iron, may be so planned that it will inevitably result not only in students' amassing information of practical and scientific importance in botany, zoology, chemistry, physics, and other sciences, but also (what is more significant) in their becoming versed in methods of experimental inquiry and proof.

That the elementary curriculum is overloaded is a common complaint. The only alternative to a reactionary return to the educational traditions of the past lies in working out the intellectual possibilities resident in various arts, crafts, and occupations, and reorganizing the curriculum accordingly. Here, more than elsewhere, are found the means by which the blind and routine experience of the race may be transformed into illuminated and emancipated experiment.

CONDITIONS TO BE MET TO RENDER "PROJECTS" EDUCATIVE

Constructive occupations have in recent years found their way increasingly into the schoolroom. They are usually known as "projects." In order that they may be truly educative, there are certain conditions that should be fulfilled.

The first condition, that of interest, is usually met. Unless the activity lays hold on the emotions and desires, unless it offers an outlet for energy that means something to the individual himself, his *mind* will turn in aversion from it, even though externally he keeps at it. But interest is not enough. Given interest, the important matter is *what kind of object and action* enlists it. Is it something transitory or is it enduring? Is the interest mainly one of excitement or is thought involved?

Hence the second condition to be met is that the activity be worth while intrinsically. This statement does not signify, as we have just seen in another connection, that its outcome be something externally useful from the adult point of view. But it does

2. See page 154.

mean that merely trivial activities, those that are of no consequence beyond the immediate pleasure that engaging in them affords, should be excluded. It is not difficult to find projects that
are enjoyable while at the same time they stand for something
valuable in life itself.

The third condition (really only an amplification of the point
just made) is that the project in the course of its development
present problems that awaken new curiosity and create a demand for information. There is nothing educative in an activity,
however agreeable it may be, that does not lead the mind out into
new fields. The new field cannot be entered unless the mind is led
to ask questions that it had not thought of before and unless the
presence of these questions creates a thirst for additional information to be obtained by observation, by reading, by consulting
persons expert in that particular field.

Finally, as a fourth condition, the project must involve a considerable time span for its adequate execution. The plan and the
object to be gained must be capable of development, one thing
leading on naturally to another. Unless it does so, new fields cannot be entered. It is the province of the adult to look ahead and
see whether one stage of achievement will suggest something else
to be looked into and done. An occupation has continuity. It is
not a succession of unrelated acts, but is a consecutively ordered
activity in which one step prepares the need for the next one and
that one adds to, and carries further in a cumulative way, what
has already been done.

15.   From the Concrete to the Abstract

I. What Is the Concrete?

The maxim enjoined upon teachers, "proceed from the concrete to the abstract," is familiar rather than wholly intelligible. Few who read and hear it gain a clear conception of the starting point, the concrete; of the nature of the goal, the abstract; and of the exact nature of the path to be traversed in going from one to the other. At times the injunction is positively misunderstood, being taken to mean that education should advance from things to thought—as if any dealing with things in which thinking is not involved could possibly be educative. So understood, the maxim encourages mechanical routine or sensuous excitation at one end of the educational scale—the lower—and academic and unapplied learning at the upper end.

Actually, all dealing with things, even the child's, is immersed in inference; things are clothed with the suggestions they arouse. They are significant as challenges to interpretation or as evidences to substantiate a belief. Nothing could be more unnatural than instruction in things without thought, in sense-perceptions without judgments connected with them. And if the abstract to which we are to proceed denotes thought apart from things, the goal is formal and empty, for effective thought always refers, more or less directly, to things.

RELATION TO DIRECT AND INDIRECT MEANING

Yet the maxim has a meaning which, understood and supplemented, states the direction of logical development. What is this meaning? "Concrete" denotes a meaning definitely marked off from other meanings so that it is readily apprehended by itself. When we hear the words, *table, chair, stove, coat,* we do not have to reflect in order to grasp what is meant.[1] The terms convey meaning so directly that no effort at translation is needed. The meaning of some terms and things, however, is grasped only by first calling to mind more familiar things and then tracing out connections between them and what we do not understand. Roughly speaking, the former kind of meaning is concrete; the latter is abstract.

DEPENDENCE ON THE INTELLECTUAL STATUS OF THE INDIVIDUAL

To one who is thoroughly at home in physics and chemistry, the notions of *atom* and *molecule* are fairly concrete. They are constantly used without involving any labor of thought in apprehending what they mean. But the layman and the beginner in science have to remind themselves of things with which they already are well acquainted, and then go through a process of slow translation. Moreover the terms *atom* and *molecule* lose their hard-won meaning only too easily if familiar things and the line of transition from them to the strange drop out of mind. The same difference is illustrated by any technical terms: *coefficient* and *exponent* in algebra, *triangle* and *square* in their geometric as distinct from their popular meanings; *capital* and *value* in political economy, and so on.

The difference as noted is purely relative to the intellectual progress of an individual; what is abstract at one period of growth is concrete at another; or even the contrary, as one finds that things supposed to be thoroughly familiar involve strange factors and unsolved problems. There is, nevertheless, a general line of cleavage that decides upon the whole what things fall within, and what fall without, the limits of familiar acquaintance. This line accordingly marks off the concrete and the abstract in a fairly permanent way. *The limits are fixed mainly by the demands of practical life.* Things such as sticks and stones, meat and potatoes, houses and trees, are constant features of the environment of which we have to take account in order to live. Hence their important meanings are soon learned and are indissolubly asso-

1. See page 236.

ciated with objects. We are acquainted with a thing (or it is familiar to us) when we have so much to do with it that its strange and troublesome corners are rubbed off. The necessities of social intercourse convey to adults a like concreteness upon such terms as *taxes*, *elections*, *wages*, *the law*, and so on. Things the meaning of which I personally do not take in directly, appliances of cook, carpenter, or weaver, for example, are nevertheless unhesitatingly classed as concrete, since they are directly connected with our common social life.

RELATION TO THINKING AS A MEANS AND AS AN END

By contrast, the abstract is the *theoretical*, that not intimately associated with practical concerns. The abstract thinker (the "man of pure science," as he is sometimes called) deliberately abstracts from application in life; that is, he leaves practical uses out of account. This, however, is a merely negative statement. What remains when connections with use and application are excluded? *Evidently only what has to do with knowing considered as an end in itself.* Many notions in science are abstract, not only because they cannot be understood without a long apprenticeship in the science (which is equally true of technical matters in the arts), but also because the whole content of their meaning has been framed for the sole purpose of facilitating further knowledge, inquiry, and speculation. *When thinking is used as a means to some end, good, or value beyond itself, it is concrete; when it is employed simply as a means to more thinking, it is abstract.* To a theorist an idea is adequate and self-contained just because it engages and rewards thought; to a medical practitioner, an engineer, an artist, a merchant, a politician, it is complete only when employed in the furthering of some interest in life—health, wealth, beauty, goodness, success, or what you will.

DEPRECIATION OF "MERE THEORY"

The great majority of men under ordinary circumstances find the practical exigencies of life almost, if not quite, coercive. Their main business is the proper conduct of their affairs. Whatever is of significance only as affording scope for thinking is pallid and remote—almost artificial. Hence the contempt felt by the practical and successful executive for the "mere theorist"; hence his conviction that certain things may be all very well in theory, but that they will not do in practice; hence, in general, the depreciatory way in which he uses the terms *abstract, theoretical,* and *intellectual.*

This attitude is justified, of course, under certain conditions. But depreciation of theory does not contain the whole truth, as common or practical sense recognizes. There is such a thing, even from the common-sense standpoint, as being "too practical," as being so intent upon the immediately practical as not to see beyond the end of one's nose or as to cut off the limb upon which one is sitting. The question is one of limits, of degrees and adjustments, rather than one of absolute separation. Truly practical men give their minds free play about a subject without asking too closely at every point for any advantage to be gained. Exclusive preoccupation with matters of use and application narrows the horizon and in the long run defeats itself. It does not pay to tether one's thoughts to the post of use with too short a rope. Power in action requires largeness of vision, which can be had only through the use of imagination. Men must at least have enough interest in thinking for the sake of thinking to escape the limitations of routine and custom. Interest in knowledge for the sake of knowledge, in thinking for the sake of the free play of thought, is necessary to the *emancipation* of practical life—to making it rich and progressive.

We now recur to the pedagogic maxim of going from the concrete to the abstract and call attention to three aspects of the process.

BEGINNING WITH PRACTICAL MANIPULATIONS

1. Since the *concrete* denotes thinking applied to activities for the sake of dealing with difficulties that present themselves practically, "begin with the concrete" signifies that we should, at the outset of any new experience in learning, make much of what is already familiar, and if possible connect the new topics and principles with the pursuit of an end in some active occupation. We do not "follow the order of nature" when we multiply mere sensations or accumulate physical objects. Instruction in number is not concrete merely because splints or beans or

dots are employed. Whenever the use and bearing of number relations are clearly perceived, a number idea is concrete even if figures alone are used. Just what sort of symbol it is best to use at a
given time—whether blocks, or lines, or figures—is entirely a
matter of adjustment to the given case. If the physical things used
in teaching number or geography or anything else do not leave
the mind illuminated with recognition of a *meaning* beyond
themselves, the instruction that uses them is as abstruse as that
which doles out ready-made definitions and rules, for it distracts
attention from ideas to mere physical excitations.

The notion that we have only to put physical objects before the
senses in order to impress ideas upon the mind amounts almost
to a superstition. The introduction of object lessons and sense-
training scored a distinct advance over the prior method of linguistic symbols, but this advance tended to blind educators to the
fact that only a halfway step had been taken. Things and sensations develop the child, indeed, but only when he *uses* them in
mastering his body and coordinating his actions. Continuous occupations involve the use of natural materials, tools, modes of energy, and do it in a way that compels thinking as to how they are
related to one another and to the realization of ends. But the
mere isolated presentation of things to sense remains barren and
dead. A few generations ago the great obstacle in the way of reform of primary education was belief in the almost magical efficacy of the symbols of language (including number) to produce
mental training; at present, belief in the efficacy of objects just as
objects blocks the way. As frequently happens, the better is an
enemy of the best.

TRANSFERRING INTEREST TO
INTELLECTUAL MATTERS

2. The interest in results, in the successful carrying on of
an activity, should be gradually transferred to the *study* of objects—their properties, consequences, structures, causes, and
effects. The adult when at work in his life calling is rarely free to
devote time or energy—beyond the necessities of his immediate
action—to the study of what he deals with.[2] The educative activities of childhood should be so arranged that the activity creates

2. See page 152.

a demand for attention to matters that have only an indirect and an intellectual connection with the original activity. To take an instance to which reference has already been made, the direct interest in carpentering or shop work should gradually pass into an interest in geometric and mechanical problems. The interest in cooking should grow into an interest in chemical experimentation and the physiology and hygiene of bodily growth. The original casual making of pictures should pass to an interest in the technique of representation of perspective, the handling of brush, pigments, etc. This development is what the term "go" signifies in the maxim "*go* from the concrete to the abstract"; it represents the dynamic and educative phase of the process.

DEVELOPING DELIGHT IN THINKING

3. The outcome, the *abstract* to which education is to proceed, is an interest in intellectual matters for their own sake, a delight in thinking for the sake of thinking. It is an old story that acts and processes that at the outset are incidental to something else develop and maintain an absorbing value of their own. So it is with thinking and with knowledge; at first incidental to results and adjustments beyond themselves, they attract more and more attention to themselves till they become ends, not means. Children engage, unconstrainedly and continually, in reflective inspection and testing for the sake of what they are interested in doing. Habits of thinking thus generated may increase in amount till they become of importance on their own account. It is part of the business of a teacher to lead students to extricate and dwell upon the distinctively intellectual side of what they do until there develops a spontaneous interest in ideas and their relations with one another—that is, a genuine power of abstraction, of rising from engrossment in the present to the plane of ideas.

II. What Is the Abstract?

EXAMPLES OF THE TRANSITION FROM CONCRETE TO ABSTRACT

The three instances cited in Chapter 6 represent an ascending cycle from the concrete to the abstract. Taking thought to keep a personal engagement is obviously of the concrete kind. Endeavoring to work out the meaning of a certain part of a boat is an instance of an intermediate kind. The original reason for the existence and position of the pole is practical, so that to the designer the problem was purely concrete—the maintenance of a certain system of action. But for the passenger on the boat, the problem was theoretical, more or less speculative. It made no difference to his reaching his destination whether he worked out the meaning or not. The third case, that of the appearance and movement of the bubbles, illustrates a strictly abstract case. No overcoming of physical obstacles, no adjustment of external means to ends, is at stake. Curiosity, intellectual curiosity, is challenged by a seemingly anomalous occurrence; and thinking tries simply to account for an apparent exception in terms of recognized principles. Intellectual means are adjusted to an intellectual result.

ABSTRACT THINKING NOT THE WHOLE END AND NOT CONGENIAL TO MOST PERSONS

Abstract thinking, it should be noted, represents *an* end, not *the* end. The power of sustained thinking on matters remote from direct use is an outgrowth of thinking on practical and immediate matters, but not a substitute for it. The educational end is not the destruction of power to think practically in overcoming obstacles, utilizing resources, and achieving ends; it is not its replacement by abstract reflection. Nor is theoretical thinking a higher type of thinking than practical. A person who has at command both types of thinking is of a higher order than he who possesses only one. Methods that, in developing abstract intellectual abilities, weaken habits of practical or concrete thinking fall as much short of the educational ideal as do the methods that, in cultivating ability to plan, to invent, to arrange, to forecast, fail to secure some delight in thinking, irrespective of practical consequences.

Educators should also note the very great individual differences that exist; they should not try to force one pattern and model upon all. In many (probably the majority) the executive tendency, the habit of mind that thinks for purposes of conduct and achievement, not for the sake of knowing, remains dominant to the end. Engineers, lawyers, doctors, merchants, are much more numerous in adult life than scientists and philosophers.

While education should strive to make men who, however prominent their professional interests and aims, partake of the spirit of
the scholar, philosopher, and scientist, no good reason appears
why education should esteem the one mental habit inherently superior to the other and deliberately try to transform the type
from concrete to abstract. Have not our schools been one-sidedly
devoted to the more abstract type of thinking, thus doing injustice to the majority of pupils? Has not the idea of a "liberal"
and "humane" education tended too often in practice to the production of technical, because overspecialized, thinkers?

EDUCATION SHOULD AIM TO SECURE
A WORKING BALANCE

The aim of education should be to secure a balanced interaction of the two types of mental attitude, having sufficient regard to the disposition of the individual not to hamper and
cripple whatever powers are naturally strong in him. The narrowness of individuals of strong concrete bent needs to be liber-
alized. Every opportunity that occurs within practical activities
for developing curiosity and susceptibility to intellectual problems should be seized. Violence is not done to natural disposition; rather the latter is broadened. Otherwise, the concrete becomes narrowing and deadening. As regards the smaller number
of those who have a taste for abstract, purely intellectual topics,
pains should be taken to multiply opportunities for the application of ideas, for translating symbolic truths into terms of everyday and social life. Every human being has both capabilities, and
every individual will be more effective and happier if both powers are developed in easy and close interaction with each other.
Otherwise the abstract becomes identical with the academic and
pedantic.

16. Language and the Training of Thought

I. Language as the Tool of Thinking

Language has such a peculiarly intimate connection with thought as to require special discussion. The very word logic, coming from logos (λόγος), means indifferently both word or speech and thought or reason. Yet "words, words, words" denote intellectual barrenness, a sham of thought. Schooling has language as its chief instrument (and often as its chief subject matter) of study. Yet educational reformers have for centuries brought their severest indictments against the current use of language in the schools. The conviction that language is necessary to thinking (is even identical with it) is met by the contention that language perverts and conceals thought. There is a genuine problem here.

VIEWS OF THE RELATION OF THOUGHT AND LANGUAGE

Three typical views have been maintained regarding the relation of thought and language: first, that they are identical; second, that words are the garb, or clothing, of thought, necessary not for thought but only for conveying it; and third (the view we shall here maintain), that, while language is not thought, it is necessary for thinking as well as for communication. When it is said, however, that thinking is impossible without language, we must recall that language includes much more than oral and written speech. Gestures, pictures, monuments, visual images, finger movements—anything deliberately and artificially employed as a *sign* is, logically, language. To say that language is necessary for thinking is to say that signs are necessary. Thought deals not with bare things, but with their *meanings*, their suggestions; and meanings, in order to be apprehended, must be embodied in sensible and particular existences. Without meaning, things are nothing but blind stimuli, brute things, or chance sources of pleasure and pain; and since meanings are not themselves tangible things, they must be anchored by attachment to some physical existence. Existences that are especially set aside to fixate and convey meanings are *symbols*. If a man moves toward another to throw him out of the room, his movement is not a sign. If, however, the man points to the door with his hand, or utters the sound *go*, his act becomes a vehicle of meaning: it is a sign, not a complete thing in itself. In the case of signs we care nothing for what they are in themselves, but everything for what they signify and represent. *Canis, hund, chien, dog*—it makes no difference what the outward thing is, so long as the meaning is presented.

Natural objects are signs of other things and events. Clouds stand for rain; a footprint represents game or an enemy; a projecting rock serves to indicate minerals below the surface. The limitations of *natural* signs are, however, great. First, physical or direct sense excitation tends to distract attention from what is meant or indicated. Almost every one will recall pointing out to a kitten or puppy an object of food, only to have the animal devote himself to the hand pointing, not to the thing pointed at. Second, where natural signs alone exist, we are mainly at the mercy of external happenings; we have to wait until the natural event presents itself in order to be warned or advised of the possibility of some other event. Third, natural signs, not being originally intended to be signs, are cumbrous, bulky, inconvenient, unmanageable. A symbol, on the contrary, is intended and invented, like any artificial tool and utensil, for the purpose of conveying meaning.

ASPECTS OF ARTIFICIAL SIGNS THAT FAVOR THEIR USE TO REPRESENT MEANINGS

It is therefore indispensable for any high development of thought that there exist intentional signs. Language supplies the requirement. Gestures, sounds, written or printed forms, are strictly physical existences, but their native value is intentionally subordinated to the value they acquire as representative of meanings. There are three aspects of artificial signs that favor their use as representatives of meanings:

First, the direct and sensible value of faint sounds and minute written or printed marks is very slight. Accordingly, attention is not distracted from their *representative* function.

Second, their production is under our direct control, so that they may be produced when needed. When we can make the word *rain*, we do not have to wait for some physical forerunner of rain to call our thoughts in that direction. We cannot make the cloud; we can make the sound, and as a token of meaning the sound serves the purpose as well as the cloud.

Third, arbitrary linguistic signs are convenient and easy to manage. They are compact, portable, and delicate. As long as we live we breathe, and modifications by the muscles of throat and mouth of the volume and quality of the air are simple, easy, and indefinitely controllable. Bodily postures and gestures of the hand and arm are also employed as signs, but they are coarse and unmanageable compared with modifications of breath to produce sounds. No wonder that oral speech has been selected as the main stuff of intentional intellectual signs. Sounds, while subtle, refined, and easily modifiable, are transitory. This defect is met by the system of written and printed words, appealing to the eye. *Litera scripta manet.*

Bearing in mind the intimate connection of meanings and signs (or language), we may note in more detail what language does (1) for specific meanings, and (2) for the organization of meanings.

LANGUAGE SELECTS, PRESERVES, AND APPLIES SPECIFIC MEANINGS

In the case of specific meanings a verbal sign (*a*) selects, detaches, a meaning from what is otherwise a vague flux and blur (see p. 228); (*b*) retains, registers, stores that meaning; and (*c*) applies it, when needed, to the comprehension of other things. Combining these various functions in a mixture of metaphors, we may say that a linguistic sign is a fence, a label, and a vehicle—all in one.

a. The Word as a Fence. Everyone has experienced how learning an appropriate name for what was dim and vague cleared up and crystallized the whole matter. Some meaning seems almost within reach, but is elusive; it refuses to condense into definite form; the attaching of a word somehow (just how, it is almost impossible to say) puts limits around the meaning, draws it out from the void, makes it stand out as an entity on its own account. When Emerson said that he would almost rather know the true name, the poet's name, for a thing, than to know the thing itself, he presumably had this irradiating and illuminating function of language in mind. The delight that children take in demanding and learning the names of everything about them indicates that meanings are becoming concrete individuals to them, so that their commerce with things is passing from the physical to the intellectual plane. It is hardly surprising that savages attach a magical efficacy to words. To name anything is to give it a title, to dignify and honor it by raising it from a mere physical occurrence to a meaning that is distinct and permanent. To know the names of people and things and to be able to manipulate these names is, in savage lore, to be in possession of their dignity and worth, to master them.

b. The Word as a Label. Things come and go, or we come and go, and either way things escape our notice. Our direct sensible relation to things is very limited. The suggestion of meanings by natural signs is limited to occasions of direct contact or vision. But a meaning fixed by a linguistic sign is conserved for future use. Even if the thing is not there to represent the meaning, the word may be produced so as to evoke the meaning. Since intellectual life depends on possession of a store of meanings, the importance of language as a tool of preserving meanings cannot be overstated. To be sure, the method of storage is not wholly aseptic; words often corrupt and modify the meanings they are supposed to keep intact, but liability to infection is a price paid by every living thing for the privilege of living.

c. The Word as a Vehicle. When a meaning is detached and fixed by a sign, it is possible to use that meaning in a new context and situation. This transfer and reapplication is the key to all judgment and inference. It would little profit a man to recognize that a given particular cloud was the premonitor of a given particular rainstorm if his recognition ended there, for he would then have to learn over and over again, since the next cloud and the next rain are different events. No cumulative growth of intelligence would occur. Experience might form habits of physical adaptation but it would not *teach* anything, for we should not be able to use an old experience consciously to anticipate and regulate a new experience. To be able to use the past to judge and infer the new and unknown implies that, although the past thing has gone, its *meaning* abides in such a way as to be applicable in determining the character of the new. Speech forms are our great carriers, the easy-running vehicles by which meanings are transported from experiences that no longer concern us to those that are as yet dark and dubious.

LANGUAGE SIGNS ARE INSTRUMENTS FOR ORGANIZING MEANINGS

In emphasizing the importance of signs in relation to specific meanings, we have overlooked another aspect, equally valuable. Signs not only mark off specific or individual meanings, but they are also instruments of grouping meanings in relation to one another. Words are not only names or titles of single meanings; they also form *sentences* in which meanings are organized in relation to one another. When we say "That book is a dictionary," or "That blur of light in the heavens is Halley's comet," we express a *logical* connection—an act of classifying and defining that goes beyond the physical thing into the logical region of genera and species, things and attributes. Propositions, sentences, bear the same relation to judgments that distinct words, built up mainly by analyzing propositions in their various types, bear to meanings or conceptions; and just as words imply a sentence, so a sentence implies a larger whole of consecutive discourse into which it fits. As is often said, grammar expresses the unconscious logic of the popular mind. *The chief intellectual classifications that constitute the working capital of thought have been built up for us by our mother tongue.* Our very lack of explicit consciousness, when using language, that we are then employing the intellectual systematizations of the race shows how thoroughly accustomed we have become to its logical distinctions and groupings.

II. The Abuse of Linguistic Methods in Education

TEACHING THINGS ALONE, THE NEGATION OF EDUCATION

Taken literally, the maxim, "Teach things, not words," or "Teach things before words," would be the negation of education; it would reduce mental life to mere physical and sensible adjustments. Learning, in the proper sense, is not learning things, but the *meanings* of things, and this process involves the use of signs, or language in its generic sense. In like fashion, the warfare of some educational reformers against symbols, if pushed to extremes, involves the destruction of intellectual life, since this lives, moves, and has its being in those processes of definition, abstraction, generalization, and classification that are made possible by symbols alone. Nevertheless, these contentions of educational reformers have been needed. The liability of a thing to abuse is in proportion to the value of its right use.

THE LIMITATIONS AND DANGERS OF SYMBOLS IN RELATION TO MEANINGS

Symbols themselves, as already pointed out, are particular, physical, sensible existences, like any other things. They are symbols only by virtue of what they suggest and represent; *i.e.*, meanings.

In the first place, they stand for these meanings to any individual only when he has had *experience* of some situation to which these meanings are actually relevant. Words can detach and preserve a meaning only when the meaning has been first involved in our own direct intercourse with things. To attempt to give a meaning through a word alone without any dealings with a thing is to deprive the word of intelligible signification; against this attempt, a tendency only too prevalent in education, reformers have protested. Moreover, there is a tendency to assume that, whenever there is a definite word or form of speech, there is also a definite idea; while, as a matter of fact, adults and children alike are capable of using even formulae that are verbally precise with only the vaguest and most confused sense of what they mean. Genuine ignorance is more profitable because it is likely to be accompanied by humility, curiosity, and open-mindedness; whereas ability to repeat catch-phrases, cant terms, familiar propositions, gives the conceit of learning and coats the mind with a varnish waterproof to new ideas.

In the second place, although new combinations of words without the intervention of physical things may supply new ideas, there are limits to this possibility. Lazy inertness causes individuals to accept ideas that have currency about them without personal inquiry and testing. A man uses thought, perhaps, to find out what others believe, and then stops. The ideas of others as embodied in language become substitutes for one's own ideas. The use of linguistic studies and methods to halt the human mind on the level of the attainments of the past, to prevent new inquiry and discovery, to put the authority of tradition in place of the authority of natural facts and laws, to reduce the individual to a parasite living on the secondhand experience of others—these things have been the source of the reformers' protest against the preeminence assigned to language in schools.

In the third place, words that originally stood for ideas come, with repeated use, to be mere counters; they become physical things to be manipulated according to certain rules or reacted to by certain operations without consciousness of their meaning. Mr. Stout (who has called such terms "substitute signs") remarks that "algebraical and arithmetical signs are to a great extent used as mere substitute signs. . . . It is possible to use signs of this kind whenever fixed and definite rules of operation can be derived from the nature of the things symbolised, so as to be applied in manipulating the signs, without further reference to their signification. A word is an instrument for thinking about the meaning which it expresses; a substitute sign is a means of *not* thinking about the meaning which it symbolises." The principle applies, however, to ordinary words, as well as to algebraic signs; they also enable us to use meanings so as to get results without thinking. In many respects, signs that are means of not thinking are of great advantage; standing for the familiar, they release attention for meanings that, being novel, require conscious interpretation. Nevertheless, the premium put in the schoolroom upon attainment of technical facility, upon skill in producing external results,[1] often changes this advantage into a positive detriment. In manipulating symbols so as to recite well, to get and give correct answers, to follow prescribed formulae of analysis, the pupil's attitude becomes mechanical, rather than thoughtful; verbal memorizing is substituted for inquiry into the meaning of things. This danger is perhaps the one uppermost in mind when verbal methods of education are attacked.

III. The Use of Language in Its Educational Bearings

Language stands in a twofold relation to the work of education. On the one hand, it is continually used in all studies as well as in all the social discipline of the school; on the other, it is a distinct object of study. We shall consider only the ordinary use of language, since its effects upon habits of thought are much deeper than those of conscious linguistic study, for the latter only makes explicit what speech already contains.

The common statement that "language is the expression of thought" conveys only a half-truth, and a half-truth that is likely to result in positive error. Language does express thought, but not primarily, nor, at first, even consciously. The primary motive for language is to influence (through the expression of desire, emotion, and thought) the activity of others; its secondary use is to enter into more intimate sociable relations with them; its employment as a conscious vehicle of thought and knowledge is a tertiary, and relatively late, formation. The contrast is well brought out by the statement of John Locke that words have a double use, "civil" and "philosophical." "By their civil use, I mean such a communication of thoughts and ideas by words as may serve for the upholding of common conversation and commerce about the ordinary affairs and conveniences of civil life. . . . By the philosophical use of words, I mean such a use of them as may serve to convey the precise notions of things and to express in general propositions certain and undoubted truths."

1. See page 163.

EDUCATION HAS TO TRANSFORM LANGUAGE INTO AN INTELLECTUAL TOOL

This distinction of the practical and social from the intellectual use of language throws much light on the problem of the school in respect to speech. That problem is *to direct pupils' oral and written speech, used primarily for practical and social ends, so that gradually it shall become a conscious tool of conveying knowledge and assisting thought.* How without checking the spontaneous, natural motives—motives to which language owes its vitality, force, vividness, and variety—are we to modify speech habits so as to render them accurate and flexible *intellectual* instruments? It is comparatively easy to encourage the original spontaneous flow and not make language over into a servant of reflective thought; it is comparatively easy to check and almost destroy (so far as the schoolroom is concerned) native aim and interest and to set up artificial and formal modes of expression in some isolated and technical matters. The difficulty lies in making over habits that have to do with "ordinary affairs and conveniences" into habits concerned with "precise notions." The successful accomplishing of the transformation requires (*a*) enlarging the pupil's vocabulary, (*b*) rendering its terms more precise and accurate, and (*c*) forming habits of consecutive discourse.

a. Enlarging the Vocabulary. This takes place, of course, by wider intelligent contact with things and persons, and also vicariously, by gathering the meanings of words from the context in which they are heard or read. To grasp by either method a word in its meaning is to exercise intelligence, to perform an act of intelligent selection or analysis, and it is also to widen the fund of meanings or concepts readily available in further intellectual enterprises.[2] It is usual to distinguish between one's active and one's passive vocabulary, the latter being composed of the words that are understood when they are heard or seen, the former of words that are used intelligently. The fact that the passive is very much larger than the active vocabulary indicates power not controlled or utilized by the individual. Failure to use meanings that are understood may reveal dependence upon external stimulus and lack

2. See pages 241–242.

of intellectual initiative. This condition is to some extent an artificial product of education. Small children usually attempt to
put to use every new word they get hold of, but when they learn
to read they are introduced to a large variety of terms that they
have no opportunity to use. The result is a kind of mental suppression, if not smothering. Moreover, the meaning of words not
actively used in building up and conveying ideas is never quite
clear-cut or complete. Action is required to make them definite.

While a limited vocabulary may be due to a limited range of
experience, to a sphere of contact with persons and things so
narrow as not to suggest or require a full store of words, it is also
due to carelessness and vagueness. A happy-go-lucky frame of
mind makes the individual averse to clear discriminations, either
in perception or in his own speech. Words are used loosely in an
indeterminate kind of reference to things, and speech approaches
a condition where practically everything is just a "thing-um-
bob" or a "what-do-you-call-it," a condition that reacts to make
thought hopelessly loose and vague. Paucity of vocabulary on the
part of those with whom the child associates, triviality and mea-
gerness in the child's reading matter (as frequently even in his
school readers and textbooks), tend to shut down the area of
mental vision. Even technical terms become clear when they are
used to make either an idea or an object clearer in meaning.
Every self-respecting mechanic will call the parts of an automobile by their right names because that is the way to distinguish
them. Simplicity should mean intelligibility, but not an approach
to baby-talk.

We must note also the great difference between flow of words
and command of language. Volubility is not necessarily a sign of
a large vocabulary; much talking or even ready speech is quite
compatible with moving round and round in a circle of moderate
radius. Most schoolrooms suffer from a lack of materials and appliances save perhaps books—and even these are "written down"
to the supposed capacity, or incapacity, of children. Occasion and
demand for an enriched vocabulary are accordingly restricted.
The vocabulary of things studied in the schoolroom is very largely
isolated; it does not link itself organically to the range of the
ideas and words that are in vogue outside the school. Hence the
enlargement that takes place is often nominal, adding to the inert, rather than to the active, fund of meanings and terms.

b. Rendering the Vocabulary More Precise. One way in which the fund of words and concepts is increased is by discovering and naming shades of meaning—that is to say, by making the vocabulary more precise. Increase in definiteness is as important relatively as is the enlargement of the capital stock absolutely.

The first meanings of terms, since they are due to superficial acquaintance with things, are "general"—in the sense of being vague. The little child calls all men "papa"; acquainted with a dog, he may call the first horse he sees "big dog." Differences of quantity and intensity are noted, but the fundamental meaning is so vague that it covers things that are far apart. To many persons trees are just trees, being discriminated only into deciduous trees and evergreens, with perhaps recognition of one or two kinds of each. Such vagueness tends to persist and to become a barrier to the advance of thinking. Terms that are miscellaneous in scope are clumsy tools at best; in addition they are frequently treacherous, for their ambiguous reference causes us to confuse things that should be distinguished.

The growth of precise terms out of original vagueness takes place normally in two directions: first, toward words that stand for relationships, and second, toward words that stand for highly individualized traits;[3] the first is associated with abstract, the second with concrete, thinking. Some Australian tribes are said to have no words for *animal* or for *plant*, while they have specific names for every variety of plant and animal in their neighborhoods. This minuteness of vocabulary represents progress toward definiteness, but in a one-sided way. Specific properties are distinguished, but not relationships.[4] On the other hand, students of philosophy and of the general aspects of natural and social science are apt to acquire a store of terms that signify relations, without balancing them up with terms that designate specific individuals and traits. The ordinary use of such terms as *causation*, *law*, *society*, *individual*, *capital*, illustrates this tendency.

3. Cf. what was said about the development of meanings, p. 229.
4. The term *general* is itself an ambiguous term, meaning (in its best logical sense) the related and also (in its natural usage) the indefinite, the vague. *General*, in the first sense, denotes the discrimination of a principle or generic relation; in the second sense, it denotes the absence of discrimination of specific or individual properties.

In the history of language we find both aspects of the growth of vocabulary illustrated by changes in the sense of words: some words originally wide in their application are narrowed to denote shades of meaning; others originally specific are widened to express relationships. The term *vernacular*, now meaning mother speech, has been generalized from the word *verna*, meaning a slave born in the master's household. *Publication* has evolved its meaning of communication by means of print through restricting an earlier meaning of any kind of communication—although the wider meaning is retained in legal procedure, as publishing a libel. The sense of the word *average* has been generalized from a use connected with dividing loss by shipwreck proportionately among various sharers in an enterprise.[5]

These historical changes assist the educator to appreciate the changes that occur in individuals with advance in intellectual resources. In studying geometry, a pupil must learn both to narrow and to extend the meanings of such familiar words as *line, surface, angle, square, circle*—to narrow them to the precise meanings involved in demonstrations, to extend them to cover generic relations not expressed in ordinary usage. Qualities of color and size must be excluded; relations of direction, of variation in direction, of limit, must be definitely seized. Thus in generalized geometry the idea of *line* does not carry any connotation of *length*. To it, what is ordinarily called a line is only a *section* of a line. A like transformation occurs in every subject of study. Just at this point lies the danger, alluded to above, of simply overlaying common meanings with new and isolated meanings instead of effecting a genuine working-over of popular and practical meanings into logical concepts.

Terms used with intentional exactness so as to express a meaning, the whole meaning, and only the meaning, are called *technical*. For educational purposes, a technical term indicates something relative, not absolute; for a term is technical, not because of its verbal form or its unusualness, but because it is employed to fix a meaning precisely. Ordinary words get a technical quality when used intentionally for this end. Whenever thought becomes more accurate, a (relatively) technical vocabulary grows up.

---

5. A large amount of material illustrating the twofold change in the sense of words will be found in Jevons, *Elementary Lessons in Logic.*

Teachers are apt to oscillate between extremes in regard to technical terms. On the one hand, these are multiplied in every direction, seemingly on the assumption that learning a new piece of terminology, accompanied by verbal description or definition, is equivalent to grasping a new idea. On the other hand, when it is seen how largely the net outcome is the accumulation of an isolated set of words, a jargon or scholastic cant, and to what extent the natural power of judgment is clogged by this accumulation, there is a reaction to the opposite extreme. Technical terms are banished; "name words" exist, but not nouns; "action words," but not verbs; pupils may "take away," but not subtract; they may tell what four fives are, but not what four times five are, and so on. A sound instinct underlies this reaction—aversion to words that give the pretense, but not the reality, of meaning. Yet the fundamental difficulty is not with the word, but with the idea. If the idea is not grasped, nothing is gained by using a more familiar word; if the idea is grasped, the use of the term that exactly names it may assist in fixing the idea. Terms denoting highly exact meanings should be introduced only sparingly—that is, a few at a time; they should be led up to gradually, and great pains should be taken to secure the circumstances that render precision of meaning significant.

c. *Forming Habits of Consecutive Discourse.* As we saw, language connects and organizes meanings as well as selects and fixes them. As every meaning is set in the context of some situation, so every word in concrete use belongs to some sentence (it may itself represent a condensed sentence); and the sentence, in turn, belongs to some larger story, description, or reasoning process. It is unnecessary to repeat what has been said about the importance of continuity and ordering of meanings. We may, however, note some ways in which school practices tend to interrupt consecutiveness of language and thereby interfere harmfully with systematic reflection.

First, teachers have a habit of monopolizing continued discourse. Many, if not most, instructors would be surprised if informed at the end of the day of the amount of time they have talked as compared with any pupil. Children's conversation is often confined to answering questions in brief phrases or in single disconnected sentences. Expatiation and explanation are reserved for the teacher, who often admits any hint at an answer

on the part of the pupil, and then amplifies what he supposes the
child must have meant. The habits of sporadic and fragmentary
discourse thus promoted have inevitably a disintegrating intellectual influence.

Second, assignment of too short lessons, when accompanied
(as it usually is in order to pass the time of the recitation period)
by minute "analytic" questioning, has the same effect. This evil is
usually at its height in such subjects as history and literature,
where not infrequently the material is so minutely subdivided as
to break up the unity of meaning belonging to a given portion of
the matter, to destroy perspective, and in effect to reduce the
whole topic to an accumulation of disconnected details all upon
the same level. More often than the teacher is aware, *his* mind
carries and supplies the background of unity of meaning against
which pupils project isolated scraps.

Third, insistence upon avoiding error instead of attaining power
tends also to interruption of continuous discourse and thought.
Children who begin with something to say and with intellectual
eagerness to say it are sometimes made so conscious of minor errors in substance and form that the energy that should go into
constructive thinking is diverted into anxiety not to make mistakes, and even, in extreme cases, into passive quiescence as the
best method of minimizing error. This tendency is especially
marked in connection with the writing of compositions, essays,
and themes. It has even been gravely recommended that little
children should always write on trivial subjects and in short sentences because in that way they are less likely to make mistakes.
The teaching of high-school and college students occasionally reduces itself to a technique for detecting and designating mistakes. Self-consciousness and constraint follow. Students lose
zest for writing. Instead of being interested in what they have to
say and in how it is said as a means of adequate formulation and
expression of their own thought, interest is drained off. Having
to say something is a very different matter from having something to say.

17. Observation and Information in the Training of Mind

Thinking is ordering of subject matter with reference to discovering what it signifies or indicates. Thinking no more exists apart from this arranging of subject matter than digestion occurs apart from the assimilating of food. The way in which the subject matter is supplied and assimilated is, therefore, of fundamental importance. If the subject matter is provided in too scanty or too profuse fashion, if it comes in disordered array or in isolated scraps, the effect upon habits of thought is detrimental. If personal observation and the communication of information by others (whether in books or speech) are rightly conducted, half the logical battle is won, for these are the channels of obtaining subject matter, and the method in which they are carried on directly affects the habit of thinking. The effect is often deeper because it is so unconscious. The best digestion can be ruined by innutritious foodstuffs, by eating at the wrong time, too much at a time, or having an unbalanced diet—that is, one the materials of which are badly arranged.

I. The Nature and Value of Observation

OBSERVATION NOT AN END IN ITSELF

The protest, mentioned in the last chapter, of educational reformers against the exaggerated and false use of language, insisted upon personal and direct observation as the alternative course. The reformers felt that the current emphasis upon the linguistic factor eliminated all opportunity for first-hand acquaintance with real things; hence they appealed to sense perception to fill the gap. It is not surprising that this enthusiastic zeal frequently failed to ask how and why observation is educative, and hence fell into the error of making observation an end in itself and hence was satisfied with any kind of material under any kind of conditions. Such isolation of observation is still manifested in the statement that this faculty develops first, then that of memory and imagination, and finally the faculty of thought. From this point of view, observation is regarded as furnishing crude masses of raw material, to which, later on, reflective processes may be applied. Our previous pages should have made obvious the fallacy of this point of view by bringing out the fact that simple concrete thinking attends all our intercourse with things that is not on a purely physical level.

OBSERVATION IMPELLED BY SYMPATHETIC INTEREST IN EXTENDING ACQUAINTANCE

All persons have a natural desire—akin to curiosity—for a widening of their range of acquaintance with persons and things. The sign in art galleries that forbids the carrying of canes and umbrellas is obvious testimony to the fact that simply to see is not enough for many people; there is a feeling of lack of acquaintance until some direct contact is made. This demand for fuller and closer knowledge is quite different from conscious interest in observation for its own sake. Desire for expansion, for "self-realization," is its motive. The interest is sympathetic, socially and aesthetically sympathetic, rather than cognitive. While the interest is especially keen in children (because their actual experience is so small and their possible experience so large), it still characterizes adults when routine has not blunted its edge. This sympathetic interest provides the medium for carrying and binding together what would otherwise be a multitude of items, diverse, disconnected, and of no intellectual use. The result is a social and aesthetic organization rather than one consciously intellectual; but it provides the natural opportunity and supplies the material for conscious intellectual explorations. Some educators have recommended that nature study in the elementary schools be conducted with a love of nature and a cultivation of aesthetic appreciation in view rather than in a purely analytic spirit. Others have urged making much of the care of animals and plants. Both of these important recommendations have grown out of experience, not out of theory, but they afford an excellent exemplification of the point just made.

ANALYTIC OBSERVATION IMPELLED BY NEED ARISING IN ACTIVITY: SOME FALLACIES ABOUT SENSE-TRAINING

In normal development, specific analytic observations are originally connected almost exclusively with the imperative need for noting means and ends in carrying on activities. When one is *doing* something *intelligently*, one is compelled, if the work is to succeed (unless it is purely routine), to use eyes, ears, and sense of touch as guides to action. Without a constant and alert exercise of the senses, not even plays and games can go on; in any form of work, materials, obstacles, appliances, failures, and successes must be intently watched. Sense perception does not occur for its own sake or for purposes of training, but because it is an indispensable factor of success in doing what one is trying to do. Although it is not designed for sense-training, this method effects sense-training in the most economical and thoroughgoing way. Various schemes have been designed by teachers for cultivating sharp and prompt observation of forms, as by writing words (even in an unknown language), making arrangements of figures and geometrical forms, and having pupils reproduce them after a momentary glance. Children often attain great skill in quick seeing and full reproducing of even complicated meaningless combinations. But such methods of training, however valuable as occasional games and diversions, compare very unfavorably with the training of eye and hand that comes as an incident of work with tools in wood or metals, or such activities as gardening, cooking, or the care of animals. Training by isolated exercises leaves no deposit, leads nowhere; and even the technical skill acquired has little radiating power or transferable value. Criticisms made upon the training of observation, on the ground that many persons cannot correctly reproduce the forms and arrangement of the figures on the face of their watches, misses the point, because persons do not look at a watch to find out whether four o'clock is indicated by IIII or by IV, but to find out what time it is, and if observation decides this fact, noting other details is irrelevant and a waste of time. In the training of observation the question of purpose and result is all-important.

OBSERVATION IMPELLED BY SOLVING THEORETICAL PROBLEMS

The further intellectual or scientific development of observation follows the line of the growth of practical into theoretical reflection already traced.[1] As problems emerge and are dwelt upon, observation is directed less to facts that bear upon a practical aim and more to what bears upon a problem as a problem. What often makes observation in schools intellectually ineffective is (more than anything else) that it is carried on without a sense of a problem that it helps define and solve. The evil of this isolation is seen through the entire educational system, from the kindergarten through the elementary and high schools to the college. Almost everywhere may be found, at some time, recourse to observations as if they were of complete and final value in themselves, instead of being means for getting the data that test an idea or plan and that make the felt difficulty into a question that guides subsequent thinking.[2] Moreover, intellectual method is violated because observations are not aroused and guided by any idea of the *purpose* they are to serve.

In the kindergarten observations are heaped up regarding geometrical forms, lines, surfaces, cubes, colors, and so on. In the elementary school, under the name of "object-lessons," the form and properties of objects—apple, orange, chalk—selected almost at random are minutely noted, while under the name of "nature study" similar observations are directed upon leaves, stones, insects, selected in almost equally arbitrary fashion. In the high school and college, laboratory and microscopic observations are carried on as if the accumulation of observed facts and the acquisition of skill in manipulation were educational ends in themselves.

OBSERVATION IN SCIENTIFIC WORK

Compare with these methods of isolated observations the statement of Jevons that observation as conducted by scientific men is effective "only when excited and guided by hope of

---

1. See page 190.
2. See page 201.

verifying a theory"; and again, "the number of things which can be observed and experimented upon are infinite, and if we merely set to work to record facts without any distinct purpose, our records will have no value." Strictly speaking, the first statement of Jevons is too narrow. Scientific men institute observations not merely to test an idea (or suggested explanatory meaning), but also to locate a problem or even create one and thereby guide the formation of a hypothesis. But the principle of his remark— namely, that scientific men never make the accumulation of observations an end in itself, but always a means to a general intellectual conclusion—is absolutely sound. Until the force of this principle is adequately recognized in education, observation will be largely a matter of uninteresting dead work or of acquiring forms of technical skill that are not available as intellectual resources.

II. Methods and Materials of Observation in the Schools

The best methods already in use in schools furnish many suggestions for giving observation its right place in mental training. Three features of these methods deserve mention.

OBSERVATION SHOULD INVOLVE ACTIVE EXPLORATION

First, they rest upon the sound assumption that observation is an *active* process. Observation is exploration, inquiry for the sake of discovering something previously hidden and unknown, this something being needed in order to reach some end, practical or theoretical. Observation is to be discriminated from recognition, the perception of what is familiar. The identification of something already understood is, indeed, an indispensable function of further investigation;[3] but it is relatively automatic and passive, while observation demands the mind to be alert, on the *qui vive*, searching and probing. Recognition deals with the already mastered; observation is concerned with delving into the

3. See page 227.

unknown. The common notions that perception is like writing on a blank piece of paper or like impressing an image on the mind as a seal is imprinted on wax or as a picture is formed on a photographic plate (notions that have played a disastrous role in educational methods) arise from a failure to distinguish between automatic recognition and live observation.

OBSERVATION SHOULD INTRODUCE THE DRAMATIC ELEMENT OF SUSPENSE, OF "PLOT INTEREST"

Second, much assistance in the selection of appropriate material for observation may be derived from considering the eagerness and closeness of observation that attend the following of a story or drama. Alertness of observation is at its height wherever there is "plot interest." Why? Because of the balanced combination of the old and the new, of the familiar and the unexpected. We hang on the lips of the story-teller because of the element of mental suspense. Alternatives are suggested, but are left ambiguous, so that our whole being questions: What befell next? Which way did things turn out? Contrast the ease and fullness with which a child notes all the salient traits of a story, with the labor and inadequacy of his observation of some dead and static thing where nothing raises a question or suggests alternative outcomes.

When an individual is engaged in doing or making something (the activity not being of such a mechanical and habitual character that its outcome is assured), there is an analogous situation. Something is going to come of what is present to the sense, but just what is doubtful. The plot is unfolding toward success or failure, but just when or how is uncertain. Hence the keen and tense observation of conditions and results that attends constructive manual operations. Where the subject matter is of a more impersonal sort, the same principle of movement toward a dénouement may apply. It is a commonplace that what is moving attracts notice when that which is at rest escapes it. Yet too often it would seem as if pains were taken to deprive the material of school observations of all life and dramatic quality, to reduce it to a dead and inert form. Mere change is not enough, however. Vicissitude, alteration, motion, excite observation; but if they merely excite it, there is no thought. The changes must (like the incidents of a well-arranged story or plot) take place in a certain cumulative order; each successive change must at once remind us of its predecessor and arouse interest in its successor if observations of change are to be intellectually ordered and thus are to aid in forming a logical attitude.

Observation of Structure and Function. Living beings, plants and animals, fulfill the twofold requirement to an extraordinary degree. Where there is growth, there is motion, change, process; and there is also arrangement of the changes in a cycle. The first arouses thought; the second organizes it. Much of the extraordinary interest that children take in planting seeds and watching the stages of their growth is due to the fact that a drama is enacting before their eyes; there is something doing, each step of which is important in the destiny of the plant. The great practical improvements that have occurred of late years in the teaching of botany and zoology will be found, upon inspection, to involve treating plants and animals as beings that act, that do something, instead of as mere inert specimens having static properties to be inventoried, named, and registered. Treated in the latter fashion, observation is inevitably reduced to the falsely "analytic,"[4] to mere enumeration and cataloguing.

There is, of course, a place, and an important place, for observation of the static qualities of objects. When, however, the primary interest is in *function*, in what the object does and how it operates, there is a motive for more minute analytic study, for observation of *structure*. Interest in noting an activity passes insensibly into noting how the activity is carried on; the interest in what is done passes over into an interest in the organs by which it is done. But when the beginning is made with the morphological, the anatomical, the noting of peculiarities of form, size, color, and distribution of parts, the material is cut off from significance and becomes dead and dull. It is as natural for children to look intently for the *stomata* of a plant after they have learned that, like animals, it breathes, and so must have something corresponding in function to lungs. It is repulsive to attend minutely to them when they are presented for study as mere items of structure, and no idea of their action and use is conveyed.

4. See pages 216–217.

OBSERVATION SHOULD BECOME
SCIENTIFIC IN NATURE

Third, observation that is carried on at first to help out a practical purpose or for the mere fun of seeing and hearing comes to be conducted for an intellectual purpose. Pupils learn to observe for the sake (*a*) of finding out what sort of perplexity confronts them; (*b*) of conjecturing and inventing hypothetical explanations for the puzzling features revealed by observation; and (*c*) of testing the ideas thus suggested.

In short, observation becomes scientific in nature. Of such observations it may be said that they should follow a rhythm between the extensive and the intensive. Problems become definite, and suggested explanations significant by an alternation between a wide and loose soaking in of relevant facts and a minutely accurate study of a few selected facts. The wider, less exact observation is necessary to give the student a feeling for the reality of the field of inquiry, a sense of its bearings and possibilities, and to store his mind with materials that imagination may transform into suggestions. The intensive study is necessary for limiting the problem and for securing the conditions of experimental testing. As the latter by itself is too specialized and technical to arouse intellectual growth, the former by itself is too superficial and scattering for control of intellectual development. In the sciences of life, field study, excursions, acquaintance with living things in their natural habitats, may alternate with microscopic and laboratory observation. In the physical sciences, phenomena of light, of heat, of electricity, of moisture, of gravity, in their broad setting in nature—their physiographic setting—should prepare for an exact study of selected facts under conditions of laboratory control. In this way, the student gets the benefit of technical scientific methods of discovery and testing, while he retains his sense of the identity of the laboratory modes of energy with large out-of-door realities, thereby avoiding the impression (that so often accrues) that the facts studied are peculiar to the laboratory. Scientific observation does not, however, merely replace observation that is enjoyed for its own sake. The latter, sharpened by the purpose of contributing to an art like writing, painting, singing, becomes truly esthetic, and the persons who enjoy seeing and hearing will be the best observers.

III. Communication of Information

When all is said and done, the field of fact open to any one observer by himself is narrow. Into every one of our beliefs, even those that we have worked out under the conditions of utmost personal, first-hand acquaintance, much has insensibly entered from what we have heard or read of the observations and conclusions of others. In spite of the great extension of direct observation in our schools, the vast bulk of educational subject matter is derived from other sources—from textbook, lecture, and *viva voce* interchange. No educational question is of greater import than how to get *intellectual* good out of what persons and books have to communicate.

HOW TO MAKE AN INTELLECTUAL ASSET OF LEARNING THROUGH COMMUNICATED INFORMATION

Doubtless the chief meaning associated with the word *instruction* is this conveying and instilling of the results of the observations and inferences of others. Doubtless the undue prominence in education of the ideal of amassing information[5] has its source in the prominence of the learning of other persons. The problem, then, is how to convert this form of learning into an intellectual asset. In logical terms, the material supplied from the experience of others is *testimony*: that is to say, *evidence* submitted by others that is to be employed by one's own judgment in reaching a conclusion. How shall we treat subject matter that is supplied by textbook and teacher so that it shall rank as material of reflective inquiry, not as ready-made intellectual pabulum to be accepted and swallowed just as if it were something bought at a shop?

In reply to this question, we may say first, that communication of material should be *needed*. That is to say, it should be such as cannot readily be attained by personal observation. For teacher or book to cram pupils with facts which, with little more trouble, they could discover by direct inquiry is to violate their intel-

5. See page 163.

lectual integrity and to cultivate mental servility. This does not mean that the material supplied through communication of others should be meagre or scanty. With the utmost range of the senses, the world of nature and history stretches out almost infinitely beyond. But fields within which direct observation is practicable should be carefully chosen and sacredly protected. Curiosity should not be dulled by making its satisfaction cheap and stale.

Second, material should be supplied by way of stimulus, not with dogmatic finality and rigidity. When pupils get the notion that any field of study has been definitely surveyed, that knowledge about it is exhaustive and final, they may become docile pupils, but they cease to be students. All thinking whatsoever—so be it *is* thinking—contains a phase of originality. This originality does not imply that the student's conclusion varies from the conclusions of others, much less that it is a radically novel conclusion. His originality is not incompatible with large use of materials and suggestions contributed by others. Originality means personal interest in the question, personal initiative in turning over the suggestions furnished by others, and sincerity in following them out to a tested conclusion. Literally, the phrase "Think for yourself" is tautological; any thinking is thinking for one's self.

Third, the material furnished by way of information should be relevant to a question that is vital in the student's own experience. What has been said about the evil of observations that begin and end in themselves may be transferred without change to communicated learning. Instruction in subject matter that does not fit into an interest already stirring in the student's own experience or that is not presented in such a way as to arouse a problem is worse than useless for intellectual purposes. In that it fails to enter into any process of reflection, it is useless; in that it remains in the mind as so much lumber and débris, it is a barrier, an obstruction in the way of effective thinking when a problem arises.

Another way of stating the same principle is that material furnished by communication must be such as to enter into some existing system or organization of experience. All students of psychology are familiar with the principle of apperception—that we assimilate new material with what we have digested and retained from prior experiences. Now the apperceptive basis of material furnished by teacher and textbook should be found, as far as possible, in what the learner has derived from more direct forms of his own experience. There is a tendency to connect material of the schoolroom simply with the material of prior school lessons, instead of linking it to what the pupil has acquired in his out-of-school experience. The teacher says, "Do you not remember what we learned from the book last week?"—instead of saying, "Do you not recall such and such a thing that you have seen or heard?" As a result, there are built up detached and independent systems of school knowledge that inertly overlay the ordinary systems of experience instead of reacting to enlarge and refine them. Pupils are taught to live in two separate worlds, one the world of out-of-school experience, the other the world of books and lessons. Then we stupidly wonder why what is studied in school counts so little outside.

18. The Recitation and the Training of Thought

I. False Ideas about the Recitation

In the recitation the teacher comes into his closest contact with the pupil. In the recitation focus the possibilities of guiding children's activities, arousing eagerness for information, influencing language habits, and directing observations. In discussing the significance of the recitation as an instrumentality of education, we are accordingly bringing to a head the points considered in the last three chapters, rather than introducing a new topic. The method in which the recitation is carried on is a crucial test of a teacher's ability to diagnose the intellectual state of his pupils and to supply the conditions that will arouse intellectual responses: a crucial test, in short, of his art as a teacher.

RE-CITING *VERSUS* REFLECTING

The use of the word "recitation" to designate the period of the most intimate intellectual contact of teacher with pupil and of pupil with pupil is a fateful fact. To *re-cite* is to cite again, to repeat, to tell over and over. If we were to call this period "reiteration," the name would hardly bring out more clearly than does the word "recitation" the frequent domination of instruction by rehearsal of secondhand information, and of memorizing for the sake of producing correct replies at the proper time. Everything which is said in this chapter is insignificant in comparison with the basic truth that the recitation is the place and time for stimulating and directing reflection. Reproduction of memorized matter is only an incident—even though an indispensable incident—in the business of cultivating a thoughtful attitude.

The recitation exhibits, more definitely than anything else in the school system, the domination of the ideal of amassing information without a purpose for it, because information would help master a difficulty, and without judgment in selection of what is pertinent. It is hardly an exaggeration to say that too often the pupil is treated as if he were a phonographic record on which is impressed a set of words that are to be literally reproduced when the recitation or examination presses the proper lever. Or, varying the metaphor, the mind of the pupil is treated as if it were a cistern into which information is conducted by one set of pipes that mechanically pour it in, while the recitation is the pump that brings out the material again through another set of pipes. Then the skill of the teacher is rated by his or her ability in managing the two pipe-lines of flow inward and outward.

THE EVILS OF PASSIVITY

It does not need to be mentioned that this practice puts a premium on passivity of mind. Everything which has been said in the discussion of thinking has emphasized that passivity is the opposite of thought; that it is not only a sign of failure to call out judgment and personal understanding, but that it also dulls curiosity, generates mind-wandering, and causes learning to be a task instead of a delight. It does not in most cases even serve the purpose of storing the mind with a subject matter of facts and principles that are available when they are needed. The mind is not a piece of blotting paper that absorbs and retains automatically. It is rather a living organism that has to search for its food, that selects and rejects according to its present conditions and needs, and that retains only what it digests and transmutes into part of the energy of its own being.

II. The Functions of the Recitation

What are the objects that the recitation should achieve? In general, they are these three: (1) It should stimulate intellectual eagerness, awaken an intensified desire for intelligent activity and knowledge, and love of study—attitudes that are essentially *emotional* in character. (2) In case pupils bring these interests and affections with them and in the degree in which they are aroused, the recitation should *guide* them into those channels in which they can accomplish intellectual work, just as the great potential force of a river has to be directed into a particular course in order to grind grain or to convert water power into electric energy. (3) It should assist in organizing what has been acquired, so as to *test* its quality and quantity, and test especially the existing attitudes and habits with a view to ensuring their greater efficiency in the future.

These three functions, or objects, of the recitation are worth more extended consideration.

THE RECITATION SHOULD STIMULATE INTELLECTUAL EAGERNESS

The ultimate impetus to study, to intellectual activity comes from within. Mentally as well as physically there must be an appetite. For there is intellectual as well as bodily hunger and thirst. Yet the foodstuffs of the *environment*, either those directly at hand or those found by search, finally determine what is eaten. That is, they decide what *direction* the appetite actually takes. So stimulus from without, especially that which occurs in a social situation, decides the further movement of an intellectual impetus. An infant has to have an impetus from within in order to learn to talk; it babbles, gestures, etc. These at first are formless and diffuse movements. Contact with others stimulates them to take on *meaning*, intellectual import.

A recitation should be a situation in which a class, a group organized as a social unity, with common interests, led by a more mature and experienced person, encourages mental eagerness. A pupil may come to the class intellectually empty and lethargic. Or his intellectual interests may be remote from the subject at hand. It is the business of the recitation period to stir up the mind, to get it going, as it were, to impart by contagion some degree of intellectual excitement. The statement is sometimes made that there have been teachers with no training in the theory of teaching, no scientific knowledge of psychology, etc., who nevertheless were great teachers, some of them much greater teachers than those who have had a full equipment of pedagogical courses. If the reader will go back over his own school experience, he will probably have no trouble in discovering the why and wherefore of this fact. He will note that the teachers who left the most enduring impression were those who awakened in him a new intellectual interest, who communicated to him some of their own enthusiasm for a field of knowledge or art, who gave his desire to inquire and find out a momentum of its own. This is the one thing most needful. Given this hunger, the mind will go on; while it may be stuffed to overflowing with information, if this one thing is omitted, little will be gained in the future.

The conditions to be met in communicating ardor in study have been indicated in various places in prior discussions. The teacher must have a genuine interest in mental activity on his own account, a love of knowledge that unconsciously animates his teaching. A bored, perfunctory instructor will deaden any subject. Again, textbooks must be used as means and tools, not as ends. They are useful to arouse questions and to supply information with which to answer them. But when they are permitted to dictate or even dominate the conduct of the recitation, the result is a dulling of thought. As a rule, the material of the text should be attacked indirectly, by a flank movement. It is the literal approach that confines the mind to the paths already trodden in the book. But such prerequisites as these sum themselves up in the fact that a lively give-and-take of ideas, experiences, information, between the members of the class should be the chief reliance.

A vital discussion will make the underlying problems stand out in sharply defined focus. Instead of treating all facts and statements as on the same intellectual level, thus destroying intellectual perspective, and hence giving no opportunity for judgment to appraise what is important and what secondary, the discussion should be conducted so as to centre thought on a few main points around which other considerations will be organized. It will lead the student to turn back and go over what he has learned from his prior personal experiences and what he has learned from others (to *re*flect), so as to find out what bears, both positively and negatively, on the subject in hand. Although discussion will not be allowed to degenerate into mere "argufying," a lively discussion will bring out intellectual differences and opposed points of view and interpretations, so as to help define

the true nature of the problem. Humor is always in place, as well
as sympathy for the pupil struggling with an idea that he has difficulty in laying hold of.

THE RECITATION SHOULD GUIDE PUPILS
TO GOOD HABITS OF STUDY

Since stimulation and direction should occur simultaneously, we have touched upon this function in what has just been
said. From the standpoint of direction, the point to be emphasized is that the recitation culminate, from the intellectual standpoint, in the promotion of *good habits of study*. Instead of repeating, we shall, then, say something about study.

In substance, study is simply reflective activity with especial
emphasis on matter provided through language, oral or printed.
The expression "a studious person" suggests a person who is
fond of books that have a substantial mental content. At the
same time, as the colloquial phrase "studying something *out*"
suggests, one "studies" machinery, financial and political situations, questions of personal conduct and character. A person's
automobile will not run; he "studies out" the trouble; he puzzles
over it to locate the cause of the trouble. It is obvious that this
active process of search, ending in *understanding*, is very different from repeating over and over the statements of a book or lecture notes in order to impress them firmly on memory with a
view to recalling them later on demand.

Thinking is inquiry, investigation, turning over, probing or
delving into, so as to find something new or to see what is already known in a different light. In short, it is *questioning*. A
well established feature of the traditional recitation is the asking
of questions by the teacher. But too often they are asked merely
to get an answer, not to *raise* a question for discussion by teacher
and students in common. The fact is that the separation usually
made between a preparatory "study" period, when pupils con
their lessons, and a recitation period, when they exhibit the results of their previous study, is thoroughly harmful. Students
need direction in their studying. Hence some so-called "recitation" periods should be times of supervised study, when the
teacher learns the difficulties that students are meeting, ascer-
tains what methods of learning they use, gives hints and sugges-

tions, helps a student recognize some bad habit that is holding him back. In *all* cases, the recitation should be a *continuation* of the study period, following up what has been done and leading on to further independent study.

The Art of Questioning. The art of conducting a recitation is, then, very largely the art of questioning pupils so as to direct their own inquiries and so as to form in them the independent habit of inquiry in both of its directions; namely, inquiry in *observation* and recollection for the subject matter that is pertinent and inquiry through *reasoning* into the *meaning* of material that is present. The art of questioning is so fully the art of guiding learning that hard and fast rules cannot be laid down for its exercise. Some suggestions follow.

First, in reference to material already learned, questions should require the student to *use* it in dealing with a new problem rather than to reproduce it literally and directly. For the former operation demands the exercise of judgment by the pupil and cultivates originality even in dealing with things already well known by others. Students in an advanced class who had been studying the snake, including its dissection, were asked in a written test: How does the snake move along the ground? They were already informed about the muscular system and skeleton; the question compelled them to *use* that information, to imagine the structure of the snake actually operating, to see in thought the muscles in action. There are times, however, when questions asking for direct reproduction of material are in place. When a problem is already under active consideration, and a student is blundering around aimlessly, he may be checked and called back to the topic by being asked to state as precisely as possible just the facts and principle that bear upon it.

Second, questions should direct the mind of students to subject matter rather than to the teacher's aim. This principle is violated when emphasis falls chiefly on getting the correct answer.[1] Then the recitation tends to become a guessing bee as to what the teacher is really after.

Third, questions should be such as keep the subject developing. That is, they should be factors in a continuous discussion, not asked as if each one were complete in itself so that when that

1. See page 164.

question is answered that particular matter is disposed of and another topic can be taken up. The failure to get a *situation* before the thought of students, and a situation that is large, inclusive, enough to have a movement within it from one point to another in a consecutive way,[2] breaks the continuity of ideas and renders thought choppy and disorderly.

Fourth, questions should periodically require a survey and review of what has been gone over, in order to extract its *net* meaning, to gather up and hold on to what is significant in the prior discussion and to make it stand out from side issues, from tentative and explorative remarks, etc. The recitation should usually include two or three minor organizing surveys in order to keep discussion to a point and prevent its rambling on aimlessly, "wandering all over the lot," as we say. Then there should be occasional recurrent summaries of extensive stretches of previous recitations so as to put the old material in the new perspective that later material has supplied.

Fifth, and finally, while recitations should at their close provide a sense of what has been accomplished and learned, the minds of pupils should even more be put on the *qui vive* through a sense of some *coming* topic, some problem still in suspense, just as in a cleverly constructed story or drama each section leaves the mind looking ahead, eager to resume the thread. There is an old story to the effect that the way to educate a baby is to begin with the grandparents. It may be said with more practicability that the way to arouse the mind, to awaken it to activity in any particular case, is to make sure that desire to go on has been left as a deposit by prior recitations.

THE RECITATION SHOULD TEST WHAT HAS BEEN ACQUIRED

There is not much additional to be said on the score of the third function of the recitation, testing. Testing should be a constant function. The mistake lies in supposing that the need for testing is met merely by tests of ability to reproduce subject matter that has been committed to memory. The previous discussion shows that that object is incidental. The important thing is

2. See page 164.

to test (*a*) progress in *understanding* subject matter, (*b*) ability to use what has been learned as an instrumentality of further study and learning, (*c*) improvement in the general habits and attitudes that underlie thinking: curiosity, orderliness, power to review, to sum up, and to define, openness and honesty of mind, etc.

III. The Conduct of the Recitation

We shall now go over the material already stated by considering the conduct of the recitation as a unity.

THE FIRST NEED: PREPARATION OF PUPILS

The first need is readiness, preparation on the part of students. The best, indeed the only, preparation needed is arousal to a perception of something that needs explanation, something unexpected, puzzling, peculiar. When the feeling of a genuine perplexity lays hold of any mind (no matter how the feeling arises), that mind is alert and inquiring, because stimulated from within. The shock, the bite, of a question will force the mind to go wherever it is capable of going, better than will the most ingenious pedagogical devices unaccompanied by this mental ardor. It is the sense of a problem to be mastered, a purpose to be realized, that forces the mind to a survey and recall of the past to discover what the question means and how it may be dealt with.

The teacher, in his more deliberate attempts to call into play the familiar elements in a student's experience, must guard against certain dangers. First, the step of preparation must not be too long continued or too exhaustive, or it defeats its own end. The pupil loses interest and is bored, whereas a plunge *in medias res* might have braced him to his work. The preparation part of the recitation period of some conscientious teachers reminds one of the boy who takes so long a run in order to gain headway for a jump that, when he reaches the line, he is too tired to jump far. Second, the organs by which we apprehend new material are our habits. To insist too minutely upon turning over habitual dispositions into conscious ideas is to interfere with their best workings. Some factors of familiar experience must indeed be brought to conscious recognition, just as transplanting is necessary for the best growth of some plants. But it is fatal to be forever digging up either experiences or plants to see how they are getting along. There is no mistake more common in schools than ignoring the self-propelling power of an idea. Once it is aroused, an alert mind fairly races along with it. Of itself it carries the student into new fields; it branches out into new ideas as a plant sends forth new shoots.

THE DEGREE OF PARTICIPATION BY THE TEACHER

The practical question of how much new subject matter the teacher should introduce in the course of a discussion was taken up in one of its aspects when we were discussing the place of information. In some quarters, however, the fear lest the adult instructor make the young pupil unduly dependent on others has led to a morbid fear of the teacher's taking an active part in the class. The practical problem of the teacher is to preserve a balance between so little showing and telling as to fail to stimulate reflection and so much as to choke thought. Provided the student is genuinely engaged upon a topic, and provided the teacher is willing to give the student a good deal of leeway as to what he assimilates and retains (not requiring rigidly that everything be grasped or reproduced), there is comparatively little danger that one who is himself enthusiastic will communicate too much concerning a topic. If a genuine community spirit pervades the group, if the atmosphere is that of free communication in a developing exchange of experiences and suggestions, it is absurd to debar the teacher from the privilege and responsibility freely granted to the young, that of contributing his share. The only warning is that the teacher should not forestall the contributions of pupils, but should enter especially at the critical junctures where the experience of pupils is too limited to supply just the material needed.

The objection most commonly brought against the type of free social discussion here recommended is that it becomes aimless, and gets nowhere, that discussion is dispersive, children jumping from one thing to another, till unity is destroyed and pupils are left with a sense of futility. There is no doubt of the reality of the danger thus suggested. But if the young are to be prepared when they leave school to take an effective part in a democratic society, the danger must be faced and conquered. Many of the failures of democratic government (which are used by critics to condemn the whole undertaking) are due to the fact that adults are unable to share in joint conference and consultation on social questions and issues. They can neither contribute intelligently, nor can they follow and judge the contributions of others. The habits set up in their earlier schooling have not fitted them for this enterprise; the habits even stand in the way.

MAKING THE PUPIL JUSTIFY HIS CONTRIBUTIONS

One of the most important factors in preventing an aimless and discursive recitation consists in making it necessary for every student to follow up and justify the suggestions he offers. He should be held responsible for working out mentally every suggested principle so as to show what he means by it, how it bears upon the facts at hand, and how the facts bear upon it. Unless the pupil is made responsible for developing on his own account the *reasonableness* of the guess he puts forth, the recitation counts for practically nothing in the training of reasoning power. A clever teacher easily acquires great skill in dropping out the inept and senseless contributions of pupils, and in selecting and emphasizing those in line with the result he wishes to reach. But this method (sometimes called "suggestive questioning") relieves the pupils of intellectual responsibility, save for acrobatic agility of mind in following the teacher's lead.

The working over of a vague and more or less casual idea into coherent and definite form is impossible without a pause, without freedom from distraction. We say, "Stop and think"; well, all reflection involves, at some point, stopping external observations and reactions so that an idea may mature. Meditation, withdrawal or abstraction from clamorous assailants of the senses and from demands for overt action, is as necessary at the reasoning stage as are observation and experiment at other periods. The metaphors of digestion and assimilation, which so readily occur to mind in connection with rational elaboration, are highly instructive. A silent, uninterrupted working-over of considerations by comparing and weighing alternative suggestions is indispensable for the development of coherent and compact conclusions. Reasoning is no more akin to disputing or arguing or to the abrupt seizing and dropping of suggestions than digestion is to a noisy champing of the jaws. The teacher must permit opportunity for leisurely mental digestion.

The holding, metaphorically, of a stop-watch over students in a recitation, exacting prompt and speedy responses from them, is not conducive to building up a reflective habit of mind.

AVOIDING DISTRACTION BY FOCUSSING UPON A CENTRAL TOPIC OR TYPICAL OBJECT

The teacher must avert the distraction that ensues from putting before the mind a number of facts on the same level of importance. Since attention is selective, some one object normally claims thought and furnishes the centre of departure and reference. This fact is fatal to the success of the pedagogical methods that put before the mind a row of objects of equal importance. In reaching a generalization the mind does not naturally begin with objects *a*, *b*, *c*, *d*, and try to find the respect in which they agree. It begins with a single object or situation, more or less vague and inchoate in meaning, and makes excursions to other objects in order to render understanding of the central object consistent and clear. A mere multiplication of objects is adverse to successful reasoning. Each fact brought within the field of thought should clear up some obscure feature or extend some fragmentary trait of the primary object.

In short, pains should be taken to see that the object on which thought centres is *typical*. Material is typical when, although individual or specific, it is such as readily and fruitfully suggests the principles of an entire class of facts. No sane person, for example, begins to think about rivers wholesale or at large. He begins with the one river that has presented some puzzling trait. Then he studies other rivers to get light upon the baffling features of this one, and at the same time he employs the characteristic traits of his original object to reduce to order the multifarious details that appear in connection with other rivers. This working back and forth preserves unity of meaning, while protecting it from monotony and narrowness. The mind needs to be defended against the deadening influence of many isolated particulars and also against the barrenness of a merely formal principle. The inherent significance of generalization is that it frees a meaning from local restrictions; generalization *is* meaning so freed; it is meaning emancipated from accidental features so as to be available in new cases. The surest test for detecting a spurious generalization (a statement general in verbal form but not accompanied by discernment of meaning) is the failure of the so-called "principle" spontaneously to extend itself. A central idea moves of its own accord to application; it seeks opportunity for operation in use to bring other facts into line.[3]

IV. The Function of the Teacher

THE TEACHER AS LEADER

The older type of instruction tended to treat the teacher as a dictatorial ruler. The newer type sometimes treats the teacher as a negligible factor, almost as an evil, though a necessary one. In reality the teacher is the intellectual leader of a social group. He is a leader, not in virtue of official position, but because of wider and deeper knowledge and matured experience. The supposition that the principle of freedom confers liberty upon the pupils, but that the teacher is outside its range and must abdicate all leadership is merely silly.

FALLACIOUS NOTIONS MINIMIZING HIS LEADERSHIP

In some schools the tendency to minimize the place of the teacher takes the form of supposing that it is an arbitrary imposition for the teacher to propose the line of work to be followed or to arrange the situation within which problems and topics arise. It is held that, out of due respect for the mental freedom of those taught, all suggestions are to come from them. Especially has this idea been applied in some kindergartens and primary grades. The result is often that described in the story of a young child who, on arriving at school, said to the teacher: "Do we have to do to-day what we want to do?" The alternative to

3. See page 266.

proposals by the teacher is that the suggestions of things to do come from chance, from casual contacts, from what the child saw on his way to school, what he did yesterday, what he sees the next child doing, etc. Since the purpose to be carried out must come, directly or indirectly, from somewhere in the environment, denial to the teacher of the power to propose it merely substitutes accidental contact with some other person or scene for the intelligent planning of the very individual who, if he has a right to be a teacher at all, has the best knowledge of the needs and possibilities of the members of the group of which he is a part.

HIS NEED OF ABUNDANT KNOWLEDGE

The practically important question concerns the conditions under which the teacher can really be the intellectual leader of a social group. The first condition goes back to his own intellectual preparation in subject matter. This should be abundant to the point of overflow. It must be much wider than the ground laid out in textbook or in any fixed plan for teaching a lesson. It must cover collateral points, so that the teacher can take advantage of unexpected questions or unanticipated incidents. It must be accompanied by a genuine enthusiasm for the subject that will communicate itself contagiously to pupils.

Some of the reasons why the teacher should have an excess supply of information and understanding are too obvious to need mention. The central reason is possibly not always recognized. *The teacher must have his mind free to observe the mental responses and movements of the student members of the recitation-group.* The problem of the pupils is found in *subject matter*; the problem of teachers is *what the minds of pupils are doing with this subject matter.* Unless the teacher's mind has mastered the subject matter in advance, unless it is thoroughly at home in it, using it unconsciously without the need of express thought, he will not be free to give full time and attention to observation and interpretation of the pupils' intellectual reactions. The teacher must be alive to all forms of bodily expression of mental condition—to puzzlement, boredom, mastery, the dawn of an idea, feigned attention, tendency to show off, to dominate discussion because of egotism, etc.—as well as sensitive to the meaning of all expression in words. He must be aware not only of *their* meaning, but of their meaning as indicative of the state of mind of the pupil, his degree of observation and comprehension.

HIS NEED OF TECHNICAL, PROFESSIONAL KNOWLEDGE

The fact that the teacher has to be a student of the pupil's mind, as the latter is a student of subject matter in various fields, accounts for the teacher's need for technical knowledge as well as for knowledge in the subjects taught. By "technical knowledge" is here meant professional knowledge. Why should a teacher have acquaintance with psychology, history of education, the methods found helpful by others in teaching various subjects? For two main reasons: the one reason is that he may be equipped to note what would otherwise go unheeded in the responses of the students and may quickly and correctly interpret what pupils do and say; the other reason is that he may be ready to give proper aid when needed because of his knowledge of procedures that others have found useful.

Unfortunately this professional knowledge is sometimes treated, not as a guide and tool in personal observation and judgment—which it essentially is—but as a set of fixed rules of procedure in action. When a teacher finds such theoretical knowledge coming between him and his own common-sense judgment of a situation, the wise thing is to follow his own judgment—making sure, of course, that it is an enlightened insight. For unless the professional information enlightens his own perception of the situation and what to do about it, it becomes either a purely mechanical device or else a load of undigested material.

Finally the teacher, in order to be a leader, must make special preparation for particular lessons. Otherwise the only alternatives will be either aimless drift or else sticking literally to the text. Flexibility, ability to take advantage of unexpected incidents and questions, depends upon the teacher's coming to the subject with freshness and fullness of interest and knowledge. There are questions that he should ask before the recitation commences. What do the minds of pupils bring to the topic from their previous experience and study? How can I help them make connections? What need, even if unrecognized by them, will furnish a leverage by which to move their minds in the desired direction?

What uses and applications will clarify the subject and fix it in their minds? How can the topic be individualized; that is, how shall it be treated so that each one will have something distinctive to contribute while the subject is also adapted to the special deficiencies and particular tastes of each one?

V. Appreciation

THE REALIZATION OF VALUE

To experience a thing fully is in familiar phrase to get a "realizing sense" of it; or, in synonymous expressions, to have it come home to one, to have it take possession. When this happens, the person is "warm," as children say in their searching games. Barriers and obstructions that have previously come between the mind and some object, truth, or situation, fall away. The mind and the subject seem to come together and unite. This is the state of affairs that is designated by the word "appreciation." We sometimes speak of things "appreciating" in value, the opposite being "depreciation" as objects grow stale, out of date, and wanted by no one. When the mind thoroughly appreciates anything, that object is experienced with heightened intensity of value. There is no inherent opposition between thought, knowledge, and appreciation. There is, however, a definite opposition between an idea or a fact grasped *merely* intellectually and the idea or fact which is *emotionally* colored because it is felt to be connected with the needs and satisfactions of the whole personality. In the latter case, it has immediate value; that is, it is *appreciated*.

ITS ROLE IN THINKING

In what has been said throughout the book about the necessity of situations and problems that are vitally real to students[4] it has been implied that no separation exists between thinking and realization, between intellectual activity and appreciation. This implicit idea will now be briefly considered with the

4. For example, on pages 193–194.

purpose of making explicit the basic importance of appreciation to thought.

There is a tendency in schools that are breaking away from traditional methods of routine discipline, of drill and literal reproduction of subject matter, to make a sharp separation between subjects that involve mastery of facts and principles (like arithmetic, grammar, physical science, the larger part of geography) on the one side, and literature, music, and the fine arts on the other side. The need for personal appreciation is supposed to be confined to the latter group of subjects. When this idea is acted upon, the latter subjects tend to become sentimental and imaginative (in the sense of merely imaginary and unreal), while freedom of self-expression turns into something that might better be called "self-exposure."

The evil that especially concerns us in this connection, however, is failure to see that vital appreciations—that is, ideas involving emotional response and imaginative projection—are ultimately as necessary in history, mathematics, scientific fields, in all so-called "informational" and "intellectual" subjects, as they are in literature and the fine arts. Human beings are not normally divided into two parts, the one emotional, the other coldly intellectual—the one matter of fact, the other imaginative. The split does, indeed, often get established, but that is always because of false methods of education. Natively and normally the personality works as a whole. There is no integration of character and mind unless there is fusion of the intellectual and the emotional, of meaning and value, of fact and imaginative running beyond fact into the realm of desired possibilities. The final test of any recitation in any subject is the extent in which pupils secure vital appreciation of the subject matter dealt with. Otherwise problems and questions, which are the only true instigators of reflective activity, will be more or less externally imposed and only half-heartedly felt and dealt with.

19.   Some General Conclusions

We shall conclude our survey of how we think and how we should think by presenting some factors of thinking that should balance each other, but that constantly tend to become so isolated that they work against each other instead of cooperating to make reflective inquiry efficient.

I. The Unconscious and the Conscious

IMPLICIT AND EXPLICIT CONTEXT

It is significant that one meaning of the term "understood" is something so thoroughly mastered, so completely agreed upon, as to be *assumed*; that is to say, something taken as a matter of course without explicit statement. The familiar "it goes without saying" means "it is understood." If two persons can converse intelligently with each other, it is because a common experience supplies a background of mutual understanding upon which their respective remarks are projected. To dig up and to formulate this common background would be imbecile; it is "understood"; that is, it is silently sup-plied and im-plied as the taken-for-granted medium of intelligent exchange of ideas.

If, however, the two persons find themselves at cross-purposes, it is necessary to dig up and compare the presuppositions, the implied context, on the basis of which each is speaking. The implicit is made ex-plicit; what was unconsciously assumed is exposed to the light of conscious day. In this way, the root of the misunderstanding is removed. Some such rhythm of the unconscious and the conscious, of going ahead and of analysis, is involved in all fruitful thinking. A person in pursuing a consecutive train of thoughts takes some system of ideas for granted (which accordingly he leaves unexpressed, "unconscious") as surely as he does in conversing with others. Some context, some situation, some controlling purpose dominates his explicit ideas so thoroughly that it does not need to be consciously formulated and expounded. Explicit thinking goes on within the limits of what is implied or understood. Yet the fact that reflection originates in a problem makes it necessary *at some points* consciously to inspect and examine this familiar background. We have to turn upon some unconscious assumption and make it explicit.

No rules can be laid down for attaining the due balance and rhythm of these two phases of mental life. No ordinance can prescribe at just what point the spontaneous working of some unconscious attitude and habit is to be checked till we have made explicit what is implied in it. No one is wise enough to tell in detail just when and how far analytic inspection and conscious statement should be engaged in. We can say that they must be carried far enough so that the individual will know what he is about and be able to guide his thinking; but in a given case just how far is that? We can say that they must be carried far enough to detect and guard against the source of some false perception or reasoning, and to get a leverage on an investigation; but such statements only restate the original difficulty. Since our reliance must be upon the disposition and tact of the individual in the particular case, there is no test of the success of an education more important than whether it nurtures a type of mind that maintains a balance of the unconscious and the conscious.

The ways of teaching criticized in the foregoing pages as false "analytic" methods of instruction, all reduce themselves to the mistake of directing explicit attention and formulation to what would work better if left an unconscious attitude and working assumption. To pry into the familiar, the usual, the automatic, simply for the sake of making it conscious, simply for the sake of formulating it, is both an impertinent interference and a source of boredom. To be forced to dwell consciously upon the accustomed is the essence of ennuï. Methods of instruction that have that tendency dull curiosity.

On the other hand, what has been said in criticism of merely routine forms of skill, what has been said about the importance of having a genuine problem, of introducing the novel, and of reaching a deposit of general meaning weighs on the other side of the scales. It is fatal to good thinking to fail to make conscious the standing source of some error or recurring failure as well as to pry needlessly into what works smoothly. To over-simplify, to exclude the novel for the sake of prompt skill, to avoid obstacles for the sake of averting errors, is as detrimental as to try to get pupils to formulate everything they know and to state every step of the procedure by which a result was obtained. Where the shoe pinches, analytic examination is indicated. When a topic is to be clinched so that knowledge of it will carry over and be an effective resource in further topics, conscious summarizing and organization are imperative. In the early stage of acquaintance with a subject, a good deal of unconstrained unconscious mental play about it may be permitted, even at the risk of some random experimenting; in the later stages, conscious formulation and review may be encouraged. Projection and reflection, going directly ahead and turning back in scrutiny, should alternate. Unconsciousness gives spontaneity and freshness; consciousness, command and control.

AN ILLUSTRATION FROM CONTROL OF REFLECTIVE THINKING

The point may be illustrated by the analysis in this volume of the phases of reflective activity. Some readers may get the idea that it is intended that students in their study and recitation should be made consciously to note and formulate these various phases as a means of intellectual control. Such a notion is, however, foreign to the spirit of the analysis. For it holds that fundamental control is effected by means of the *conditions* under which students work—the provision of a real situation that arouses inquiry, suggestion, reasoning, testing, etc. The chief value of the analysis that has been given is therefore to suggest to teachers the ways in which reflective thought may be best secured in students without the latter being made conscious at every step of their own attitudes and processes. It is also true that, *after* the instructor has once provided the conditions most likely to call out and direct thinking, the student's subsequent activity, while conscious of ends and means, may be unconscious with respect to his own personal attitudes and procedures. The familiar fact that creative work in the arts, writing, painting, music, etc., is largely unconscious as to the motives and attitudes of the artist, his mind being fixed on the objects he is dealing with or constructing, suggests the adoption of a like course in both study and teaching. The artist should be taken as a model rather than the activities of one painfully conscious at every step of just how he is operating. Control should be exercised by the set-up of the situation itself. Yet in conditions of unusual perplexity or repeated error it will usually be a help if conscious attention goes back to such causes as lie in the attitudes and processes of the learner.

ABSORPTION AND INCUBATION

It is a common experience that after prolonged preoccupation with an intellectual topic, the mind ceases to function readily. It apparently has got into a rut; the "wheels go around" in the head, but they do not turn out any fresh grist. New suggestions cease to occur. The mind is, as the apt expression goes, "fed up." This condition is a warning to turn, as far as conscious attention and reflection are concerned, to something else. Then after the mind has ceased to be intent on the problem, and consciousness has relaxed its strain, a period of incubation sets in. Material rearranges itself; facts and principles fall into place; what was confused becomes bright and clear; the mixed-up becomes orderly, often to such an extent that the problem is essentially solved. Many persons having a complicated practical question to decide find it advisable to sleep on the matter. Often they awake in the morning to find that, while they were sleeping, things have wonderfully straightened themselves out. A subtle process of incubation has resulted in hatching a decision and a plan. But this bringing forth of inventions, solutions, and discoveries rarely occurs except to a mind that has previously steeped itself consciously in material relating to its question, has turned matters off and over, weighed·pros and cons. Incubation, in short, is one phase of a rhythmic process.

II. Process and Product

PLAY AND WORK AGAIN

A like balance in mental life characterizes process and product. We met one important phase of this adjustment in considering play and work. In play, interest centres in activity, without much reference to its outcome. The sequence of deeds, images, emotions, suffices on its own account. In work, the end holds attention and controls the notice given to means. Since the difference is one of direction of interest, the contrast is one of emphasis, not of cleavage. When comparative prominence in consciousness of activity or outcome is transformed into isolation of one from the other, play degenerates into fooling, and work into drudgery.

PLAY SHOULD NOT BE FOOLING

By "fooling" we understand a series of disconnected temporary overflows of energy dependent upon whim and accident. When all reference to outcome is eliminated from the sequence of ideas and acts that make play, each member of the sequence is cut loose from every other and becomes fantastic, arbitrary, aimless; mere fooling follows. There is some inveterate tendency to fool in children as well as in animals; the tendency is not wholly evil, for it militates against falling into ruts. Even indulgence in dreaming and fancies *may* give mind a start in a new direction. But when they are excessive in amount, dissipation and disintegration follow; and the only way of preventing this result is to see to it that the children look ahead and forecast, to some extent, the ends of their activity, the effects it is likely to produce.

WORK SHOULD NOT BE DRUDGERY

However, *exclusive* interest in a result alters work to drudgery. For by drudgery is meant those activities in which the interest in the outcome does not suffuse the process of getting the result. Whenever a piece of work becomes drudgery, the process of doing loses all value for the doer; he cares solely for what is to be had at the end of it. The work itself, the putting forth of energy, is hateful; it is just a necessary evil, since without it some important end would be missed. Now, it is a commonplace that in the work of the world many things have to be done, the doing of which is not intrinsically very interesting. However, the argument that children should be kept doing drudgery tasks because thereby they acquire power to be faithful to distasteful duties is wholly fallacious. Repulsion, shirking, and evasion are the consequences of having the repulsive imposed—not loyal love of duty. Willingness to work for ends by means of acts not naturally attractive is best attained by securing an appreciation of the value of the end, so that a sense of its value is transferred to its means of accomplishment. Not interesting in themselves, they borrow interest from the result with which they are associated.

BALANCE OF THE WORK ATTITUDE AND THE PLAY ATTITUDE

The intellectual harm accruing from divorce of work and play, product and process, is evidenced in the proverb, "All work and no play makes Jack a dull boy." That the obverse is true is perhaps sufficiently signalized in the fact that fooling is so near to foolishness. To be playful and serious at the same time is possible, and it defines the ideal mental condition. Absence of dogmatism and prejudice, presence of intellectual curiosity and flexibility, are manifest in the free play of the mind upon a topic. To give the mind this free play is not to encourage toying with a subject, but is to be interested in the unfolding of the subject on its own account, apart from any subservience to a preconceived belief or habitual aim. Mental play is open-mindedness, faith in the power of thought to preserve its own integrity without external supports and arbitrary restrictions. Hence free mental play involves seriousness, the earnest following of the development of subject matter. It is incompatible with carelessness or flippancy, for it exacts accurate noting of every result reached in order that every conclusion may be put to further use. What is termed the "interest in truth for its own sake" is certainly a serious matter, yet this pure interest in truth concides with love of the free play of thought in inquiry.

In spite of many appearances to the contrary—usually due to

social conditions either of superfluity of means that induces idle fooling or of undue economic pressure that compels drudgery— childhood normally realizes the ideal of conjoint free mental play and thoughtfulness. Successful portrayals of children have always made their wistful intentness at least as obvious as their lack of worry for the morrow. To live in the present is compatible with condensation of far-reaching meanings in the present. Such enrichment of the present for its own sake is the just heritage of childhood and the best insurer of future growth. The child forced into premature concern with economic remote results may develop a surprising sharpening of wits in a particular direction, but there is danger that this precocious specialization will be paid for by later apathy and dullness.

THE ATTITUDE OF THE ARTIST

That art originated in play is a common saying. Whether or not the saying is historically correct, it suggests a harmony of mental playfulness and seriousness that describes the artistic ideal. When the artist is preoccupied overmuch with means and materials, he may achieve wonderful technique, but not the artistic spirit *par excellence*. When the animating idea is in excess of the command of method, aesthetic feeling may be indicated, but the art of presentation is too defective to express the feeling thoroughly. When the thought of the end becomes so adequate that it compels translation into the means that embody it, or when attention to means is inspired by recognition of the end they serve, we have the attitude typical of the artist, an attitude that may be displayed in all activities, even though they are not conventionally designated "arts."

THE TEACHER AS AN ARTIST

That teaching is an art and the true teacher an artist is a familiar saying. Now the teacher's own claim to rank as an artist is measured by his ability to foster the attitude of the artist in those who study with him, whether they be youth or little children. Some succeed in arousing enthusiasm, in communicating large ideas, in evoking energy. So far, well; but the final test is whether the stimulus thus given to wider aims succeeds in transforming itself into power; that is to say, into the attention to detail that ensures mastery over means of execution. If not, the zeal flags, the interest dies out, the ideal becomes a clouded memory. Other teachers succeed in training facility, skill, mastery of the technique of subjects. Again it is well—so far. But unless enlargement of mental vision, power of increased discrimination of final values, a sense for ideas, for principles, accompanies this training, forms of skill ready to be put indifferently to any end may be the result. Such modes of technical skill may display themselves, according to circumstances, as cleverness in serving self-interest, as docility in carrying out the purposes of others, or as unimaginative plodding in ruts. To nurture inspiring aim and executive means into harmony with each other is at once the difficulty and the reward of the teacher.

III. The Far and the Near

"FAMILIARITY BREEDS CONTEMPT"

Teachers who have heard that they should avoid matters foreign to pupils' experience are frequently surprised to find pupils wake up when something beyond their ken is introduced, while they remain apathetic in considering the familiar. In geography the child upon the plains seems perversely irresponsive to the intellectual charms of his local environment, but fascinated by whatever concerns mountains or the sea. Teachers who have struggled with little avail to extract from pupils essays describing the details of things with which they are well acquainted sometimes find them eager to write on lofty or imaginary themes. A woman of education, who has recorded her experience as a factory worker, tried retelling *Little Women* to some factory girls during their working hours. They cared little for it, saying, "Those girls had no more interesting experience than we have," and demanded stories of millionaires and society leaders. A man interested in the mental condition of those engaged in routine labor asked a Scotch girl in a cotton factory what she thought about all day. She replied that, as soon as her mind was free from starting the machinery, she married a duke, and their fortunes occupied her for the remainder of the day.

Naturally, these incidents are not told in order to encourage methods of teaching that appeal to the sensational, the extraordinary, or the incomprehensible. They are told, however, to enforce the point that the familiar and the near do not excite or repay thought on their own account, but only as they are adjusted to mastering the strange and remote. It is a commonplace of psychology that we do not attend to the old or consciously mind that to which we are thoroughly accustomed. For this there is good reason; to devote attention to the old, when new circumstances are constantly arising to which we should adjust ourselves, would be wasteful and dangerous. Thought must be reserved for the new, the precarious, the problematic. Hence the mental constraint, the sense of being lost, that comes to pupils when they are invited to turn their thoughts upon that with which they are already familiar. The old, the near, the accustomed, is not that *to* which but that *with* which we attend; it does not furnish the material of a problem, but of its solution.

BALANCING THE NEW AND THE OLD

The last sentence has brought us to the balancing of new and old, of the far and that close by, involved in reflection. The more remote supplies the stimulus and the motive; the nearer at hand furnishes the point of approach and the available resources. This principle may also be stated in this form: the best thinking occurs when the easy and the difficult are duly proportioned to each other. The easy and the familiar are equivalents, as are the strange and the difficult. Too much that is easy gives no ground for inquiry; too much that is hard renders inquiry hopeless.

The necessity of the interaction of the near and the far follows directly from the nature of thinking. Where there is thought, something present suggests and indicates something absent. Accordingly, unless the familiar is presented under conditions that are in some respect unusual, there is no jog to thinking; no demand is made upon hunting out something new and different. And if the subject presented is totally strange, there is no basis upon which it may suggest anything serviceable for its comprehension. When a person first has to do with fractions, for example, they will be wholly baffling so far as they do not signify to him some relation that he has already mastered in dealing with whole numbers. When fractions have become thoroughly familiar, his perception of them acts simply as a signal to do certain things; they are a "substitute sign," to which he can react without thinking.[1] If, nevertheless, the situation as a whole presents something novel and hence uncertain, the entire response is not mechanical, because this mechanical operation is put to use in solving a problem. There is no end to this spiral process: foreign subject matter transformed through thinking into a familiar possession becomes a resource for judging and assimilating additional foreign subject matter.

OBSERVATION SUPPLIES THE NEAR, IMAGINATION THE REMOTE

The need for both imagination and observation in every mental enterprise illustrates another aspect of the same principle. Teachers who have tried object lessons of the conventional type have usually found that, when the lessons were new, pupils were attracted to them as a diversion, but as soon as they became matters of course, they were as dull and wearisome as was ever the most mechanical study of mere symbols. Imagination could not play about the objects so as to enrich them. The feeling that instruction in "facts, facts" produces a narrow Gradgrind is justified, not because facts in themselves are limiting, but because facts are dealt out as hard and fast ready-made articles. No room is left to imagination. Let the facts be presented so as to stimulate imagination, and culture ensues naturally enough. The converse is equally true. The imaginative is not necessarily the imaginary; that is, the unreal. The proper function of imagination is vision of realities and possibilities that cannot be exhibited under existing conditions of sense perception. Clear insight into the remote, the absent, the obscure is its aim. History, literature, and geography, the principles of science, nay, even geometry and arithmetic, are full of matters that must be imaginatively realized if they are realized at all. Imagination supplements and deepens observation; only when it turns into the fanciful does it become a substitute for observation and lose logical force.

A final exemplification of the required balance between near

1. See page 307.

and far is found in the relation that obtains between the narrower field of experience realized in an individual's own contact with persons and things, and the wider experience of the race that may become his through communication. Instruction always runs the risk of swamping the pupil's own vital, though narrow, experience under masses of communicated material. The mere instructor ceases and the vital teacher begins at the point where communicated matter stimulates into fuller and more significant life that which has entered by the strait and narrow gate of sense perception and motor activity. Genuine communication involves contagion; its name should not be taken in vain by terming communication that which produces no community of thought and purpose between the child and the race of which he is the heir.

Reviews

The Adventure of Persuasion

Adventures of Ideas, by Alfred North
Whitehead. New York: Macmillan Co., 1933.

Process and Reality, the book that grew out of Mr.
Whitehead's Gifford Lectures, was a hard nut to crack for those
readers who had been attracted to him by his *Science in the
Modern World*. It was anything but easy reading even for professional philosophers. But his present volume combines the human
sweep of the former with the comprehensive generality of the latter book. Cultivated persons with no specialized philosophical
knowledge or interest will find a genuine intellectual adventure
in following Mr. Whitehead's account of the march of a few great
ideas in human history. This statement applies particularly to the
first of the four sections which compose the book—their titles
being "Sociological," "Cosmological," "Philosophical" and
"Civilization." On the other hand, philosophical experts who
were more or less baffled by the intricacies of thought and novelties of terminology that abounded in *Process and Reality* will
find their understanding of Mr. Whitehead's underlying metaphysics much aided by the broad simplifications of the present
volume. One gains the impression that he now has a longer perspective in which to see ideas that were very close to him, because still in process of formation, when he gave the Gifford
Lectures.

Mr. Whitehead is preeminent among living thinkers for his extraordinary sensitiveness to the movement of things. Indeed, he is
distinguished among philosophers of all periods in this same respect. The delicacy, the "tenderness" (to use one of his own words)
of his sensitivity is indicated only in the rough by the general fact
that his philosophy is one of the universe in process, "creative advance." Other thinkers have had the same conception—notably,
in our own day, Bergson. But while the latter sums up the matter

[First published in *New Republic* 74 (19 April 1933): 285–86.]

in two leading ideas that are exemplified in a multitude of forms and ways, Mr. Whitehead brings out shade after shade of subtle distinction. He makes much of "intuition." This to my mind is a dangerous term; at least none has been more abused. But as I interpret Mr. Whitehead's use of it, it signifies a deep sensitivity to some aspect or temper of the experienced world, especially to one which is emerging and which characterizes an epoch. The emphasis that he places upon feeling, his condemnation of all philosophies that separate intellect from responsive interests, his recognition, so rare among philosophers, of the inadequacy of language to convey thoughts, and above all his sense of the multiplicity (the welter, as he calls it) of characteristics found in every object and institution, all testify alike to the fact that in spite of the unusually technical garb of his thought, it is rooted in a sensitivity of experience to the movement of things.

I would emphasize that it is *movement* to which he responds most directly and easily; it is this which sets his problems, especially his basic problem: namely, the question of how eternal objects can be influentially embodied in the processes of change that constitute the actuality of the universe. Now rationalistic philosophers, the school with which Mr. Whitehead prefers to identify himself (so far as he is "patient" of classification), have generally been open only to the *content* of things, as this content is translatable into ideas. Mr. Whitehead came to philosophy mainly through the medium of mathematics. There is a current notion, perhaps fallacious and due to the Cartesian and Lockeian identification of mathematics with clear and distinct ideas, with ideas wholly explicit and aboveboard, that a mathematician is sensitive *only* to the content of ideas. In more ways than one, Mr. Whitehead's problem is to harmonize the content of things with their *movement*. Perhaps the very thoroughness of his acquaintance with the static and eternal character of mathematical conceptions has made him the more aware of the discrepancy existing between them and the flux of existent things, while the function of mathematics in the science of these changing things has precipitated itself in a consciousness of what seems to be his basic metaphysical problem.

These conditions surely account for his devotion to Plato and for the points of contact between his own views and those of

Plato. It goes to show that Plato's attempt to unite a mathematical and religious interpretation of the universe is not the merely "mystical" thing it is often taken to be. At all events, such statements as are found in the two following quotations are characteristic of Mr. Whitehead's own combination of the two. "I hazard the prophecy that that religion will conquer which can render clear to popular understanding some eternal greatness incarnate in the passage of temporal fact." And, "there is a freedom beyond circumstance, derived from the direct intuition that life can be grounded upon its absorption in what is changeless amid change."

The second part, the cosmological, of Mr. Whitehead's treatment sums up his interpretation of the "immanent" character of law in opposition to its imposed character. For, in his mind, this doctrine culminates in speculative or systematic theology. Realization of the true philosophy of the case would culminate in "the New Reformation." The "institutional and dogmatic forms" of Protestant Christianity are in steady decay. Nevertheless, the attack of "liberals" upon systematic theology, while justified as far as the dogmatism of the latter is concerned, is entirely misconceived, for in principle it is an attack upon reason, upon systematic thought itself. The religious reformation, to be of fortunate issue, must primarily base itself upon "moral and metaphysical intuitions" scattered throughout the germinal epoch lying between the Hebrew prophets and Plato and the stabilization of Western theology by St. Augustine. The elements that Mr. Whitehead believes the new reformation must recover and develop are, first of all, the fact brought out by Plato, that "the divine element in the world is to be conceived as a persuasive agency and not as a coercive agency"; second, the exemplification of this principle by Christ in act; and third, the formulations of the Greek school of theologians in Alexandria and Antioch, since they "demanded a direct doctrine of immanence," thus pointing out the only way in which the Platonic idea of the persuasive agency of God could consistently develop. I doubt if the Protestant theologians to whom Mr. Whitehead appeals will grasp the revolutionary implication of his statement that "the leaders of religious thought should to-day concentrate upon the Christian tradition and more particularly upon its historical origins." They are used to depending upon the past as authority. Perhaps he shares the doubt. For at the end he asks: "Must 'religion' always remain as a synonym for 'hatred'?"

I have selected this particular chapter for special reference partly because of Whitehead's identification of the cosmological with (ultimately) the theological, but more because it brings the idea of "persuasion" to the front. It would not be true that this is the most important concept of Mr. Whitehead's thought. On the contrary, more than most thinkers he has a number of concepts of coordinate importance in that each is necessary to an understanding of the system. But it is, I think, the centralizing idea in the four main topics discussed in the volume. The mutual relations of coercion and persuasion in Western history are the chief theme of the sociological section, which traces the means by which the idea of persuasion, formulated by Plato in connection with the general character of "soul" and freedom, finally found its way, in conflict against ideas of slavery and coercion of circumstances, into power in Western civilization. That it is the culminating idea of the second portion I have already noted. Its significance is less marked in the section labeled "Philosophical," but this portion in reality deals with a number of special problems largely explanatory of the author's *Process and Reality*. It is implicit in the final section on Civilization, which differs basically from the sociological section in that it considers "Truth, Beauty, Adventure and Peace" as characters which measure civilization.

The exact meaning of "persuasion" is to be gained by feeling that has become intuition rather than by formal definition. It names the career and growing victory of ideas in the world of actuality that is dominantly a world of coercions. "Ideas" in his sense exist prior to human consciousness; they denote the general as governing the particular, and possibility as transcending actuality. "The Adventure of Ideas" is thus in some sense the process by which "the world of civilized order is created, the victory of persuasion over force." Mr. Whitehead's book is thus both a philosophy of human history and an exposition of the principles that, in his view, metaphysically underlie and constitute this history.

For reasons which obviously cannot be gone into here, I cannot align myself with the general school to which Mr. Whitehead professes that he belongs—which indeed, according to him, is alone worthy of the name of philosophy, Rationalism. This latter doctrine has, however, become conventionalized and academic. It is hardly too much to say that Mr. Whitehead has given it a radically fresh interpretation, one that must command the attention of all those outside the rationalistic school who had become wearied with the complacent repetition of outworn stalenesses characteristic of most who call themselves rationalists. I even doubt whether, when Mr. Whitehead's ideas have become developed and digested, they can be linked with historic rationalism in any but a Pickwickian sense. Of one thing I am sure. He has exemplified his own interpretation of the meaning of the Platonic transcendence of ideas. He has originated intuitions which will initiate new adventures: at first, adventures of thought, and then of action. For his ideas are not the concepts of historic rationalism, but are modes of valuing.

I am unwilling to close without quoting a number of aphoristic sentences selected at random. "The progress of religion is defined by the denunciation of gods." "Human life is driven forward by its dim apprehension of notions too general for its existing language." "Wherever there is a creed, there is a heretic round the corner or in his grave." "The literary exposition of freedom deals mainly with the frills." "State-systems are transient expedients upon the surface of civilization." "Life is an offensive, directed against the repetitious mechanism of the Universe." "The nearest analogues to the Alexandrian theological debates are the modern debates among mathematical physicists on the nature of the atom"—not said in derogation of either. "Aristotle dissected fishes with Plato's thoughts in his head"—an illustration of the relation of much scientific research to prior philosophical speculation.

A Challenge to Criticism

Academic Illusions in the Field of Letters and the Arts, by Martin Schütze. University of Chicago Press, 1933.

Professor Schütze's book is a critical and constructive account of the nature of literature as art. Speaking generally, it deals with theories of literary interpretation and, more specifically, with the effect of these theories upon the university teaching of literature—hence the title. The book brings together three strands. The first, which bulks largest in volume, has to do with the disastrous effects of Kantian and post-Kantian philosophies upon German esthetic theories. The second is an exposition both of the various theories that have governed the field in Germany and of Mr. Schütze's own conception of the nature of a literary work of art. The third strand concerns the educational phase of the discussion: in addition to attacking the methods which he finds dominant in the university teaching of literature, the author also proposes a definite plan for a thoroughgoing reform of its aims and methods.

For the details of the exposition of the leading ideas that have controlled the various writers who have drawn upon German rational idealism for their philosophies of literature, I shall have to refer to the volume itself—not only for reasons of space but because the writers themselves are outside the field of my acquaintance. But Mr. Schütze's account carries lightly a large load of learning, and his exposition is marked by concentrated generalization. His own sympathies are entirely with the genetic naturalism of Herder. He finds that the supplanting of Herder's intellectual influence by that of Kant was detrimental to the whole development of German literary criticism for the last century and a half, while the transfer of Goethe's allegiance from the former to the latter (under the influence of Schiller) coincided with a relative decline in the quality of Goethe's literary output, and was

[First published in *New Republic* 76 (16 August 1933): 24–25.]

indeed partly due to permitting Kant's opposition of reason and sense to benumb his own inherent sense of nature and life.

Persons who are not particularly interested in the theories that are set forth, but who are interested in the period of Germany's climax in creative literature, cannot fail to find instruction in the author's specific remarks about the Storm and Stress period, the different phases of the Romantic movement, and Goethe's own development. He seems to me to be at his best when, by way of illustrating the inevitable consequences of the rigid conceptualism inherited from Kant and Hegel, he shows how concrete differences among a whole group of writers have been obscured by bringing them all arbitrarily under certain concepts which were supposed to constitute, a-priori, the essence and unity of Romanticism.

Speaking from my own experience, I should say that those whose interest is philosophical cannot fail to learn a great deal from the accounts of the esthetics of literature propounded by critics who depended upon philosophic direction. Seeing their basic ideas reflected in the field of literature has the effect of a stereoscopic vision. If the evidence were not so comprehensive and weighty, one could hardly believe that men of natural ability and scholarship could have so subordinated personal insight to pre-formed general concepts. Certain antitheses and certain formulas for resolving them seem to have paralyzed natural and cultivated understanding of both individual authors and general movements. Rationalism and irrationalism, connected with the notion that sense, emotion and imagination are inherently irrational and with the daemonic character of the German mind; variations on the themes of permanence and change; of the "closed" nature of the classic in opposition to the "open" character of the Romantic, and similar oppositions, seem to have provided pigeonholes for classifying literary production that fatally made understanding of works of art in their individual wholeness quite unnecessary—and indeed, aside from the true mark. Dr. Schütze gives a thoroughly scholarly exposition of the many forms which this "dialectic absolutism" assumed.

I imagine that the general reader who is not particularly concerned with what would be vagaries of literary criticism, did not they follow so logically from basic philosophic concepts (which still have a great vogue outside of a literary application) will get most direct enlightenment from Chapter VII, dealing with the relation of poetry to the experience of the poets who produced it, and Chapter X, which concerns itself with the relation of the artist's environment to style. I do not see how anything could be more successful than the former in showing that the poem itself as a vital whole is not just an expression of the artist's experience but *is* that experience in its fullest form. Dr. Schütze turns this truth (which ought to be axiomatic in all artistic interpretation) against the attempt of critics to explain works of art in terms of *other* experiences of the poet and also against their attempt to deduce other experiences from the authentic poetic ones. Both of these operations are so common among critics who are quite innocent of the philosophic basis which German critics have used to support the practice, that adequate understanding of the point made by Mr. Schütze would throw out of employment a large number of existing critics—but it might also provide a beginning of intelligent objective criticism in the arts generally.

The chapters just mentioned provide the natural transition to the other school of literary criticism with which the author deals. This he terms "factualism," attributing its influence to Scherer. He does not claim that the method of "dialectic absolutism" had any especial influence on the teaching of literature in American universities. But this other "academic illusion" he finds dominating instruction in literature, especially in graduate schools and in work for the doctor's degree. Its influence is by no means to be attributed in all fields to Scherer, but it follows from the same causes that led Scherer to his conclusions: in gist, the desire to make instruction in, and interpretation of, literature thoroughly "scientific." To "factualism" Dr. Schütze assigns a value not possessed by the conceptualistic method. But the value is linguistic, not literary, in character, and at best is preliminary to an understanding of the literary work as literature. When it is permitted to invade literature it results in substituting external facts, identical or constant everywhere (as in the proper function of science) for the integrated variables that express a complete experience and constitute the work of art *per se*. The criticism of Mr. Schütze is thoroughgoing here and raises a question of the most fundamental importance not only for education in all the fine arts but also for criticism in them. The position he takes in respect to literature seems to me to have marked similarities, as far as concern the conception of what makes any product a work of art, with that taken by Dr. Barnes with respect to painting.

Criticisms of the so-called scientific teaching of literature are common enough. They are likely to end, however, in setting up something called "appreciation at large" in its place. This usually turns out to be a union of gushing sentiment with literary chatter. The solidity of Dr. Schütze's grasp of his theme saves him from every such excursion from the frying pan into the fire. He has developed, and expounds in the concluding chapters, a clear conception of the nature of a work of literature, and of what is meant by understanding it for what it is. He has had the courage to show what its adoption would signify for the university teaching of literature. His challenge deserves to be taken up. The extent to which it may become the starting point of a reconsideration of the whole subject seems to me to offer a fair measure of the vitality of intelligence in the university quarter.

The Industrial Discipline and the Governmental Arts, by Rexford G. Tugwell. New York: Columbia University Press, 1933.

The implications of the title are numerous and significant. There is the contrast of the present age with the conditions of thousands of years that extend almost to the present generation, for in the long agrarian period the discipline of daily life was enforced by nature itself. There is the suggestion that the chaos of the present is due to the fact that the discipline inherent in industry is neither intellectually recognized nor practically executed. And one does not have to read far to discover the reason why industry has not effected an organization analogous to that once enacted by direct contact with the forces of nature. It is because "business," namely, production and trading for a profit, has dominated industry and automatically institutes a series of conflicts that are socially disturbing and personally demoralizing.

The presentation is in my judgment by far the most intelligent analysis of our present economic situation and its impact upon the social order that exists. It is neither a condemnation, a laudation nor an exposition of a dubious philosophy of history. It is an intelligent analysis of forces at work, with a statement of how they work and a comprehensive grasp of the unutilized possibilities latent in these forces. Its temper is well expressed in these words: "What seems most desirable is that we should, for the moment, accept the conditions of our existence, but should try to build on these conditions a future which would be more desirable. It would be comparatively easy to dynamite the industrial system; it requires a long and rigid discipline of creative thinking to bring it into the service of human needs." The whole analysis points to the means by which we can create "the kind of world we all of us would like, very different from the present, yet built on it as a foundation."

[First published in *Occupations* 12 (December 1933): 40–41. For excerpts from Tugwell's *The Industrial Discipline*, see this volume, Appendix 1.]

The contents of the book are varied to the point of a pretty complete statement of all the elements, mechanical and human, in the present industrial and business systems, and yet it is highly compact. These facts make an adequate review in brief space practically impossible. The section on "Industrialized Society" brings out the fact that existing methods of industry compel the formation of groups and of compulsion within groups, but makes no provision for keeping a balance among groups—unless conflict can be called a provision. It points out that the traditional idea is that the function of government is simply to prevent monopolization and thus keep group conflict going. But with further development of present forces the real choice is "between a supertrust outside our political forms (which may swamp the State in the backwash of its progress) and an assimilation to the State of the going·system. They cannot exist together and yet separately."

Mechanization is also bound to go on. It is futile to complain of machinery. The need is for the "divination of a strain of tough, continued force which we must grasp and use if it is not to destroy our civilization. . . . Perhaps our only chance for cure is the substitution of preoccupation with the future for contemplative leaning above the past." From the earliest age men have engaged in inventions that would free them from labor. They never, however, envisaged this as a generalized end, merely working at it piecemeal and with reference to some immediate advantage. The great problem of and for an industrialized society is whether we can deliberately set out to achieve the end of abolition of mere labor, an end that so far has been brought about through pursuit of purposes irrelevant to it. This problem, with the question of the means by which orderly methods can be substituted for conflict (misnamed competition), form the strands that run through the book.

The relation of Dr. Tugwell to the Administration has given a somewhat factitious prominence to the closing section on "Government and Industry." It expresses clearly the philosophy on which he personally would like to see the government proceed. Unfortunately there is no evidence, so far as I can see, that the Administration has adopted the policies recommended in any thoroughgoing way. Whether half-measures will help in substituting cooperation for conflict or in the end add to the existing confusion is not yet decided. But it at least may be mentioned that some steps contemplated by Dr. Tugwell have not been attempted, such as an Integration Board, adequate representation of the weaker businesses, and of technicians, while the representation of consumers is, so far, formal and inert. Nor is there the slightest evidence that any one in the existing government has any conception of what Dr. Tugwell means when he says that "income must be dissociated from jobs," much less is interested in carrying out the idea.

There are multitudes of significant points that I have not touched upon. But I cannot close without saying that I know of no work from which hot-headed radicals and supposedly hard-headed business men can learn as much, if they would, as from this book. For those, the great majority, who are in between, it provides a map of the present alignment of forces and a chart of future possibilities.

Appendixes

Appendix 1
Excerpts from
The Industrial Discipline
By Rexford G. Tugwell

. . . For industry is going on. Concentration takes place; elaboration of facilities about the concentrative spheres also. And they made specific demands for defined abilities and for special training which are somehow, even if not rationally, met. Steadily even if slowly, we fit men for and into the new tasks. Without generalizing, or without exactly realizing what we are doing, we make of one individual a salesman, of another a designer of machines, of another a riveter, and of another, alas, a simple tender of machines. All through this process of selection and social promotion there runs a tragic note. There is a residue of unfitness, of inability to make adjustment to the new kinds of work; and into this class many of us seem doomed to fall. This is not true of all those who may, at any one time, be found there, for there are many fortuitous circumstances which determine these things quite outside inherent capability. The lack of opportunity may be as determinative as the lack of ability in a society which still lives partly in and partly out of poverty, and in which opportunities are still restricted. This group seems to possess a sufficient number, however, of individuals who have a general lack of capability for any of the tasks in the upper ranges of industrial effort, to create concern as to what may eventually become of them. If we are correct in supposing that machines are destined to take over physical tasks because they can do them more efficiently than the cheapest price at which life for workers can be supported, the unfit will eventually come to be a dead load on society. But this is another problem. Just as serious a one, perhaps, also, is the presumable trend which will increase the qualifications of skill necessary to employment. Such a development

[First published in *Occupations* 12 (December 1933): 41–44. For Dewey's review of Tugwell's book, see this volume, pp. 364–66.]

would increase the size of this unfit group. These considerations point to difficulties; but they will not stop industrial advance. One thing is clear from a humanitarian viewpoint: it is not the fault of the unfit that they are so. We shall have to keep back a portion of our increasing surplus for their support. . . .[1]

Education and Society

It is not necessary to point out the individual's inevitable dependence on education, both as child and as adult, if any better adjustment lies above rather than below. Education is a ladder by which it may be reached. There are, of course, other necessary conditions besides availability. An autocratically controlled system will always play favorites; a purely profit-seeking system will not develop even obvious social programs; a competitive system will not achieve sufficient stability to give anyone in it assurance of continuous employment or of enlarged opportunity. The worker must press for revision in all these respects; but also he must refuse to be a machine and to do machine work and he must fit himself for the really human tasks of managing natural materials and forces. . . .[2]

Education, formal and informal, is developing as a major social activity. And, from the point of view to which we are committed here, it is only one more of those social facilitations of which we have spoken. Industry in its modern phase could no more function without the educational system than it could without our railroads or organized markets. Changes in education reveal some perception, at least, of its possible utilitarian value. It slowly loses its meretricious, gentlemanly taint and becomes more relevant to common tasks and everyday problems. If this progress goes on, we shall discover in education an instrument which will be better and better adapted to the creation of a system in which expertness will not be confined to one field, but will extend throughout the whole range of industrial activity. . . .[3]

What does matter is that, from whatever industrial system we

1. From Chapter IV, pp. 95–96.
2. From Chapter IV, p. 97.
3. From Chapter IV, p. 102.

have, we should be able to get what we require in the way of goods and in the way of forms of effort which are suited to man's obvious interests and capabilities. . . .

Discovering Abilities

The discovery of ability is, in itself, something of a science. This is the expertness about expertness to which allusion has already been made. One difficulty about this science, as about so many others, is that its limitations are not seen with sufficient clarity so that what is done is distinguished from what is not done. For abilities are specific, not general. And when a test of ability is made, it is a test of intelligence at work with limited materials and at a given task. It is not a condemnation of a person that he cannot do one thing, when he can do many others. What he can do may not, at the time, be valued; but that is not his fault; and it is not necessarily an evidence of limited intelligence. Many of our tests of intelligence or of ability have given rise to unwarranted generalizations from the fact of failure or success in given examinations.

Some of this testing work has been done in industry; some in education, where its uses are perhaps more obvious. There is a certain sense of futility involved in any attempt to make a silk purse out of a sow's ear, and it has always been roughly recognized. To attempt to teach people kinds of knowledge which we know beforehand they cannot acquire, is just as easily recognizable as futile. The intelligence test is a device by which this foreknowledge can be made available. Even in education this procedure, though it is by now pretty thoroughly worked out, is not universally used. In industry it is hardly used at all. Our failure to make use of these devices has several causes. For one thing, there are relatively few really competent technicians in the field, but this is perhaps because there has been so little demand for them. For another, we still cling stubbornly to the notion that all men are created equal, and we refuse to accept the notion that there are degrees of intelligence or that there are different kinds of it. Only the terrific recent pressure on educational facilities has enabled educators to insist on some qualitative standards for the higher opportunities. The bare fact that there were not enough of these to go round made assent to selection compulsory. The necessity for some selection provided the entry for a theory that it ought to be carried out on the basis of ability to take advantage of opportunity. . . .[4]

When there is no attempt at the prediction of success, many inefficient ones must be tried and weeded out only after their failure has become apparent. But this is costly both for the industry and for the individual. The industry has lost the difference between the efficiency of a good man and the inefficiency of a poor one. It has also wasted time and effort in his training; and the individual has lost the time which might have been spent in getting started at a more fitting task and has suffered the humiliation of failure and discharge.

The cause of efficiency, both for industry and for the individual's career, is therefore served if all this costly trial and error can be prevented, or, at least, reduced. As has been said, failure in an examination for fitness means only that the individual ought not to try to do the specific thing for which the test was made, whether it happened to be the pursuing of collegiate education, the operation of a crane, the management of a lathe, the draughting of prints, or the leadership of a group of other men. The success of such tests in the educational field suggests, indeed, the possibility of a very wide application of the testing idea. For we might devise means not only for negative selections, such as we are beginning to make now, but also for positive ones. Instead of telling a man, on separate occasions, of fifty things he cannot do, we might tell him of the one thing which he can do best.

Discovering the Right Jobs

The activities of industry are sufficiently varied so that every degree and kind of intelligence might easily discover a fitting task to be done. If individuals could see that this is best for them, and if executives could be persuaded of the profitableness of selection, it is certain, from our experience up to now, that a long step might very quickly be taken in this direction. The resulting gains in effectiveness and happiness to the individual and

4. From Chapter IV, pp. 103–4.

in reduced costs and increased efficiency for the industry would be immense. The number of good mechanics who have wasted their time trying to be foremen, salesmen, or clerks must be enormous. And the same general misfitting of individuals and jobs by the trial-and-error methods of the past and the present must have been about as frequent as more happy marriages of this sort; or even more frequent, for the assumption of a job often comes about through accident rather than design, and inertia often holds men to tasks they hate and can only perform with indifferent success. Escape from this situation would be of the greatest benefit to workers. As an item in their own constructive program it ought to have an important place. . . .[5]

No suggestion of actual means for carrying out this particular program has been made, for obvious reasons. Measurement of ability and of achievement is a highly technical task. It is one of those fields in which expertness must be left to function freely. What has been said has been intended only as persuasion in this direction. . . .[6]

A democratic arrangement which had as one of its tenets the strictly objective measuring of abilities for given tasks could advance the efficiency of industry immeasurably. The accidents of relationship, or of pleasantness of personality, could then be discounted as they never are at present. It might also be said that as the number of responsible, thinking jobs grow in proportion to those of the routine, physical sort, these considerations become more important.[7]

5. From Chapter IV, pp. 105–6.
6. From Chapter IV, p. 107.
7. From Chapter IV, p. 109.

Appendix 2
Foreword

This book results from the union of two lines of events. On the one hand, the authors in relative independence had individually concluded that the social-economic situation now makes the outstanding demand on education. On the other, the National Society of College Teachers of Education requested of them a yearbook in the philosophy of education.

The initial decision was to deal directly with the social-economic situation and its interaction with education, and in this way to show the philosophy of education properly at work. It was further agreed to present as far as possible one unified treatment rather than a collection of separately written essays. What here appears is the result of these decisions. Extended conferences have sought through earnest discussion to effect a single outlook and a consistent argument. The actual writing, however, has perforce been apportioned, with no effort to "iron out" individuality. The observant eye will accordingly discern amid obvious differences of style some remaining differences of emphasis.

In the sense thus explained, the several chapters may be assigned as follows: Chapter I to Professor Bode; Chapter II to Professors Dewey and Childs, a joint product of thought written out by Professor Dewey; Chapter III to Professor Raup; Chapter IV to Professor Kilpatrick; Chapter V to Professor Hullfish; Chapter VI to Professor Hullfish and Dr. Thayer, the former doing the writing; Chapter VII to Dr. Thayer; Chapter VIII to Professor Kilpatrick; Chapter IX to Professors Dewey and Childs, again as before. Professor Kilpatrick has served as editor with the help of Professors Raup, Childs, and Hullfish.

The hearty thanks of the authors are hereby tendered to Miss

[First published in *The Educational Frontier*, ed. William H. Kilpatrick (New York and London: Century Co., 1933), pp. v–vi.]

Marion Y. Ostrander, Secretary of the Committee, for her generous and helpful contribution to the making of the book.

The authors offer this book to their fellow members of the profession and to all thoughtful citizens with the most earnest hope that it may serve to foster thinking in what seems surely to be the chief problem of our times.

Pagination Key to the 1933 *How We Think*

Scholarly studies in the past have referred to the 1933 D. C. Heath and Company publication of *How We Think: A Restatement of the Relation of Reflective Thinking to the Educative Process.* The list below relates that pagination to the pagination of the present edition. Before the colon appear the 1933 edition page numbers; after the colon appear the corresponding page numbers from the present edition.

iii : 107	24 : 130–31	51 : 153	78 : 176–77
iv : 107–8	25 : 131–32	52 : 153–54	79 : 177–78
v : 109	26 : 132–33	53 : 154–55	80 : 178
vi : 109	27 : 133–34	54 : 155	81 : 178–79
1 : 111	28 : 134–35	55 : 156	82 : 179–80
2 : 112	29 : 135–36	56 : 156–57	83 : 180–81
3 : 113	30 : 136	57 : 157–58	84 : 181–82
4 : 113–14	31 : 136–37	58 : 158–59	85 : 182
5 : 114–15	32 : 137–38	59 : 159–60	86 : 182–83
6 : 115–16	33 : 138–39	60 : 160	87 : 183–84
7 : 116–17	34 : 139	61 : 160–61	88 : 184–85
8 : 117–18	35 : 140	62 : 161–62	89 : 185–86
9 : 118	36 : 140–41	63 : 162–63	90 : 186
10 : 118–19	37 : 141–42	64 : 163–64	91 : 187
11 : 119–20	38 : 142–43	65 : 164	92 : 187–88
12 : 120–21	39 : 143–44	66 : 165	93 : 188–89
13 : 121–22	40 : 144	67 : 165–66	94 : 189–90
14 : 122	41 : 144–45	68 : 166–67	95 : 190–91
15 : 122–23	42 : 145–46	69 : 169	96 : 191
16 : 123–24	43 : 146–47	70 : 170	97 : 191–92
17 : 125	44 : 147–48	71 : 171	98 : 192–93
18 : 125–26	45 : 148–49	72 : 171–72	99 : 193–94
19 : 126–27	46 : 149	73 : 172–73	100 : 194–95
20 : 127–28	47 : 149–50	74 : 173–74	101 : 195
21 : 128–29	48 : 150–51	75 : 174	102 : 196
22 : 129	49 : 151–52	76 : 174–75	103 : 196–97
23 : 130	50 : 152–53	77 : 175–76	104 : 197–98

Textual Apparatus

Index

Textual Commentary

Volume 8 of *The Later Works of John Dewey, 1925–1953* comprises, in addition to Dewey's revised *How We Think*, seven items for 1933: two co-authored chapters for *The Educational Frontier*, three book reviews, and two articles for the *Encyclopaedia of the Social Sciences*. One 1934 item—a discussion of Philosophy for the *Encyclopaedia of the Social Sciences*, contracted for and written with the two 1933 articles—has also been included. The remainder of Dewey's writings for 1933 appear in volume 9 of *The Later Works*.

None of these items presents copy-text problems; the only previous authoritative appearance of each item has necessarily served as copy-text.[1] While the existence of a single prior text obviates textual problems, some commentary on the origin and reception of these works can illuminate Dewey's philosophical concerns and writing activity during 1933.

As professor emeritus of philosophy in residence at Columbia University, Dewey continued during 1933 to meet with individual graduate students in philosophy and education. Additionally, he responded to the worsening American economic crisis by his involvement in the League for Independent Political Action; he attempted to buoy up the country's educational system, foundering in the 1930s; and he fought the communist bid to take over New York Teachers Union Local No. 5. Dewey's writings reflect all those turbulent contemporary events as well as his long-standing commitment to educational, philosophical, and peace issues.

---

1. All textual decisions for this volume have been based upon Fredson Bowers, "Textual Principles and Procedures," *The Later Works of John Dewey, 1925–1953*, ed. Jo Ann Boydston (Carbondale and Edwardsville: Southern Illinois University Press, 1984), 2:407–18.

Contributions to *Encyclopaedia of the Social Sciences*

By late 1932 Dewey had contracted with the *Encyclo-paedia of the Social Sciences* to write extensive discussions of Logic, Outlawry of War, and Philosophy.[2] Salmon O. Levinson, Dewey's friend and co-worker in the outlawry of war movement,[3] wrote that a student of international politics was thinking of writing up "that phase of the history of Outlawry which shows the direct connection between it and the new 'Stimson' doctrine of non-recognition. . . . Now I notice that you will probably be next with your article in the Enc. of the Social Sciences. If you are contemplating writing on that phase of it, I certainly do not want him to write an article on that subject."[4]

With characteristic generosity, Dewey replied that about all he could do in the *Encyclopaedia* article was "to call attention to

2. For "Human Nature," Dewey's 1932 contribution to *Encyclopaedia of the Social Sciences*, see *Later Works* 6:29–39.
3. As early as 1918, Levinson's essay "The Legal Status of War," *New Republic* 14 (9 March 1918): 171–73, prompted Dewey's "Morals and the Conduct of States," *New Republic* 14 (23 March 1918): 232–34 [*The Middle Works of John Dewey, 1899–1924*, ed. Jo Ann Boydston (Carbondale and Edwardsville: Southern Illinois University Press, 1982), 11:388–92 and 122–26]. Dewey also wrote a foreword to Levinson's 1921 *Outlawry of War* [*Middle Works* 13:411]. This pamphlet was published by the newly organized American Committee for the Outlawry of War, founded by Levinson.
    After Walter Lippmann's critical essay " 'The Outlawry of War' " appeared in *Atlantic Monthly* 132 (August 1923): 245–53 [*Middle Works* 15:404–17], Dewey responded in the *New Republic* with "What Outlawry of War Is Not" on 3 October 1923 and "War and a Code of Law" on 24 October 1923 [*Middle Works* 15:115–21 and 122–27]. These two articles became the sixteen-page pamphlet published by the American Committee for the Outlawry of War with the title *Outlawry of War: What It Is and Is Not, A Reply to Walter Lippmann* (Chicago, 1923).
    Dewey's essay "America's Responsibility," urging adoption of Senator William E. Borah's resolution to outlaw the war system, appeared in *Christian Century* on 23 December 1926 [*Later Works* 2:167–72]. In 1927 Dewey wrote a foreword to Charles Clayton Morrison's *The Outlawry of War: A Constructive Policy for World Peace* and the article "Outlawing Peace by Discussing War," *New Republic* 54 (16 May 1928): 370–71 [*Later Works* 3:348–58 and 173–76].
4. Levinson to Dewey, 28 October 1932, Salmon O. Levinson Papers, Box 16, Folder 5, Department of Special Collections, University of Chicago Library, University of Chicago.

the fact that the Stimson doctrine is a logical development of the Outlawry of war movement. . . . I think your friend ought to write his article along the lines of his suggestion; there certainly would be no conflict and I judge his article would be very helpful to me."[5]

That Dewey valued Levinson's reactions concerning his Outlawry article is clear from his 4 February 1933 letter:

> I enclose carbon of my Encyclopedia article, for your criticism and suggestions. Unfortunately, they limited me in space so much so that I have overrun as it is the alloted space by about a third—if they insist on cutting it down, which I dont believe they will, I shall cut out the last section.
>
> This limitation affected the character of the article somewhat. It seemed to me that the history of the movement deserved first right of way if anything had to be sacrificed.
>
> Please be wholly free in your criticisms—I am pretty much without pride and sensitiveness of authorship and I want to do the best I can in the allotted space.[6]

For the Outlawry article *Encyclopaedia* editor Alvin Johnson sent Dewey a "check for $40. in payment. We have made very few changes except some minor condensations in order to save space, . . . subject to your approval."[7] Dewey apparently approved; he wrote to Levinson, "I enclose the other pages of the Outlawry article They cut it down a little in the office but nothing essential is out I think."[8]

Upon reading the final version, Levinson wrote to Dewey, "I am exceedingly pleased with your article which you seem to have burnished up since I last saw it. I don't see how it could be improved upon."[9]

Although the *Encyclopaedia of the Social Sciences* was reissued in 1937 (combining volumes 1 and 2) and reprinted in 1942 and 1944, Dewey did not revise his contributions. The first impression (New York: Macmillan Co., 1933; 1933; 1934) has served as copy-text for his three articles in the present volume.

5. Dewey to Levinson, 1 November 1932, Levinson Papers, Box 16, Folder 5.
6. Dewey to Levinson, 4 February 1933, Levinson Papers, Box 16, Folder 5.
7. Johnson to Dewey, 12 April 1933, Levinson Papers, Box 16, Folder 5.
8. Dewey to Levinson, 24 April 1933, Levinson Papers, Box 16, Folder 5.
9. Levinson to Dewey, 1 May 1933, Levinson Papers, Box 16, Folder 5.

Contributions to *The Educational Frontier*

In August 1932, immediately after completing his *How We Think* revision (discussed below), Dewey began work on his contributions to *The Educational Frontier*, a collection of essays edited by Columbia University Teachers College Professor William Heard Kilpatrick. From his vacation retreat in Hubbards, Nova Scotia, Dewey wrote to Sidney Hook:

> I have to get a kind of manifesto year book in the philosophy of education now. It is in the hands of Kilpatrick and his two asst profs at T[eachers] C[ollege] and [Boyd H.] Bode and Hollfish [H. Gordon Hullfish] at Ohio State. . . . [John L.] Childs of T C and myself are to do the first and last chpaters, the first on existing social institutions in their educative bearings leading up to the conflict between their actual effect and the professed aims of the schools and the consequent messiness of the education given by the latter, and the final chapter brin[g]ing out the phil implications of the book as a whole.[10]

This "manifesto" had been requested by the National Society of College Teachers of Education and prompted by the depression's traumatic effect on American education. Though little noticed at its 1933 publication by Century Company, *The Educational Frontier* presented an educational philosophy by progressivists who were breaking away from traditional theory. The book became a reference point in educational controversies that, having evolved at a time of desperate need for change in the 1930s, continued unabated in the 1940s. Dewey and his Teachers College colleagues were at the center of this storm.

Actual writing of *The Educational Frontier* was apportioned differently than Dewey had first envisioned it. Dewey and Childs collaborated on the second and last chapters ("The Social-Economic Situation and Education" and "The Underlying Philosophy of Education"), leaving the first chapter for Ohio State University Professor Bode. In the foreword, Kilpatrick described the

10. Dewey to Hook, 22 August 1932, Sidney Hook/John Dewey Collection, Special Collections, Morris Library, Southern Illinois University at Carbondale.

Dewey-Childs chapters as "a joint product of thought written out by Professor Dewey" (this volume, page 374).

Other contributors included Teachers College Professor R. Bruce Raup for chapter 3 and editor Kilpatrick for chapters 4 and 8. Professor Hullfish contributed chapter 5 and collaborated on chapter 6 with V. T. Thayer (educational director, Ethical Culture schools), who also wrote chapter 7. The foreword states that the authors

> agreed to present as far as possible one unified treatment rather than a collection of separately written essays. . . . Extended conferences have sought through earnest discussion to effect a single outlook and a consistent argument . . . with no effort to "iron out" individuality. The observant eye will accordingly discern amid obvious differences of style some remaining differences of emphasis.[11]

Dewey confided to Hook that "we had some meetings and some rather hot discussions laying out the plan. . . . Of course part of the trouble is that Bode is the only one beside myself who has had a philosophical trai[n]ing as such—Hollfish has had it vicariously through Bode tho."[12]

The joint effort ultimately proved rewarding, as Dewey indicated in his letter to Ohio State University collaborator Hullfish: "I hardly need say that I reciprocate warmly what you say about the opportunity to meet with you and Bode in discussion. I got a great deal of stimulus out of the gatherings, and hope that the product in the Year-Book may be as educative to others as I feel it has been to us to work in preparing it."[13]

In the single review, Sidney Hook called *The Educational Frontier* "a penetrating socio-economic analysis," one that "defends the philosophy of experimentalism as a basis for immediate social action."[14] Writing for the *New Republic*, Hook noted that the authors espoused the democratic ideal of each person's right to realize his potential capacities. A blend of individuality and social interaction within the educational system can create

11. See this volume, p. 374.
12. Dewey to Hook, 22 August 1932, Hook/Dewey Collection.
13. Dewey to Hullfish, 30 November 1932, H. Gordon Hullfish Papers, Special Collections, Ohio State University Library, Columbus, Ohio.
14. Hook, *New Republic* 75 (24 May 1933): 49.

a commonality of purpose, Hook agreed. If the classless society that is part of the democratic ideal "is to be achieved, it is not by closing one's eyes to existing class struggles but by prosecuting them more widely and vigorously and intelligently." [15]

The Educational Frontier was not reprinted; copyright deposit copy A 60336 (New York and London: Century Co., 1933) has served as copy-text for the present volume. The Century Company also published the identical book under its incorporated imprint (New York and London: D. Appleton-Century Co., 1933). *The Educational Frontier* was also published as Yearbook 21 of the National Society of College Teachers of Education, Studies in Education (Chicago: University of Chicago Press, [1933]), the only difference being that the yearbook includes, after the index, the constitution, membership list, and officers of the society.

How We Think: A Restatement of the Relation of Reflective Thinking to the Educative Process

Dewey's biggest undertaking during this period was revising his 1910 *How We Think*.[16] He had planned to begin work on it early in 1932; on 19 February he wrote to Joseph Ratner, "I have finished up the ethics [*Later Works* 7] and am going to work on the revision of the How We Think next." [17] More than a month later, however, he wrote to Ratner, "I've had no time to do anything more with H W T." [18] Not until the summer did Dewey finally find time for the revision. From Hubbards he outlined his plan to Ratner:

> I haven't had much time for working on H W T, what with picnics & work about my cabin   Im breaking up the second part. Give the illustrations as a chapter by themselves. Then another brief chapter on Inference & Testing based on the three illustrations of the previous chapter. Then one of analysis of Reflective Thinking, first section on Facts & Ideas (Mean-

15. Ibid., p. 50.
16. *Middle Works* 6:177–356.
17. Dewey to Ratner, 19 February 1932, Joseph Ratner/John Dewey Papers, Special Collections, Morris Library, Southern Illinois University at Carbondale.
18. Dewey to Ratner, 30 March 1932, Ratner/Dewey Papers.

ing) as the two necessary factors, & section two, the old "steps"—There is considerable repetition but perhaps easier as a text.

Then I think Ill have a chapter on Conceptions & Unders[tanding]—then on Judgment, & then the one on Systematic inference.[19]

Dewey concentrated on Part Two. He reported to Ratner: "I have been working especially this week on H W T. I have done the chapters in Part Two which is the important part to revise. I have broken them up, changed the order somewhat, and by some omissions and more additions have I hope added to the clarity and teachability of the book The chapter on concrete and abstract Ive carried over into Part III, the educational portion."[20] Dewey also described his progress to colleague and protégé Sidney Hook:

I have spent a restful five weeks here, and have got a lot of work done in [r]evising H W T, in fact have it most completed. . . . My thrist for logic is strong enough to take me thru this job with a good deal of interest—it is the second part, the logical part, which has incited the larger part of the revising. I hope to show you that part before getting it off to the publishers. Of course the changes arent revolutionary, but I hope I have clarified as well as simplified.[21]

The initial publication of *How We Think* in 1910 had revolutionized American educational theory by presenting a practical approach to thought processes for students in elementary logic courses. Dewey had moved away, in that one brief textbook, from a theoretical, formalistic treatment of logic; the 1910 *How We Think* addressed the beginner directly, outlining a problem-solving process that would train students to be critical consumers of discourse, with an emphasis on the psychology of the thought process and logical argumentation.[22]

But during the twenty-three years since the first edition had

19. Dewey to Ratner, 2 August 1932, Ratner/Dewey Papers.
20. Dewey to Ratner, [ca. 22 August 1932], Ratner/Dewey Papers.
21. Dewey to Hook, 22 August 1932, Hook/Dewey Collection.
22. Willis Moore, oral interview with Bridget Walsh, 20 June 1984, Center for Dewey Studies, Southern Illinois University at Carbondale. Moore, professor emeritus of philosophy at Southern Illinois University at Carbondale, used both the 1910 and 1933 *How We Think* in his classes for several years.

appeared, critics had raised questions that Dewey wanted to answer. From the left of the philosophical spectrum came queries from teachers who, in using *How We Think* as a text, had pointed out some problems with this new approach to teaching a logical thought process. From the right came criticisms from Hegelian formalists who questioned Dewey's abandonment of theoretical logic and who "dubbed his kind of logic as mere psychology."[23]

In his "Preface to the New Edition," Dewey wrote that he had done "extensive rewriting," involving some excision and "considerable expansion," and that the revision was "nearly a quarter" longer than the original account. Dewey's "restatement" was "made with a view to increased definiteness and clearness of statement."[24] For the textual relationship of the 1933 edition to the 1910 edition, see Summary of Substantive Revisions in the 1933 *How We Think*, this volume, pp. 397–414.

Part Three, "The Training of Thought," addressed teachers' concerns and included a "practically all new" chapter on the problems of recitation.[25] Part Two, "Logical Considerations," in which Dewey explained the meaning of his terms to old-line logicians, reflected numerous changes defending his approach to the thought process. Dewey's alterations here indicate the gravity of his shift from idealism, his ceasing to make a rather sharp distinction between forms of thinking and the actual activity of problem solving. Dewey's more formal usage of language in this part makes clear he was addressing Hegelian logicians rather than students.[26]

Considered "a classic among educators and psychologists,"[27] the 1933 *How We Think: A Restatement of the Relation of Reflective Thinking to the Educative Process* pleased reviewers[28] as

23. Moore to Walsh, 20 June 1984.
24. See this volume, p. 107.
25. See this volume, p. 108.
26. Moore to Walsh, 20 June 1984.
27. Sidney Hook, *New Republic* 78 (21 March 1934): 165.
28. The following reviews appeared: *A. L. A. Booklist* 29 (July 1933): 349; Eugene G. Bugg, *American Journal of Psychology* 46 (1935): 528; John Anderson, *Australasian Journal of Psychology and Philosophy* 15 (September 1937): 224–30; E. N., *Boston Evening Transcript*, 21 June 1933, p. 2; *British Journal of Educational Psychology* 4 (November 1934): 323–24; Thomas H. Briggs, *Educational Outlook* 8 (1933): 56–57; J. C. Meadows, *High School Quarterly* 22 (October 1933): 42; *Junior-Senior High School Clearing House* 8 (January 1934): 319–20; Sidney Hook, *New Republic* 78 (21 March 1934): 165; Sven Nilson, *Philosophical Review* 44 (1935): 75–76; *Saturday Review of Literature* 9 (1 July 1933): 682; W. McAndrew,

an "acute, profound and valuable analysis of the processes and meanings of reflective thought."[29] In the *New Republic*, Sidney Hook found the revision noteworthy for its "consideration given to objections which have accumulated over a period of more than twenty years."[30]

Sven Nilson, of the *Philosophical Review*, noted structural changes:

> The text has been increased by something like sixty-eight pages, and the typography has been considerably improved. The number of chapters has similarly grown from sixteen to nineteen, while the last chapter of Part One in the first edition has been made the first chapter of the Second Part in the new. Most of the chapters have been renamed, although the changes are often quite slight; the various chapters have also been enriched with additional subheadings, just as the volume as a whole has been blessed with an index.[31]

More importantly, Nilson wondered what effect a quarter century of changes in educational theory and practice might have had on the mind of the author. He concluded that the 1933 revision informs the reader "quite truthfully," just as promised in the volume's new preface, that " 'the basic ideas, those that gave the original work its distinctive character, have not only been retained but have also been enriched and developed further.'"[32] At the same time, Nilson questioned "the retention of so many dubious notions that have served to mar this thought-provoking little volume," such as "Professor Dewey's belief that thought has but a problem-solving function to perform."[33]

To this criticism Hook inadvertently responded in his review: "The most outstanding feature of Dewey's analysis of thinking is his demonstration that at some determinate point in the thought process, concrete activity is involved. This is not to say that thinking exists for the sake of action, but that activity is an integral part of the total life history of any thought."[34]

School and Society 38 (1 July 1933): 24; Isidore Starr, *Social Education* 34 (November 1970): 820, 838.

29. E. N., *Boston Evening Transcript*, 21 June 1933, p. 2.
30. Hook, *New Republic* 78 (21 March 1934): 165.
31. Nilson, *Philosophical Review* 44 (1935): 75.
32. Ibid.
33. Ibid.
34. Hook, *New Republic*, p. 165.

In the *American Journal of Psychology*, Eugene G. Bugg, observant of Dewey's changed attitude toward the psychology of the thinking process, found "many valuable pedagogical suggestions drawn from the author's wide experience." However, he expressed concern that Dewey's "rather free use of a terminology adapted to the level of the average grade teacher (*i.e.* non-professional psychologist)" would frequently result in "mere verbalization and psychological inaccuracy."[35]

The 1933 edition constituted a "rebirth," according to W. McAndrew in *School and Society*; he delighted in Dewey's attack upon "re-citation" as "an ideal of amassing information without a purpose for it. The pupil is treated as a phonograph record. The practise puts a premium on passivity."[36]

Less complimentary of Dewey's revision, John Anderson in the *Australasian Journal of Psychology and Philosophy* questioned the book's basic premise:

> The appeal to actual processes of thinking, as against formal logic, has no educational force, and the important matter remains that of the choice of subjects. An analysis of the social forces (including the influence of teachers) which inhibit absorption in culture might be of considerable value, but moralisings on the rousing of interest in unattractive subjects, on the "ideal mental condition" in which the attitudes of work and play are balanced, on the combining of largeness of vision with skill in execution, can hardly be so.[37]

Perhaps most typical, however, was the *Saturday Review of Literature*'s observation that

> the renovation is well carried through and reflects the clarity characteristic of our Nestorian sage. Its appeal . . . remains as timely as ever. The book itself contributed to the reforming movement, which with all its persisting faults has made the atmosphere of schooling more wholesome, more fresh-airy than when the Dewey campaign began.[38]

35. Bugg, *American Journal of Psychology* 46 (1935): 528.
36. McAndrew, *School and Society* 38 (1 July 1933): 24.
37. Anderson, *Australasian Journal of Psychology and Philosophy* 15 (September 1937): 229–30.
38. *Saturday Review of Literature* 9 (1 July 1933): 682.

On behalf of D. C. Heath and Company, which published both the 1910 and 1933 editions of *How We Think*, General Manager John T. Harney stated that "files on this title are very thin and I have no reference to the 1933 contract. In all probability D. C. Heath simply implemented the clause from the 1910 contract which permitted the company to publish the work in a new edition."[39]

Although the exact number of impressions of the 1933 *How We Think* cannot be determined, an extensive search confirms that it was reprinted at least six times before Dewey's death in 1952. Copy-text for the present edition is copyright deposit copy A 62942, registered in the name of John Dewey following publication in April (Boston: D. C. Heath and Co., 1933).

In 1912 D. C. Heath had established a printing code to identify the month and year of publication on a volume's copyright page. Eugene R. Bailey of Heath's production and editing department explained this code: "The numbers refer to the year of the printing and the alphabetical character refers to the month in which the printing occurred. *A* designates January; B, February; . . . L, December. Thus, for example, the designation 2D1 indicates a printing in April of 1921."[40]

Thus, number and letter combinations found on the copyright page of impressions held at the Center for Dewey Studies indicate that the 1933 *How We Think* was reprinted during Dewey's lifetime in June 1934, July 1938, September 1945, February 1947, September 1947, and February 1950. Machine and sight collations of the initial April 1933 impression against the copyright deposit copy and against the February 1950 impression revealed no variants in the text, indicating that D. C. Heath probably used the 1933 plates to print all subsequent impressions.

The front matter of the April 1933 and February 1950 impressions differ in two respects. The 1933 publication date that appeared on the title page in April 1933 was not present in February 1950, an omission that first occurred in the July 1938 impression. Secondly, at the end of the "Preface to the New Edition" and "Preface to the First Edition," the places and dates of

39. Harney to Jo Ann Boydston, 20 July 1973, Center for Dewey Studies.
40. Bailey to Jo Ann Boydston, 12 March 1974, Center for Dewey Studies.

Dewey's writing ("New York City, May, 1933." and "New York City, December, 1909.") that appeared in the April 1933 impression did not appear in the February 1950 impression, an omission that first occurred in the September 1947 impression.

According to D. C. Heath Vice-President John T. Harney, "The 1933 edition is still in print and we continue it very much as an active title."[41] Between 1964 (when D. C. Heath began its current recordkeeping procedures) and 1984, domestic and foreign sales amounted to 7,321 copies.[42]

The enduring relevance of Dewey's revised *How We Think* is highlighted in Isidore Starr's 1970 review. Saying that it "has haunted social studies educators since the date of its revision in 1933," Starr continued: "An increasing number of teachers have been intrigued and influenced by this slim volume, while the more thought-provoking social studies methods books of recent years represent variations on a theme by Dewey." Starr concluded his review with the reminder: "It is remarkably easy for any of us to travel the ruts of routine to the point of staleness and dogmatism. One of the best antidotes to this occupational hazard is a periodic pilgrimage to Dewey's classic."[43]

B. A. W.
H. F. S.

41. Harney to Jo Ann Boydston, 23 April 1974, Center for Dewey Studies.
42. Linda Laredo to Bridget Walsh, 2 August 1984, Center for Dewey Studies.
43. Starr, *Social Education* 34 (November 1970): 820, 838.

Emendations List

All emendations in both substantives and accidentals introduced into the copy-text are recorded in the list that follows, with the exception of the changes in formal matters described below. No titles appear for the four items that had no emendations. The copy-text for each item is identified at the beginning of the list of emendations for that item. The page-line number at left is from the present edition; all lines of print except running heads are counted. The reading to the left of the square bracket is from the present edition; the bracket is followed by an abbreviation for the source of the emendation's first appearance.

W means Works—the present edition—and is used for emendations made here for the first time. The symbol WS (Works Source) is used to indicate emendations made within Dewey's quoted material that restore the spelling, capitalization, and some required substantives of his source (see Substantive Variants in Quotations).

For emendations restricted to punctuation, the curved dash ~ means the same word(s) as before the bracket; the inferior caret ∧ indicates the absence of a punctuation mark.

A number of formal, or mechanical, changes have been made throughout:

1. Chapter headings have been deleted and arabic numbers placed before chapter titles of *How We Think*.

2. Book and periodical titles are in italic type; articles and sections of books are in quotation marks.

3. Ligatures have been separated.

4. Periods and commas have been brought within quotation marks.

5. Single quotation marks have been changed to double when not inside quoted material; however, opening or closing quotation marks have been supplied where necessary and recorded. Opening and closing quotation marks around extracts have been omitted; however, quotation marks within extracts have been retained.

The following spellings have been editorially regularized to the known Dewey usage appearing before the brackets:

centre(s)] center 7.10, 7.20, 24.33, 49.25, 65.33, 83 n.2, 145.13, 233.9, 286.8, 329.31, 336.13, 336.26, 346.5

cooperate (all forms)] coöperate 51.1, 64.25, 66.38, 68.6–7, 69.38,
    70.39, 74.35–36, 74.36–37, 80.35, 85.30–31, 101.40,
    102.33, 109.28, 152.35, 285.15, 342.5
coordinate (all forms)] coördinate 281.24, 297.18, 358.10
meagre] meager 147.9, 324.3
preeminence (all forms)] preëminence 85.38, 90.20, 161.26, 179.4,
    290.22, 307.20, 355.25
role] rôle 91.32, 254.19, 283.22, 284.14, 320.4, 340.27
zoology] zoölogy 260.8, 261.20, 291.8, 321.17

Logic

Copy-text for this article is its publication in *Encyclopaedia of the Social Sciences*, ed. Edwin R. A. Seligman and Alvin Johnson (New York: Macmillan Co., 1933), 9:598–603.

9.9	*concerning*] W; *on the*
10.19	synthesis] W; snythesis
12.26	Rjazanov] W; Ryazanov
12.28	*Methods*] W; *The Methods*

Outlawry of War

Copy-text for this article is its publication in *Encyclopaedia of the Social Sciences*, ed. Edwin R. A. Seligman and Alvin Johnson (New York: Macmillan Co., 1933), 11:508–10.

13.13	towards] WS; toward
18.9–10	Sanction, International] W; Sanction
18.12	Be] W; be
18.12	'Enforced'?∧"] W; ∧~∧?,"
18.14	no.] W; nos.
18.16	War] W; Man
18.17	"'As] W; "∧~
18.17	Nations'"] W; ~∧"
18.23	"'The] W; "∧~
18.24	War'"] W; ~∧"
18.37	*Aechtung*] W; *Achtung*

Philosophy

Copy-text for this article is its publication in *Encyclopaedia of the Social Sciences*, ed. Edwin R. A. Seligman and Alvin Johnson (New York: Macmillan Co., 1934), 12:118–29.

39.36   1927–34] W; 1928–32

How We Think: A Restatement of the Relation of Reflective Thinking to the Educative Process

Copy-text for this work is the copyright deposit copy A 62942 (Boston: D. C. Heath and Co., 1933).

126.23   brute,] W; ~;
129.23   any thing] WS; anything
132.30   neighbours] WS; neighbors
133.2   humour] WS; humor
133.5   round-about] WS; roundabout
133.9   traffick] WS; traffic
133.26   any thing] WS; anything
133.30   unbiassed] WS; unbiased
133 n.2–3 favourable terms] WS; favorable terms
133 n.3   favourable ideas] WS; favorable ideas
133 n.8   Assent,] W; ~∧
134.14   mould] WS; mold
134.29   neighbourhood] WS; neighborhood
142.14   scrabbles] WS; scrambles
193.5   Other] W; Others
214.7   connexion] WS; connection
232.27   satellite] W; stellite
238.15,16 Sedgwick] W; Sidgwick
238.22   Sedgwick] WS; Sidgwick
238.24   realise] WS; realize
247.29   statically] W; statistically
248.14–15 Chapter 7] W; Chapter VI
258.14   snow-like] WS; snowlike
267.1   colleges∧] W; ~,
275.9   towards] WS; toward
275.21   cases";] W; ~;"
302.13   *hund*] W; *Hund*
307.29   symbolised] WS; symbolized
307.33   symbolises] WS; symbolizes

310.17   "what-do-you-call-it,"] W; "~∧"
311.2   fund] W; funds
312 n.2   *Elementary Lessons*] W; *Lessons*
319.15   resources] W; resourses
328.16   foodstuffs] W; food stuffs
331 n.1   page 164] W; page 47

The Adventure of Persuasion

Copy-text for this review is its publication in *New Republic* 74 (19 April 1933): 285–86.

358.25   Truth, Beauty, Adventure and Peace] WS; truth, beauty, adventure and peace
359.23   State-systems] WS; ~∧~

Review of Rexford G. Tugwell's *The Industrial Discipline and the Governmental Arts*

Copy-text for this review is its publication in *Occupations* 12 (December 1933): 40–41.

365.22   leaning above] WS; learning about

Summary of Substantive Revisions in the 1933 *How We Think*

This section shows the textual relationship of the revised edition of *How We Think*[1] to the first edition.[2] In his "Preface to the New Edition" (this volume, pp. 107–8), Dewey explains his revision; this section documents his explanation. The following information appears for each 1933 revised chapter:

1. A summary of its relationship to the corresponding 1910 text in terms of length, extensive revision, and new material.[3]

2. An organizational scheme designating the corresponding 1910 text.[4] For instance, 1933 Chapter 1, Section I, is a revision of 1910 Chapter 1, Section 1; 1933 Chapter 2, Section II, is a revision of 1910 Chapter 2, Section 3 and part of Section 4. (Section titles are preceded by roman numerals in 1933 and by arabic in 1910; this summary preserves that distinction. However, section titles, which appear in italics in 1910, do not appear in italics here.) For extensively reorganized text (Chapter 5, Section II) the 1933 rearranged order of the 1910 paragraphs is given.

3. A list of extensive substantive revisions.[5] The revisions list follows

1. *How We Think: A Restatement of the Relation of Reflective Thinking to the Educative Process* (Boston: D. C. Heath and Co., 1933) (this volume, pp. 105–352).
2. *How We Think* (Boston: D. C. Heath and Co., 1910) (*Middle Works* 6:177–356).
3. This summary indicates where Dewey's "considerable expansion" made the 1933 edition "nearly a quarter" longer, and where he added "more illustrative material" (this volume, p. 107).
4. This scheme indicates where Dewey rearranged "the position of entire chapters" (p. 107).
5. In his Preface (p. 107), Dewey distinguishes "slight verbal changes" from "an extensive rewriting"; this revisions list includes additions, deletions ("material excised"), and extensive revisions, but not "slight verbal changes." A complete list of substantive revisions is available at the Center for Dewey Studies. Using this revisions list together with the 1933 and 1910 editions of *How We Think* makes it possible to identify revisions that illustrate Dewey's stated purposes: revisions "made with a view to increased definiteness and clearness of statement" (as, for example, at 126.39–127.1, 183.16–19, 222.39–223.2); and revisions that "enriched and developed further the basic ideas, those that gave the work its distinctive character" (as, for example, at 144.9–26, 242.11–243.28).

this formula: to the left of the bracket appear the page-line number and revised text from this volume, either in full or with an ellipsis; to the right of the bracket appears the corresponding 1910 text, either in full or with an ellipsis. Roman numerals designating 1910 subsections have been included. A paragraph sign [¶] indicates the beginning of a paragraph. For instance, the entry at 113.4–20 indicates that the 1933 paragraph is an extensive revision of the 1910 paragraph in Chapter 1, Section 1, beginning "No" and ending "senses" (in this case, a complete paragraph). The corresponding 1910 text may be more than a paragraph, as at 115.17–116.23, or part of a sentence, as at 116.30–32.

Descriptions, such as "paragraph deleted" [*para. del.*] or "three sentences transposed" [*3 sents. tr.*], appear in italics and, where necessary, within brackets; "*added*" indicates new material. To indicate a revision with new material added, "[*w. add.*]" appears after the corresponding 1910 text, as at 141.10–142.5.

Abbreviations used:
chap(s). = chapter(s)
sec(s). = section(s)
para(s). = paragraph(s)
sent(s). = sentence(s)
intro. = introduction
tr. = transposed
w. = with
w. add. = with new material added

1933	1910
Part One. The Problem of Training Thought	Part One. The Problem of Training Thought
chaps. 1–4	*chaps. 1–4*

Chap. 1

Summary: The 1933 revision is approximately the same length as the corresponding 1910 text. Material is added at the ends of 5 paras. 7 paras. of Sec. I, the last para. of Sec. II and Sec. IV, and the first para. of Sec. III are extensively revised or new. Material is added in Sec. I on thought as belief and in Sec. II on the function of suggestion.

Organization:

1933	1910
Chap. 1. What Is Thinking?	**Chap. 1. What Is Thought?**
Sec. I. Different Meanings of Thought	Sec. 1. Varied Senses of the Term

Sec. II. The Central Factor in Thinking	Sec. 2. The Central Factor in Thinking
Sec. III. Phases of Reflective Thinking	Sec. 3. Elements in Reflective Thinking
Sec. IV. Summary	Sec. 4. Summary

Revisions:
113.4–20   [¶] No . . . given.] [¶] No . . . senses.
113.22–114.9   [¶] All . . . behind.] [¶] I. In . . . hope. [*w. 2 sents. added, 1 sent. tr.*]
114.29–31   There . . . end.] *added*
114.34–36   [¶] The second . . . tasted.] [¶] II. Even . . . touch.
115.12–14   In . . . pictures.] *added*
115.17–116.23   [¶] In . . . unconsciously.] But *they* . . . correct belief.
116.30–32   conclusions . . . evidence.] judgments . . . evidence.
116.32–117.9   Even . . . commitment.] *added*
117.9–37   Beliefs, . . . inquiry.] [¶] IV. Thoughts . . . facts. [*w. add.*]
118.34–36   clouds, . . . storm.] clouds and a coming shower.
118.36–119.3   This . . . consideration.] *added*
119n.3–4   some . . . law.] something else.
120.2–8   Reflection . . . latter.] *added*
120.23–121.4   *what* . . . perplexity.] *the latter* . . . suggested belief.
121.28–33   For . . . operation.] The purport . . . negate it.
123.26   experience,] experience . . . imagination,
123.27   Even] [*sent. del.*] Even
123.30–124.13   [¶] There . . . found.] [¶] If . . . thinking.

Chap. 2

Summary: The 1933 revision is one-third longer than the corresponding 1910 text. One-half of Sec. I and more than one-half of Sec. II are extensively revised or new. Material is added in Sec. I on control and in Sec. II on beliefs and attitudes.

Organization:

1933	1910
Chap. 2. Why Reflective Thinking Must Be an Educational Aim	Chap. 2. The Need for Training Thought
Sec. I. The Values of Thinking	Sec. 1. The Values of Thought and

		Sec. 2.	Importance of Direction in order to Realize these Values
Sec. II.	Tendencies Needing Constant Regulation	Sec. 3.	Tendencies Needing Constant Regulation *and*
		Sec. 4.	Regulation Transforms Inference into Proof, *para. 3*

Revisions:

125.6–27   [¶] We . . . come.] [¶] To . . . aware. [*1910 Sec. 1 begins at 125.11*]

126.14–17   Only . . . possible.] Upon . . . calculation.

126.37–127.1   discovers . . . etc.] invents . . . needed.

127.18–128.28   the collection . . . meantime.] each has . . . Newton to apprehend. [*w. add.*]

129.7–18   [¶] These . . . greater.] [*1910 Sec. 2 begins*] [¶] What . . . ill-exercised.

130.1   [¶] While] [*sent. del.*] While

130.9   point, the necessities] point, . . . The necessities

130.32–131.10   because . . . rest.] because existing customs . . . fabric of misconception. [*w. add.*]

131.25–31   When . . . conquest.] Dreams . . . conquest. [*tr. from preceding para.*]

134.31–135.37   [¶] We . . . specialities.] [¶] Both Bacon . . . produced. [*w. add.*]

136.3–13   [¶] What . . . use.] [*1910 Sec. 4*] [¶] While . . . Mind.

136.14–139.33   [¶] *a. Open-mindedness* . . . unity.] *added*

Chap. 3

Summary: The 1933 revision is one-fourth longer than the corresponding 1910 text. The intro., one-half of Sec. I, paras. 1–2 of Sec. II, para. 1 of Sec. III, and all of Sec. IV are extensively revised or new. Material is added in the intro., Sec. I, and Sec. IV on the teacher's role, in Sec. I on curiosity in childhood, in Sec. II on ideas, and in Sec. III on the process of reflective thinking.

Organization:

1933	1910
Chap. 3. Native Resources in Training Thought	**Chap. 3. Natural Resources in the Training of Thought**

Intro.		*Intro.*	*paras. 1–2*
Sec. I.	Curiosity	Sec. 1.	Curiosity
Sec. II.	Suggestion	Sec. 2.	Suggestion
Sec. III.	Orderliness	Sec. 3.	Orderliness: Its Nature
Sec. IV.	Some Educational Conclusions		

Revisions:

140.2–141.8   [¶] We . . . employed.] [¶] In . . . himself. [*para. del.*]

141.10–142.5   [¶] Every . . . thinking.] [¶] The most . . . itself. [*w. add.*]

143.13–31   finding . . . evaporates.] *problems* . . . blunted.

144.9–26   it; . . . spirit.] it. . . . things.

144.29–145.6   [¶] Many . . . them.] [2 *sents. del.*] Many . . . so." [*w. add.*]

145.8–146.2   [¶] Ideas, . . . thought.] *added*

146.35–36   Moreover, . . . over.] *added*

149.15–16   for . . . differ] *added*

150.5–21   [¶] The mere . . . *trust*worthy.] [¶] Facts, . . . proof. [*w. add.*]

151.12   and . . . attained] *added*

152.3–4   —provided . . . routine] *added*

152.9–13   From . . . operations.] *added*

154.20–155.32   [¶] The . . . theme.] *added*

Chap. 4

Summary: The 1933 revision is two-fifths longer than the corresponding 1910 text. Paras. 2, 3, and 5 of Sec. I, para. 4 of Sec. III, and one-half of Sec. IV are extensively revised or new. Material is added in Sec. I on method of training thought and role of the teacher, in Secs. III and IV on faults of the scholarly specialist, and in Sec. IV on transfer of habits of thought.

Organization:

1933		1910	
Chap. 4.	**School Conditions and the Training of Thought**	**Chap. 4.**	**School Conditions and the Training of Thought**
Sec. I.	Introductory: Methods and Conditions	Sec. 1.	Introductory: Methods and Conditions
Sec. II.	The Influence of the Habits of Others	Sec. 2.	Influence of the Habits of Others
Sec. III.	The Influence of the Nature of Studies	Sec. 3.	Influence of the Nature of Studies

| Sec. IV. | The Influence of Current Aims and Ideals | Sec. 4. | The Influence of Current Aims and Ideals |

Revisions:
156.22–157.12   a problem . . . ideas.] the occasion . . .
        investigation.
157.12–28   These . . . thought,] *added*
158.10–11   *bad* habits.] habits. [*sent. del.*]
158.13–29   [¶] There . . . habits.] *added*
163.3–4   [¶] A false . . . understanding.] [¶] (*c*) Much . . .
        information.
163.4–12   One . . . thought.] *added*
165.25–167.11   [¶] The point . . . experiences.] *added*

1933	1910
Part Two. Logical Considerations	**Part Two. Logical Considerations**
chaps. 5–13	*chaps. 5, 6, 2, 6, 8, 9, 7, 11*
"There the whole logical analysis of reflection has been rewritten and, it is believed, very considerably simplified in statement" (p. 107).	

Chap. 5

Summary: The 1933 revision is two-thirds longer than the corresponding 1910 text. All of Sec. I, more than one-half of Sec. II, and the first one-third of Sec. III are extensively revised or new. Material is added in Sec. I on the form and process of thinking, in Sec. II on the role of education in teaching habits of thinking, and in Sec. III on the conception of discipline.

Organization:

1933	1910
Chap. 5. The Process and Product of Reflective Activity: Psychological Process and Logical Form	Chap. 5. The Means and End of Mental Training: The Psychological and the Logical [*tr. from Part One*]
Sec. I. Thinking as a Formal and as an Actual Occurrence	Sec. 1. Introductory: The Meaning of Logical, *paras. 3, 12*

Sec. II.   Education in Relation to   Sec. 1.   *paras. 4, 7, 8, 9, 6, 10,*
           Form   *5, 12, 11, 2*
Sec. III. Discipline and Freedom   Sec. 2.   Discipline and Freedom

Revisions:
171.7–175.8   [¶] When . . . doing.] *added*
175.9–176.4   [¶] A person . . . permit.] [¶] In this sense, . . . formal
   on the other. [*w. add.*]
176.6–26   [¶] The "psychological," . . . it.] The natural . . . could be.
   [*w. add.*]
176.29–177.32   [¶] From . . . qualities.] [¶] No argument . . . logical
   power. [*w. add.*]
177.36–38   [¶] Curiously . . . schools.] [¶] The conception . . . educational theory.
178.1–12   [¶] One . . . pupils.] *added*
178.13–14   [¶] An . . . statements.] [¶] This description . . .
   illustration.
179.18–28   [¶] It . . . achievement.] [¶] The other school . . .
   rebellious.
180.18–27   [¶] The other . . . growth.] To one school, . . . intellectual nurture. [*w. add.*]
180.37–181.17   [¶] Thus . . . operation.] [¶] In truth, . . . truly educative. [*w. add.*]
181.31–36   He will . . . adopted.] *added*
181.37–182.13   [¶] That which . . . them.] [¶] What is . . . *point of
   departure.* [*w. add.*]
182.15–27   [¶] We . . . *art.*] [¶] In its broadest sense, . . . artificial
   thought.
182.30–183.3   [¶] It was . . . then] *added*
183.3–4   discipline . . . a] [¶] Discipline, . . . a
183.16–19   is engaged . . . operation.] is developing mental . . .
   servility.
183.20–32   [¶] In truth, . . . sake.] [¶] Discipline of mind . . . constructive. [*w. add.*]
183.34–38   [¶] This fact . . . capable] [¶] When discipline . . .
   capable

Chap. 6

Summary: The 1933 revision is twice as long as the corresponding 1910
text. The intro. para., the first and last para. in Sec. I, all of Sec. II except
para. 3, and all of Sec. III are extensively revised or new. Material is
added in Sec. II illustrating ways of testing inferences, and in Sec. III illustrating the function of reflective thought.

Organization:

1933	1910
Chap. 6. Examples of Inference and Testing	**Chap. 6. The Analysis of a Complete Act of Thought** *and* Chap. 2, Sec. 4
Sec. I. Illustrations of Reflective Activity	Chap. 6. *first one-third*
Sec. II. Inference to the Unknown	Chap. 2. Sec. 4. Regulation Transforms Inference into Proof, *paras. 1–2*
Sec. III. Thinking Moves from a Doubtful to a Settled Situation	

Revisions:

187.2–20   [¶] We . . . type.] [¶] After . . . experience.
190.12–18   [¶] In . . . one.] We . . . types.
190.21–191.24   [¶] In . . . *proof.*] [¶] Thinking . . . *proof.*
192.10–11   *assent . . . justified.*] *assent yielded.*
192.13–195.36   [¶] All . . . values.] *added*

Chap. 7

Summary: The 1933 revision is two and one-half times longer than the corresponding 1910 text. Everything except 1 para. in Sec. II is extensively revised or new. Material is added in Sec. I on the role of facts and ideas in reflection and in Sec. II on phases of reflective thought.

Organization:

1933	1910
Chap. 7. Analysis of Reflective Thinking	**Chap. 6. The Analysis of a Complete Act of Thought**
Sec. I. Facts and Ideas	
Sec. II. The Essential Functions of Reflective Activity	*last two-thirds*

Revisions:

196.3–200.7   [¶] When . . . falls.] *added*
200.10–204.34   [¶] In . . . one.] [¶] Upon . . . extremes (*ante*, p. 72). [*w. add.*]
204.35–205.23   [¶] Mathematics . . . form.] *added*

205.26–27 [¶] The . . . *experimental*] [¶] 5. The . . . *experimental*
206.6–38   [¶] Of course, . . . it.] [¶] Observation . . . solution.
207.1–209.18   [¶] There . . . account.] *added*

Chap. 8

Summary: The 1933 revision is approximately the same length as the corresponding 1910 text. Paras. 1–3, the last para., and 6 sents. are extensively revised or new. Material is added in Sec. I illustrating judgments as units of thought.

Organization:

1933	1910
Chap. 8. The Place of Judgment in Reflective Activity	**Chap. 8. Judgment: The Interpretation of Facts,** *Secs. 1 and 3*
Sec. I. Three Factors in Judging	Sec. 1. The Three Factors of Judging
Sec. II. Analysis and Synthesis: The Two Functions of Judgment	Sec. 3. Analysis and Synthesis

Revisions:
210.4–211.6   [¶] We . . . judgment.] To know . . . account? [*w. add.*]
211.6–9   A man . . . academic standing.] [¶] A man . . . literacy.
212.22–23   They . . . questions:] *added*
215.2   educed.] educed. [*sent. del.*]
215.26–29   In short, . . . chase.] *added*
216.10–11   The clearing . . . *synthesis*.] *added*
218.34–37   It unites . . . value.] *added*
220.9–15   [¶] Whenever . . . judgment.] *added*

Chap. 9

Summary: The 1933 revision is one-third longer than the corresponding 1910 text. The first 2 and last 2 paras. of Sec. I, most of paras. 1–3 of Sec. II, and one-half of Sec. III are extensively revised or new. Material is added in Sec. I illustrating the role and formation of ideas, in Secs. II and III illustrating the process by which things acquire meaning, and in Sec. III on the educational significance of this process.

Organization:

1933	1910
Chap. 9. Understanding: Ideas and Meanings	Chap. 9. Meaning: or Conceptions and Understanding, *Secs. 1–2, and* Chap. 8, Sec. 2
Sec. I. Ideas as Suggestions and Conjectures	Chap. 8. Sec. 2. The Origin and Nature of Ideas
Sec. II. Things and Meanings	Sec. 1. The Place of Meanings in Mental Life
Sec. III. The Process by Which Things Acquire Meaning	Sec. 2. The Process of Acquiring Meanings

Revisions:

221.3–222.6 [¶] We . . . considered.] [¶] This brings . . . *judgment.* [*and Chap. 9, Sec. 1*] [¶] As in . . . direct and indirect. [*w. add.*]

222.39–223.2 such phenomena as . . . etc.] the phenomena in question.

223.15–18 This . . . animals.] *added*

223.37–224.11 On the . . . of them.] On the . . . problems in geometry. [*w. add.*]

224.14–225.11 [¶] It . . . expressions.] *added*

225.17 value.] value. [*sent. del.*]

225.17–18 It . . . of.] *added*

225.34–226.3 To grasp . . . grasped.] To grasp . . . nonsense, insanity.

226.4–22 [¶] Since . . . place.] [¶] All knowledge, . . . when desired.

228.23–25 once . . . them.] as meanings . . . things themselves.

231.30–233.2 [¶] In . . . language.] *added*

233.5–27 [¶] We . . . invented.] [¶] Familiar . . . wavering. [*w. add.*]

233.28–234.11 [¶] The . . . understood.] *added*

Chap. 10

Summary: The 1933 revision is two-thirds longer than the corresponding 1910 text. All of Sec. I except 2 paras. and most of Sec. II are extensively revised or new. Material is added in Sec. I illustrating the nature of concepts and their educational significance and in Sec. II illustrating the development of concepts and synthesis.

Organization:

1933	1910
Chap. 10. **Understanding: Conception and Definition**	Chap. 9. **Meaning: or Conceptions and Understanding,** *Secs. 3–5*
Sec. I. The Nature of Conceptions	Sec. 3. Conceptions and Meaning
Sec. II. How Conceptions Arise	Sec. 4. What Conceptions are Not
Sec. III. Definition and Organization of Meanings	Sec. 5. Definition and Organization of Meanings

Revisions:

235.4–14   [¶] In . . . significance.] *added*

235.16–237.3   [¶] The . . . up.] [¶] The word *meaning* . . . personal changes.

237.4–21   [¶] When . . . experience.] *added*

237.24   [¶] Stating . . . conceptions,] [*sent. del.*] We shall . . . conceptions,

238.32–240.3   [¶] It . . . turn.] *added*

240.8–15   [¶] It . . . to all.] [¶] The idea . . . in which they agree.

241.9–28   [¶] It . . . concept.] and as this process . . . get body and clearness. [*w. add.*]

241.30–31   [¶] By . . . *generality.*] *added*

242.10   general.] general. [*sent. del.*]

242.11–243.28   [¶] What . . . differences.] *added*

245.11   , the *kind* . . . subclasses] *added*

Chap. 11

Summary: The 1933 revision is slightly shorter than the corresponding 1910 text. Almost all of Sec. I and paras. 1–4 of Sec. II are extensively revised or new; most instances of "induction" are deleted or revised. Material on data is added.

Organization:

1933	1910
Chap. 11. **Systematic Method: Control of Data and Evidence**	Chap. 7. **Systematic Inference: Induction and Deduction,** *Secs. 1–3 and 4*
Sec. I. Method as Deliberate Testing of Facts and Ideas	Sec. 1. The Double Movement of Reflection

Sec. II.   The Importance of   Sec. 2.   Guidance of the Induc-
            Method in Judging   tive Movement *and*
            Data   Sec. 3.   Experimental Variation
                                                    of Conditions *and*
                                         Sec. 4.   *para. 2*

Revisions:
248.5–249.2   [¶] Judgment, . . . data.] [¶] The characteristic . . .
               meanings.
249.4–19   [¶] Method . . . errors.] [¶] This more systematic . . .
            short).
249.20–35   [¶] We . . . class.] [¶] A commonplace . . . facts.
249.36–250.11   [¶] The original . . . clearer.] *added*
250.14–251.10   [¶] This . . . calculations.] [¶] So far . . . scien-
                 tifically carried on.
251.13–252.12   [¶] From . . . up.] [¶] Control . . . inferences. [*and*
                 1910 Sec. 4] [¶] The control . . . haphazard.
252.14   interpretation.] inductive interpretation.
252.16–22   There . . . experts.] *added*
252.34   inference] induction
253.3   method includes,] induction means,
255.3   method] control in induction
255.6–7   method . . . development] inductive method
255.8   controlled] inductive
255.16–17   a suggested inference] that induction
255.19   cited,] cited (p. 83) was inductive, . . . examined.
255.24–25   introduce scientific method into] make inductive
255.26   inference] induction
256.30–31   control of method,] inductive method, [*1910 Sec. 3*
             begins]
257.7   methods on the fact side] inductive methods

Chap. 12

Summary: The 1933 revision is one-half longer than the corresponding 1910 text. Almost all of Sec. I and the first and last 2 paras. of Sec. II are extensively revised or new; most instances of "deduction" are deleted or revised. Material is added in Sec. I illustrating the purpose and value of concepts and in Sec. II on education's failures.

Organization:

1933	1910
Chap. 12. Systematic Method: Control of Reasoning and Concepts	Chap. 7. Systematic Inference: Induction and Deduction, *Secs. 4–5 and 1*
Sec. I. The Value of Scientific Conceptions	Sec. 4. Guidance of the Deductive Movement *and* Sec. 1, *para. 4*
Sec. II. Significant Applications to Education: Characteristic Inadequacies	Sec. 5. Some Educational Bearings of the Discussion

Revisions:

259.4–21   [¶] We . . . formation.] [¶] Before dealing . . . fruitful form.

259.24–260.26   [¶] We . . . together.] [*1910 Sec. 1*] [¶] The importance . . . *properties.* [*w. add.*]

260.27–37   [¶] Popular . . . nature] *added*

261.2–25   science . . . provided] science is to provide

261.36–262.9   facilitating . . . had.] facilitating . . . tested. [*w. add.*]

262.11–263.6   [¶] To . . . yet] *added*

263.6   test] test of deduction

263.11   theoretical] the deduced

263.12   rational conclusion] deduction

263.21–264.16   [¶] Some . . . information.] [¶] Some . . . ignored. [*w. add.*]

265.23   Suggestion] Induction

265.25   reasoning] deductive

266.7–9   Moreover, . . . inquiry.] *added*

266.12   general ideas] deduction

266.15   rational] deductive

267.13–31   [¶] The counterpart . . . promoted.] *added*

Chap. 13

Summary: The 1933 revision is slightly longer than the corresponding 1910 text. 3 paras. and the ends of 2 paras. are extensively revised or new. Material is added in Sec. I on empirical thinking and in Sec. II illustrating abstraction.

Organization:

1933	1910
Chap. 13. Empirical and Scientific Thought	Chap. 11. Empirical and Scientific Thinking

Sec. I.	What Is Meant by Empirical	Sec. 1.	Empirical Thinking
Sec. II.	Scientific Method	Sec. 2.	Scientific Method

Revisions:
268.3–13   [¶] Many . . . it.] [¶] Apart . . . purposes. [*w. add.*]
269.29–31   Attention . . . dogmatism.] *added*
270.15   conjunction.] conjunction. [*sent. del.*]
272.25–28   In . . . effect.] *added*
273.7–8   fact. . . . key] fact, . . . key
277.1–2   considerations . . . evident.] considerations . . . clear.
277.3–22   [¶] Abstraction . . . stem.] *added*
277.22–27   Abstracting . . . inference.] A certain power . . . fruitful.
278.9–12   and lazy . . . value] *added*

1933	1910
Part Three. The Training of Thought	Part Three. The Training of Thought
chaps. 14–19	*chaps. 12, 10, 13–16*

Chap. 14

Summary: The 1933 revision is one-sixth longer than the corresponding 1910 text. 2 sents. in Sec. I, 2 paras. in Sec. II, and the last one-half of Sec. III are new. Material is added in Sec. II on the significance of work and in Sec. III on educative "projects."

Organization:

1933		1910	
Chap. 14.	Activity and the Training of Thought	Chap. 12.	Activity and the Training of Thought
Sec. I.	The Early Stage of Activity	Sec. 1.	The Early Stage of Activity
Sec. II.	Play, Work, and Allied Forms of Activity	Sec. 2.	Play, Work, and Allied Forms of Activity
Sec. III.	Constructive Occupations	Sec. 3.	Constructive Occupations

Revisions:
283.19–21   In learning . . . them.] *added*
285.35   mind?] mind? [*sent. del.*]
286.22–287.8   [¶] The word . . . child.] *added*
291.21–292.26   [¶] Constructive . . . done.] *added*

Chap. 15

Summary: The 1933 .revision is approximately the same length as the corresponding 1910 text. 6 sents. are extensively revised or new.

Organization:

1933	1910
Chap. 15. From the Concrete to the Abstract	**Chap. 10. Concrete and Abstract Thinking**
	[*tr. from Part Two*]
Sec. I. What Is the Concrete?	*first two-thirds*
Sec. II. What Is the Abstract?	*last one-third*

Revisions:

296.6   *intellectual.*] *intellectual*—as distinct from *intelligent.*
296.31–37   [¶] 1. Since . . . occupation.] [¶] 1. Since . . . materials.
298.25–30   It is . . . ideas.] *added*
299.15   Intellectual . . . result.] *added*
299.22–23   think practically . . . ends;] think so as . . . ends;
300.21–22   Otherwise, . . . deadening.] *added*
300.29–30   Otherwise . . . pedantic.] *added*

Chap. 16

Summary: The 1933 revision is approximately the same length as the corresponding 1910 text. 4 sents. of Sec. I and 13 sents. of Sec. III, most at the ends of paras., are extensively revised or new. Material is added in Sec. III on education's responsibility in transforming language into an intellectual tool.

Organization:

1933	1910
Chap. 16. Language and the Training of Thought	**Chap. 13. Language and the Training of Thought**
Sec. I. Language as the Tool of Thinking	Sec. 1. Language as the Tool of Thinking
Sec. II. The Abuse of Linguistic Methods in Education	Sec. 2. The Abuse of Linguistic Methods in Education
Sec. III. The Use of Language in its Educational Bearings	Sec. 3. The Use of Language in its Educational Bearings

Revisions:
301.13–14   There . . . here.] *added*
302.10–11   his act . . . itself.] his movement . . . symbol.
302.29–31   A symbol, . . . meaning.] *added*
303.1–2   There . . . meanings:] *added*
308.15–16   conscious . . . contains.] conscious study.
309.33–35   The fact . . . individual.] The fact . . . individual.
310.8   Action . . . definite.] *added*
310.17–18   a condition . . . vague] *added*
310.22–27   Even . . . baby-talk.] *added*
312.22–25   Thus . . . line.] *added*
314.30–35   Self-consciousness . . . say.] The resulting self-consciousness . . . negative ideal.

Chap. 17

Summary: The 1933 revision is approximately the same length as the corresponding 1910 text. 3 sents. of the intro., 3 sents. of Sec. I, 8 sents. of Sec. II, and 2 sents. of Sec. III, most at the ends of paras., are extensively revised or new. Material is added on method and scientific observation.

Organization:

1933		1910	
Chap. 17.	Observation and Information in the Training of Mind	Chap. 14.	Observation and Information in the Training of Mind
Sec. I.	The Nature and Value of Observation	Sec. 1.	The Nature and Value of Observation
Sec. II.	Methods and Materials of Observation in the Schools	Sec. 2.	Methods and Materials of Observation in the Schools
Sec. III.	Communication of Information	Sec. 3.	Communication of Information

Revisions:
315.7–8   supplied . . . importance.] furnished . . . point.
315.14–19   , and the method . . . arranged] *added*
316.29–32   The result . . . conscious] These systems . . . conscious
318.15–17   being means . . . thinking.] the means . . . its solution.
318.17–19   Moreover, . . . serve.] *added*
319.20   Three . . . mention.] *added*
319.31–32   observation . . . probing.] observation . . . deliberate.

320.6   live observation.] the searching . . . observation.
321.5–6   intellectually . . . attitude.] logically fruitful.
321.34–322.5   have learned . . . purpose.] have become . . . quality.
322.34–39   Scientific . . . observers.] *added*
324.7–8   Curiosity . . . stale.] *added*
325.15–16   Then . . . outside.] *added*

Chap. 18

Summary: The 1933 revision, "practically all new" (p. 108), is one-half longer than the corresponding 1910 text. One-half of Sec. I, all of Secs. II, IV, and V, and one-fourth of Sec. III are extensively revised or new. Material is added on the evils, function, and value of the recitation, and. the role of the teacher.

Organization:

1933		1910	
Chap. 18.	**The Recitation and the Training of Thought**	**Chap. 15.**	**The Recitation and the Training of Thought**
Sec. I.	False Ideas about the Recitation	*Intro.*	
Sec. II.	The Functions of the Recitation	Sec. 1.	The Formal Steps of Instruction, *paras. 2–4*
Sec. III.	The Conduct of the Recitation	Sec. 2.	The Factors in the Recitation
Sec. IV.	The Function of the Teacher	Sec. 1.	*paras. 6–7*
Sec. V.	Appreciation	Sec. 2.	*last 2 paras.*

Revisions:

326.30–327.28   [¶] The recitation . . . being.] *added*
327.30–328.10   [¶] What . . . consideration.] [¶] If we compare . . . developing thought.
328.13–331.4   [¶] The ultimate . . . study.] *added*
331.5–333.5   [¶] *The Art* . . . etc.] [¶] By preparation . . . Connecticut. [*w. add.*]
333.7–11   [¶] We . . . students.] [¶] Bearing in mind . . . and presentation.
333.19–20   problem . . . realized,] problem
334.3–7   There . . . shoots.] Constraint, . . . familiar experiences.
334.10–16   [¶] The . . . class.] [¶] It is unnecessary . . . with it.
334.24–335.14   If a . . . He should] *added*

336.5−7   [¶] The holding, . . . mind.] *added*
336.15−16   that put . . . generalization] that endeavor . . .
comparing,
336.36   narrowness.] narrowness. [*sent. del.*]
336.38−337.1   principle. The inherent] principle. . . . The inherent
337.7−9   A central . . . line.] The essence . . . application.
337.12−340.5   [¶] The . . . one?] [¶] Lack of any preparation . . .
own mind. [*w. add.*]
340.8−341.33   [¶] To . . . with.] [¶] The true purpose . . . principles.
[*w. add.*]

Chap. 19

Summary: The 1933 revision is slightly longer than the corresponding
1910 text. 2 paras. of Sec. I and 2 sents. of Sec. II are extensively revised
or new. Material is added in Sec. I illustrating conscious and unconscious processes of thought.

Organization:

1933		1910	
Chap. 19.	**Some General Conclusions**	Chap. 16.	**Some General Conclusions**
Sec. I.	The Unconscious and the Conscious	Sec. 1.	The Unconscious and the Conscious
Sec. II.	Process and Product	Sec. 2.	Process and Product
Sec. III.	The Far and the Near	Sec. 3.	The Far and the Near

Revisions:
342.26   , of going . . . analysis,] *added*
343.15−17   No one . . . engaged in.] No one . . . carried.
343.36−37   Methods . . . curiosity.] to pursue methods . . . interest.
344.23−345.35   [¶] The point . . . process.] *added*
346.22−24   Even indulgence . . . direction.] *added*
346.26−28   to see . . . produce.] to make regard . . . freest play
activity.
350.33   upon hunting . . . different.] upon what . . . understood.

H. F. S.

Line-End Hyphenation

I. Copy-text list.

The following are the editorially established forms of possible compounds that were hyphenated at the ends of lines in the copy-text:

13.19	precondition	150.21	*trust*worthy
18.15	Cooperation	153.37	self-expression
51.38	self-criticism	181.12	self-expression
53.5	subject-matter	188.38	Tugboats
54.19	school-children	193.32	ferryboat
57.6	semi-military	233.37	so-called
57.22	"pork-barrel"	243.36	*mis*-understanding
58.2	reinterpreted	249.5	safeguard
58.10	watchwords	261.12	radio-active
73.35−36	world-wide	270.17	trustworthiness
73.38−39	interdependence	271.35	semi-sacred
98.15	remaking	297.16	halfway
99.23	foothold	307.4	catch-phrases
101.40	intercommunication	310.27	baby-talk
103.12	straightforward	320.16	story-teller
126.28	shipwreck	325.5	schoolroom
139.3−4	open-mindedness	347.28	open-mindedness
141.14	framework	365.25	piecemeal
145.3	worth-while		

II. Critical-text list.

In transcriptions from the present edition, no line-end hyphens in ambiguously broken possible compounds are to be retained except the following:

23.26	politico-moral	51.30	slow-going
31.21	self-manifestation	57.38	hold-overs
51.29	fellow-men	69.10	man-made

73.35	world-wide	200.4	*post*-reflective
79.31	non-social	218.24	clear-cut
87.15	self-interest	237.34	new-forming
88.39	pipe-line	239.26	worth-while
92.17	self-continuing	261.11	ultra-violet
139.3	open-mindedness	297.13	sense-training
158.24	open-mindedness	342.22	im-plicit
199.37	cleared-up	366.11	hard-headed

Substantive Variants in Quotations

Dewey's substantive variants in quotations have been considered important enough to warrant this special list. Dewey represented source material in varying ways, from memorial paraphrase to verbatim copy, in some places citing his source fully, in others mentioning only authors' names, and in others omitting documentation altogether. All material inside quotation marks, except that obviously being emphasized or restated, has been searched out; Dewey's citations have been verified and emended when necessary. All quotations have been retained as they appear in the copy-text, with the exceptions noted in the following paragraph, which are recorded in the Emendations List; it is, therefore, necessary to consult the Emendations List in conjunction with this list.

Although Dewey, like other scholars of the period, was unconcerned about precision in matters of form, many of the changes in quotations may well have occurred in the printing process. For example, comparing Dewey's quotations with the originals reveals that some editors and compositors house-styled the quoted materials as well as Dewey's own. Therefore, in the present edition, the spelling and capitalization of the source have been restored; these changes are recorded in the Emendations List with the symbol WS (Works—the present edition—emendations derived from Dewey's Source). Similarly, in cases of possible compositorial or typographical errors, changes in substantives or accidentals that restore original readings are noted as WS emendations. Dewey frequently changed or omitted punctuation in quoted material; if it has been necessary to restore the punctuation of the source, these changes are also recorded in the Emendations List with the symbol WS.

Dewey often did not indicate that he had omitted material from his source. Omitted short phrases appear in this list; omissions of more than one line are noted by a bracketed ellipsis [. . .]. Italics in source material have been treated as substantives. Both Dewey's omitted and added italics are noted here.

Differences between Dewey's quotations and the source attributable to the context in which the quotation appears, such as changes in number, tense, or subject, are not recorded.

In cases where Dewey translated the source, the reference appears in the Checklist of Dewey's References, but no variants in the quotation are included here.

Notations in this section follow the formula: page-line number from the present edition, followed by the lemma, then a bracket. After the bracket, the original form appears, followed by the author's surname, shortened source-title from the Checklist of Dewey's References, and the page-line reference to the source, all in parentheses.

The Social-Economic Situation and Education

74.38   educators] educators, however, (Tugwell, "Social Objectives," 109.17)
75.3   upon] on (Tugwell, "Social Objectives," 109.22)
75.6   their minds] minds (Tugwell, "Social Objectives," 109.24)
75.7   learn] learn how (Tugwell, "Social Objectives," 109.25)
75.9   how to reach] to reach (Tugwell, "Social Objectives," 109.27)
75.9–10   manipulate] operate (Tugwell, "Social Objectives," 109.28)

How We Think: A Restatement of the Relation of Reflective Thinking to the Educative Process

129.1–2   is . . . accordingly] [rom.] (Mill, Logic, 5.52–6.1)
129.4–5   It . . . engaged.] [rom.] (Mill, Logic, 6.5–6)
129.34   aright] right (Locke, Conduct, 3.24)
129.35   judgments] the judgments (Locke, Conduct, 3.25)
132.32   troubles] trouble (Locke, Conduct, 6.17)
132.34   This kind] The second (Locke, Conduct, 6.19)
133.2   party.] party; [. . .] it. (Locke, Conduct, 6.23–29)
133.5   large, . . . sense] [ital.] (Locke, Conduct, 7.2)
133.13   when all] all (Locke, Conduct, 11.20)
133.16   and notions] notions (Locke, Conduct, 11.23)
133.17   mind] minds (Locke, Conduct, 11.24)
133.20   which] what (Locke, Essay, 601.20)
133.20   principles] [rom.] (Locke, Essay, 601.20–21)
133.26   established rules] [rom.] (Locke, Essay, 601.26)
133.29   in] into (Locke, Essay, 601.42)
133 n.1   inclinations] inclinations by this way (Locke, Conduct, 91.6)
133 n.2   discourse] their discourse (Locke, Conduct, 91.10)
133 n.5   precise] the precise (Locke, Conduct, 91.14)

134.1 (and this] (equally, (Locke, *Essay*, 601.43)

134.12–13 controversies. 2. Secondly,] controversies. [. . .] Secondly, (Locke, *Essay*, 602.7–45)

134.21 ever] never (Locke, *Essay*, 603.38)

134.24–25 batteries. 4. Authority. The] batteries; [. . .] Authority.—Fourthly, The (Locke, *Essay*, 603.41–606.19)

134.27 others] other (Locke, *Essay*, 606.21)

134.27–28 is the] is that which I have mentioned in the foregoing chapter: I mean the (Locke, *Essay*, 606.21–23)

142.11 their] the (Hobhouse, *Mind*, 195.32)

142.12 tendency] tendency of his rats (Hobhouse, *Mind*, 195.32)

142.12 Rats] They (Hobhouse, *Mind*, 195.32)

213.38 method] mode (Mill, *Logic*, 126.50)

214.3 principles] principle (Mill, *Logic*, 127.2)

214.5–6 could therefore] therefore could (Mill, *Logic*, 127.3–4)

214.6 own skill] skill (Mill, *Logic*, 127.4)

214.6 individual] the individual (Mill, *Logic*, 127.4)

214.10 case,] cases, (Mill, *Logic*, 127.7)

214.10 *infer . . . employed*] [*rom.*] (Mill, *Logic*, 127.7–8)

238.17 if it were really] then added, if really (Darwin, *Life and Letters*, 48.11)

238.19 because] as (Darwin, *Life and Letters*, 48.13)

238.24 had] had ever (Darwin, *Life and Letters*, 48.19)

238.24 realise] realise, though I had read various scientific books, (Darwin, *Life and Letters*, 48.20)

238.24–26 *that science . . . them.*] [*rom.*] (Darwin, *Life and Letters*, 48.20–22)

257.35 amber.] amber (*electrum*). (Jevons, *Logic*, 232.32)

258.17 three] the three (Jevons, *Logic*, 233.17)

270.32, 33 met] met with (Clifford, *Lectures*, 144.18, 20)

270.34–35 the application] an application (Clifford, *Lectures*, 147.28)

270.35 old] past (Clifford, *Lectures*, 147.28)

270.35 new] new and different (Clifford, *Lectures*, 147.29)

275.7 have] have had (James, *Psychology*, 2:342.7)

275.8 rays] the rays (James, *Psychology*, 2:342.9)

275.9 as cases of] as (James, *Psychology*, 2:342.9)

276.30 effort.] effect. (Bain, *Senses and Intellect*, 492.34)

307.26 arithmetical signs] arithmetical symbols (Stout, *Analytic Psychology*, 193.34)

308.29 upholding of] upholding (Locke, *Essay*, 386.11)

308.31 a use] an use (Locke, *Essay*, 386.15–16)

The Adventure of Persuasion

357.8–9   beyond] lying beyond (Whitehead, *Adventures*, 86.19)
358.25   Adventure and Peace] Adventure, Art, Peace (Whitehead, *Adventures*, 353.17)
358.34   the world . . . the victory] The creation of the world—that is to say, the world of civilized order—is the victory (Whitehead, *Adventures*, 31.3–4)

Review of Rexford G. Tugwell's *The Industrial Discipline and the Governmental Arts*

364.28   of creative] of training and of creative (Tugwell, *Industrial Discipline*, 64.2)
365.15–16   yet separately] separately (Tugwell, *Industrial Discipline*, 19.20)
365.19   grasp] seize (Tugwell, *Industrial Discipline*, 23.20)
365.20   our only] the only (Tugwell, *Industrial Discipline*, 23.31)
365.21   for] for all this (Tugwell, *Industrial Discipline*, 23.32)
366.7   must] has to (Tugwell, *Industrial Discipline*, 223.21)

Checklist of Dewey's References

This section gives full publication information for each work cited by Dewey. Books in Dewey's personal library (John Dewey Papers, Special Collections, Morris Library, Southern Illinois University at Carbondale) have been listed whenever possible. When Dewey gave page numbers for a reference, the edition has been identified by locating the citation; for other references, the edition listed here is his most likely source by reason of place or date of publication, general accessibility during the period, or evidence from correspondence and other materials.

Adamson, Robert. *A Short History of Logic*. Edited by W. R. Sorley. Edinburgh: William Blackwood and Sons, 1911.

Bain, Alexander. *The Senses and the Intellect*. 3d ed. New York: D. Appleton and Co., 1879.

Borah, William E. *See Congressional Record*.

Bradley, Francis Herbert. *The Principles of Logic*. 2 vols. 2d ed., rev. London: Oxford University Press, 1922.

Brunschvicg, Léon. *Le progrès de la conscience dans la philosophie occidentale*. 2 vols. Paris: Felix Alcan, 1927.

Clifford, William Kingdon. *Lectures and Essays*. Edited by Leslie Stephen and Frederick Pollock. Vol. 1. London: Macmillan and Co., 1901.

Cohen, Morris Raphael. *Reason and Nature: An Essay on the Meaning of Scientific Method*. New York: Harcourt, Brace and Co., 1931.

Congressional Record. 67th Cong., 4th sess., 1923. Vol. 64, pt. 4:3605.

Council on Foreign Relations. *Survey of American Foreign Relations*. Edited by Charles Prentice Howland. New Haven: Yale University Press, 1929.

Darwin, Charles. *The Life and Letters of Charles Darwin*. Edited by Francis Darwin. Vol. 1. New York: D. Appleton and Co., 1897.

Dempf, Alois. "Kulturphilosophie." In *Handbuch der Philosophie*, edited by Alfred Baeumler and Manfred Schröter, pt. 4. Munich: R. Oldenbourg, 1934.

Dewey, John. *Essays in Experimental Logic*. Chicago: University of Chicago Press, 1916.

————. *Philosophy and Civilization*. New York: Minton, Balch and Co., 1931.

————. *Reconstruction in Philosophy*. New York: Henry Holt and Co., 1920. [*The Middle Works of John Dewey, 1899–1924*, edited by Jo Ann Boydston, 12:77–201. Carbondale and Edwardsville: Southern Illinois University Press, 1982.]

————. "'As an Example to Other Nations.'" *New Republic* 54 (7 March 1928): 88–89. [*The Later Works of John Dewey, 1925–1953*, edited by Jo Ann Boydston, 3:163–67. Carbondale and Edwardsville: Southern Illinois University Press, 1984.]

————. "If War Were Outlawed." *New Republic* 34 (25 April 1923): 234–35. [*Middle Works* 15:110–14.]

————. "Political Combination or Legal Cooperation?" *New Republic* 34 (21 March 1923): 89–91. [*Middle Works* 15:105–9.]

————. "Rejoinder to James T. Shotwell." *New Republic* 54 (28 March 1928): 194–96. [*Later Works* 3:168–72.]

————. "War and a Code of Law." *New Republic* 36 (24 October 1923): 224–26. [*Middle Works* 15:122–27.]

————. "What Outlawry of War Is Not." *New Republic* 36 (3 October 1923): 149–52. [*Middle Works* 15:115–21.]

Dilthey, Wilhelm. *Gesammelte Schriften*. 8 vols. Leipzig: B. G. Teubner, 1921–31. ["Das Wesen der Philosophie," 5:339–416; "Über das Studium der Geschichte der Wissenschaften vom Menschen, der Gesellschaft und dem Staat," 5:31–73.]

Engels, Friedrich. "Dialektik und Natur." In *Marx-Engels Archiv*, edited by D. Rjazanov, 2:117–395. Frankfurt: Verlags-Gesellschaft, 1927.

Enriques, Federigo. *Per la storia della logica*. Bologna: N. Zanichelli, 1922. Translated by Jerome Rosenthal as *The Historic Development of Logic: The Principles and Structure of Science in the Conception of Mathematical Thinkers*. New York: Henry Holt and Co., 1929.

Fenwick, Charles G. "War as an Instrument of National Policy." *American Journal of International Law* 22 (1928): 826–29.

Groethuysen, Bernhard. "Philosophische Anthropologie." In *Handbuch der Philosophie*, edited by Alfred Baeumler and Manfred Schröter, pt. 3. Munich: R. Oldenbourg, 1931.

Hard, William. "The Nonstop Peace Advocate." *World's Work* 58 (March 1929): 76–83.

Harms, Friedrich. *Geschichte der Logik*. Vol. 2 of *Die Philosophie in ihrer Geschichte*, edited by Adolf Lasson. Berlin: Theodor Hofmann, 1881.

Hatvany, Antonia, and Kellor, Frances Alice. *Security against War.*
2 vols. New York: Macmillan Co., 1924.

Hobhouse, Leonard Trelawney. *Mind in Evolution.* London: Macmillan and Co., 1901.

James, William. *The Principles of Psychology.* 2 vols. New York: Henry Holt and Co., 1893.

Jevons, W. Stanley. *Elementary Lessons in Logic: Deductive and Inductive.* New ed. London: Macmillan and Co., 1896.

Kellor, Frances Alice, and Hatvany, Antonia. *Security against War.*
2 vols. New York: Macmillan Co., 1924.

Levinson, Salmon O. "Can Peace Be 'Enforced'? A Study of International Sanctions." *Christian Century* 42 (8 January 1925): 46–47.

———. "The Legal Status of War." *New Republic* 14 (9 March 1918): 171–73. [*Middle Works* 11:388–92.]

———. "The Sanctions of Peace." *Christian Century* 46 (25 December 1929): 1603–6.

Lippmann, Walter. "'The Outlawry of War.'" *Atlantic Monthly* 132 (August 1923): 245–53. [*Middle Works* 15:404–17.]

Locke, John. *An Essay concerning Human Understanding.* New rev. ed. Edited by Thaddeus O'Mahoney. London: Ward, Lock, and Co., 1881.

———. *Locke's Conduct of the Understanding.* 5th ed. Edited by Thomas Fowler. Oxford: At the Clarendon Press, 1901.

Madariaga, Salvador de. *Disarmament.* New York: Coward-McCann, 1929.

Marck, Siegfried. *Die Dialektik in der Philosophie der Gegenwart.*
2 vols. Tübingen: Mohr, 1929–31.

Mill, John Stuart. *A System of Logic, Ratiocinative and Inductive.*
New York: Harper and Brothers, 1850.

Miller, David Hunter. *The Peace Pact of Paris: A Study of the Briand-Kellogg Treaty.* New York: G. P. Putnam's Sons, 1928.

Morrison, Charles Clayton. *The Outlawry of War: A Constructive Policy for World Peace.* Chicago: Willett, Clark and Colby, 1927.

Murray, Gilbert. "The Failure of Nerve." In his *Four Stages of Greek Religion,* pp. 103–54. New York: Columbia University Press, 1912.

Myers, Denys Peter. *Origin and Conclusion of the Paris Pact: The Renunciation of War as an Instrument of National Policy.* World Peace Foundation Pamphlets, vol. 12, no. 2. Boston: World Peace Foundation, 1929.

Page, Kirby. *The Renunciation of War: An Evaluation of the Strength and Weakness of the Recent Multilateral Treaty Renouncing War as an Instrument of National Policy.* Christianity and World Problems, no. 16. Garden City, N.Y.: Doubleday, Doran and Co., 1928.

Paulsen, Friedrich. *Einleitung in die Philosophie*. 24th ed. Stuttgart: J. G. Cotta, 1912. Translated from 3d German ed. by Frank Thilly as *Introduction to Philosophy*. 2d ed. New York: Henry Holt and Co., 1898.

Peirce, Charles S. *Collected Papers of Charles Sanders Peirce*. Edited by Charles Hartshorne and Paul Weiss. 2 vols. Cambridge, Mass.: Harvard University Press, 1931–32.

Prantl, Carl von. *Geschichte der Logik im Abendlande*. 4 vols. Leipzig: S. Hirzel, 1855–70. Reprinted at Leipzig: G. Fock, 1927.

"The Preservation of Peace." Edited by Parker Thomas Moon. In *Proceedings of the Academy of Political Science*, vol. 13, no. 2 (January 1929), pp. 197–254.

Santayana, George. *The Life of Reason; or, The Phases of Human Progress*. 5 vols. New York: Charles Scribner's Sons, 1922.

Schiller, Ferdinand Canning Scott. *Logic for Use: An Introduction to the Voluntarist Theory of Knowledge*. London: George Bell and Sons, 1929.

Schücking, Walther Max Adrian. *Die Revision der Völkerbundssatzung im Hinblick auf den Kelloggpakt*. Wissenschaftliche Beitrage zu aktuellen Fragen, no. 1. Berlin: Emil Ebering, 1931.

Schütze, Martin. *Academic Illusions in the Field of Letters and the Arts*. Chicago: University of Chicago Press, 1933.

Shotwell, James Thomson. *War as an Instrument of National Policy and Its Renunciation in the Pact of Paris*. New York: Harcourt, Brace and Co., 1929.

———. "Divergent Paths to Peace." *New Republic* 54 (28 March 1928): 194. [*Later Works* 3:415–16.]

Social Science Research Council. *Methods in Social Science: A Case Book Compiled under the Direction of the Committee on Scientific Method in the Social Sciences of the Social Science Research Council*. Edited by Stuart A. Rice. Chicago: University of Chicago Press, 1931.

Stout, George Frederick. *Analytic Psychology*. Vol. 2. London: Swan Sonnenschein and Co., 1896.

Tugwell, Rexford Guy. *The Industrial Discipline and the Governmental Arts*. New York: Columbia University Press, 1933.

———. "Social Objectives in Education." In *Redirecting Education*, edited by Tugwell and Leon H. Keyserling, 1:3–112. New York: Columbia University Press, 1934.

Varisco, Bernardino. *I massimi problemi*. 2d ed. Milan: Libreria Editrice Milanese, 1914. Translated by R. C. Lodge as *The Great Problems*. London: G. Allen and Co., 1914.

Ward, Lester F. *The Psychic Factors of Civilization*. 2d ed. Boston: Ginn and Co., 1906.

Wehberg, Hans. *Die Aechtung des Krieges*. Berlin: Franz Vahlen, 1930.

Wheeler-Bennett, John W. *Information on the Renunciation of War, 1927–1928*. Information Service on International Affairs, Information Series, no. 4. London: George Allen and Unwin, 1928.

Whitehead, Alfred North. *Adventures of Ideas*. New York: Macmillan Co., 1933.

Wordsworth, William. "Expostulation and Reply." In *Poems of Wordsworth*, edited by Matthew Arnold, pp. 131–32. London: Macmillan and Co., 1879.

Wright, Quincy. "The Outlawry of War." *American Journal of International Law* 19 (1925): 76–103.

Index

This index incorporates Dewey's original index for How We Think: A Restatement of the Relation of Reflective Thinking to the Educative Process *(Boston: D. C. Heath and Co., 1933).*

The Collected Works of John Dewey, 1882–1953

Index to The Collected Works of John Dewey, 1882–1953

The Later Works, 1925–1953